THE TIGER

The World at War, 1939–1945
The Boer War
Protest in Arms: The Irish Troubles, 1916–1923
The Strangest War: The Story of the Maori Wars
The Opium Wars in China
The Carlist Wars in Spain
Giuseppe Mazzini: The Great Conspirator
Risorgimento: The Making of Italy, 1815–1870
Plon-Plon: The Life of Prince Napoleon

EDGAR HOLT

THE TIGER

The Life of Georges Clemenceau
1841 – 1929

HAMISH HAMILTON
LONDON

*First published in Great Britain 1976
by Hamish Hamilton Ltd
90 Great Russell Street London WC1B 3PT*

Copyright © 1976 by Edgar Holt

SBN 241 89294 5

**Printed in Great Britain by
Western Printing Services Ltd, Bristol**

To PAT and PAUL CHAIX

CONTENTS

Contents

ILLUSTRATIONS

Nos. 1, 2, 5, 10, 11 and 18 are reproduced by permission of Librairie Hachette; no. 3 by permission of Photographie Giraudot; nos. 4, 12, 15 and 16 by permission of Radio Times Hulton Picture Library; nos 7 and 13 by permission of the Bibliothèque Nationale; no. 9 by permission of Baschet et Cie (*L'Illustration*); and nos. 14, 17 and 19 by permission of Roget-Viollet. Acknowledgment is made elsewhere for permission to reproduce illustrations nos. 6 and 8.

ACKNOWLEDGMENTS

The author has to acknowledge the gracious permission of Her Majesty the Queen to make use of material from the Royal Archives at Windsor Castle.

He must also thank the Archives du Sénat de la République for allowing him to reproduce the drawing of Clemenceau as senator by Noël Dorville; the Estate of Viscountess Milner for permission to include quotations from Lady Milner's *My Picture Gallery* and the photograph from the same book of Lady Milner and her father in the Bois with Clemenceau; and the Hamlyn Group for permission to include a quotation from Winston Churchill's *Great Contemporaries*.

Further thanks are due to M. Georges Wormser for his interest and help, and to the staffs of the London Library, the British Museum reading room and newspaper library, the Institut Français du Royaume-Uni, and in Paris the staffs of the Bibliothèque Nationale, the Bibliothèque de la Sorbonne and the Musée Clemenceau for their assistance with the author's researches.

FOREWORD

In a review of a recent symposium of essays on Clemenceau by Jacques Chastenet and others a writer in *Le Figaro* regretted that the contributors had not given an adequate picture of Clemenceau's life as he lived it. The remark was heartening to the author of the present book, for that is the very objective which he has had in mind from the beginning of his researches. No one, of course, could write about 'the Tiger' without dealing at length with his long parliamentary career and his rôle as France's 'Father of Victory', but other aspects of his life, such as his many years as a working journalist, the books he wrote, the friends he made, and his relations to his wife and his family, are often given short shrift by his biographers. The purpose of the following pages is to try and dovetail together the different parts of Clemenceau's story, in the hope of presenting a faithful portrait of the man Clemenceau and his life as he lived it.

PART ONE

MAKING THE
REPUBLIC

CHAPTER ONE

THE YOUNG REPUBLICAN

1. *Vendean Blue.* 2. *Father and son.* 3. *Student days.* 4. *Friends and mentors.* 5. *Thesis approved.*

[1]

IN THE AUTUMN of 1906 Georges Clemenceau, minister of the interior in the French government, made an official tour of the Vendée, the westernmost part of the old province of Poitou, lying between Nantes and La Rochelle and looking out across the Atlantic. He was sixty-five, and he was holding his first ministerial post after an already long career in politics and journalism.

A year or two earlier, when he was editor of the daily newspaper *L'Aurore*, one of his writers had nicknamed him the Tiger, but the name had not yet passed into general use. It would take a world war to bring cartoons of the French tiger at grips with the German eagle, or of a secretary pointing to a document for Clemenceau's signature and saying, 'If the prime minister would put his claw there . . .'

Georges Clemenceau was at home in the Vendée, which is one of the most rural departments of France. He had been born there, and throughout his life he delighted in the Vendean countryside—the plain, the marshland and especially the *bocage*, that rugged, gently undulating area of woodland, hillocks, valleys, small farms, secluded villages and sunken roads, along which, as he recalled in later life, one could ride for two or three miles without once seeing the sun. As a young man, he once wrote, it was his joy to 'drink in' the sky, the wind and the rain, to become drunk with the scent of the grass, to marvel at the beauty of the land. During his ministerial tour a ceremony at La Roche-sur-Yon gave him an opportunity for expressing his devotion to his own countryside.

He had seen, he said, something of the world, but nothing he had seen anywhere else could affect his love for the land of his birth. 'Its charm won me, its charm has held me. Plain, marsh, *bocage*, I have remained faithful to our good earth.' Vendeans, he declared, were part of France, but they wanted to be French with their own regional characteristics; and he gaily admitted that he owed the best of his enmities to his Vendean traits of independence, readiness to criticise, obstinacy and pugnacity. 'Our life,' he said, 'was a series of struggles against the invader. There are no better Frenchmen than we are.'

Clemenceau's praise of the Vendée caused some surprise in Paris, where he had lived for the past thirty-six years and was regarded as entirely Parisian. Yet no one could understand his career or his personality without taking account of his geographical background, which had given him the characteristics he mentioned in his speech, and particularly his keen sense of partisanship. No one, it is said, is neutral in the Vendée.

The Clemenceaus had lived there for many generations, at first in the manor house of Colombier, in the village of Mouchamps, and later in the gloomy, fortress-like mansion of L'Aubraie, in the hamlet of Féaule, with its 'expressionless, three-story façade' and 'latticed, funereally black windows' which Georges Clemenceau would later describe in his only novel, *Les Plus Forts*. They were proud to have bought the property before the French Revolution, and not, as was sometimes alleged, at one of the sales of *biens nationaux*—confiscated property of the Crown, the Church and the emigrant nobles—during the revolutionary era. A seventeenth-century Clemenceau had been given the right to bear arms by Louis XIII, and the family lived with a certain style in a poor region. Georges Clemenceau's uncle Paul liked to pretend that they were aristocrats, but in fact they were small landed gentry who were neither nobles nor bourgeois. The head of the family was usually a doctor of medicine, though the doctor's degree was acquired more as a hobby than with the intention of seriously practising as a physician.

In the revolutionary years the Clemenceaus were Republican, and took no part in the Vendean revolts against the new *régime*. They were Blues, as the Republicans were called, in contrast with the Whites—the nobles and clergy who fought for the return of the *ancien régime* and the peasants who took up arms against the Revolution because it favoured the towns and increased the economic hardships of the countryside. In the nineteenth century their Republican faith was stoutly maintained by Benjamin Clemenceau, Georges's father, who had followed the family tradition by qualifying as a doctor of medicine.

[2]

Though Dr. Benjamin Clemenceau and his wife were living at L'Aubraie in the 1840s, Georges was born at his mother's family home in the Vendean village of Mouilleron-en-Pareds, not far from Fontenay-le-Comte, on 28 September, 1841. Madame Clemenceau, who was Emma Gautherau before her marriage, was not on good terms with her father-in-law, who also lived at L'Aubraie, and she preferred to bear her child in more congenial surroundings. King Louis-Philippe, the former Duc d'Orléans, then reigned in France; the Second Republic ran its brief course while Georges was a small boy; he grew to manhood under the Second Empire.

He had a remarkable father. Dr. Clemenceau did not take his profession very seriously, though for some time he had a surgery at Nantes; most of his time was spent in reading, riding and walking and a rather haphazard management of his estate. He was Republican, materialist and anticlerical, and he had a reputation for misanthropy, ferocity, bitter hatreds and wounding irony. Yet he would always talk kindly to the peasants, who called him '*Not' maître*'.

'I think,' Georges Clemenceau once said, 'that the only influence which had any effect on me was my father's. . . . My father was at bottom a romantic who had carried the literary theories of Victor Hugo and others into politics and sociology. . . . At table . . . he spoke largely of his reading, enunciated his philosophy by fits and starts, and, little by little, I absorbed it.' As Georges grew up, father and son took long walks together through the *bocage*, either with heavy walking-sticks or with guns for rabbit-shooting, and the doctor would often burst into furious tirades against nobles, priests and rich farmers. He passed on to his son his eighteenth-century materialism, his faith in science and reason, his belief in the gradual progress of humanity towards a free and perfect society, and above all his anticlericalism and his Republicanism, which was deeply rooted in the Jacobin tradition. It was to his Jacobin upbringing, and perhaps also to the portraits of Robespierre, Saint Just and other Jacobin heroes that his father hung on the walls at L'Aubraie, that Georges Clemenceau owed the realism and the ruthlessness which were to mark his political career.

Madame Clemenceau bore the doctor six children—Georges (the eldest son), Albert and the much younger Paul, and Emma (the eldest of the family), Adrienne and Sophie. The girls' education was left to their mother, who learned Latin so that she could teach it to them; the doctor was more concerned with the boys, and particularly with Georges. The family moved to Nantes when Georges went to the *lycée* there, but returned to L'Aubraie each summer and to Mouilleron-en-Pareds in the autumn. Georges had ample opportunity for getting to know the *bocage*.

His schooldays were unremarkable; he showed no sign of brilliance, but did well enough to be admitted to the medical school of Nantes in 1858. This was a year in which his father was in serious trouble with the authorities of the Second Empire.

Throughout his later life Dr. Clemenceau had remained in touch with Etienne Arago and other Republicans whom he had met as a medical student in Paris. Such friendships became dangerous after 1851, when Prince Louis-Napoleon (the future Napoleon III) made his *coup d'état* which ended the Second Republic and led France into the Second Empire; the doctor was then arrested and held in custody for a short time while the new *régime* established itself. Worse was to follow in 1858, when Napoleon III and his wife, the Empress Eugénie, had a lucky escape from attempted assassination by the Italian revolutionary, Orsini, and his fellow conspirators. Though Orsini was quickly arrested (and subsequently executed) the attempt alarmed the Imperial government, which enacted a stringent public safety law, authorising the arrest and deportation without trial of suspected enemies of the *régime*. The minister of the interior ordered that a fixed number of arrests should be made in each department, and the list for the Vendée included Dr. Clemenceau's name. He was known to the police as one of a group of advanced liberals who met at a bookshop for political discussions. They needed no further evidence against him.

The doctor was arrested, and after a month in prison at Nantes was sentenced to be deported to Algeria; he was then placed in a *fourgon*—a cell-like vehicle in which one could neither sit nor stand—to be taken to Marseilles. Georges, who had come to see his father's departure, said emotionally: 'I will avenge you, father.' 'If you wish to avenge me, work,' the doctor answered.

The episode had a happier ending than might have been expected. One of the features of the Imperial administration was that Napoleon III always took careful note of local feeling, which he did not wish to offend unnecessarily. In Nantes the bourgeoisie were seething with indignation at the harsh treatment of a respected citizen. News of their anger reached official quarters in Paris, with the result that Dr. Clemenceau was released and sent home as soon as he arrived at Marseilles.

For two years the intimate and formative relationship between father and son was resumed, but in 1860 Georges left Nantes to continue his medical studies in Paris. The Vendean was about to become a Parisian, but he would never lose touch with his native land.

[3]

The city which Georges Clemenceau now saw for the first time was changing dramatically under the masterful direction of Baron Haussmann, prefect of the Seine. Wide new boulevards were giving Paris light and air and providing the military with easy access to all districts in the event of a rising; the boulevard de Strasbourg, formerly the boulevard du Centre, had been driven across the Seine into the heart of the Latin Quarter, home of the University of Paris, students, artists and writers, and its extension on the left bank had been named the boulevard Saint-Michel. New roads were also piercing the Mont Sainte-Geneviève area, the section of the student quarter in which Dr. Clemenceau found a small apartment for his son in the rue de l'Estrapade.

When Clemenceau came to the Latin Quarter the general feeling among students was Republican and anti-Imperialist. There were occasional demonstrations against professors who were known to be sympathetic to the Empire; some students joined workers' groups or launched ephemeral reviews; but most of them were busy with their work and their love-affairs, and with the process, so movingly described in Maurice Barrès's *Les Déracinés*, of turning themselves from provincials into Parisians.

The young Vendean, who was slight in stature, with a beard and long wavy hair, and was always correctly dressed, soon became a popular figure among the medical students. When they formed a students' association they made him president. His father, who came to see him in prison in 1862, was proud to find that Georges was 'king of the Odéon theatre gallery' (a traditional meeting-place for revolutionary students) and 'the lion of the Latin Quarter'. His medical studies, like his school work at Nantes, were satisfactory without being exceptional; in his first examination in 1861 he was tenth out of 330 candidates, and two years later he was accepted as a temporary house-surgeon, first at the Bicêtre hospital and later at that of La Pitié. An intervening spell in prison did not interfere with his university career.

Republican activities were the cause of his imprisonment. During his second year in Paris he and some other students founded *Le Travail*, an anti-government newspaper which was intended to appear weekly, though its readers were warned that '*Le Travail* appears when it can'. It survived for eight issues, the first appearing on 22 December, 1861 and the last on 22 February, 1862, so that its young editors did not fall far short of making it a weekly while it lasted.

Under the Second Empire the press was strictly controlled, but there were ways of defeating the Imperial censorship. Just as Mazzini, a generation earlier, had concealed revolutionary arguments in the literary articles he wrote for the *Indicatore Genovese*, so *Le Travail*, which described itself as a literary and scientific weekly, found subtle ways of expressing its opposition to the Imperial government.

In some ways the paper lived up to its self-description. It published book reviews, theatre notices, literary articles and poems, including one by a young man called Emile Zola, whom Clemenceau met in the office of Hachette, the book publisher. Zola responded eagerly to an invitation to contribute to *Le Travail*, and submitted a number of poems, of which one, entitled 'Doubt', drew the comment 'Rotten!' from Clemenceau, probably because of its religious tone and a reference to Jesus Christ and the Cross. 'Doubt' was published, but Clemenceau, who was a year younger than Zola, felt it his duty to warn him that he was not cut out for the literary life. 'Do anything you like,' he said. 'Sell mustard or women's hats. But give up literature. *You will never be a writer.*'

The real message of *Le Travail* could be read between the lines of apparently innocuous articles. For example, a new play by Edmond About, the gifted journalist and much-read novelist, was fiercely attacked in its columns; the attack was not so much for the play's dramatic faults but because About, who had once been anti-Imperialist, had now accepted the *régime* and had even attended one of the emperor's glittering house-parties at Compiègne. One can find, too, a strongly Republican trend in a passage from Clemenceau's article on 'The Martyrs of History', which appeared in *Le Travail*'s final issue. Anticipating his famous statement in the Chamber of Deputies that *'La Révolution est un bloc'*, he developed, at the age of twenty, the same contention that the French Revolution must be accepted as a whole.

> There are people (*he wrote*) who think themselves very advanced and seriously tell us, 'We accept with all their consequences the principles of '92, but we reject with horror the violences of the Revolution'. People who talk in this way are either ninnies or men of bad faith: do they not know that the violences are only the inevitable consequences of the appearance of these principles on the political scene? Do they really believe that one can gain victory for a new idea by peaceful means?

And a few lines lower down he asked how one could expect to deprive the king of his throne and the nobles of their estates and privileges without conflict and terror.

The police were not so blind to this kind of thing as Clemenceau and his friends may have hoped. They showed an embarrassing interest in *Le Travail*, and the editors had to change its office from week to week for fear of a raid. But it was not because of anything Clemenceau wrote in its pages that he found himself in the Mazas prison at the end of February 1862.

His arrest was due to his taking part in the printing and distribution of leaflets summoning workers to the place de la Bastille for a demonstration on the anniversary of the foundation of the Second Republic. The police had clear proof of his complicity in this illegal enterprise, and they came to his lodgings to arrest him. He was taken to the old Mazas gaol, where rats infested the cells, and he was ordered to take a bath in grimy, soup-like water already used by ten other prisoners. After waiting more than a month for his trial he was sentenced to a month's imprisonment and ordered to pay half the costs; but the period of his detention before trial was not offset against his sentence, so that he was actually in gaol for seventy-three days. He was not intimidated by his experiences, and before long he helped to launch another underground newspaper, *Le Matin*, which, like *Le Travail*, had only a short life.

[4]

While Clemenceau had been suffering the rigours of Mazas gaol, two of his friends, who had distributed an anti-Imperialist poem and recited it at the Bastille demonstration, had also been arrested and sent to Sainte-Pélagie prison. There they got to know another prisoner, Auguste Blanqui. After their release they went to Sainte-Pélagie to visit him, and took Clemenceau with them. His new acquaintance was to strengthen his Republican and anticlerical sentiments.

Blanqui, who spent a large part of his life in gaol, was then fifty-seven years old. He was a revolutionary agitator who believed in a Socialist dictatorship rather than in democratic Socialism. Roger L. Williams says that 'he was an egalitarian, an atheist, with great compassion for the poor, and he found it inconceivable that Socialism in any form could ever be established without the violent destruction of religion, the bourgeoisie and the State.' His extreme views had already brought him a death sentence (later commuted to life imprisonment) in the reign of King Louis-Philippe and periods of imprisonment under the Second Republic and the Second Empire. (He was to suffer eight more years of detention under the Third Republic.) Though Clemenceau's views were never as revolutionary as Blanqui's, his friendship with the single-minded and persuasive agitator was one of the formative elements in his student years.

After their first meeting Clemenceau visited Blanqui frequently. The old rebel urged him never to yield, never to compromise, but always to press ahead with the realisation of his ideas; he showed his confidence in his young friend by sending him to Brussels to bring back a forbidden printing press. Their friendship ended abruptly when Blanqui learnt that Clemenceau was a friend of the revolutionary journalist, Charles Delescluze, who had been Blanqui's enemy since the time of the Second Republic; but he continued, as will be seen later, to take a keen interest in Clemenceau's career. Clemenceau, too, did not forget his elderly mentor. Twenty years later, when he was director of his first daily newspaper, *La Justice*, a newcomer to the office found that hardly an evening went by without Blanqui's name being mentioned in one context or another.

Clemenceau made other important and useful friends in his student days. A letter from his father introduced him to the house of Etienne

Arago, playwright, scientist and ardent Republican; under Arago's roof
he met Henri de Rochefort, Jules Méline and Arthur Ranc, future politicians of the Third Republic, and he encountered other able young men,
such as Léon Gambetta and Henri Brisson, in cafés and artists' studios.
He was introduced to Claude Monet, who was then in his twenties and
was glad to get fifty francs for a picture, but he met the artist only a few
times and it was not until the 1880s that they began their long and close
friendship. He made, too, a number of American friends, some of whom
were very helpful to him when he went to New York.

Two friendships with older men—Gustave Jourdan and Auguste
Scheurer-Kestner—were of special significance. Jourdan had been a
government lawyer in the reign of King Louis-Philippe, but he was so
deeply convinced of the rights of the individual that he became a Republican
and even led one of the small local revolts against Prince Louis-Napoleon's
coup d'état. He spoke well at secret Republican meetings, and Clemenceau
thought him the most eloquent man he had ever heard. In many conversations Jourdan encouraged him to take up the defence of liberty;
they continued their discussions by letter when Clemenceau went to
America in 1865, but the correspondence was ended by Jourdan's death
from cholera two years later. Georges Wormser, who was Clemenceau's
last *chef de cabinet*, thinks that of all his friends in Paris Jourdan and
Blanqui were the two who had most influence on him.

Auguste Scheurer-Kestner, who was about twenty years older than
Clemenceau, was an Alsatian who had studied at the Paris medical school
but had entered industry, becoming manager of his father-in-law's
chemical works at Thann. He too was a Republican; Clemenceau met him
at Sainte-Pélagie when he was imprisoned for writing politically indiscreet
letters which were opened by the police. Their friendship was never to be
broken, though there must have been long periods when they saw little of
each other.

If Clemenceau had had his way in those early years, their relationship
would have been closer still; for Scheurer-Kestner had an unmarried
sister-in-law, Hortense Kestner, whom Clemenceau met when he stayed
with his friend at Thann in 1863. He fell in love with her and wanted to
marry her.

Hortense was the youngest and prettiest of the five daughters of Charles
Kestner, owner of the chemical works. She was a year older than
Clemenceau, and she had twenty proposals of marriage before she married
Charles Floquet, a successful barrister and future prime minister, in 1869.
The depth of Clemenceau's feelings for her is indicated in his letters to
Scheurer-Kestner in 1864 and by his friend's notes in his journal. For
nearly a year Clemenceau pleaded with him to intercede with Hortense;

his life, he said, would be greatly changed by the reply that she gave him. But Hortense was not attracted by him, and her parents did not like him at all; they all found him domineering, his exuberance clashed with their quiet bourgeois ways, and it was considered wrong for Hortense to have a husband younger than herself. Clemenceau's suit was finally rejected in a letter from Charles Kestner at the end of October.

Clemenceau was deeply grieved by the decision, and Scheurer-Kestner thought that it had a harmful effect on his career. 'If he had had an intelligent and ambitious wife like Madame Floquet,' he wrote in his journal, 'he might have overcome his instability of character.' But Hortense may have been wise in rejecting Clemenceau's addresses. Time would show that he was far from being an ideal husband.

[5]

Though the Paris medical school was so large that the professors knew few of the students by sight, Clemenceau was friendly with one of its best-known lecturers, Dr. Charles Robin, a member of the Académie des Sciences and a frequenter of the literary world, who was later to be one of the six guests at Sainte-Beuve's controversial Good Friday dinner.[1] Robin's lecture courses and occasional writings were the basis of the thesis, *De la génération des éléments anatomiques*, which Clemenceau submitted to the University of Paris for his doctorate in 1865.

Nothing that he had experienced since leaving the Vendée had weakened his faith in the eighteenth-century materialism he had learned from Dr. Clemenceau. ('I am a terrible materialist,' he wrote to Scheurer-Kestner in 1863.) To his father's views he had now added a certain amount of positivism, the philosophy of Auguste Comte which was, in essence, 'the assertion that science provides the model for all knowledge, so that everything we claim to know must be capable of empirical verification.' Like most of those who became prominent politicians under the Third Republic he shared Comte's belief in the inevitability of progress and the futility of such 'superstitions' as theology and metaphysics; he accepted, too, the Comtean view that only scientific method can provide a positive approach to problems of human behaviour and social organisation. Yet he was not a whole-hearted disciple of Comte, for he objected to the conservatism of Comte's political programme and to the religious emphasis of his last years.

[1] In 1868 Sainte-Beuve scandalised orthodox Parisians by giving a dinner-party on Good Friday and regaling his guests with crayfish, salmon trout, fillet of beef and pheasant stuffed with truffles. The distinguished company consisted of Prince Napoleon (Plon-Plon), who suggested the date for the party, Renan, Flaubert, About, Taine and Dr. Robin. (*See* Sainte-Beuve, *Souvenirs et Indiscrétions*, p. 216).

His thesis, as its title indicates, was a search for the secret of growth. In a foreword Clemenceau asserted that exact observation of phenomena was the point of departure for science; he did not claim to provide new observation, he had only assembled facts. With a touch of arrogance he added: 'The opinions which I shall express are entirely my own. I do not hold them because I have written this essay; I have written it because I hold them.'

His arguments are old-fashioned now, but they passed muster in their day. He accepted the theory of spontaneous generation, and rejected any idea of a supernatural influence on human life. 'We shall never know anything about first causes,' he wrote, 'for the simple reason that there are no first causes and never could be any.' He touched on a number of metaphysical problems, made some criticisms of Comtean assumptions and generally presented a materialistic view of the universe.

He admitted in later years that his thesis was only 'a compilation', based on Dr. Robin's researches. It is a long work, and footnotes on nearly every page refer to articles or papers by Robin, who is frequently quoted in the text. One can admire the young man's effrontery in submitting a thesis with so little medical content, when other students were writing on subjects like neuralgia, cardiac pathology, blood pressure and typhoid fever; but Robin himself presided over the examination board, and Clemenceau's offering was duly accepted. He believed that the other examiners did not even read it, for the only question he was asked in his oral test was about the treatment of scarlet fever. It was a fair enough question, since there was nothing in *De la génération des éléments anatomiques* to show that Clemenceau would be an efficient doctor.

The thesis did not pass unnoticed. After being published, like those of other successful candidates, in 1865, it appeared in a second edition in 1867, with an introduction by Robin. By that time Clemenceau was in the United States.

After completing his medical studies his next step should have been to gain further clinical experience in the Paris hospitals. He did nothing of the kind. The political world was already beckoning to him; he decided to go to the United States, where the Civil War had just ended, to see democracy in action. His father agreed, and gave him a modest allowance for his travels. Another reason for his leaving France was that he was still hurt by the failure of his courtship of Hortense Kestner. In writing to Scheurer-Kestner about his journey, he said pointedly: 'You know why I am going . . . I shall leave behind me only one genuine sorrow, my father's . . . I shall be free of all attachments, and I shall go where the wind takes me.' He was not to be 'free of all attachments' when he returned to live in France.

CHAPTER TWO

AMERICAN INTERLUDE

1. *In search of democracy.* 2. *'Letters from the United States.'* 3. *Mary Plummer.*
4. *Country doctor.*

[1]

THE YOUNG FRENCHMAN who sailed from Liverpool to New York in the steamer *Etna* in the summer of 1865 was dark-haired, dark-moustached and dark-bearded, of rather less than average height, with a high forehead, prominent cheekbones and sharp eyes flashing under bushy eyebrows. He had a pleasant voice, and would talk very rapidly while his ideas were pouring out, but more slowly when he wished to make some point particularly clear. His conversation might be light-hearted at one moment and deeply serious at the next; though he was keenly interested in politics he could also talk fluently on many other topics, such as books, pictures, theatres, science, philosophy and the countryside. He arrived in America with a good knowledge of the English language, which he had studied at home as well as at school, as he had wanted to read *Robinson Crusoe* in English.

His father came with him to England to see him off; it was the first of Clemenceau's many crossings of the English Channel. In London father and son called on John Stuart Mill and Herbert Spencer. Mill had written a book on Comte and positivism; Georges Clemenceau asked if he might be allowed to translate it into French, and Mill readily gave his permission. It turned out to be a useful bargaining counter, for a French publisher agreed to bring out the second edition of Clemenceau's thesis in return for the right to publish his translation of Mill's book.

Clemenceau did not intend to be merely a sightseer in America. Gustave Jourdan wrote to him on 10 February, 1866: 'I did not shudder in the very least to hear you say that you want to study America in the light of the positivist method.' The remark suggests that he was proposing to examine the influences of environment and heredity in the United States, and to extend his survey from the biological to the social plane; but the harsh necessity of earning a living evidently compelled him to give up this grandiose plan. The articles on American politics he wrote for

Le Temps showed democracy in action but hardly amounted to a study in depth of the American way of life.

It was a fascinating time for visiting the United States. The civil war was over, the union was to remain intact, and the abolition of slavery would involve a great work of political and social reconstruction. Clemenceau had sympathised with the American negroes ever since, as a boy at Nantes, he had wept over *Uncle Tom's Cabin* at the local theatre. He greatly admired Abraham Lincoln, and had been distressed by his death. He felt, too, that he was not going to the United States as a complete stranger, for some of the American friends he had made in Paris had now returned to their own country.

Soon after his arrival in New York he settled down in the still semi-rural Greenwich Village, the suburb which housed the French colony, together with many of the city's liberals, intellectuals, artists and journalists. Eugene Bushe, a lawyer whom he had met in Paris, made him welcome, and he was soon well known in the Bohemian circles of New York. He had his regular table at Pfaff's, the Broadway restaurant, and he was invited to the Union Square Club. He attended meetings in Union Square and went to Tammany Hall, the centre of New York's municipal politics. He became acquainted with Horace Greeley, editor of the *New York Tribune*, and learnt much from him about American political life. He was often to be seen in the French bookshop.

He had not meant to make a long stay. He had told his father he would be away for six months at the most, but he had under-estimated America's magnetism. He returned briefly to France in 1866, probably to find a publisher for his translation of Mill's book and the second edition of his thesis, but he was soon back in the United States. While he was in Paris he met several of his old student friends, and joined them in signing a declaration of atheistical principles, promising 'never to receive any religious sacrament—no priest at birth, no priest at marriage, no priest at death.' (One part of this vow was to cause him some embarrassment two years later.)

Resuming his life in New York, he was anxious to add to his father's allowance by his own efforts. He opened a small surgery, but patients were few, and he soon gave up the idea of earning his living as a doctor. He did better with journalism, though his first earnings as a writer were small indeed.

[2]

Clemenceau began to contribute to the Parisian newspaper *Le Temps* in his early days in New York, and he continued to write for it until November 1869, though his final American commentaries were actually written in France. His articles were published as 'Letters from the United States', but they appeared over the name of the member of the editorial staff who prepared them for publication. It would doubtless have been indiscreet of *Le Temps* to have published them over the name of Georges Clemenceau, which could be found in the police records of the Second Empire.

There were ninety-five letters in all. They were well written, with flashes of humour and irony, and they provided a fair conspectus of the difficulties facing the United States after the death of President Lincoln.

He had much to write about. Among his subjects were the long conflict between President Andrew Johnson and Congress which led to the president's impeachment (and eventual acquittal); the American attitude towards French intervention in Mexico; American relations with Cuba; negro suffrage and the effects of racial segregation in the southern States, which he went to see for himself in Virginia and in North and South Carolina.[1] His lifelong passion for justice was shown in his warm sympathy with the negroes; he thought that they should be given civil, political and social equality, though he realised that social equality was something which could not be provided by law.

As they appeared in *Le Temps*, Clemenceau's articles were exclusively political. Though he was a keen reader of English literature, he never mentioned Charles Dickens's triumphant tour of the States in 1867–8; when he became a part-time teacher he never amused his French readers with glimpses of life in an American girls' school. It was a different matter when he wrote daily for *La Justice* in later years and was always ready to turn from social and political articles to comments on an art exhibition or a satirical description of a strip-tease show.

Clemenceau's Republicanism was confirmed and strengthened by his experience of American democracy. His hatred of monarchical rule was expressed in a letter to a woman correspondent (who has never been identified), written on 6 September, 1867. His correspondent had apparently shown some sympathy with the unfortunate Emperor Maximilian and Empress Charlotte of Mexico; he told her he could not share her feelings. All these emperors, kings, archdukes and princes might be noble, sublime, generous and superb, and their princesses everything that was lovely: 'but I hate them, with a merciless hatred, as one hated Louis XVI in 1793. . . . Between us and these people there is war to the death.'

---

[1] Clemenceau never forgot his visit to the southern States. As an old man he recalled his surprise on finding there 'a remarkably refined society in which the selfish prejudice in favour of slavery was mingled with the most delicate sentiment. Almost every evening I found on my table some work in which it was proved that slavery was sanctioned in the Bible.' (*See* Clemenceau, *In the Evening of my Thought*, p. 399n.)

His father would certainly have approved of such sound Jacobin sentiments.

One can understand, therefore, why he was in no hurry to return from the freedom of American democracy to the authoritarian rule of Napoleon III. But his financial problems had become acute. His father's allowance covered only his basic expenses; his hopes of running a successful medical practice had been disappointed; and he was poorly rewarded for his articles in *Le Temps*, which was then paying him by the line and finally settled for the modest fee of 150 francs a month. As he wondered where to turn for money, a new thought came to him. This was the period when many Americans were laying the foundations of huge fortunes in the Chicago and Great Lakes area. He spent a month in Chicago and wrote home enthusiastically to say that he could make some marvellous investments there if his father would send the money he needed.

Georges Clemenceau was not destined to become a Franco-American millionaire. His father not only declined to send the money, but told Georges that he would stop his allowance unless he came back to France. But Georges was not yet ready to leave America. He decided to stay in New York, to go on writing for *Le Temps* and to find some other way of increasing his income.

[3]

His friend Eugene Bushe came to his rescue. Clemenceau told him that he would like a post as a teacher of French, and Bushe introduced him to Miss Catherine Aiken, who kept a boarding-school for young ladies at Stamford, Connecticut, some thirty-four miles north-east of New York City, on Long Island Sound. He gaily told her that he was ready to teach anything except the Catechism and revealed religion, and he was engaged as a teacher of French. When Miss Aiken learned that he was a good horseman she asked him to teach the girls riding as well.

Stamford was conveniently placed for a young man who wished to combine teaching with journalism. The train journey from New York took little more than an hour; Clemenceau was able to go to Stamford on Monday morning, give lessons for two days and be back in New York on Tuesday evening, leaving him with the rest of the week for his study of America and his letters for *Le Temps*.

It can be imagined that he made a considerable impression on the pupils at Miss Aiken's academy. He was foreign and good-looking, and though he was already beginning to grow bald he was now wearing side-whiskers in the fashionable style of General Burnside, one of the less successful northern commanders in the Civil War. Some of the girls were a little frightened by him, but they liked him too. At the end of his first year at Stamford they gave him a beautiful edition of Washington Irving's *Sketch Book*.

Miss Aiken thought there had never been a better French teacher, and a pleasant appreciation of his classroom manner is given in a letter quoted in Georges Wormser's *La République de Clemenceau*. The writer was one of his former pupils, who spent six years at the school. She also found him a good teacher, who was able to present information in an arresting way and to simplify the rules of grammar so as to make them easier to understand. She remembered how impulsive he was: in the middle of explaining something to his class he might suddenly leap from his seat, go towards the open door, close it with a well-aimed kick at the handle and return to his seat with the utmost gravity.

Everything suggests that he enjoyed teaching his American young ladies and amusing them with his dry humour. While he was giving his first riding lesson he said politely: 'You are all firm on your saddles, but allow me to say that when you begin to gallop it is unnecessary to give the war-cry of the Cherokee Indians.' And when a pupil came to him at the end of a lesson to ask for further enlightenment on the use of the past participle, he made her write on the blackboard, '*J'ai mangé la pomme; la pomme que j'ai mangée.*' 'Ever since Eve,' he said, 'young ladies understand things better with an apple.'

The girl who asked for enlightenment was Mary Plummer, daughter of a New Hampshire dentist who had moved to Wisconsin for his health's sake and had died there while she was still a child. Fortunately for the now impoverished family, Mrs. Plummer had a wealthy brother, Horace Taylor, who lived in New York. He had become Mary's guardian and was paying for her education at Miss Aiken's select academy.

She was a pretty girl, with light brown hair and brown eyes, who had been much admired in Wisconsin and was popular with her fellow pupils. Clemenceau soon found himself attracted by her, and was impressed by her intelligence as well as her good looks. A colleague once came across a tiny sketch he had made on a scrap of paper, and exclaimed: 'Those eyebrows are like Mary Plummer's!' Clemenceau crumpled the paper up, and it was a long time before he drew any more sketches.

Mary, too, was attracted by her teacher. They went for walks together, and they went on meeting after Mary had left school and was living at her uncle's house on Fifth Avenue. Some time in 1868 Clemenceau asked Horace Taylor for his niece's hand. Mr. Taylor did not like the idea of a marriage between his niece and a French teacher, but to please Mary he would have given his consent, had not Clemenceau himself raised an apparently insuperable obstacle to their union. Mr. Taylor insisted that the young couple should be married in church; Clemenceau refused to take part in a church service because of his vow that he would never accept a religious sacrament.

It was a deadlock. Neither Clemenceau nor Mr. Taylor would yield, and though Mary did not insist on a church wedding she would not marry against her uncle's wishes. But Clemenceau did not give up hope. He felt confident that the marriage would take place, and he decided to go home and ask for his father's consent. Dr. Clemenceau raised no objection, but made the condition that Georges and his bride should live in the Vendée; Clemenceau readily agreed, and spent the winter in L'Aubraie and Paris, apart from a brief return to America at the end of the year. At L'Aubraie he read, rode and made his first attempts at being a country doctor. In Paris he resumed old friendships, quarrelled with a house surgeon and fought the first of his twenty-two duels. Pistols were the chosen weapons, and neither of the duellists was injured.[1]

He was still certain that Mary Plummer would marry him. In a letter to Scheurer-Kestner in February he said that he was engaged to a young American girl and would bring her to France in July. He described her as a brunette of medium height, and added, rather prosaically, that she had twenty-nine teeth, with three still to come. Her ideas, he said, were 'in process of formation'.

His confidence was justified. Mary wrote to say that she had persuaded her uncle to sanction a civil marriage, and he returned to New York in the early summer. The young couple were married at Mr. Taylor's house on 23 June, 1869; the ceremony was conducted by the Mayor of New York. But for all Mr. Taylor's apparent good will, he did not really approve of the wedding. He made no settlement on Mary when she married, he left her nothing in his will. Malicious gossip of later years, suggesting that Clemenceau had squandered his wife's fortune, had no foundation, for no such fortune existed.

Five days after the wedding *Le Courrier des Etats-Unis* (New York's French newspaper) reported that Dr. Clemenceau and his lady had sailed for Brest and Le Havre in the *Lafayette*. On landing in France they went at once to the Vendée, where Clemenceau had found a house at Sainte-Hermine.

---

[1] Clemenceau had a great reputation as a duellist. He was an excellent swordsman and a brilliant shot, and he kept in good practice. Yet his duels were singularly bloodless; only one of his opponents seems to have been wounded at all seriously. He explained to an American journalist: 'I left my mark several times with pistol and *épée*, and in turn I carry scars.... More often, especially in encounters with distinguished adversaries, I had the good sense to cool off and to fire in the air. They may have had the same idea, for the blood of any of us might have had an evil political effect.' (*See* Wythe Williams, *The Tiger of France*, p. 39.)

[4]

French politics were in a state of flux in that summer of 1869. Napoleon III was taking tentative steps towards the liberalisation of the Second Empire and the surrender of some, at least, of his absolute powers; but liberalisation was not enough for the political Left, which was now established as the Republican opposition and had found a strong leader in Léon Gambetta, the thirty-one-year-old lawyer whom Clemenceau had met occasionally in the Latin Quarter. Gambetta's election address at Belleville, the Parisian working-class district which returned him to the largely powerless Legislative Body, set a pattern for French Radicalism and was long remembered as 'the Belleville manifesto'. Though ostensibly prepared by the electors, it clearly represented Gambetta's own views. It called for disendowment and disestablishment of the Church, free elementary education and freedom of the Press and of meeting and association.

The Belleville manifesto was a programme which Clemenceau would soon take as his model, and would, indeed, continue to uphold long after its author had abandoned it; but for the time being he was content to be a country doctor, making his round of visits on horseback and looking in at L'Aubraie for long talks with his father about the expected collapse of the Second Empire. His professional rewards were modest. A notebook he preserved till his old age gave the names of his patients, with records of his visits and the fees he received. There were entries like Baumard, two visits at 2 fr. 50, one visit at 3 fr.; Barbot, seven visits at 5 fr., total 35 fr., one visit at 0 fr.; Marie Biré, six visits at 4 fr., total 24 fr. A consultation and an operation cost only five francs, and his entire earnings in 1869–70 were 1,900 fr. 50.[1]

In June 1870 Mary Clemenceau gave birth to her first child, a daughter who was named Madeleine. But Clemenceau had little time to enjoy the pleasures of fatherhood, for a few weeks later excited Parisian crowds were shouting '*A Berlin!*' as France fell into Bismarck's trap and declared war on Prussia.

He had mixed feelings at the outset of the Franco-Prussian War. He loved France deeply, but his English friend H. M. Hyndman heard him say in later years; 'It was almost impossible for a patriotic Republican to desire victory for the French armies. That would have meant a new life for the Second Empire.' But he was not in this state of uncertainty for long.

---

[1] In the nineteenth and early twentieth centuries 25 francs were the equivalent of £1 sterling or 4·86 U.S. dollars. Clemenceau was thus receiving four shillings or just under a dollar for an operation, and his yearly earnings were equal to about £76 or 370 dollars.

The Prussian army's superiority in the early encounters quickly showed that Napoleon III had come to the end of the road. So, too, had Clemenceau's career as a country doctor. Leaving his wife and child in his father's care at L'Aubraie, he went to Paris, anxious to be at the centre of whatever great events were about to unfold themselves.

CHAPTER THREE

MAYOR OF MONTMARTRE

1. *'Long live the Republic'*. 2. *Parisian deputy*. 3. *The Eighteenth of March*. 4. *Retreat and return*.

[1]

CLEMENCEAU ARRIVED in Paris as a young provincial doctor with no political standing. Less than a year later he had been mayor of Montmartre and a deputy of the National Assembly. The end of the Second Empire was the beginning of his long career in public life.

Arriving, as he did, with no definite purpose, he was soon in touch with the more politically-minded friends of his student days. With Arthur Ranc he was one of the crowd outside the Palais-Bourbon, seat of the Legislative Body, on the afternoon of 4 September, 1870, when the news of Napoleon III's surrender at Sedan reached Paris. The two young men were among the first to push past the ushers and burst into the debating chamber, where they were just in time to hear Gambetta and Jules Favre, leaders of the Republican opposition, announce that the Second Empire had ceased to exist. The Republican deputies then moved to the Hôtel de Ville, where they proclaimed the Third Republic and appointed a government of national defence, with Favre as foreign minister, Gambetta as minister of the interior and General Trochu, military governor of Paris, as prime minister (*président du conseil*). The Republicans were resolved to go on fighting and to win back for France what the Second Empire had lost. Clemenceau no longer had any reservations about wishing for his country's victory.

One of Gambetta's first actions was to ensure the loyalty of Paris by nominating good Republicans as mayors of Paris and its twenty *arrondissements*. Etienne Arago, whose house Clemenceau had often visited, became mayor of Paris, and Ranc was made mayor of the nineteenth *arrondissement*. On Arago's advice, Gambetta chose Clemenceau as mayor of the eighteenth *arrondissement*, covering the Montmartre area. Many people must have been surprised by the choice of a young Vendean for the mayoralty of a Parisian working-class area; the appointment was obviously due to Clemenceau's personal friendships, though he claimed in later years that the Second Empire had made such a clean sweep in Montmartre that there was no one left who was suitable for the post.

Clemenceau was named mayor on 5 September. Six days later he showed his warlike spirit in a proclamation to the people of Montmartre:

Citizens,

Shall France sink and disappear or resume her former place in the vanguard?

That is the question today, and it is our duty to solve it. The enemy is at the gate of the city. The day may not be far distant when our breasts will be the country's last rampart.

Everyone knows his duty.

We are the children of the Revolution. Let us be inspired by the example of our fathers in 1792, and like them, *we shall conquer*.

Long live France! Long live the Republic!

France, the Revolution, the Republic: three of the guiding principles of Clemenceau's political thought were thus enunciated in his first official declaration.

At that time Montmartre still seemed to be separate from the city of Paris, in which it had only recently been incorporated. Its hill, on which Sacré Coeur had not yet been built, offered an illusion of safety, and refugees streamed there from other districts as the German armies invested the city. These newcomers added to the mayor's responsibilities, but Clemenceau took up his work with great enthusiasm and soon showed that he had natural gifts for administration.

His duties were manifold. On the military side he had to ensure that the ramparts were guarded, to give warning of any Prussian attempt to enter the city, and to organise and arm the National Guard, the old citizen militia of the French Revolution which had been hastily revived in the last days of the Second Empire, when the departure of so many regular troops for the front left Paris without enough trained men to guard the fortifications. Then there was much to be done for the citizens' welfare. From 19 September the Prussian ring round Paris was complete, and the city was cut off from the rest of France; it was the mayor's duty to see that food supplies were maintained, that there was milk for the children, that coal and paraffin were fairly distributed, and that lodgings of some kind were available for the refugees.

This was not all. With power in his hands for the first time in his life, Clemenceau decided that he would put at least one of his political ideas into practice. As an anticlerical, he felt that the Church's hold on education must be loosened. He sent a circular to the Montmartre schools announcing that Church and State were to be separated and that education would be entirely lay. In particular, he told teachers that they need no longer obey their parish priest's orders to take their schoolchildren to catechism classes, though the children were free to go alone if they wished.

But the teachers of Montmartre were not prepared to change their ways because of a mayoral circular. Only one teacher in the eighteenth *arrondissement* followed Clemenceau's instructions. This was the forty-year-old Louise Michel, who ran a small school in the rue Houdon with the help of her mother and a junior teacher. After a religious upbringing Louise had become Republican and violently anti-clerical; she was glad to carry out Clemenceau's instructions, and she was soon on friendly terms with the young mayor. He visited her school, and as food became scarcer, he took care to see that Louise's pupils had their due supplies.

His work as mayor was appreciated by the citizens. In November the government gave orders for an election of mayors and deputy mayors in Paris, since those chosen by Gambetta in September had no legal standing. Montmartre showed its gratitude to Clemenceau by electing him to continue his duties, but his friends Arago and Ranc both lost their posts.

This was the winter of siege and starvation, when no food could enter Paris. The rich lived for a time on the meat of bears, zebras, elephants and camels from the zoo, while the poor had to make do with rats; yet the city's defenders dourly defied the Prussians, and Gambetta, now minister of war, flew from Paris to Tours by balloon and made heroic but un-availing efforts to organise an efficient army in the provinces.

Ordinary communications between Paris and the rest of France had ceased when the Prussians completed their ring round the city; messages could be sent only by pigeon post or the occasional balloon, and it was by balloon post that Clemenceau sent two affectionate letters to his wife in December. Both letters were in English. In the first he said: 'My very dear love, all my thoughts never leave you. Here we are doing all that is possible to win. Patience and courage. I am impatient to hold you to my heart. We shall hold firm.' And a few days later: 'My dear little wife Mary, another balloon is leaving tonight. I would like so much to go with it and make a short stay at Féaule where you are, but at this moment I cannot think of such a thing. . . . Courage and confidence. Courage and patience.'

[2]

Courage was not enough. The French armies were soundly beaten, and on 26 January, 1871, the government accepted armistice terms which

Jules Favre had negotiated with Bismarck, the German chancellor. They provided for a war indemnity and the cession to the new German Empire (proclaimed at Versailles a few days earlier) of Alsace and the greater part of Lorraine.

The Republicans were shocked by the government's submission to Prussia. From the provinces Gambetta called desperately for further resistance, but Paris, which had held out so bravely for so long, could do no more. It was being bombarded by the Prussians; food supplies had run out; it could only capitulate to the enemy.

It was clear, however, that the government of national defence, which the Republican deputies had appointed on 4 September, had not been elected by the people and had no authority to make peace. A condition of the armistice was that free elections for a National Assembly should be held at once, so that peace could be made by a fully representative government.

Clemenceau, like many other Parisians, saw the armistice as a betrayal of France. He told his subordinates at the Montmartre *mairie*: 'You have been cruelly abandoned. All resistance has been made impossible.' He believed that war should be resumed and that no peace should be made on Bismarck's conditions. To promote his views he stood for election to the National Assembly in February, and was one of forty-three deputies—all Republicans—who were returned for Paris. With few exceptions all the Parisian deputies wished for a resumption of the war.

The majority of the Assembly took a different view. The Republican fervour which had swept over Paris after Sedan had not been shared by the provinces, except in a few of the larger towns. Though the Second Empire had fallen and France had been proclaimed a Republic, the monarchists formed the majority of the new National Assembly. Of its six hundred members some four hundred were avowed royalists, fairly evenly divided between legitimists (followers of the Comte de Chambord, Bourbon pretender to the French throne) and Orleanists (who upheld the rival claim of the Comte de Paris, grandson of King Louis-Philippe), and Republicans held less than a third of the seats. Weary of war and longing for peace and order, the rural districts of France had elected a reactionary Assembly whose members were largely drawn from established bourgeois families.

Since Paris was still unsettled after its months of famine and bombardment, Bordeaux was chosen as the Assembly's first meeting-place. Clemenceau took his seat in the middle of February, and joined Victor Hugo, Louis Blanc, Edgar Quinet and other Republicans in expressing deep sympathy with the deputies from Alsace-Lorraine who were soon to lose their constituencies to Germany. He signed a letter to them, saying:

'We declare that the National Assembly and the people of France are incompetent to make a single one of your constituents a Prussian subject; like you, we hold in advance as null and void any act or treaty, any vote or plebiscite, by which any part of Alsace or Lorraine should be ceded. Whatever happens, the citizens of those two areas will remain our compatriots and our brothers.' On 1 March he was one of the 107 Republicans who voted against the law ratifying the preliminary peace negotiations— the negotiations which led, on 10 May, to the signing of the Treaty of Frankfort. Thus at the very beginning of his parliamentary career Clemenceau took the first steps in his long crusade for the restoration of Alsace-Lorraine.

It was during the National Assembly's meetings at Bordeaux that he caused some stir among his fellow deputies by laying on the table, on behalf of the Republican Positivist Club of Paris, a motion demanding that Corsica should cease to be a part of the territory of the French Republic. The motion was obviously intended to be a sneer at Napoleon III and all other Bonapartes, since Corsica was their family home and remained the centre of their cult; but it was also arguable that Franco-Italian relations would have been improved by the cession of Corsica to Italy, and Paris would have been happy to say good-bye to its many, and unpopular, Corsican policemen. But the motion remained on the table. Having agreed to give away a large area of French territory under duress, the Assembly was not prepared to surrender still more as an anti-Bonapartist gesture.

Clemenceau's presentation of this motion does not necessarily mean that he supported it, or even that he expected it to be taken seriously. Evidently he was still in touch with positivist circles, and felt that he could hardly refuse his friends when they asked him to lay their motion before the Assembly. Yet his action was a *gaffe* which revealed his political immaturity, and his enemies would revert to it later as a means of deriding him. Edouard Drumont, the scurrilous antisemitic journalist, brought it up in 1889 in his book *La Fin d'un Monde*, in which he accused Clemenceau of trying to give away part of France. Even in 1942 Joseph Caillaux, still smarting from the Tiger's treatment of him in the First World War, referred to the Corsican motion in his memoirs, and asserted that the deputies 'shrugged their shoulders' when it was laid on the table.

Early in March Clemenceau and his Republican friends had a serious rebuff in the Assembly. Bordeaux had never been meant to be more than a temporary meeting-place, and the Assembly might soon have been expected to move to Paris; but the country-based royalist majority—the dukes and other nobles, squires and squireens and pillars of the *haute bourgeoisie*—saw Paris as a hotbed of revolution and wished to keep away from it until they had been able to restore the monarchy. Though the Parisian deputies strongly opposed the 'decapitalisation' of their city, Adolphe Thiers, the ageing Orleanist statesman who had been chosen by the Assembly as 'chief of the executive power' (a title which neatly avoided using the word 'Republic'), agreed with the majority. Fontaine-bleau and Bourges were considered as possible meeting-places, but the final choice was Versailles, which the German high command had occupied and was already leaving. To appease the Parisian deputies Thiers conceded that ministers and government offices should remain in Paris.

Strategic reasons had much to do with the choice of Versailles, for Thiers realised that it would be a good base for a government army invading Paris in the event of an insurrection. It was also near enough to Paris to allow ministers to travel easily between the Assembly and their offices. Clemenceau himself was able to combine his mayoral duties in Montmartre with occasional attendance at the Assembly.

He found, however, a new and difficult problem awaiting him when he returned from Bordeaux to his *mairie*. This was the affair of the cannons, which came to a head on 18 March.

[3]

A significant event had taken place in Paris during the absence of the government and the National Assembly. A central committee had been formed by the National Guard, which was now a citizen defence force of more than 300,000 men, who were paid 1 fr. 50 centimes a day, with an extra 75 centimes for a wife and 25 centimes for each child.

The unpopular General Clément Thomas, who was remembered for the severity with which he had helped to crush the workers' insurrection in 1848, was its first commanding officer under the government of national defence. He aroused further hatred through his attempts to bring the Guardsmen under strict military discipline, and he was replaced by General d'Aurelle de Paladines after the general election. At the same time representatives of 215 out of the 260 battalions met to elect the central committee, which was to play a big part in the events of the next few weeks.

It was this committee which made the first move in the affair of the cannons. Under the terms of the armistice the Prussians were to occupy the western districts of Paris on 1 March, and more than 250 cannons, some of which had been paid for by National Guard subscriptions, were still in the future Prussian zone. Fearing that they would fall into enemy hands, the central committee ordered that they should be transferred to safer places; this was successfully done by National Guardsmen, assisted by army reservists and civilians, and 171 cannons were placed in Montmartre, 74 in Belleville and others in the place des Vosges.

To Adolphe Thiers it seemed that these guns were directly threatening the city of Paris; he instructed Ernest Picard, who had succeeded Gambetta as minister of the interior, to tell the mayors of the *arrondissements* concerned that they must persuade the local National Guard to hand over the cannons to the government. Picard passed on the order to Clemenceau, whose first impression was that the National Guard in Montmartre would fall in with the government's wishes. In preliminary talks it was almost agreed that the cannons should be transferred to the Ecole Militaire in the Champ-de-Mars; but the National Guard were in no hurry to move them, as they felt no confidence in a government backed by a largely royalist Assembly.

Thiers was impatient at the delay in arranging the transfer. He had promised, through Picard, to warn Clemenceau if he meant to take any action in Montmartre; when the time came, he did not keep his promise. At a meeting of military chiefs on 17 March he gave orders for the immediate seizure of the cannons. Early on the following morning troops and gendarmes marched through the narrow streets of Montmartre to the artillery park at the top of the hill.

The events which followed were so important to Clemenceau that in 1872 he dictated to a secretary and corrected in his own hand a long account of his movements on the disastrous 18 March. The main points of his story are fully confirmed by other reports and by the findings of the court-martial on the chief offenders which was held in November. From his account it is clear that he first learned of the government's action at 6 a.m., when one of his assistants at the *mairie* came to his lodgings to tell him that Montmartre was occupied by troops who had seized the cannons. They seemed to be in complete command of the situation.

And so, to a point, they were, but the position was changing. General Lecomte, who was in charge of the operation, had taken the National Guard by surprise and seized the cannons with very little shooting: about a hundred National Guardsmen had been taken prisoner and one had been wounded; but the teams of horses needed to drag the guns away had not yet arrived. In the meantime the gendarmerie had taken over a National Guard headquarters in the rue des Rosiers (which no longer exists) and were guarding the prisoners there.

On hearing the news Clemenceau hurried to the centre of the troops' operations. Passing through quiet streets, in which soldiers were chatting with local people and buying rolls at bakers' shops, and no National Guardsmen were to be seen, he found General Lecomte on the heights and urged him to take the guns away as quickly as possible. He then went to the rue des Rosiers, treated the injured Guardsman's wound and sent for a stretcher to take him to hospital. But this was forbidden by General Lecomte, who feared that taking a stretcher through the streets would be too much like the well-known insurrectionary ploy of 'parading the corpse'. Clemenceau had to accept the general's decision and thought it best to go to the *mairie*. On his way he noticed that crowds were beginning to grow, and that many soldiers had laid down their rifles on the pavement.

He was now in an ambiguous position, suspected by both sides. To Lecomte he appeared as a potential revolutionary who might arouse the mob against the military; but the ominous silence of the senior National Guardsmen waiting at the *mairie* showed that they regarded the mayor as being in league with the government. He stayed in the *mairie* to await developments.

He had not long to wait. Soon after 8 a.m. a bugler of the National Guard sounded the call to arms; men came running from all sides and formed up in companies, with some of Lecomte's soldiers among them. A threatening crowd, supported by National Guardsmen, surrounded Lecomte and his staff and took them prisoner; they were held in custody at the Château Rouge, a dance-hall in the rue de Clignancourt. A number of other officers and gendarmes were also captured and were taken to the *mairie* for safe keeping.

News of Lecomte's capture was brought to Clemenceau by Captain Simon Mayer, a National Guard company commander. Clemenceau said to him: 'I count on you to guard the prisoners.' Later in the morning another prisoner was seized: the much-hated General Clément Thomas ill-advisedly came out to see what was going on, and was recognised by National Guardsmen as he walked along the boulevard in civilian clothes. He was taken to the house in the rue des Rosiers, and Lecomte was also taken there from the Château Rouge.

By this time General Vinoy, commander-in-chief of the troops in Paris, had realised that the operation had failed; he sent orders for the troops to be withdrawn, leaving the prisoners behind. Montmartre was still in a state of turmoil, and at half-past four Captain Mayer came back to the *mairie*, to warn Clemenceau that Lecomte and Clément Thomas would be killed unless he went at once to the rue des Rosiers. Wearing his mayoral sash as the symbol of his authority, Clemenceau forced his way through the crowded, winding streets, but before he reached the house in the rue des Rosiers a passer-by shouted that the generals had been shot.

A hostile demonstration greeted him outside the house. He was now generally suspected of having acted in connivance with the government and against the National Guard; he always believed that if he had arrived five minutes earlier he would have been shot with the generals. They had been killed in the garden, and while Clemenceau was talking to National Guardsmen about the safety of the other prisoners, he suddenly heard a great noise, as a crowd of soldiers, Guardsmen, women and children, who had filled the courtyard of the house, surged out into the street, singing and dancing.

All were shrieking like wild beasts without realising what they were doing (*he wrote in 1872*). I observed then that pathological phenomenon which might be called blood lust. A breath of madness seemed to have passed over this mob: from a wall children brandished indescribable trophies; women, dishevelled and emaciated, flung their arms about while uttering raucous cries, having apparently taken leave of their senses. I saw some of them weeping while they shrieked louder than others. Men were dancing about and jostling one another in a kind of savage fury. It was one of those extraordinary nervous outbursts, so frequent in the Middle Ages, which still occur among masses of human beings under the stress of primeval emotion.

Prudently he decided not to go into the house, but went instead to the Château Rouge to assure himself of the safety of the officers held there; then he regained the calm of the *mairie*, where there were other prisoners to protect. There were no more killings that evening.

Clemenceau's conduct on this astonishing day was often discussed in later years. Some people (Queen Victoria among them) mistakenly thought that he took part in the murders; a more pertinent comment was that, if he had kept in closer touch with events and had gone to the rue des Rosiers earlier, he could have saved the generals.

No doubt he was reluctant to leave the *mairie* because he felt himself responsible for the prisoners who were held there. But even if he had gone out earlier, could he, in fact, have saved the generals' lives? The uproar was caused by the frenzied mob and disgruntled Guardsmen rather than the leaders of the National Guard who had originally instigated resistance to the government troops. As Jeanne Gaillard points out, 'On 18 March the ringleaders restrained the crowd more than they excited it. General Lecomte was killed, it seems, by a soldier of the line. As for Clément Thomas, the officers of the National Guard tried their hardest to save him from a summary execution, but in the eyes of the Guardsmen he symbolised the military rule which he wished to impose on them when he commanded them.' Intervention by the mayor of Montmartre would hardly have had much effect on the disgruntled sergeant who had resolved to kill his commanding officer; and if the National Guard's own officers could not protect the rash, intruding Clément Thomas, Clemenceau would have had little hope of doing any better. It should also be remembered that brutal murders had not been expected at that time, which was some weeks before the horrors of the Commune and its repression by the government army.

[4]

The affair of the cannons showed that Paris refused to recognise the authority of the National Assembly and the chief of the excutive power. Faced with such open defiance, Thiers decided to abandon the capital: all army units were at once withdrawn from the city, and he and his ministers left for Versailles. By ordering the seizure of the cannons he had started the insurrection, by leaving Paris he turned it into a revolution—a revolution which the central committee of the National Guard had neither intended nor prepared.

For the time being Paris was calm. On the morning after the generals' murder shops were open, cafés were full, omnibuses were running and citizens went about their ordinary business. The central committee, which had taken over the Hôtel de Ville, issued a reassuring statement that it intended to preserve the Republic and would shortly hold elections for a Commune, or municipal council, of Paris.

The mayors of Paris, of whom some were deputies and all had been elected by their fellow citizens, challenged this cool assumption of power by a committee which had no legal authority. They sent a deputation to the Hôtel de Ville, where Clemenceau told the committee that it did not represent Paris and that the city had no right to defy the National Assembly. The committee ignored his protests, and retaliated on the next day by seizing the *mairies* and expelling the mayors.

Having failed to restrain the central committee, Clemenceau went to Versailles, hoping to forestall the National Guard by getting the Assembly to order municipal elections for Paris. He asked the deputies to pass the necessary law as a matter of urgency, but he found that the rural majority was in no mood to conciliate Paris, and that many of them wanted to settle with the capital once and for all. 'But you surely do not want to besiege Paris?' he cried, as he saw that no concession would be made. But a siege of Paris was just what the Assembly wanted, though Thiers declared that there would be no march on the city.

Clemenceau made one last effort to mediate between Paris and the Assembly. On 23 March he returned to Versailles with a deputation of mayors and deputy mayors, all dressed in black and wearing their tricolor scarves. As they entered the public gallery a Left wing deputy called out 'Long live the Republic!', and the mayors, who had been told that they must keep silent, unwisely echoed the cry. The president of the Assembly suspended the sitting; the last chance of reconciling Paris and Versailles had been lost. The two sides were now aligning themselves for civil war.

Without the authority of the government or the Assembly the central committee of the National Guard held municipal elections for Paris on 26 March. The eighty-three elected members formed the Commune, but the twenty-two moderates among them quickly resigned, leaving power in the hands of Jacobins, Blanquists and others associated with different aspects of the French revolutionary tradition. Only two members could rightly be called Marxian Communists; the Commune was not a Socialist body, but the outcome of a spontaneous reaction against the blunderings of a provincially-minded and anti-Parisian National Assembly. The Communards, as Guy Chapman observes, 'were not Socialists but decentralisers.'

After the municipal election Clemenceau formally resigned the mayoralty of Montmartre. He also resigned from the National Assembly, as he did not wish to be associated with any military attack on Paris. Yet even when, at the beginning of April, the Versailles army began the second siege of Paris, he did not entirely give up hope of acting as a mediator. With other Radicals he founded the *Ligue d'Union républicaine pour les droits de Paris*, which pressed for the legalisation of Parisian municipal autonomy; but the *Ligue* made no impression on either the Assembly or the Commune.

In spite of his rebuff by the central committee, Clemenceau showed no hostility towards the National Guard. Foreshadowing his famous tours of the battle front during the First World War, he paid at least one visit to the National Guard detachments which were defending the city against the Versailles army. At the fort of Issy he found the fire-eating Louise Michel, who had given up her school to enrol in the National Guard; she was in military uniform, with peaked cap and hobnailed boots, and she used her rifle so effectively that she was believed to have killed several Versailles soldiers. 'She killed to stop others killing,' Clemenceau commented. 'I never saw her in a calmer mood. How she was not killed a hundred times before my eyes is something I cannot understand. And I only saw her for an hour.'

He was still in Paris on 30 April, for on that day Edmond de Goncourt, who was later to know him well, met him in the office of *Le Temps* and thought that he had 'lost his Satanic appearance' and that his conversation was intelligent, animated and 'rather hesitantly amusing, in the manner of a Palais-Royal farce.' But in the first week of May he left Paris with Charles Floquet and three other members of the *Ligue* to attempt to organise provincial Republican committees on similar lines. They hoped to summon a congress of municipal representatives which would have sufficient moral strength to force the combatants to lay down their arms.

They had no success. Government troops pursued them, three were arrested, Floquet escaped to the Pyrenees, and though Clemenceau managed to visit Alençon, Nantes and Bordeaux his mission was fruitless. He returned to Paris on 16 May to find the gates of the city closed: government troops had entered a few hours earlier and civil war was being waged in the streets of Paris, where the Communards killed their hostages and suffered the fearful vengeance of indiscriminate slaughter by Thier's army. Neither side can be defended for its deeds in the 'week of blood': the Republican patriotism which launched the Commune became a murderous challenge to social order, while the government's brutal repression went far beyond what was decent or necessary. 'It was one of the maddest madnesses in all history,' Clemenceau recalled in his old age. 'No one even knew what the Commune was about. Those people killed, burned, got themselves killed, at times magnificently, but they never knew why!' The closed gates kept him out of the terrible carnage. He made his way to the Vendée and stayed with his wife and parents while the Commune was smashed and order restored in Paris, where the savage punishment of the Communards intensified class conflict and helped to create a permanent breach between the workers and the governments of the Third Republic.

Clemenceau returned to Paris in time for the by-elections for the National Assembly which were due to be held on 1 July. Now that the war between Paris and Versailles was over, he was anxious to re-enter the Assembly, and he stood again for Montmartre; but his supposedly ambivalent attitude on 18 March told against him, and he was not elected.

It was now clear that he would have to wait several years before he could re-enter parliament, but his experiences as mayor and deputy had given him the taste for public life. His chance came in September. Paris was legally authorised to elect a municipal council, though one with less power than the Commune had seized or the *Ligue d'Union républicaine pour les droits de Paris* had advocated. He stood as a candidate for the eighteenth *arrondissement*, and this time the voters were ready enough to elect him. To establish himself still more firmly in Montmartre, he opened a surgery there, and was thus able to combine medical practice with local politics. A career in public life was opening before him.

CHAPTER FOUR

DOCTOR AND DEPUTY

1. Rue des Trois-Frères. 2. Amnesty speech. 3. A letter from Blanqui. 4. La Justice.

[1]

THOUGH THERE would always be controversy about Clemenceau's conduct on 18 March his reputation was officially cleared at the court-martial, held later in 1871, of the soldiers and National Guardsmen involved in the assassinations. The evidence proved that he could not be blamed for them, and a military witness who made a disparaging remark about him was promptly challenged to a duel. It was fought with pistols; Clemenceau said magnanimously, 'I could kill you, but you are a French soldier, and I shall content myself with giving you a warning.' He deliberately shot the officer in the thigh, thus establishing himself as a crack pistol-shot.

Paris was now his home, but his wife and daughter were still in the Vendée, where his mother, who was devoted to children, was delighted to help Mary with the upbringing of her first child (and also of the two others, Thérèse and Michel, who were born in the next few years).[1] Unhampered by family ties Clemenceau had ample time for 'nursing' his old parliamentary constituency of Clignancourt, in the eighteenth *arrondissement*, serving as a municipal councillor and being a 'poor man's doctor' at his surgery in the rue des Trois-Frères.

The municipal council of Paris had eighty members, four from each of the twenty *arrondissements*. It had little power, since financial affairs were dealt with by the prefect of the Seine and law and order were in the hands of the prefect of police, both of whom were appointed by the government.

---

[1] Since most of Clemenceau's biographers say little or nothing about his married life, it may be interesting to note that Mary Clemenceau had a great admiration for her mother-in-law. She once said of the elder Madame Clemenceau: 'She took me to her heart with such simple and wise kindness when I came, young and inexperienced, from America that I love her as dearly as any child she has. It was she who taught my two daughters how to read, write and to be excellent grammarians. One was with her eleven years, and the other eight. She must be always teaching some child or other.' (*See* 'The Clemenceau Case', *New York World*, 14 March, 1892.)

The council, therefore, was mainly advisory, but it offered scope to anyone who was genuinely concerned for social welfare. Clemenceau took particular interest in education and public assistance, two subjects which closely affected his future constituents, and he became expert in administrative detail. He was re-elected to the council in 1874, and became its chairman a year later, only a few months before the parliamentary elections.

In these years he kept in touch with the work of the National Assembly through Louis Blanc and other Left wing deputies, and his old friendship with Scheurer-Kestner was also useful to him. Gambetta had alarmed the bourgeois by claiming that a new social stratum (*nouvelles couches sociales*) of the working classes was beginning to take its part in politics. Scheurer-Kestner was anxious to prove to his rich friends that they need not be frightened by this claim, and he gave dinners and *soirées* at which prosperous bourgeois, mainly former Orleanists who had become conservative Republicans, could meet members of the Left. In addition to Gambetta's followers he invited a trio from the extreme Left whom Gambetta called 'the three musketeers'—Clemenceau, Edouard Lockroy and Georges Périn. Clemenceau's presence at such functions marked him out in political circles as a coming man.

His professional work was also a factor in advancing his parliamentary interests. Many doctors were members of the National Assembly and the subsequent Chamber of Deputies—sixty, for example, in 1881 and seventy-two in 1898; one reason for their presence was that a doctor's surgery brought him into constant touch with the electors. The contact was all the more agreeable to the elector—and presumably productive to the candidate—when the doctor, like Clemenceau in Montmartre, gave free consultations.

The surgery was at 23 rue des Trois-Frères, one of the narrow streets which climb tortuously up between the boulevard Rochechouart and the heights of Montmartre. (The house still exists, and a plaque over the doorway commemorates Clemenceau's use of it.) It consisted of three rooms—a waiting-room, a consulting-room and a small kitchen—and people came to see Clemenceau both as doctor and as councillor. His dual rôle once led to an odd confusion, as he recalled in a newspaper article twenty years later. One day, so his story goes, he saw an obvious consumptive entering his consulting-room; he pointed to a corner and told the man to undress. While he was doing so another consumptive came in, and Clemenceau told him to undress in another corner. Then came a third visitor, who was tall and strong, with a florid complexion and apparently in the best of health; without waiting to be told, he quickly took off his jacket, waistcoat and trousers. 'What have *you* come for?' Clemenceau asked. 'I'd like a job in the post office,' the man replied. He had heard

1 Dr Benjamin Clemenceau
(Musée Clemenceau)

2 Madame Benjamin Clemenceau
(Musée Clemenceau)

3 Georges Clemenceau, aged ten
(from a painting by his father)

4 Georges Clemenceau as a young man

5 Mary Plummer (Musée Clemenceau)

6. Clemenceau with Admiral and Violet Maxse in the Bois de Boulogne

Clemenceau's orders to the other men and had concluded that all callers were expected to undress.

After surgery hours there were calls to be made, for he readily visited patients in the most squalid streets, and he believed that he saw all that there was to see of the infirmities and sufferings of the lower classes. He did not himself live in Montmartre. He had a small apartment at 15 rue de Miromesnil in the fashionable eighth *arrondissement*, which touches the eighteenth at the place de Clichy; and although he was nearer to the Champs-Elysées than to Montmartre he was within walking distance of his surgery. It was to this apartment that his four-year-old daughter Madeleine came to spend the winter with him in 1874.

Madeleine Clemenceau-Jacquemaire's book of childhood memories, *Le Pot de Basilic*, gives a pleasant glimpse of Clemenceau as a proud father. During her stay in Paris the little girl was made much of by an elegant Parisian lady, 'a beautiful brunette, pale and with regular features'. This was Clemenceau's old flame Hortense Kestner, now married to Charles Floquet, who, like Clemenceau, had been out of parliament since 1871 but was to be re-elected in 1876. Hortense loved children, though she had none of her own; one afternoon she took a bevy of them, including Madeleine, to the puppet-show in the Champs-Elysées. Clemenceau was also there, and after the performance he lifted Madeleine on to the 'stage', holding her by the legs like a puppet, and asked her to recite a fable to the audience. She did so with great success. It was a happy scene which would have surprised the politicians of later years who quaked at the Tiger's roar.

[2]

In the general election of 1876 Clemenceau was nominated as candidate for the Chamber of Deputies by the Radical Republican committee of the eighteenth arrondissement. In his election address he emphasised the contrast between the more conservative Republicans, such as those who followed Gambetta, and the Radicals. 'The conservative Republicans ask for the minimum Republic,' he said. 'We ask for the maximum. We, the Radical Republicans, want the Republic for its natural consequences—the great and fruitful social reforms it brings with it.' He easily won the seat.

The election was the first to be held under the constitution of the Third Republic, which the National Assembly had voted in 1875. The constitution provided for a three-tier system of government, consisting of President, Senate and Chamber of Deputies, the President to hold office for seven years, the senators for nine (apart from seventy-five who were elected for life) and the deputies for four. It was only through a late amendment that France was formally named a Republic.

The years in which Clemenceau had been working as doctor and municipal councillor had been a frustrating period for the Republicans, who were still a minority party, both in the National Assembly and in the country as a whole. It took the entire decade to achieve the political change which made France a Republican nation. Even the change of Thiers's title from chief of the executive power to President of the Republic had been a gesture without serious meaning, for the royalist majority in the Assembly, first under Thiers and then under Marshal MacMahon, who succeeded him in 1873, was waiting for the opportunity of restoring the monarchy and making the Bourbon heir, the Comte de Chambord, king of France. But Chambord, who was childless, lost his chance of the throne by insisting that the Bourbon white flag should replace the familiar and well-loved tricolor. This was politically inexpedient, and thereafter the monarchists could wait only for Chambord's death, which would leave the Orleanist pretender, the Comte de Paris, as a more amenable claimant to the throne.

Though nominally Republican, the constitution of 1875 was made to suit the requirements of the Comte de Paris. The president's powers resembled those of a constitutional monarch rather than those of the President of the United States; the monarchists hoped that if (as seemed likely and actually happened) the Comte de Chambord died during MacMahon's seven years' presidency, the Comte de Paris would be able to succeed MacMahon as president and later be proclaimed as king. But that was not to be, for the days of Right wing ascendancy were ending. The Chamber of Deputies in which Clemenceau returned to parliament contained 360 Republicans and only 153 monarchists, of whom seventy-five were Bonapartists. The change was impressive but not unexpected. In Professor Bury's words, 'This was largely the success that follows success—now that the Republic had been legally established many electors would have seen no sense in not supporting it.' Yet the Republicans were not in full control, for they were confronted by a monarchist President and an anti-Republican majority in the Senate.

Both Chamber and Senate met, like the old National Assembly, at Versailles, and Clemenceau must have had mixed feelings on going back to the town where, as deputy for Paris and mayor of Montmartre, he had found so little sympathy in 1871. On taking his seat he joined Louis Blanc and the small group of advanced Republicans who formed the extreme Left. He was thus separated from the main body of Republicans under Gambetta's leadership, and even more so from the moderate Republicans of the Left Centre and the liberals of the Right Centre—two bourgeois parties whose refusal to coalesce caused much of the political instability of the Third Republic. Though he was still on friendly terms with Gambetta he now differed from him over the Republican approach to politics and over the constitution. He and Blanc believed that a single-chamber system, with neither President nor Senate, was the most democratic form of government, and they would not accept Gambetta's assurance that the constitution was the best which could be obtained from the National Assembly.

Clemenceau was to speak little in his first three years as a deputy, partly through lack of congenial subjects and partly because he served in 1877–8 as one of the Chamber's eight secretaries, a post which required many hours to be spent on the preparation of parliamentary reports; but within a few weeks of taking his seat he made a speech which established him as one of the Chamber's most impressive orators. It was a plea for an amnesty for the 5,496 condemned Communards still serving sentences of deportation (3,609), hard labour (240) or imprisonment and solitary confinement (1,647) and for the further 100,000 who had fled the country to avoid arrest and were living abroad. It was the first of many speeches dealing with various aspects of social justice, and it was one which touched him personally, for among the men and women sentenced for their activities under the Commune were Blanqui, imprisoned at Clairvaux, and Louise Michel, deported to New Caledonia. Although he was no longer in contact with Blanqui he corresponded with Louise and sent her occasional money orders to alleviate her exile.

The total amnesty bill was introduced in the Chamber on 21 March by F.-V. Raspail, but the speech which won the closest attention was Clemenceau's. He spoke with great moderation, and found an historical precedent for amnesty in his own part of France, where pardon had been granted for crimes committed in the Vendée during the Revolutionary period. He observed caustically that other offenders against the State, such as the organisers of Louis-Napoleon's *coup d'état* and the politicians who led France into war in 1870, had not been punished for their misdeeds; why, he asked, should there be so much indulgence on one side and so much severity on the other? He urged the government to proclaim an amnesty while it could do so as a sign of its own strength, and without waiting to be forced to act by public opinion. As he saw it, the amnesty would be a first step towards the reconciliation of the classes, which was needed to create the social appeasement that everyone wished to see.

Neither Clemenceau's eloquence in the Chamber nor Victor Hugo's in the Senate, where a similar motion was tabled, could win over the conservative Republicans, who felt that to grant an amnesty would be to justify the Commune; even Gambetta would not support it, though at one time in the debate he thought he might 'strike a blow' in favour of a partial amnesty. But Clemenceau's speech was warmly applauded by his fellow deputies and favourably noticed in the press. The clarity of his thought, his tact and his restraint, his forceful if rather staccato way of speaking, and the loftiness of his ideas laid the foundations of his parliamentary career. The ruthlessness and love of combat which won him his nickname were to be shown later.

The amnesty issue brought a new word into French politics. During the election campaign many of Gambetta's followers had accepted an amnesty in principle but would not commit themselves to putting it into action; their caution was condemned as opportunism by Henri de Rochefort, the formidable Left wing deputy and journalist. 'The Opportunist', he wrote in his paper, *Les Droits de l'Homme*, 'is the sensitive candidate who, deeply affected by the evils of civil war and full of solicitude for the families it deprived of their mainstays, declares that he is in favour of the amnesty, but that he will wait to vote for it at the "opportune time". . . . Electors, take heed; *at the opportune time* is a term of parliamentary slang, meaning: Never.'

In spite of Rochefort's irony Gambetta willingly accepted the new word, and told the Chamber that it should substitute a policy of opportunism for a policy of chimeras. His attitude widened his breach with Clemenceau, who once told a young Austrian friend (Berta Szeps): 'Gambetta had created the Opportunist party; myself, the Radical party. Clashes were inevitable. His great work had been to demand the Republic and to guide its first steps. Mine was to react against an Opportunism which ran the risk of dimming the Republic's lights.' Such criticism was fully justified. France had a series of Opportunist governments for nearly two decades, but J. E. C. Bodley, writing at the end of the nineteenth century, said that the Opportunist party never revealed 'that it had any principle more definite than that of securing the spoils of office. Hence the word Opportunist became a term of reproach in the appreciation of all other groups.'

[3]

Clemenceau had little part in the *seize Mai*—the clash between President MacMahon and the Chamber which began on 16 May, 1877, and ended two years later with MacMahon's resignation and the election of the first Republican president. The cause of the crisis was MacMahon's attempt to assert his authority by virtually dismissing a Republican prime minister and then dissolving the Chamber after only one year of its allotted four. Gambetta organised Republican victory in the election by forming an alliance of deputies of all shades of Republican opinion, known as 'the 363' and ranging from the old Orleanists of the Left Centre to Clemenceau, Blanc and their supporters on the extreme Left. Though losing a few seats, the Republicans were returned with a comfortable majority. MacMahon had gained nothing, and his failure precluded every future president of the Third Republic from exercising his constitutional right to dissolve the Chamber, if the Senate concurred, before the end of its four-year term.

Clemenceau approved of Gambetta's handling of the crisis; he had saved the Republic and created a new situation in which, at no distant date, MacMahon would have to 'give in or get out'. 'Gambetta has been admirable—admirable!—from start to finish,' Clemenceau told Scheurer-Kestner. 'He has organised everything.' Having retained his seat in Montmartre, Clemenceau was one of four members of the extreme Left invited to sit on the Committee of Eighteen, a Republican committee set up to guard against monarchist or clerical threats to the Republic. It included most of the Third Republic's prime ministers for the next twenty years.

A succession of Opportunist governments followed the general election; each of them was largely composed of the remnants of its predeccessor, and Clemenceau scornfully said of one of them, 'It's nothing but a re-plastering of a re-plastering.' At last, on 30 January, 1879, MacMahon resigned, and Clemenceau was one of several friends who urged Gambetta to stand for the presidency. But Gambetta, who was only forty, thought he was too young, and was not sure that he could beat Jules Grévy, a Republican rival with great experience and prestige, in the presidential election. He preferred to be elected to the comfortable and influential post of president of the Chamber (the equivalent of the Speaker of the House of Commons), while waiting for the day when he would be called on to form a government.

Grévy was duly elected President. His accession to power meant that the day of 'the Republicans' Republic' had dawned at last; but Clemenceau still felt that there was too much compromise and too little action. In a speech at the Cirque Fernando in Paris he made a virtual declaration of war upon Opportunist government.

The men in power, he declared, had no sense of direction. They lacked the authority needed to speak to the Republican party and above all to the old Republicans. The Republic, he said, should keep its promises, and give up a policy which had led only to 'irritation, equivocation and anaemia.'

Many Republicans, including Scheurer-Kestner and Jules Ferry, the minister of education, were shocked by this forthright attack on the

Opportunist government, but it was welcomed by provincial Radicals, who now looked to Clemenceau as the unchallenged leader of the extreme Left. His growing prestige was also noticed by one of the friends of his younger days, Auguste Blanqui, who had been imprisoned at Clairvaux since 1872. On 18 March, 1879, he sent a long letter to Clemenceau, whom he addressed as 'XX', presumably in the naive hope of shielding the recipient's name if the letter were opened by the police.[1]

Blanqui writes of Clemenceau in glowing phrases. The struggle has begun, he says; Clemenceau must not return to his tent, for 'You alone have the weapon to wield in the present peril. . . . The immense acclamation given to your first speech shouts on high how formidable you are. But do not let yourself be disarmed by the hand of man or woman. Above all, do not disarm for the sake of tranquillity. That would be to sacrifice the Republic. You have no right to do it.'

Blanqui says that in spite of the nominal Republicanism of the Chamber of Deputies, there were at most a hundred Republicans in it. The extreme Left had always shown deplorable weakness, and had been a model of gentlemanly behaviour; what was needed was a man, and the three speeches which Clemenceau had made in the Chamber showed that he was the man. He must take care that he was not put aside in the ranks as a sergeant or corporal; he was the great orator of the extreme Left, and he must be murderous when necessary, allowing no one to decide the strength of his weapon or the number of his blows. 'I say it again. Only one man can lead an assembly, and you are that man. . . . In England and elsewhere they now look on you as the leader of the Left. It is impossible for you to withdraw from this mission. . . . In the Chamber you must become the man of the future, the head of the Revolution. It has not known or been able to find one since 1830. Chance gives it a leader, do not take that chance away.'

Clemenceau could hardly fail to be flattered by such high praise from the great old revolutionary; though in later years, as Maurice Paz observes, he 'had a keen interest in remaining silent on his "Blanquist" youth', in 1879 he was ready enough to show his high regard for his former friend. Indeed, when Blanqui was elected to the Chamber in a Bordeaux by-election, and was declared ineligible because he was in prison, it was

[1] Clemenceau's earliest biographers did not know of the existence of this letter, which was found among Blanqui's papers in the Bibliothèque Nationale. Alexandre Zévaès published a small part of it in his *Clemenceau* in 1949, and Georges Wormser gave extracts from it in *La République de Clemenceau* in 1962. It was only in September 1973 that the complete text was published by Maurice Paz in the *Historical Journal*. Paz says of it: 'Through this letter we can trace a passing on of a certain strain in the French Left from Blanqui. . . . Through Clemenceau Blanqui would extend his own influence deep into the Third Republic.'

Clemenceau who pleaded on his behalf before the election was formally annulled.

One may doubt whether the future Tiger really needed Blanqui's exhortation to be 'murderous' in politics; such an attitude was ingrained in his nature. He had already, in the third of the speeches mentioned by Blanqui, foreshadowed the reputation he was soon to acquire as the *tombeur de ministères*—overthrower of ministries.

His weapon in this kind of political warfare was always the interpellation—the parliamentary term for a speech, of which a deputy had given previous notice, discussing, and usually denouncing, the conduct or policy of the prime minister or some other minister. The matter was then debated and voted on, and if the interpellation were successful, a minister or a government would be forced to resign. Early in March Clemenceau made an interpellation about scandals in the prefecture of police which were being disclosed in the press, but in attacking the police he was really aiming at de Marcère, minister of the interior. De Marcère retaliated by calling for a vote of confidence, and resigned when the Chamber declined to support him.

Clemenceau had overthrown his first minister. His next victims would be entire ministries.

[4]

As the year 1879 advanced, Clemenceau had business outside the Chamber which called for his attention. He was about to begin his long career in journalism—that remarkable second career which allowed Sacha Guitry to describe him, towards the end of his long life, as 'a very old journalist who, from time to time, had given up journalism in order to be a deputy, a senator, a prime minister.'

It was on 15 January, 1880, that the first issue of a new daily paper, with Georges Clemenceau as political director and Camille Pelletan as editor, appeared in Paris. It was appropriately called *La Justice*, since justice in all its aspects, social, political and legal, was one of the cornerstones of Clemenceau's political thinking. It filled a gap in French journalism, for until it was founded the Left wing had no militantly Radical daily newspaper.

Clemenceau was not, and never became, a wealthy man. He could not have founded *La Justice* without his father's help. But the old doctor was delighted to help his son to promote Republican doctrines. He sold a farm to launch the paper, and Clemenceau was able to open modest offices in the rue du Faubourg Montmartre, close to the *grands boulevards*.

Since *La Justice* was an important part of Clemenceau's life for seventeen years, it may be worth considering it in some detail. The offices were simple, with plain wooden chairs and tables; Clemenceau himself had a big room with three large windows looking out on to the street. The staff was both talented and enthusiastic. Pelletan, who wrote the chief political articles, was the best Radical journalist of his time; Gustave Geffroy, who joined the paper on the day before the first issue appeared, was a sensitive critic of the arts; others who worked on the paper for varying periods were Stephen Pichon, a serious student of foreign affairs, Charles Martel, who wrote humorous fantasies, Edouard Durranc, who coined the cynical and often quoted phrase, 'How beautiful the Republic was—under the Empire', Alexandre Millerand, future prime minister and President of the Republic, Charles Longuet, the son-in-law of Karl Marx, and Jean Ajalbert.

They were not well paid. *La Justice* took no advertisements and had no regular subscribers; each issue was sold on its merits, and these were enough to gain a very creditable circulation of 10,000; but it was never on a sound financial basis. Clemenceau had hoped to get a regular income from it, for the articles of incorporation allotted salaries of 30,000 francs a year to himself and 20,000 francs to Pelletan. 'These were high sums, (£1,200 and £800 respectively),' writes D. R. Watson, 'and it is unlikely that the paper ever made enough profit to cover that sort of expense.' A friendly commentator had to admit that 'The end of every month was tragic. . . . The manager was always looking round for a thousand-franc note'; and in 1888 Edmond de Goncourt heard that Geffroy was owed 2,500 francs by *La Justice* and could not get a centime of it. Yet the paper kept going from 1880 to 1897; its continued existence was proof alike of the loyalty and competence of the staff and the need for a good Radical newspaper.

Politically, the paper exposed the inertia and sterility of the Republican majority in the Chamber; in its very first issue it attacked the moderate Republicans of the Left Centre, whom it accused of trying to corner the Republic. Its programme was strongly anticlerical: it stood for compulsory lay education and the separation of Church and State. It also embraced the whole range of its political director's parliamentary objectives, such as a general amnesty for Communard prisoners, abolition of the death penalty and freedom to hold meetings and to form associations.

Clemenceau wrote little in the first thirteen years of *La Justice*. In those days he thought best when he was standing on his feet. Writing came hardly to him, and Pelletan, who had a gift for drawing, made a witty sketch of *le patron* sitting at an office table and looking at a sheet of paper, completely blank except for a single blot. Even so, he managed to write nine or ten articles in the paper's first year, though afterwards he contributed little except short notes.

Yet he was not a figurehead in the office; he discussed the subjects of the principal articles with Pelletan and the other writers, and Charles Martel said that 'he really made the paper'. In the previous November parliament had at last returned to Paris, the Chamber of Deputies to the Palais-Bourbon, the Senate to the Palais de Luxembourg; President Grévy had previously taken up residence in the Elysée. The decapitalisation of Paris was ended, and Clemenceau could move easily between the Palais-Bourbon and the rue du Faubourg Montmartre, thus keeping his writers informed about the latest political developments. He kept a watchful eye on the contents of the paper, and paid particular attention to the work of the critics; one of his rules was that they should always be scrupulously fair to his political enemies. Then there was the business side to be attended to, and time to be found for a friendly word with some of the many callers—artists like Monet, Carrère and Raffaelli, who came to see Geffroy, novelists like Lucien Descaves and J.-H. Rosny *aîné*, soldiers like General Boulanger and business men like Cornelius Herz, whose connection with *La Justice* was to prove unfortunate for Clemenceau.

In the evening he often deserted his staff to go to the theatre or the opera, but he would come back afterwards to see how they were getting on. Both Léon Daudet and Goncourt have described his midnight appearances at the office, elegant in tail-coat and white tie, a cigar in his mouth, a gardenia in his buttonhole, faintly scented with *eau de cologne*. According to Daudet, he would say an appropriate word to each of his writers and then hurry away to rejoin his *belle amie*; Goncourt, who got his information from Jean Ajalbert, says that sometimes he would lie full length on one of the tables, like a Roman on a *triclinium*, and begin a long political discussion with men who had finished their work and would rather have gone home.

On some of these midnight visits he had a light meal in his room. As was his custom throughout life, he drank only water, but on one occasion, which must have been in the middle years of *La Justice*, he brought his daughter Madeleine with him after a theatre and sent out for half a bottle of champagne. The staff, who were supping frugally on cider and roast chestnuts, observed cynically: 'Champagne in the drawing-room, cider in the office!' The quip was repeated to Clemenceau, who at once sent out for two magnums of champagne for his faithful writers.

Jean Ajalbert says that Clemenceau was despotic in the office: Rosny *aîné* once saw him seize an offending journalist by the shoulders, turn him round and give him a hard and well-placed kick. Yet his despotism must have been taken in good part, since Pelletan, Pichon and Geffroy stayed with *La Justice* for years. The last two, indeed, became his friends and admirers for life.

CHAPTER FIVE

MINISTRY-BREAKER

1. Clemenceau in 1880. 2. The Marseilles programme. 3. Anti-colonial. 4. English visits. 5. Ferry defeated.

[1]

IN 1880 CLEMENCEAU was beginning the central period of his life, which would last from the founding of *La Justice* to his resignation from his first prime ministership in 1909. Since entering the Chamber he had virtually abandoned medicine, though a few friends occasionally came to him for treatment, and his name, with the information that he could be consulted daily by appointment from 1 to 2 p.m., continued to appear in a medical directory until 1906. By now he had served his apprenticeship in local and national politics and was soon to become known as the redoubtable *tombeur de ministères*. He was also the director of a newspaper.

His public duties were combined with the amiable relaxations of the *boulevardier* and amateur of the arts. With his impeccable dress and his hat on the side of his head, it seemed that he had become the complete Parisian. He rode in the Bois de Boulogne and was a close friend of the famous equestrian, James Fillis. He was a familar figure at theatrical first nights, he loved music and and pictures and could talk fluently about both, he delighted in opera, especially the works of Mozart, and he was one of the mixed gathering of ambassadors, politicians, financiers, men of letters, artists and idlers who chatted with ballet-girls in the *foyer de danse* of the Opera, a spacious green-room where fashionable gentlemen could be seen without arousing suspicion that they were there for ulterior purposes.

Some of Clemenceau's biographers say that by this time he was separated from his wife. This is not so. When he returned to Paris after the Commune he at first lived alone in the small apartment where his elder daughter stayed with him in 1874; Mary remained at L'Aubraie while her second and third children were born. In 1876, when he began to draw a deputy's salary, he took a larger apartment in the avenue Montaigne, off the avenue des Champs-Elysées, and Mary joined him there, leaving the children in the Vendée in their grandmother's care. (Paul Cambon, the diplomat, mentioned the avenue Montaigne apartment in one of his letters, observing that the living-room was furnished with considerable taste, and there were chairs upholstered with old tapestries, an interesting collection of Japanese *objets d'art* and some pictures which were 'not bad'. The 'not bad' pictures were probably Monets and Manets.) Here, it seems, the whole family were reunited in 1881.[1]

In the early years in the avenue Montaigne Mary Clemenceau did her share of the entertaining which was expected from a deputy's wife; she moved in Paris society and was a popular guest at the parties given by Manet's wife and mother. Both she and Clemenceau had their portraits painted by Manet. In 1883, after the artist's death, Clemenceau bought Mary's portrait—a pastel—from Madame Manet for five hundred francs.

Up to this time there was no sign of a break-up of their marriage, though the love of their honeymoon period seems to have vanished for ever during the five years when Mary was in the Vendée and Clemenceau was alone in Paris. It is true that in 1884, when he was about to visit a dangerous cholera-ridden district, he signed a paper entrusting the care of his children, in the event of his death, to his friend Cornelius Herz; but years later, in describing this episode to Jean Martet, he observed: 'At that time I happened to be on bad terms with my wife.' (The remark surely implies that at other times he was on good terms with her.) Yet their marriage was certainly heading for disaster, for, as time went on, Clemenceau's affections were given to his mistresses rather than his wife, and when 'all Paris' talked about his *affaires* Mary could hardly have failed to know about them.

Jean Ajalbert wrote in 1931 that one could never get together the necessary documentation to compose '*La vie amoureuse de Georges Clemenceau*'. This remains true, but there is no doubt that he deserved his reputation for gallantry. His first notorious *affaire* was with Léonide Leblanc, an already middle-aged actress and courtesan, of whom wits had said under the Second Empire, 'Put her on the summit of Mont Blanc, she will still be accessible.' There was a certain piquancy in this relationship, for Léonide had long been the mistress of the Duc d'Aumale, son of King Louis-Philippe; gossips told stories of the rivalry between the royalist and the Republican, and hinted that an *affaire* with a duke's mistress was a sign of Clemenceau's snobbishness. Rose Caron, the opera-singer, and Suzanne Reichenberg, of the Comédie-Française, were among his other notable mistresses; Rose Caron, indeed, has been described as 'Clemenceau's most dazzling conquest in the world of the theatre.' There was also the

---

[1] The date is indicated by Mary Clemenceau's remark, quoted in the *New York World* for 14 March, 1892, that her mother-in-law looked after her daughters for eleven and eight years respectively. Madeleine, the elder, was born in 1870.

'ravissante femme d'un diplomate complaisant' mentioned by Léon Daudet: this was certainly the American-born Comtesse d'Aunay, who (if we can believe Clemenceau's grandson, the not always reliable Georges Gatineau-Clemenceau) had a son closely resembling Clemenceau as a young man.

During his long conflict with Jules Ferry his opponents tried to make capital out of his private life. There were whispers about him in the corridors of the Palais-Bourbon: 'Didn't he sleep with famous actresses? Wasn't he often seen among the ballet-girls at the Opera?' Such whispers did him no harm. Other rumours would damage him later, but at the beginning of the 1880s he was too firmly established to be displaced by gossip.

[2]

The basic political division under the Third Republic was between the parties of established order and of movement. 'On the one hand,' writes J. M. Roberts, 'stood those Frenchmen who distrusted the use which might be made of politics by democracy; this was the side of Order. On the other stood those Frenchmen who wished to press further the implications of the Republican regime, the side of Movement.' The dividing line between the two groupings ran between the influential bourgeois parties of Right and Left Centre. Further to the Right were the monarchists; further to the Left the moderate Republicans—the Republican Left (Jules Ferry) and the Republican Union (Gambetta)—and the Radicals of the extreme Left (Clemenceau). The moderate Republicans provided the leaders of the Opportunist governments which Clemenceau so bitterly attacked and so often overthrew, though he would say later, and with some justice: 'People exaggerate. I only overthrew one ministry. It was always the same one.'

He had already indicated the differences between the Radicals and the Opportunists in his speech at the Cirque Fernando in 1879. At Marseilles in October 1880 he expounded the full programme of the extreme Left. It was a call for a social and democratic Republic, a demand for radical action far beyond the wishes of the Opportunists, of whom he said caustically that 'they set themselves up as judges of the opportune time for reforms, not to arrange priorities and to carry them out, but to postpone them.'

The Marseilles programme was both political and social. Politically, it called for the separation of Church and State, a reduction in the period of military service, revision of the constitution (which would include the abolition of the presidency and the Senate), local autonomy and the introduction of income tax; socially, it demanded far-reaching reforms in industry, such as a reduction in the permitted hours of work, prohibition of child labour and arrangements for worker-management consultations about factory conditions, as well as pensions for retired workers, the nationalisation of railways, canals and mines, and freedom of association for trade unions.

The speech was also a call for peace. Clemenceau was not, as is sometimes suggested, a fire-eater, working recklessly for *revanche*—a war of revenge against Germany to recover Alsace-Lorraine. Like other patriotic Frenchmen, he accepted Gambetta's advice on *revanche*—'Speak of it never, think of it always', but he did not regard Alsace-Lorraine as a reason for disturbing the peace of Europe. At Marseilles he said firmly: 'We desire Republican reforms, and consequently peace. . . . Violence founds nothing. Permit peace to accomplish its work among all the peoples of Europe, and it will be promptly seen that it is the best ally of France and the Republic.'

In its social aspects the programme bore signs of being devised by intellectuals. Clemenceau and his friends had few contacts with the working classes; when the workers became a force in politics they would look elsewhere for leadership. Certainly the Marseilles speech had borrowed extensively from a workers' programme drawn up by a Socialist congress in Paris earlier in the year; but it included only the minimum demands of that congress. Though sitting on the extreme Left in the Chamber, Clemenceau was not on the extreme Left of France's political thought. The Radicals, while favouring a limited amount of nationalisation, had no intention of attacking either capital or private property. Only alarmed conservatives could regard Clemenceau's party as Socialist.

It will be noticed that an amnesty for Communards no longer appears in his programme. It had now been granted. Since 1876 individual pardons had been given to most of the prisoners and deportees, and a total amnesty for the remaining eight hundred was voted in June 1880 on the initiative of Charles de Freycinet, the prime minister. Clemenceau's friend Louise Michel had been pardoned in the previous October, but had refused to return to France until a total amnesty was granted; when at last she arrived in Paris in November 1880 Clemenceau was waiting on the station platform to meet her.

Fortified by the Marseilles programme, Clemenceau stood for three seats—two in Montmartre, where his old constituency had been divided, and one at Arles—in the general election of 1881. He was returned for all three, and he chose to sit for one of the Montmartre constituencies.

The election strengthened the Republicans and reduced the Right to a mere ninety seats. Republican majorities controlled both the Senate and the Chamber of Deputies, where Gambetta's Republican Union was the strongest group; the extreme Left, which had begun to call itself Radical Socialist, also gained in the election. There was thus adequate support for Jules Ferry's important educational reforms, which were designed to take education out of the hands of the Church.

As an old campaigner for free, compulsory and lay education, Clemenceau was generally in favour of Ferry's bill, which finally passed into law in 1882, when religious and clerical supervision was removed from all State primary schools and members of 'unauthorised' religious communities were forbidden (by the controversial Article 7) to teach in any educational establishment; he grew more restive when Gambetta formed his 'great ministry' in November 1880 and put forward a plan for constitutional revision which fell far short of the Marseilles programme. Gambetta proposed to set up a revising congress, consisting of senators and deputies, which was to work only on an agreed agenda; Clemenceau felt that this limitation would make the congress ineffective, since the Senate would hardly consent to put its own abolition on the agenda. On this occasion Gambetta's ministry survived Clemenceau's criticisms, but it soon fell on a proposal to introduce *scrutin de liste*, i.e. the election of all the deputies for a department by voting for lists of like-minded candidates, instead of the existing single-member system known as *scrutin d'arrondissement*.

This was a proposal on which Republicans were divided, even in the office of *La Justice*. Clemenceau preferred single-member constituencies, but Camille Pelletan thought that *scrutin de liste* was the only voting system compatible with Republican doctrine. '*Scrutin d'arrondissement*,' he said, 'is the vote for a man, *scrutin de liste* is the vote for a programme.' In general, deputies were reluctant to change the system under which they had been elected; the committee appointed to consider the proposals reported against it, and when its report was discussed in the Chamber the Radicals, led by Clemenceau, joined with the Right and part of the Centre to defeat the government.

Gambetta resigned. His 'great ministry' had lasted a mere eighty-one days. He was never to be prime minister again, for he died, at the age of forty-four, on the last day of 1882.

[3]

The rights and wrongs of colonial expansion occupied much of Clemenceau's attention in the 1880s. This was the period in which Jules Ferry, during two spells as prime minister, gave France a colonial policy.

Ferry was not the originator of French overseas development. As Theodore Zeldin observes, 'It was civil servants, explorers, soldiers and sailors, acting under their own initiative, who carried the French flag to new lands. But Ferry supported them, once they had involved themselves, in order to save its honour.' In the first instance he believed that colonies would be valuable markets for French exports; it was only later that France realised their greater importance as sources of raw materials.

Clemenceau consistently opposed colonial expansion. He thought it irrelevant, costly and dangerous. Though he did not advocate a war of revenge against Germany, he insisted that France needed all her troops and resources in her homeland, so that she might be able to resist any further German aggression; the eyes of deputies, he was always to urge, should be on 'the blue line of the Vosges', behind which lay the menace of Prussia. He objected to the increased taxation imposed to finance overseas expeditions; he feared that colonial adventures would cause bad feeling between France and Britain, and would thus push France into diplomatic dependence on Germany.

His first attempt to restrain colonial expansion overthrew a ministry, but did not check the growth of the French Empire. Early in 1881, when Ferry was prime minister, the French governor-general in Algeria appealed for help against raiders from the neighbouring and still independent country of Tunisia; and a few weeks later French residents in Tunisia sent their own call for help. Realising that the occupation of Tunisia would give France the fine harbour of Bizerta, Ferry agreed to send help to north Africa; credit for an expeditionary force was almost unanimously agreed by parliament; and the arrival of French troops was enough to induce the Bey of Tunis to sign the Treaty of Bardo making his country a French protectorate.

For the moment Ferry seemed to have parliament on his side. Clemenceau was the only dissentient when the Chamber was asked to approve the draft treaty. But then came the election campaign, in which Clemenceau attacked Ferry on the ground that he had been led by Bismarck into a fatal adventure.

He was not the only one who believed that the German chancellor was trying to weaken France in Europe by encouraging her to send troops overseas; Lord Lyons, the British ambassador in Paris, told the Foreign Office that the French had walked into Bismarck's trap with their eyes open. When still more troops were sent out to quell an insurrection in southern Tunisia, the Radicals followed Clemenceau's lead and joined the monarchists (who feared that colonial successes would strengthen the Republic) in attacking Ferry's government.

When the new Chamber of Deputies met in November Clemenceau made a vigorous onslaught on the prime minister, claiming that he had violated the constitution by engaging in war without the Chamber's consent and had thrown a patriotic cloak over low financial interests. 'I see nothing in these enterprises,' he said, 'except men who want to do business and make money on the Bourse.' Other deputies also put down hostile interpellations, and though Ferry was not actually defeated the stormy debate caused him to resign and make way for Gambetta's ministry.

Clemenceau's belief that overseas ventures must fatally weaken France in Europe was criticised in the press. 'Whatever MM. Leroy-Beaulieu and Clemenceau may think,' said *Le Siècle*, 'it seemed to us that we could have one eye on Tunis and the other on the Vosges. . . . Cannot a lesson be administered to the Bey of Tunis without our being constrained to embrace M. de Bismarck?' But Clemenceau's Vendean obstinacy would not allow him to accept such plausible reasoning. For him the blue line of the Vosges was sacrosanct. Freycinet, who had another innings as prime minister after Gambetta's defeat, was the next to suffer for taking an interest in north Africa.

This time the argument turned on Egypt, where France had been the paramount influence from the time of Napoleon I's Egyptian expedition to the opening of the Suez Canal in 1869. Britain had appeared there in 1875, when Disraeli bought 40 per cent. of the Suez Canal shares from the Khedive of Egypt for £4m., and a year later Britain and France set up a dual control of Egypt's shaky finances. But Egyptian xenophobia soon raised problems for the controlling powers; a nationalist revolt was threatened, and in 1882 Britain and France agreed on joint military intervention.

If Ferry had been prime minister, the intervention would almost certainly have taken place, and the French parliament would have been asked to approve of a *fait accompli*. But Freycinet, who was nicknamed 'the white mouse', was a cautious, middle-of-the-road politician who was liked by the Chamber because he regarded himself as its servant rather than its master. He went to the Palais-Bourbon in July to ask for credits of 9m. francs for 'meeting the expenses required by events in Egypt', but in the face of hostile criticism he reduced his demand, and said that French forces would be engaged only in the occupation of the northern end of the Suez Canal.

Even this was too much for Clemenceau. His policy had already been outlined in *La Justice*: it was one of complete non-intervention, of leaving Egypt to the Egyptians. Now, from the rostrum of the Chamber of Deputies, he subjected Freycinet to the full force of his satire and invective.

Ironically he asked: 'Is it peace? No, because we are sending troops. Is it war? No, because we are not going to fight.' But whether it was peace or war, had the government considered the complications which might arise through the jealousy of other European countries? If France pulled the chestnuts out of the fire for England, as she had done in the Crimea and in China, France would have the danger, England the profit. And why, he asked, should France seek to impose on Egypt a government which it did not want?

He ended with a grim warning against involvement in unnecessary operations. 'It seems,' he said, 'that somewhere a fatal hand is preparing a terrible explosion in Europe. . . . Europe is covered with soldiers, everyone is waiting, all the powers are keeping their freedom of action for the future. Let France keep hers!'

Freycinet wrote in his memoirs that the effect of these final words was shattering. It raised the fear of war, and suggested that incalculable dangers might follow military intervention in Egypt. Clemenceau had the Chamber on his side, and the credits were refused by 450 votes to 75. Freycinet resigned. France withdrew from Egypt, leaving Britain to begin a supposedly temporary occupation on her own.

The reversal of the government's policy and the overthrow of the Freycinet ministry by a single, forceful speech were a notable demonstration of Clemenceau's power over the Chamber; but many knowledgeable people thought that he had made a mistake in forcing the government to withdraw from Egypt. Gambetta declared, 'If we lose Egypt, we also lose our influence in the Mediterranean'; Paul Cambon said of the British occupation of Egypt, 'Its consequences are almost as disastrous for France as the war of 1870'; Théophile Declassé, a young journalist who was later to be one of the Third Republic's most distinguished foreign ministers, wrote a pamphlet attacking French policy for its weakness over Egypt.

These views found greater support in later years, as French opinion gradually accepted the Imperial principle and Clemenceau had to bear the odium of having lost Egypt for France. Remembering the value of Egypt to the Western Allies in two world wars, Jacques Chastenet suggests that Clemenceau was suffering from 'a strange myopia' when he thought that possession of the African coast-line could do nothing to ward off the German peril. This may well be true, but the occupation of Egypt would not have been an unmixed blessing to France, any more than it was to Britain. Clemenceau should at least be thanked by his countrymen for having kept France out of the wars with the Mahdi and the difficult problems involved in Egypt's claim to independence after the First World War.

[4]

Clemenceau's reference to 'pulling chestnuts out of the fire for England' was not a symptom of Anglophobia. England was his second country. He often visited London, where he usually stayed at Admiral Frederick Maxse's house in Onslow Square.

Maxse, who had retired from the navy in his thirties with the intention (which was never fulfilled) of entering the House of Commons, was a great friend of the novelist George Meredith, and was the prototype of Beauchamp in Meredith's *Beauchamp's Career*. He was a keen Francophil, and he was one of three Englishmen who signed a public protest in 1871 against the German annexation of Alsace-Lorraine. (The other signatories were John Morley and Frederic Harrison.) In the following year Louis Blanc introduced him to Clemenceau, and the close friendship which then began was ended only by the admiral's death in 1900. As she grew up, Maxse's daughter Violet also became one of his greatest friends.

On one of his visits to England Charles Longuet introduced him to Karl Marx and Professor Edward Beesly, a keen student of positivism and a leading Socialist thinker, but he remained unrepentantly anti-Socialist. On another visit his presence in England was viewed with some disfavour by Queen Victoria.

This was in 1884, when Clemenceau came to London with Senator Richard Waddington, one of two English brothers who had taken French nationality. The senator was the inventor of the neat remark that 'government consists of holding France at the end of a telegraph wire starting from Paris'; his brother William, who had briefly held office as prime minister a few years earlier, had become French ambassador to London.

The two visitors had come to study the British government's handling of social and economic affairs, for the enlightenment of a French parliamentary commission on the position of industrial and agricultural workers in France. Clemenceau was chairman of the commission, and Senator Waddington one of its members. They arrived in London on 14 February, and Clemenceau went to hear an Egyptian debate in the House of Commons. A watchful reporter of *The Times* noticed that Joseph Chamberlain, Sir Charles Dilke, Charles Stewart Parnell and George Trevelyan (Macaulay's nephew, soon to become Sir George Trevelyan) all spoke to him during the evening.

Evidently Dilke, who was a cabinet minister, invited Clemenceau to call at his house, and the news found its way to Queen Victoria at Osborne, for on 16 February she telegraphed to Gladstone, the prime minister:

> Trust that you will not invite Clemenceau to your house. Whatever his language may be now, he was concerned in some of the most horrible acts of the Commune.

She also gave instructions that Lord Granville, the foreign secretary, should be told of her message to Gladstone and of her regret at the action that Sir Charles Dilke appeared to have taken.[1]

The Queen's telegram suggests that she was mistakenly holding Clemenceau responsible for the murders of Generals Thomas and Lecomte in 1871. Her ministers knew better, but in any case Gladstone was in the happy position of being able to tell the Queen that he had already decided it would not be desirable for him to meet Clemenceau.[2]

Granville was not so fortunate. He wrote to the Queen to say that he had consulted the French ambassador about Clemenceau's visit, and the ambassador had said 'that he did not approve of some of his political principles, but that he was a distinguished man.' The ambassador had also said that he had invited Clemenceau to dine at the French Embassy, and he thought there was no reason why Granville should not invite him too. So Granville had to confess that he had invited the French ambassador, his wife and Clemenceau to dine in Carlton Terrace on Thursday. He wistfully added that 'He would be delighted, especially after receiving your Majesty's message, if, as is probable, M. Clemenceau is engaged.'[3]

As the awful moment drew nearer when he might be entertaining a French Radical to dinner against his Sovereign's wishes, Granville wrote to the Queen to deal with her point about the Commune. The ambassador had probably told him that Clemenceau had tried to mediate between Paris and the government and had no responsibility for the acts of the Commune; and he was able to assure the Queen that he regarded Clemenceau's categorical denials of the Commune murders as conclusive. The ambassador, he added,

> says that M. Clemenceau is a strong Radical, would be glad to abolish the Senate, and is desirous that Trade Unions should have the same legal protection as they have in this country, but that his opinions are strongly anti-Socialistic.[4]

This last assurance may have slightly consoled the Queen, and there is no further correspondence about Clemenceau's visit in the Royal Archives.

Probably he was already engaged on the evening suggested by Lord Granville, for on his departure *The Times* mentioned that he was entertained to dinner at the French Embassy, but made no reference to a visit to Carlton Terrace. During his ten days' stay he spoke at the Cobden and Cosmopolitan clubs, but had to refuse an invitation to address the

---

[1] Royal Archives A 59/58.   [2] RA A 59/49.
[3] RA B 35/106,   [4] RA B 35/108,

Liverpool Junior Reform club. He had no meetings with trade unionists.[1]

[5]

On his return to Paris Clemenceau was busy with the report of the commission on the workers' position in industry and agriculture. It had been appointed after a miners' strike at Anzin, in the Pas-de-Calais, and the report was notable for its strong indictment of the power of the mining companies. Though Clemenceau, as William Waddington had told Lord Granville, was not a Socialist, the commission's report made out a strong case against capitalist domination of the mineworkers. It compared the companies' big profits with the miners' poverty, and suggested that the government's concessions to the companies should be reviewed. More adventurously still, it proposed that employers should be compelled to give the miners a share of the profits. Such a report was much too advanced for the 1880s. Mining unrest continued, and was one of the problems confronting Clemenceau when he at last came to power more than twenty years later.

At this time industrial reorganisation was less important to him than the issues of constitutional reform and colonial expansion. Ferry, who had resumed office as prime minister in 1883, was prepared to consider minor revisions of the constitution, but these were far short of the demands formulated in the Marseilles programme.

A new phase in the battle for wider change had been opened in *La Justice* on 22 March, 1883, when the manifesto of a newly formed *Ligue républicaine pour la révision des lois constitutionelles* appeared in its columns. The league was supported by all members of the extreme Left; Clemenceau spoke at its public meetings, and took up the subject in the Chamber. If the presidency and the Senate were not to be abolished, he claimed as a minimum reform that senators should be elected by universal suffrage, and not by the votes of special electoral groups, as laid down in the 1875 constitution.

The campaign failed. When Chamber and Senate met together as the National Assembly at Versailles in August 1884, they went only a small part of the way towards meeting Clemenceau's wishes. The presidency and the Senate remained; the electoral colleges for senatorial elections would be enlarged, though they would still be composed of those

[1] Prince von Bülow, the German statesman and diplomat, was in London that summer, and met a number of diplomats from other countries, including 'the Frenchman d'Aunay, later the friend and confidant of Clemenceau, and his ambitious and coquettish American wife.' (*See* Bülow, *Memoirs, 1849–1897*, p. 553.) This was the *'femme ravissante d'un diplomate complaisant'* who became Clemenceau's mistress. Possibly they met for the first time at the French Embassy dinner.

bourgeois elements which were likely to oppose social reform; but no more life senators would be appointed, and the seats of existing life senators would be filled by ordinary elections as their occupants died. Though the last concession was to be of considerable importance in Clemenceau's career, the 1875 constitution had survived his attacks. He continued for a few years to demand a further revision, but finally dropped the subject from his electoral programme.

With revision disposed of, he could turn again to his fight against colonial expansion. It was Indo-China which led to the new battle between the government and the anti-colonialists.

French missionaries had been active in Indo-China since the days of Louis XIV, but it was only in the closing years of the Second Empire that France had occupied the territory of Cochin-China, in the south of the peninsula. The next objective was the great northern territory of Tonkin, in the kingdom of Annam, which was a Chinese dependency. Both Chamber and Senate gave Ferry the credits he wanted for Indo-China in 1883–4, in spite of the consistent opposition of Clemenceau, who at one time induced two hundred deputies to vote against the government.

After some months of what was virtually an undeclared war with China, hostilities seemed to be ended in May 1884 by the Franco-Chinese Treaty of Tientsin, under which France promised to protect China's western frontiers from aggression and China agreed to withdraw her troops from Tonkin and to renounce her claim to suzerainty over Indo-China. But Chinese troops remained in Tonkin. At the end of the year Ferry decided to resume the war, and at once encountered the bitter opposition of Clemenceau and his allies from the monarchist Right. The government got the credits it wanted, but only by 342 votes to 170.

Early in 1885 a French expeditionary force marched north from Cochin-China and occupied Langson, on the road to Hanoi. At the end of March an alarmist telegram from the commander-in-chief, indicating that the French had been driven out of Langson and needed reinforcements, gave Clemenceau his opportunity for bringing Ferry down.

It was discovered later that the evacuation of Langson had been unnecessary, and that the action in which it occurred was really a French victory. But the shock of the blundering telegram caused Ferry to be jeered in the streets as '*le Tonkinois*'; and when he appeared in the Chamber on 30 March, to ask for credits of 200m. francs, he found that Clemenceau had assembled a formidable opposition, consisting of the Radical Socialists, the devoted patriots with their eyes on the Vosges, the Roman Catholics who hated Ferry because of his anti-clerical educational policy, and the rural deputies who knew that their constituents were against war in Tonkin or anywhere else.

The prime minister's defence of the apparent disaster was noble and dignified. France, he declared, was the second maritime power in the world and should not surrender any of her overseas territories; on the contrary, she should prepare new areas for the activity and labour of future generations. Langson must be avenged, 'not only for the security and future of our possessions in Indo-China, but for our honour in the world at large.'

Such words were wasted on Clemenceau. The Tiger was ready to pounce on his prey. A foretaste of his speech had been given in that morning's issue of _La Justice_, which had commented on the supposed loss of Langson: 'There will be a single cry of rage and pain throughout France.' He replied to Ferry in what Alexandre Zévaès calls 'beyond doubt the most violent speech of his whole career.' It pronounced sentence of death on the ministry.

Annexation and conquest, he declared, were contrary to the principles of the Revolution. Colonial policies gave profit to financial oligarchies at the expense of France, and wasted men and money that were needed at home. France was not an island like England, but was placed in the middle of Europe: 'We shall be strong only if we keep all the resources we have at our disposal.'

After a savage review of the recent events in Tonkin he turned on Ferry and his ministers:

> Everything is finished between us. We do not wish to hear you any more. We can no longer discuss with you the great affairs of the country. We do not know you any more, we do not wish to know you any more. . . .
>
> These are no longer ministers whom I see before me. They are men charged with high treason, on whom, if there remains in France a principle of responsibility and justice, the hand of the law will soon fall.

This ringing denunciation was greeted with wild cheers from Left and Right; even the deputies of the Left Centre, on whom Ferry could usually rely, joined the opposition. The credits were refused by 306 votes to 149.

Ferry resigned. He never held ministerial office again, though he remained an active figure in politics and was a contender for the presidency in 1887. He was murdered by a madman in 1893. Ironically, the Tonkin affair was almost settled when he fell from power. Sir Robert Hart, inspector-general of Chinese Customs, had been asked by the Chinese government to negotiate peace terms with France; agreement was reached in April, and Chinese troops left Tonkin. Clemenceau's invective would have had less power if deputies had known that a settlement was so near.

As the architect of Ferry's defeat, Clemenceau had a reasonable claim to be invited to form the next government. But President Grévy preferred weak prime ministers to strong ones, and he certainly would not appoint a strong man from the extreme Left. 'I shall never call on M. Clemenceau,' he once told René Goblet. 'He would turn France upside down.' Instead he chose the moderate Henri Brisson to succeed Ferry.

Three months after Ferry's defeat victor and vanquished met again in a debate which Raoul Girardet calls 'the essential text' for the colonial controversy of the 1880s. In the Chamber of Deputies on 28 July Ferry defended his policies on the grounds of France's need for export markets, the duty of superior races to bring the benefits of civilisation to inferior races, and the importance of maintaining France's national prestige. Three days later Clemenceau opposed the realities of home needs—*la politique du pot au feu*—to the illusions of 'the colonial dream'. Colonial expeditions, he said, were an unnecessary luxury when so much was needed at home for the development of the French genius and the increase of industrial production. Ferry's ambition, he thought, must be very lofty if he could not find sufficient scope for it in increasing the sum of knowledge and enlightenment in France and developing the country's well-being, in extending liberty and the rule of law, in fighting ignorance, vice and misery, and in organising a better use of social resources. He was not impressed by Ferry's argument about the duty of superior races, for he remembered German professors proving scientifically that France deserved to be beaten in the Franco-Prussian War because the Frenchman was of an inferior race to the German. Since that time, he observed, he had thought twice before calling men or civilisations 'inferior'.

So Clemenceau had broken another ministry and seemed to have won a victory for anti-colonialism, though he did not, in fact, try to carry his victory to the point of forcing an evacuation of Indo-China; but Ferry's work lived on, and France continued to develop the colonial Empire he had founded in Indo-China, Madagascar, the Congo and Tunisia. In the fifteen years from 1880 to 1895 the extent of France's overseas possessions grew from one million to nine-and-half million square kilometres, and the population from five to fifty millions.

Though time has shown that such empires have no permanence, it was Ferry's colonial policy, rather than Clemenceau's *politique du pot au feu*, which served France well in the First World War. If, as Clemenceau had urged, she had kept her eye exclusively on the German problem, she would have had to do without the 600,000 soldiers and 200,000 labourers whom the French colonies sent to Europe in that war, together with $2\frac{1}{2}$m. tons of foodstuffs, raw materials and other supplies.

It has been said, and is probably true, that Clemenceau's anti-colonial policy was partly based on his personal dislike of Ferry. This was an unworthy motive for taking sides on a great national issue, and even his worthier motive of preserving French security was inspired by a rather short-sighted patriotism, as he himself began to understand in later years. 'Perhaps I was wrong in my violent attacks at other times on colonial conquests,' he admitted in a public speech in 1919. 'It was because I wanted to keep for France the totality of her men and resources.' His mistake was in failing to see that colonial expansion increased this totality rather than diminished it, and would continue to do so until the whole colonial concept was shattered by the upsurge of nationalism after the Second World War.

CHAPTER SIX

BOULANGER

1. Cornelius Herz. 2. The Republic in danger. 3. Dangerous protégé.
4. Decorations scandal. 5. The end of Boulangism.

[1]

IN THE years when Clemenceau was emerging as the great Radical leader he had the misfortune to become friends with Cornelius Herz, a financial charlatan who had amassed a fortune by devious methods. Herz's parents were German Jews, but he was born at Besançon and could claim French nationality. Two years younger than Clemenceau, he worked in a pharmacy before 1870 and served in the ambulance service during the war. He then went to America, where he found his way into the new industry of electric lighting.

Returning to France in 1877, as agent for an American firm of electric lighting manufacturers, he founded a paper, *La Lumière Électrique*, and established several companies, some of which were successful. His connection with a new and important industry gave him the entry into political and business circles; he was soon on good terms with deputies and ministers, and President Grévy treated him as a family friend. In due course he was given the Legion of Honour and later promoted to be a Grand Officer of the order.

Clemenceau was one of those who were taken in by Herz's suavity and knowledge of high finance. Perhaps he was not to blame. 'I must say that Cornelius Herz was a thoroughly bad lot,' he said to Jean Martet in 1928. 'Unfortunately it wasn't written all over his face.' His decision to entrust his children to Herz's care, in case he had died during his visit to the cholera-ridden Midi in 1884, was a proof of his confidence in the Jewish financier.

For a time Herz gave financial help to *La Justice*. In the second year of its publication the original shareholders surrendered their shares to Clemenceau, on the understanding that he would be responsible for the newspaper's liabilities; in 1883 half of these shares were assigned to Herz in return for advances to cover the paper's expenses. Herz was not, as was rumoured, a partner in *La Justice*, and after two years Clemenceau was able to buy the shares back, presumably with the loans from other friends. Thereafter the financier had nothing to do with the newspaper, but his brief association with it gave Clemenceau's enemies a weapon to use against him. They asserted that in return for Herz's purchase of shares Clemenceau had boosted the financier's business interests in *La Justice* and had recommended him for the Legion of Honour.

Neither of these charges was true. In reply to a spiteful article in *Le Monde* Clemenceau gave an account of the share transactions in *La Justice* of 3 November, 1886, and declared that he had never recommended Herz to any minister or anyone else in connection with any business matter or to ask any favour.

There is no need to doubt the truth of this assertion, or to wonder, as Edouard Drumont did in his book *La Fin d'un Monde*, why an astute financier should invest money, even temporarily, in a newspaper which had never paid a dividend and was never likely to pay one. (Clemenceau, wrote Drumont sneeringly, had apparently said to Herz: 'Sir, I agree to accept your 500,000 francs, but on one condition, that you will never ask for a recommendation or a favour!') It must, after all, have been of great value to Herz to be known as a friend and business associate of such a prominent deputy as Clemenceau. That alone was adequate return for his money.

Though Clemenceau's answers to *Le Monde's* charges seem irrefutable, his financial dealings with Herz are still open to a certain amount of suspicion. This was a period in which he was both maintaining a family home and enjoying a crowded social life, which must have involved expenses far beyond his apparent means; and while there is no evidence of any sort of corrupt practice one may surmise that Herz gave him some assistance in his private finances as well as helping to keep *La Justice* alive. He would pay heavily in time for his friendship with the shady financier.

[2]

After defeating Ferry's second ministry in 1885 Clemenceau was the unchallenged master of the Chamber of Deputies. Yet it was a disillusioning time for him, as for all Republicans. Edmond de Goncourt quotes a remark Clemenceau made at a dinner-table. As a young man hostile to the Empire he had believed, he said, that two things would be provided by new men—a revival of intelligence and of morals; but among those currently governing the country both intelligence and morality were inferior to those of the men of the Empire.

Certainly the eight years following the *seize Mai*, years of Opportunist government and conservative Republicanism, had brought little but ministerial instability, budget deficits, economic crises, unemployment and intellectual confusion. With an obstinate Right, an impatient Left and a neutral Centre genuine government seemed impossible.

Clemenceau, as *tombeur de ministères*, is sometimes blamed for the ministerial instability of the Third Republic, but the weakness was mainly due to the Chamber of Deputies, which was elected for a fixed term of four years and was not dissolved when a government was overthrown. Since the MacMahon débâcle the president's right to dissolve the Chamber, with the Senate's concurrence, had never been used; no president was willing to risk his office to teach the Chamber a lesson, and deputies could be sure of keeping their seats (and their salaries) for the statutory four years, however often they might overthrow the government. Ministerial instability was thus built into the constitution and was not created by Clemenceau. With three notable exceptions (the ministries of Waldeck-Rousseau, Combes and Clemenceau himself) governments were just as short-lived when he had ceased to be a deputy as they were when he dominated the Chamber.

The year of Ferry's second defeat was also the year of a general election, in which Clemenceau stood for peace and social reform, and made an unsuccessful attempt to bring the small but growing Socialist party into temporary alliance with the Radicals, 'up to the point where Radical and collectivist doctrines divide'. The Socialist leader, Jules Guesde, would not be tempted. 'Since we do not believe in your peaceful methods,' he said, 'what should we be doing in your boat?'

But the Socialist vote was of minor importance in this election. The crucial factor was the split among the Republicans, between Clemenceau's Radicals and the moderates, who included Opportunists like Ferry and men of the Left Centre like Alexandre Ribot. The division between conservative and advanced Republicans had been widened by the colonial controversy; members of the two groups now opposed each other all over the country, and the clash was all the more dangerous because the old Chamber had finally voted in favour of *scrutin de liste*, so that Paris, for example, had become one vast constituency with thirty-nine seats. In all districts separate lists were presented by the Radicals, the moderates and the reactionary, anti-Republican Right.

The first results of the election were disastrous for the Republicans. In department after department the split in their vote gave seats to the reactionaries, of whom 177 were returned on the first ballot, against 129 Republicans.

Clearly the Republic was in danger, in graver danger than it had been at any time in the previous eight years. An anti-Republican government was again a real possibility. But the Republicans saw the danger in time; on the second ballot moderates and Radicals stood down in each other's favour. thus leaving a single Republican list in each department. The strategy succeeded. The second vote gave 243 seats to the Republicans, and only 25 to the Right. The Republicans now had a safe majority, but it had been an uncomfortably near thing.

Clemenceau was returned for both Paris and the Var, which he had visited during the recent cholera outbreak. In spite of his long association with Montmartre, he decided to sit for the Var. This was really a tactical move; he knew that his old Paris constituency was certain to stay Republican, but in the Var, which was more reactionary, the Right might have regained the seat if he had given it up in favour of Paris. He now represented the Draguignan district, which was to fill many columns in the European press eight years later.

The Republicans had won the election, but it was not a happy result. The Chamber was divided into three groups—205 on the Right, 257 moderate Republicans and 115 Radicals. It was a time for Republican consolidation, to meet the growing challenge from the Right, but the Republican leaders were content to remain separated.

Jean Jaurès, the future Socialist leader, who had just entered the Chamber as a moderate Republican, once said that the 'capital error' of Clemenceau's life was his failure to bring the Republicans together after the 1885 election. Such a union would have been very desirable, but it would have been practicable only if each side had been ready to sacrifice some of its principles. All forms of compromise were foreign to Clemenceau's Vendean nature. He preferred to fight for the Republic in his own way, even though division meant weakness.

The election was barely over before it was time to elect a president, as Jules Grévy's seven-year term of office was ending. The Republicans thought it best to play for safety, and they invited Grévy to stand again, though he was seventy-eight and would be eighty-five when his second term was completed. He was re-elected without serious opposition on 28 December, and he and his family, including his tall, red-bearded son-in-law, Daniel Wilson, continued to live at the Elysée.

One of Grévy's first tasks in his second term of office was to appoint a new prime minister, for Brisson, who had succeeded Ferry, found his majority dwindling after a few months and decided to resign. Since any Republican government would need Radical support, people wondered if Grévy would send for Clemenceau at last; but the President still distrusted him and turned instead to his old friend Freycinet, who was always his first choice in any crisis. Freycinet's ministry lasted till the end of the year, and was chiefly notable for the new men who were brought into the cabinet.

Freycinet tried to unite the Republicans by including, for the first time, Radicals in the government. Clemenceau was regarded as too dangerous, but posts were given to other Radicals—Edouard Lockroy, René Goblet, Ferdinand Sarrien and Félix Granet, who was one of Clemenceau's closest associates. He also invited General Georges Boulanger to become his minister of war.

There is some dispute about how Boulanger was chosen. Freycinet says in his memoirs that he was recommended by the outgoing war minister, General J. B. Campenon, but the story current at the time was that Clemenceau imposed Boulanger on Freycinet as a Republican general who could be trusted to democratise the army. Certainly Clemenceau favoured Boulanger's appointment, and *Le Figaro* said definitely: 'It is to M. Clemenceau's friendship that General Boulanger owes his portfolio. The Radicals have put their hand on the ministry of war.'

[3]

Like Clemenceau, who was four years his junior, Georges Boulanger went to the *lycée* at Nantes, but thereafter their ways diverged. While Clemenceau was still at school, Boulanger went to the Saint-Cyr military academy, from which he passed out in 1857; under the Second Empire he served in Algeria, Italy and Cochin-China; in the Franco-Prussian War he won rapid promotion in the defence of Paris, and a fortunate wound saved him from having to take part in the government troops' attack on the Communards. After the war he spent a few years at Saint-Cyr as an instructor, became colonel of the 133rd regiment and was appointed chief inspector of infantry.

It was during his two years as infantry inspector (1882–4) that he began to make political friendships, notably with Clemenceau and Paul Déroulède, a fervent nationalist who founded the *Ligue des Patriotes* in 1882. Originally a scheme for training boys in gymnastics and rifle-shooting, the league became a paramilitary organisation with the declared objectives of securing the revision of the Treaty of Frankfort and the return of Alsace-Lorraine. When Déroulède met Boulanger he thought that he had 'at last found a man, I would even say, *our* man.'

Boulanger's next post was as army commander in Tunisia, where he quarrelled with Paul Cambon, the civilian resident-general, and lost his command. He was thus in Paris, sporting a magnificent blond beard and enjoying the prestige of being the youngest general in the army, when Freycinet was forming his cabinet.

In sponsoring Boulanger as minister of war Clemenceau had not relied only on his own opinion. He had also consulted the general's military files, of which he observed later to Berta Szeps: 'I was royally deceived. That will teach me not to look at files when it's a matter of judging a man.' His view was that Boulanger would be an instrument for republicanising the army by removing monarchist officers from their high places, and he found it pleasant to have a minister of war at his beck and call. In the early days of Boulanger's appointment he used to call at the war ministry in the rue Saint-Dominique every morning, and every evening an aide-de-camp would come round to the office of *La Justice* with the latest news from the ministry. He seemed to regard the general as someone to be 'shown off' to his friends, for on one occasion he took Cornelius Herz to the war ministry, and on another his new mistress, the Comtesse d'Aunay, who wanted, he explained, to see Boulanger and to congratulate him on riding so well.

At first all went in accordance with Clemenceau's plans. 'Boul-boul', as he called the general, had a flair for army reform. He improved the food, clothing and quarters of the troops, and made army discipline more intelligent and flexible—for example, by allowing private soldiers to grow beards and to return to barracks at later hours than had been usual. He also sponsored the introduction of new and more efficient weapons, especially the Lebel rifle and melinite (lyddite) for high-explosive shells.

It was soon clear that 'Boul-boul' had a personal magnetism unsuspected by Clemenceau. He was one of those rare men whom the French people take to their hearts. At the annual military review at Longchamp on 14 July few onlookers paid much attention to the ageing President of the Republic; everyone was looking at the handsome, blond-bearded general on his black horse Tunis. The crowds which watched the parade felt they were at last seeing the rebirth of French military glory. That evening the café-concert singer Paulus launched a new song, '*En revenant de la revue*', which established Boulanger as the symbol of the army and the man who could win back Alsace-Lorraine.

Even Bismarck helped to build up the new hero's reputation. In January 1887 he told the German Reichstag that Boulanger was 'the greatest danger to good relations between France and Germany'. Three months later the Schnaebele incident gave 'General *Revanche*' a chance to stand up to the German chancellor.

Schnaebele was a French frontier official and under-cover organiser of espionage in Alsace. He was found on German soil and arrested. The French government at once demanded his release, and as long as he remained under arrest it seemed as though France might declare war to avenge her honour. Fortunately it was discovered that Schnaebele had been invited to cross the frontier on official business; Bismarck released his prisoner and even offered a vague apology; and the enraptured

French public mistakenly believed that the national honour had been saved by Boulanger. In fact, his only contribution to resolving the crisis had been his foolhardy readiness to send the French army into a war for which it was not prepared. It was this recklessness which made Clemenceau remark in the office of *La Justice*, 'War is too serious a matter to be left to soldiers.'

Boulanger remained at the war ministry when Freycinet resigned at the end of 1886 and the Radical René Goblet became prime minister, but his ministerial career was ended when the Opportunists turned against Goblet and defeated him after the Schnaebele crisis. Though he was still the Radicals' nominee, the Opportunists distrusted his popularity and feared a *coup d'état*. The Senate refused to support any new ministry of which he was a member.

Grévy thought it essential to appoint an Opportunist prime minister, but it was clear that the Opportunists would lose Radical support if Boulanger were dropped, and would have to pick up votes from the Right. This was the course adopted. Maurice Rouvier, an able and resolute Opportunist who was to have a long and chequered career in politics, formed a ministry in the expectation of receiving enough support from Right wing deputies to ensure a majority. In that ministry there was no place for Boulanger.

The Radical press, and particularly *La Justice*, complained bitterly of the general's dismissal. Clemenceau tried to out-manoeuvre Rouvier by persuading General Ferron, who had been nominated to succeed Boulanger as war minister, to refuse the post; and he was deeply offended when Ferron, after agreeing to refuse it, allowed himself to be talked round by Grévy and joined the ministry.[1] This was his last effort on Boulanger's behalf; whatever faith he still had in the general was dispelled by the hysterical scenes at the gare de Lyon on 8 July, when frantic crowds tried to keep back the train which was taking their hero to an army command at Clermont-Ferrand.[2]

---

[1] The incident provides a good example of Clemenceau's gift for the appropriate use of literary allusions. After agreeing to join the Rouvier ministry Ferron met Clemenceau in the Palais-Bourbon and hurried forward with outstretched hand. Clemenceau put his hand in his pocket, and said coldly: '*Albe vous a nommé, je ne vous connais plus*'—'Alba has named you, I do not know you any more.' (*See* Zévaès, *Histoire de la Troisième République*, p. 171.) The quotation is from Corneille's *Horace*, Act II, scene 3.

[2] Demonstrators at the gare de Lyon may have had other motives besides their love for Boulanger. Frederick H. Seager suggests that the demonstration was a Republican protest against the Rouvier ministry's association with the Right; by cheering Boulanger the crowds were implicitly denouncing the government. (*See* Seager. *The Boulanger Affair*, pp. 67–8.)

Clemenceau felt that no good could come from the public frenzy over Boulanger. *La Justice* declared that the scenes at the gare de Lyon were 'the negation of Republican doctrine. . . . The first duty of Republicans is not to exalt an individual to this point. It is to the idea, and the idea alone, that they should pay homage.' And in the Chamber Clemenceau said of Boulanger:

I say that this popularity has come too quickly to someone who liked noise too much, or who, to speak more equitably, did not avoid it enough. The Boulanger question is a misfortune; it is a misfortune for all of us, for you [Rouvier] as well as for me.

The misfortune, in his opinion, was that Boulanger had been allowed to divide the Republicans, so that the Rouvier ministry now found allies among its former enemies. But though he no longer believed in the general, he had not yet broken with him. They were to meet again before Boulanger began to look for backers from other quarters.

[4]

In October 1887, three months after Boulanger's departure for Clermont-Ferrand, reports of a scandalous traffic in honours and decorations began to appear in the French press. They were the prelude to a major constitutional crisis in which the President was to find himself opposed by all his senior ministers and ex-ministers.

The opening disclosure in what became known as 'the decorations scandal' or 'the Wilson affair' was that a senior officer at the war ministry had been adding to his pay by selling decorations at prices ranging from 25,000 fr. to 50,000 fr. The trail then led to the Elysée, where it was found that Daniel Wilson, President Grévy's son-in-law, was conducting a virtual 'ministry of recommendations and contacts' from a suite of offices on the first floor.

Wilson was the son of a Scottish engineer who had settled in France and made a fortune out of gas installations. He was a deputy and the owner of a chain of some twenty provincial newspapers, which provided the cover for his operations at the Elysée. Everything was done discreetly. People who wanted honours or favours were not asked for cash down, but were invited to subscribe generously to one of Wilson's papers. He had seven or eight secretaries, gave 150 interviews a week and used the presidential free postage for the tens of thousands of letters he wrote every year.

When the scandal broke, Grévy might have saved himself by disowning Wilson and turning him out of the Elysée; but the President made no move, naively regarding the attacks on his son-in-law as being due to jealousy of his successful newspapers. The uproar grew. Rochefort wrote of 'the King Log of the Elysée' and referred to Wilson as 'the first son-in-law of France'; a popular cabaret song lamented, '*Ah! quel malheur d'avoir un gendre*'; and the misfortune of having a son-in-law became only too evident when the Chamber of Deputies agreed to waive Wilson's parliamentary immunity so that he could be placed on trial. Many people already thought that for France's honour Grévy should resign from the presidency.

Wilson's immunity was lifted on 17 November. On the same day Clemenceau and other Republican deputies met to discuss ways of forcing Grévy to resign. The President had committed no offence which obliged him to forfeit his office, and the deputies' problem was to find a method of removing him which would not be in breach of the constitution. The plan which found most favour was that Rouvier's ministry should be overthrown, and that all potential prime ministers should either refuse to form a government or declare themselves unable to do so, so that only Grévy's resignation would allow the government of France to be carried on.

The overthrow of the government was a job for the *tombeur de ministères*. When the Chamber met, he interpellated the government on its handling of the decorations scandal. Without mentioning Grévy by name he declared that the political system had collapsed. There was loud applause from the Left when he asked: 'Supposing there were some foreign contingency which I cannot foresee, to whom would the nation turn? Where is the flag? Who keeps it? Who carries it? Where is the government?' His staccato questions fulfilled their purpose. Rouvier was defeated, and Grévy announced that he would summon another minister to form a government.

The task was beyond him. There were no blacklegs in the ministers' strike. Freycinet, Goblet, Brisson and Ribot all declined or were unable to form a ministry. In despair Grévy turned to Clemenceau, but he too refused the post which he would gladly have accepted in other circumstances. He made it clear that only the President's resignation could resolve the ministerial crisis. Grévy held out for as long as he could, but towards the end of November he promised to resign and said that he would send a letter of resignation to the Chamber and the Senate in the following week.

It seems to have been only at this point that the plotters realised they were getting rid of a president without having decided who was to take his place. The obvious successor was the highly experienced Ferry, who was fifty-five, but Clemenceau detested him, and knew that he would have no chance of becoming prime minister if Ferry were at the Elysée. Other names were mentioned in the press, but it seemed likely that Ferry would get an adequate majority in the presidential election.

Attempts to work out a plan to 'stop Ferry' were made at two meetings attended by Clemenceau and other deputies and newspaper directors on the evenings of 28 and 29 November—evenings which the participants afterwards called *'les nuits historiques'*, though in fact they achieved nothing. Déroulède, the Right wing nationalist, and Boulanger, playing truant from Clermont-Ferrand, were present at the meetings.

The first of the 'historic nights' was at Durand's restaurant at the corner of the place de la Madeleine, on the site now occupied by Thomas Cook's; its object was to bar Ferry from the presidency, even at the cost of allowing Grévy to stay at the Elysée and finding, after all, a ministry which would take office under him. One proposal was to form a ministry which would include Clemenceau, Freycinet, Floquet and Boulanger; but neither Freycinet nor Floquet was present, and messengers sent to ask for their opinions came back to report that neither would join the projected ministry, evidently because they both meant to stand for the presidency if Grévy resigned. It was then suggested that Clemenceau and Boulanger should form a government, but Clemenceau declined the honour, fearing that he would be forced to take a back seat while Boulanger exploited his popularity with the masses.

On the second 'historic night' the conspirators met at the house of Georges Laguerre, a young Radical deputy who was soon to become a fervent Boulangist, and his charming wife, Marguerite Durand of the Comédie-Française. At first there was some talk of allowing Andrieux, a former prefect of police, to form a government, but it was soon realised that such a makeshift cabinet would be defeated as soon as it faced the Chamber. The discussions confirmed Clemenceau in his belief that Boulanger was of no further use to the Radicals; for it was clear that some of the plotters were thinking more in terms of a *coup d'état* than of constitutional action, and that Boulanger was prepared to go along with them. Clemenceau showed his distaste for the whole affair by leaving the discussion and gossiping with Marguerite Durand in the dining-room.

The 'historic nights' showed only that the idea of allowing Grévy to stay at the Elysée in order to bar Ferry was impracticable, since no viable ministry could be formed. Some other way of defeating Ferry would have to be found, but Clemenceau, for one, had little hope of finding it. While Grévy's letter of resignation was still awaited, he told Rochefort: 'We are lost. Ferry's election is certain.' Yet it was he, in the end, who kept Ferry out by casting himself in the new rôle of king-maker.

Grévy's letter was received on 2 December, and Chamber and Senate were summoned to meet at Versailles to elect his successor. As was usual on such occasions, a preliminary vote was taken by the Republican deputies before the meeting of the National Assembly. Clemenceau persuaded Floquet to stand down and leave the field clear for Freycinet, but even so the voting put Ferry comfortably ahead, with Freycinet next and some modest support for Brisson and Sadi Carnot, who had been finance minister in Rouvier's government.

Clemenceau now saw a way of beating Ferry: Freycinet would never win, but a heavy transfer of votes to one of the outsiders might change the situation. Which should it be, Brisson or Sadi Carnot? The phrase long associated with Clemenceau's decision is '*Votons pour le plus bête*', but though the remark seems characteristic enough, most historians do not believe that he really urged deputies to 'vote for the stupidest'. He is more likely to have said something like the remark he made to Rochefort: 'Carnot is not very great, but he has a Republican name.'

Certainly Carnot had a good name. He was the grandson of Lazare Carnot, the 'organiser of victory' in the first phase of the French Revolution, and a son of Hippolyte Carnot, a minister of the Second Republic in 1848; he was thus an admirable representative of the great bourgeois dynasties of Republican France. Many deputies and senators followed Clemenceau's advice, and when the National Assembly met to choose the new president, the previously unconsidered Carnot led on the first ballot and was subsequently elected by a big majority.

So Carnot replaced Grévy, and a new ministry was formed at last, with the undistinguished Pierre Tirard as prime minister. The decorations scandal was ended by Wilson's trial and conviction, but 'the first son-in-law' was acquitted on appeal, on the legal nicety that he had not stated definitely that honours would be conferred at a particular time.

After Clemenceau's successful 'stop Ferry' campaign it was ironical that he should have been the first doctor to go to Ferry's assistance when a malcontent tried to assassinate him in the Palais-Bourbon a few days after the presidential election. The wound was not serious.[1]

[5]

Though the idea of a *coup d'état* had been mentioned on the 'historic nights', neither Boulanger nor his close friends were seriously envisaging a *coup* on the lines of Louis-Napoleon's *deux-Décembre*. Frederick H. Seager, Boulanger's American biographer, observes that the general 'repeatedly emphasised

---

[1] Berta Szeps once chaffed the Tiger on the oddity of his giving medical treatment to his greatest enemy. He explained that he was observing the English doctrine of 'fair play': 'After giving your opponent the "knock-out" you salute him!' (*See* Szeps, *Clemenceau tel que je l'ai connu*, pp. 45–6.)

his devotion to the Republic', and that the charge of Caesarism, brought against him by his opponents, was not justified. His aim was a new Republican constitution, which would transfer power from parliament to the executive, and in that executive he expected to take the leading part. He had no scruples about posing as a champion of either Left or Right in order to get financial or other backing.

Boulangism became a political programme in March 1888, when the general put his name forward as a candidate in a by-election in the Aisne department, calling for the dissolution of the Chamber and revision of the constitution. His candidature was an infringement of army regulations, and he was promptly discharged from the service. He was now free to pursue his political ends more openly.

By this time Clemenceau was fully aware of the general's threat to parliamentary authority, and he fought Boulangism both inside and outside the Chamber. In collaboration with Camille Pelletan (who was now a Radical deputy as well as editor of *La Justice*) he tried to steal Boulanger's thunder by putting down a Radical demand for constitutional revision, so that France, as he told the Chamber, might have at last 'a truly Republican constitution'. The motion was also supported by Boulangists and monarchists, who hoped that revision might favour their own causes, and was passed, against the government's wishes, by 268 votes to 237. Once again Clemenceau had overthrown a ministry. Tirard resigned, and was succeeded by Floquet, who asked for calm and reflection before revision was reconsidered.

Clemenceau's next aim was to rally all Republicans in a common front against Boulangism. In association with Ranc, who was now one of the leading Opportunists, and Joffrin, a Socialist of the 'possibilist' group (i.e. non-Marxists who believed in restricting the Socialist programme to what was politically possible), he formed the *Société des Droits de l'Homme et du Citoyen*, which was designed, as he announced at its inaugural meeting, 'to establish an entente between all those who remain faithful to the Republic, and to put an end to the Boulangist adventure which is so humiliating for our country.' While accepting the principle of constitutional revision, the society rejected its exploitation 'by a general who poses as a pretender and recruits his followers from all parties.'

To René Waldeck-Rousseau, a former minister of the interior who was later to be an outstanding prime minister, it seemed that the linking of the three names of Clemenceau, Ranc and Joffrin was '*un trait de génie*' and '*un coup de maître*'; he enthusiastically told Ranc that they had saved the *régime*. But the new society was not really the flash of genius and masterstroke that Waldeck-Rousseau acclaimed. To make its programme more constructive than one of mere opposition to Boulanger, Clemenceau included a number of social and industrial reforms, such as a public health service and legal provision for safety and hygiene in factories and workshops. These proposals kept many Opportunists out of the society, and encouraged monarchists to back Boulanger as a defence against the encroachments of Socialism. Boulanger himself recognised the divisive effects of the society's programme and ironically commented: 'I hardly expected M. Clemenceau to aid my cause, and I thank him.'

The society was further weakened when the Socialists left it, but Clemenceau continued to fight Boulangism in the Chamber and the columns of *La Justice*. Anatole France, writing in 1906, said that it was to Clemenceau, more than to any other man, that the Republic owed its safety in these crucial years.

Soon after the formation of the *Société des Droits de l'Homme et du Citoyen* Clemenceau clashed with Boulanger in the Chamber of Deputies. The general had withdrawn from the Aisne by-election after his dismissal from the army in March, but had soon won a seat in the Nord department. In his maiden speech on 4 June he condemned the existing form of parliamentary government, and was sharply reproved by both Floquet and Clemenceau. Boulanger, who was then fifty-one, had referred to Napoleon I in his attack on parliament; Floquet drily retorted, 'At your age, sir, Napoleon was dead.' Clemenceau picked up the general's assertion that there was too much talking in parliament: these discussions, he said, did the deputies honour, and proved that they were eager to defend the ideas they held to be just and productive. 'If it is the system of discussion that you think you are stigmatising under the name of parliamentarianism,' he continued, 'understand that it is the representative system itself, it is the Republic on which you wish to lay hands.'

Unabashed by the cold reception of his first speech, Boulanger spoke again in July, calling for dissolution of the Chamber as a prelude to revision of the constitution; his exchanges with Floquet in this debate became so heated that the prime minister was obliged to challenge him to a duel. Floquet, who was several years older than the general and extremely near-sighted, asked Clemenceau to be one of his seconds. When the duel was fought Boulanger was expected to overwhelm his adversary, but in fact he was wounded by Floquet, who was himself unhurt. This surprising *dénouement* was apparently due to wise advice from Clemenceau.[1]

[1] The duel took place at the house of Count Dillon, one of Boulanger's monarchist friends. Stephen Bonsal, an American journalist in Paris in the 1880s, was one of many newspaper men who waited in the main garden, where cooling drinks were served by charming young ladies in muslin dresses, while the duel took place in a rear garden hidden by plants and shrubs. They heard a clash of steel, which lasted only a second, and soon afterwards Floquet emerged, 'on the arm of M. Clemenceau, who was laughing in what seemed to us a most unseemly manner.' Clemenceau explained

In spite of his humiliating defeat by an elderly politician, Boulanger remained a popular hero for several months. His political career reached its zenith in January 1889, when he contested a by-election in Paris and was returned with a huge majority.

This was the moment of decision. As the general dined with his friends at Durand's after the declaration of the poll, an excited crowd waited in the place de la Madeleine, ready to escort him to the Elysée. Clemenceau felt that a *coup d'état* was inevitable; on chancing to meet a friend who had been exiled to New Caledonia he jokingly asked him what life was like there. But Boulanger was a weak man. Was it necessary, he wondered, to seize power illegally when the public seemed certain to give him a landslide victory in the coming general election? He left the restaurant to consult his mistress, and came back to announce that he would take no action that night. One of those present looked at his watch. It was five minutes after midnight. 'Boulangism is going down,' he said.

Saved from the danger of a *coup d'état*, the government found an ingenious way of driving the general out of France. Ernest Constans, the minister of the interior, spread the news that Boulanger was about to be arrested and put on trial. The general fled to Brussels, leaving his friends to organise Boulangist candidatures for the general election.

Two timely measures reduced the Boulangists' chances. One was the restoration of single-member constituencies (*scrutin d'arrondissement*), which encouraged electors to choose deputies for their personalities and knowledge of local affairs rather than for their support of a particular political programme. The other was a new law prohibiting candidates from standing for election in more than one constituency, thus thwarting the Boulangists' intention to turn the election into a plebiscite by putting the general's name forward in hundreds of constituencies.

The general's flight, the electoral changes and the continuing anti-Boulangist campaign (waged with especial vigour by Clemenceau in securing re-election at Draguignan) were all factors in the collapse of Boulangism. Only thirty-eight Boulangist deputies were returned to the Chamber. The threat to the parliamentary Republic was ended.

It remained for Clemenceau to write Boulanger's epitaph. The general stayed in Brussels and never returned to France. His mistress, who had gone into exile with him, died in 1891, and two months later he shot himself on her grave. Clemenceau wrote in *La Justice*: 'He died as he had lived—like a second lieutenant.'

that he had told Floquet that his only chance was to extend his sword-arm and hope that Boulanger would run into it. 'And that,' said Clemenceau, 'is exactly what happened. Boulanger rushed at him like an enraged bull and spitted himself on Floquet's rapier.' (*See* Bonsal, *Heyday in a Vanished World*, pp. 117–20.)

CHAPTER SEVEN

THE PANAMA YEARS

1. Friends and enemies. 2. Canal failure. 3. Defending the Revolution. 4. Amateur diplomat. 5. End of a marriage. 6. The scandal breaks. 7. Defeat at Draguignan.

[1]

ONE OF the unexpected traits in Clemenceau's character was his gift for enjoying easy, intimate and entirely innocent friendships with young girls who were greatly his junior. Two such girls were Berta Szeps, younger daughter of Moritz Szeps, director of the *Neuer Wiener Tageblatt*, and Violet Maxse, elder daughter of his old friend Admiral Frederick Maxse. Their reminiscences give pleasant glimpses of Clemenceau's personal life during his years as Radical leader in the Chamber of Deputies.

Moritz Szeps met Clemenceau in Paris and asked him to stay at his house in Vienna. Berta was about sixteen at the time of his first visit in 1883; she was impressed by his looks and by the beauty of his diction, which made the French language seem more beautiful than she had thought possible. In 1886 she married a Professor Zuckerkandl, and at the end of the same year the Szeps and Clemenceau families were linked by the marriage of Georges's much younger brother Paul to Berta's elder sister, the beautiful and elegant Sophie.

When Berta was in Paris after her wedding she felt that Clemenceau was growing more powerful every day. Everything succeeded for him, everything obeyed his wishes. He had a charming mistress and a wide circle of literary and artistic friends, yet he could always spare time for entertaining the young Austrian girl. He took her to Rodin's studio, he introduced her to General Boulanger, and they met at Madame Menard-Dorian's distinguished *salon*, where she remembered how eloquently he praised the Impressionist school of painting.

Violet Maxse, too, had pleasant memories of Clemenceau in 1887–9, when she spent a couple of years of her late teens in Paris with her father and her sister Olive. (She was studying drawing.) Clemenceau took her to the Opera and the Comédie-Française, where she was impressed by his 'superb and ruthless' criticisms; he commented on her clothes, saying paradoxically, 'Eccentric clothes suit you very well—I advise you not to wear them'; and he often joined her and her father for their morning ride in the Bois. 'Politics,' she wrote later, 'ran very high at this time in Paris— it was the era of the Boulanger election—and once or twice we were greeted with cries of "*A bas Clemenceau*" as we cantered up the avenue du Bois de Boulogne (now the avenue Foch). That was a real "thrill".' She went back to England in the winter of 1889, to prepare for her 'coming out'; but she and her father continued to make short visits to Paris. Each time they arrived Clemenceau would hurry round to their hotel 'with plans for our stay, which included any amount of political talks, picture galleries, artists' studios and theatres.'

In the political world he had many enemies as well as friends. Ferry, for one, never forgave him for his hostility in the Chamber and his sponsorship of Sadi Carnot for the presidency. Déroulède turned against him after his desertion of Boulanger and became one of his bitterest opponents. But the most savage of all his denigrators was the antisemitic writer, Edouard Drumont, author of the two-volume *La France Juive*, of which more than 100,000 copies were sold within nine months of its publication in 1886, and of its sequel, *La Fin d'un Monde*.

Drumont has been described as a 'hard-working, respectable, ambitious and frustrated journalist', who was inspired by a great love for France's past. He was also a vicious propagandist, whose attacks on rich Jewish families and their Christian friends started a new and powerful wave of antisemitic feeling in France. The Jews, he declared, were the primary cause of all France's troubles, particularly since 1870. The title of his second book indicated that the whole world, and not only France, was facing the 'chaos created by the Jews'.

Clemenceau was one of Drumont's targets because of his friendship with Herz. In *La Fin d'un Monde* he was described as 'finished' and 'empty'; Drumont sneered at him for having succeeded a prince (the Duc d'Aumale) in the favours of a *cocotte* (Léonide Leblanc), for passing his life in the wings of the Opera, for having squandered all his own money and some of his father's, for raising funds by borrowing and for having 'the most costly of vices'—a newspaper which no one would read and on which Herz and other financiers had poured out large sums of money. Drumont admitted that Clemenceau was not a hypocrite, but denounced him as a cold cynic and a false Vendean who insulted all the beliefs of his fellow countrymen. Why, then, did deputies of both Left and Right keep on good terms with him and feel honoured by his friendship? The reason, Drumont suggested, was his skill with a pistol, with which he could make a perfect ring in a piece of twenty centimes thrown into the air.

This wild invective had no immediate effect on Clemenceau's career, though it gave ammunition to the enemies who brought him down a few years later. But in 1888 he was so firmly established that only a foolish practical joke, which turned a friend into an enemy, prevented his election as president of the Chamber of Deputies.

The election became necessary when Floquet, the previous president of the Chamber, succeeded Tirard as prime minister. The two candidates were Clemenceau and the experienced but less distinguished Méline. They received an equal number of votes, and according to the rules the older man—Méline—was declared elected. But Clemenceau would have had a majority of two if he had not offended a deputy who would otherwise have voted for him.

Accounts of the trick played on the unfortunate deputy differ in detail; both Berta Szeps and Georges Gatineau-Clemenceau claim to have been told about it by Clemenceau, but their stories do not agree. The version which finds most favour is that the deputy always stuffed his pocket with sandwiches and other buffet delicacies when he attended official receptions, and Clemenceau humiliated him by exposing his greed in public. If Berta Szeps is right, the exposure was in front of the President of the Republic, and Clemenceau said afterwards: 'I regret nothing. The moment when the *foie gras* spread over Sadi Carnot's shoe was worth all the presidencies there are.' The prank, at any rate, was something of that nature, and Charles Péguy, who mentioned it in one of his *Cahiers de la Quinzaine* some years later, cannot have been alone in regarding it as a *mauvaise plaisanterie*.

One may still wonder why Clemenceau should have wanted a post in which, like the Speaker of the House of Commons, he would have been unable to take part in debates. Probably he thought that the prestige of having been president of the Chamber would help him to become prime minister at some later date, and since he was only forty-seven he could afford to withdraw from political controversy for a year or two. It must also be remembered that the presidency of the Chamber brought with it a salary of £3,000 a year and a delightful house; these advantages would have substantially relieved his financial difficulties. But Maurice Barrès was certainly wrong when he wrote in *L'Appel au Soldat*, his semi-fictional, semi-historical reconstruction of the Boulanger era, that Clemenceau wanted the presidency of the Chamber because he was afraid of taking power as prime minister. Time would show Barrès that this was a misreading of the Tiger's character.

[2]

Though Clemenceau, like most politicians of the Third Republic, had little knowledge of business or industry, he was on friendly terms with a number of financiers and *entrepreneurs*. One, as we have seen, was Cornelius Herz; another was the wealthy and influential Baron Jacques de Reinach, a native of Frankfort, whose Paris house overlooking the parc Monceau was a meeting-place for financiers, artists and politicians. It was Clemenceau's friendship with Baron Reinach which brought him into contact with the affairs of the Panama canal company.

The project of cutting a canal through the isthmus of Panama had been mooted in the first half of the nineteenth century, and was considered more seriously in the 1870s after Ferdinand de Lesseps's success in building the Suez canal. An investigating mission went out to Colombia in 1876 and came back to report that a canal was feasible; and Lesseps, though now seventy-four, had no hesitation in putting himself at the head of the enterprise. 'The great Frenchman,' as Gambetta had dubbed him, was always optimistic, rash and obstinate. These characteristics had served him well at Suez. They were fatal at Panama.

From its launching in 1881 to its dissolution in 1889 the Panama canal company had a disastrous record. The investigating mission had estimated that a canal would cost 1,200m. francs and would take twelve years to build; Lesseps then went to Panama to see for himself, and returned to assert that it would cost only 658m. francs, which could be reduced by economies to 600m., and that it could be completed in eight years. It was proposed to raise 300m. francs by the issue of shares and 300m. by loans.

As usual, Lesseps was too optimistic. The raising of funds grew more and more difficult, and the canal was much harder to build than Lesseps had imagined. By the middle of 1885 the company had raised 450m. francs and spent 490m., but only 7m. cubic metres of earth had been extracted out of an estimated total of 1,200m. Yellow fever was claiming a terrible toll of both labourers and office workers in the canal zone. The local cemeteries were filled, and three new ones had to be built.

The foundations of the 'Panama scandal' now began to be laid. Public subscriptions to the company's loan issues were drying up; the directors decided that only a lottery loan, giving small investors the chance of winning substantial prizes, would attract adequate funds.

But lottery loans had to be approved by parliament. A parliamentary commission appointed in 1886 reported against the proposal, and Lesseps now took the fatal step of putting himself, in Guy Chapman's phrase, 'in the hands of one whose business was "fixing" '. The 'fixer' was Baron Reinach, who had many friends in parliament, ministers as well as deputies, and was sure that he could get parliamentary approval for the lottery loan. He was promised 10m. francs for his services, or more strictly, for distributions to deputies, ministers, newspaper owners and editors. By June 1888 the lottery bond issue was authorised by both Chamber and Senate, but it was too late to save the company. Less than half of the issue was taken up by the public.

It was after the lottery bond failure that Clemenceau made his first personal intervention in the Panama affair. Reinach was out of pocket on his 'fixing' activities, for the company was reluctant to pay him the 10m. francs it had promised. The payment was vital to him, for Herz, who had also been involved in the Panama 'fixing', was blackmailing him and threatening to expose his transactions unless he was at once given 2m. francs. The unhappy baron appealed to Clemenceau for help in persuading the Panama directors to honour their debt.

To oblige his friend, Clemenceau went with Ranc to see Freycinet, then minister of war, and asked him to make the company give Reinach his money. We do not know whether he was fully aware of what Reinach was being paid for, or why he needed the money so urgently; his argument was simply that the Panama company would be exposed to scandal if it became known that it did not honour its debts. Freycinet saw the point and sent for Charles de Lesseps, son of 'the great Frenchman' and managing director of the company. He was induced to give Reinach 5m. francs, of which 2m. went to the voracious Herz.

But the 'fixing' days were over. The public had lost faith in the company, and in February 1889 it was wound up by order of the civil tribunal of the Seine. Small savers, who had subscribed most of the company's funds, had lost everything, but neither the government nor the courts were in any hurry to establish the civil responsibilities of those in charge of the enterprise. It was only in 1892 that the secrets of Panama began to be publicly uncovered.

[3]

The Chamber of Deputies elected in 1889 was happily free from the menace of Boulangism, but its record was undistinguished. An uneasy alliance of Opportunists, Left Centre and moderate Radicals produced a succession of weak governments which were always liable to be overthrown by *ad hoc* coalitions of Left and Right. Government was largely a matter of domestic quarrels, in which there was little regard for national greatness.

Before the explosion of the Panama affair Clemenceau made few important interventions in debate. But three of his speeches made a deep impression on his listeners. In the first he defended the totality of the French Revolution; in the second he warned his bourgeois colleagues to come to terms with the emerging proletariat; in the third he reasserted his anticlerical principles in opposition to the proposed *ralliement* between Catholics and the Republic.

At the end of January 1891 a new play about the French Revolution by Victorien Sardou, one of the leading dramatists of the day, was produced at the Comédie-Française. It was called *Thermidor*, and it attacked Robespierre's Reign of Terror which ended with the rising against him on 27 July, 1794, the date known in the Revolutionary calendar as the ninth of Thermidor. The play was based on the widely held view that Robespierre's fall, which represented the defeat of Jacobin authoritarianism, was a happy deliverance for France.

To Clemenceau and others of the extreme Left this denigration of Robespierre seemed to be counter-Revolutionary propaganda. The play was denounced in *La Justice*, the Socialist *La Bataille* and other Left wing newspapers. At the second performance there were demonstrations and disturbances in the theatre, encouraged by Clemenceau and Lissagaray, editor of *La Bataille*. Fearful of worse trouble, the government banned further performances of *Thermidor* at the Comédie-Française.

The matter was then raised in the Chamber, where Joseph Reinach, the entirely reputable nephew and son-in-law of Baron Jacques de Reinach, said he saw no reason why the play should be banned. He approved of its point of view, praising Danton and the Girondins and condemning 'this political Tartuffe called Robespierre'. His speech brought Clemenceau to his feet, to pronounce his memorable and controversial dictum, '*La Révolution est un bloc.*' This was the theory he had first outlined in *Le Travail* in his student days.

Reinach, he complained, was trying to pick over (*éplucher*) the French Revolution, saying 'I accept this, I reject that'; but the Revolution was a *bloc*, from which nothing could be subtracted, because historical truth would not allow it. Why, he asked, had so much emotion been aroused by the production of a bad play? It was because the Revolution was not yet ended, it was still in being, and the same men were still at grips with the same enemies. 'I loudly assert,' he concluded, 'that we shall not allow the French Revolution to be tarnished by theorising of any kind. We shall not tolerate it, and if the government had not done its duty, the citizens would have done theirs.'

The speech was warmly applauded by the Left and part of the Centre, and the government maintained its ban on the play. But the press, apart from *La Justice* and those papers which had been shocked by the first performance, deplored Clemenceau's attitude because it was hostile to freedom of the stage. Coquelin, who was the leading actor in *Thermidor*, told Berta Szeps that 'We are living under a Clemenceau monarchy.' In the end Sardou did not suffer financially, as *Thermidor* was revived with great success at the Porte Saint-Martin theatre a few years later.[1]

Clemenceau's theory that Frenchmen are not entitled to pick and choose among the different phases of the Revolution has always been a matter of controversy. It can be argued, as Gordon Wright argues, that the Revolution 'was never a monolithic and homogeneous unity' and that 'Clemenceau failed (or refused) to see that the revolutionary myth might have different meanings to different Frenchmen.' Clemenceau faced this kind of criticism in his lifetime, and was not shaken by it. In defending Zola in the *J'Accuse* trial he condemned 'the scaffolds of the Revolution', and was then taken to task by Francisque Sarcey for having contradicted his own theory of the *bloc*.

Clemenceau replied in *L'Aurore* that he had condemned the guillotine a hundred times, but this did not affect his standpoint. What he meant by the *bloc* theory was there was nothing so impertinent for a man of the present day as to claim to stop the Revolution at some date that suited his own convenience; the acts of violence and the benefits of the Revolution were linked together as correlated manifestations of the same spirit of action. The Revolution must be accepted as a whole with all its grandeurs and its violences.

The Third Republic never accepted Clemenceau's theory. In a study of nearly two hundred years of Revolutionary myths and interpretations Alice Gérard asserts that 'the Third Republic was predominantly Dantonist and, one might say, neo-Thermidorian.' Sardou's play, depicting the Robespierre period as a regrettable episode in Revolutionary history, is generally representative of public opinion; Clemenceau was going against the tide in arguing that Robespierre's violence was necessary in its day and must be accepted as an indispensable part of the Revolution.

A few months after the *Thermidor* incident a tragic clash between strikers and troops at Fourmies, a small industrial town in northern France, where twelve civilians were killed and about thirty wounded, was the occasion for one of Clemenceau's most moving speeches. The government defeated a Left wing demand for an official enquiry into the shooting, but on 8 May the subject was reopened by Pelletan, who called for an amnesty for imprisoned strikers. Clemenceau supported his colleague.

Reports of workers' demonstrations on May Day showed, he said, that

---

[1] Léon Daudet gives an amusing account of what happened when Clemenceau went to the Var to explain his speech to his electors. The honest peasants had never heard of Sardou, *Thermidor* or Robespierre, but they cheered Clemenceau loudly and shouted, 'He's right, our deputy! Long live Clemenceau! Down with *Thermidor*! Death to Sardou!' Sardou believed that if he had gone to the Var at that time he would not have come back alive. (*See* Daudet, *La Vie Orageuse de Clemenceau*, pp. 98–100.)

the Fourth Estate was rising and was about to assume power. At Fourmies there had been a frightening disproportion between the events preceding the shooting and the shooting itself, and he warned the government: 'Take care. The dead are great proselytisers; we must pay attention to the dead ... I assert that the central fact of the current political situation is the inevitable revolution which is being prepared. . . . You must take your side: either you receive the Fourth Estate with violence, or you welcome it with open arms. It is the moment to choose.'

Later in his speech he appealed to Freycinet, who was again prime minister, to grant an amnesty to the strikers. 'I ask you to have pity on the Republic,' he said. 'I ask you to have pity on France. Grant an amnesty. Let us forget.' But the government, supported by the Right, refused the amnesty. Nothing was done to close the ever-widening breach between industrial workers and the governments of the Third Republic.

Clemenceau's last speech in the Chamber before his involvement in the Panama scandal was made in February 1892, after the opening, on instructions from the Vatican, of the new policy of *ralliement*, or co-operation between Roman Catholics and the State. The intention, which was never entirely fulfilled, was that Catholic politicians should merge with Republican moderates to form a large and solid conservative party; the practical result was the formation of a clerical-monarchist alliance, which became a significant factor in French politics.

Freycinet was willing to accept the *ralliement* as a political fact. The Left saw it as a piece of Vatican trickery. In a debate initiated by a Socialist deputy Clemenceau insisted that a lay government should have nothing to do with a Pope, and that there was no possibility of any understanding between Church and State. 'Conflict is possible between the rights of man and what are called the rights of God; an alliance is not.'

Alliance was impossible, he said, because the Church had to be every-thing or nothing, and to bring the Pope within the Republican fold was a superhuman task. 'It is an enterprise beyond your powers, beyond human powers, because the two elements that you claim to unite are irreconcilable and contradictory; in a word, they are mutually exclusive.' The Church, he declared, wanted exactly the opposite of what the Republic wanted. To Freycinet he said coldly: 'I leave you to your *tête-à-tête* with the authorised friends of the Roman Church. Make your terms with them. I have nothing more to say to you.'

Clemenceau's rigid anticlericalism found many supporters, and for the last time in the Chamber of Deputies he appeared in his old rôle of *tombeur de ministères*. Radical opponents of *ralliement* were joined by monarchists, like Paul de Cassagnac, who wanted the Church to stand aloof from the Republic, and the government was defeated by 282 votes to 210. Freycinet resigned. The debate had no immediate effect on the progress of *ralliement*, but it reminded the country that the separation of Church and State was still part of the Radical programme.

[4]

A curious episode in Clemenceau's last years as a deputy was his single-handed attempt to establish a Franco-British *entente*. For some years he had been anxious about France's isolation in Europe, and he had discussed the prospects for a Franco-Austrian alliance with Crown Prince Rudolf of Austria, whom he met through his friendship with the Szeps family. But Rudolf, who shared his distrust of Germany, died in the hunting lodge at Mayerling. Clemenceau felt that the hope of a Franco-Austrian alliance had died with him, and that France must look elsewhere for allies.

At the beginning of the 1890s many of his compatriots had taken up the idea of a Franco-Russian alliance. A French naval squadron had been invited to visit Kronstadt; the Russian Grand Duke Alexis had an almost hysterical reception when he came to Paris. But Clemenceau was always sceptical about French association with Tsarist Russia. 'Will the child be Cossack or Republican?' he once asked in *La Justice*. He preferred to look across the English Channel, and a visit to Admiral Maxse in London gave him an opportunity for discussing Anglo-French relations with Joseph Chamberlain.

It was several years since he had first become acquainted with the leading English Radicals, Chamberlain, Dilke and Morley. Since that time Chamberlain had broken with Gladstone over Home Rule for Ireland, and he was now a leading figure on the Unionist side of the House of Commons. Like Clemenceau, he was friendly with Maxse, and it was in the admiral's house in South Kensington that the French Radical and the English Radical Unionist met in July 1891 and discussed European problems after dinner.

Clemenceau had no mission from the French government. He was speaking only as a private individual, but he assured Chamberlain that important French ministers knew of his visit and would be informed of what was said. His argument was that there could be no Franco-Russian alliance, since 'there could be no real sympathy between the Republic and an autocrat', and if France were not to remain isolated she must have the friendship of either Germany or England. Friendship with Germany was out of the question, since it could be purchased only by giving up all hope of the recovery of Alsace-Lorraine; but he hoped that England might give France her moral support, if existing disputes between the two countries in Egypt and Newfoundland could be settled in England's favour.

Italy, which had recently renewed her membership of the Triple Alliance with Germany and Austria-Hungary, was also mentioned. Clemenceau explained that, when he had first spoken to Maxse about a possible meeting with Chamberlain, he had hoped that Britain might advise Italy to leave the Triple Alliance. It was too late for that now, but he hoped that England would promise to be neutral in the event of a Franco-Italian war begun by Italy, on the understanding that France would promise to respect Italy's territorial integrity.

Chamberlain was impressed by Clemenceau's proposal for an Anglo-French understanding. He agreed to put it before Lord Salisbury, the Unionist leader, who was both prime minister and foreign secretary, but Salisbury would have none of it. His policy, he told Chamberlain, was to keep absolutely clear of foreign engagements and to leave Britain free to take any action she might think fit in the event of war in Europe. He thought that Germany would resent any British attempt to detach Italy from the Triple Alliance, and Britain could not afford to lose Germany's friendship; and he cynically observed that as long as France was afraid of Germany she would do nothing to injure Britain. In short, all Clemenceau's ideas were rejected, and it was left to Chamberlain to wind up the incident in a tactful letter to Maxse. 'I thoroughly appreciate our friend's generous action,' he wrote, 'and I shall not forget it, but the time is not ripe for taking any further notice of it.'

Clemenceau's amateur diplomacy had come to nothing, but it is at least to his credit that he saw the need for an *entente cordiale* many years before it was achieved. In the meantime the Russophils were in the ascendant. The French fleet was rapturously received at Kronstadt, and a Franco-Russian alliance was brought nearer. Europe was falling into two armed camps.

[5]

At the beginning of 1892 Clemenceau reached a crisis in his married life. He discovered that his wife was unfaithful to him.

Up to this time, and in spite of his own infidelities, his marriage had not entirely collapsed. He and Mary were still together in 1887, when they moved from the avenue Montaigne to the neighbouring rue Clément-Marot and their elder daughter Madeleine married Numa Jacquemaire, a wealthy barrister. But though they were under the same roof one imagines that they met rarely, and that Mary felt she had been put aside in favour of her husband's glamorous mistresses and charming young girl-friends. As she passed her fortieth year and found herself utterly neglected it is not surprising that she sought consolation elsewhere and that a young student fell readily into her arms. She was still an attractive woman.

The story of Mary Clemenceau's divorce was told by Ernest Daudet, elder brother of Alphonse Daudet, to Edmond de Goncourt, who recorded it in his *Journal* on 25 February, 1894. Clemenceau was deeply shocked when he learned that his wife had a lover, and he arranged for her to be followed by a private detective, who at first could find nothing to report. But Clemenceau guessed who the young man was, and one of his daughters suggested that it would be better to follow the lover instead of the wife. The detective did so, the erring couple were caught, and Clemenceau had his wife taken to the prefecture of police, where she was threatened with imprisonment if she did not agree to be divorced at once and to leave the country.

She could only agree. Clemenceau had her bags packed for her, she was taken to Le Havre and put on a boat for America. The whole affair was done so quickly that the French magistrates pronounced the divorce on the very day that her boat docked at New York. 'Never,' says Clemenceau's constant enemy, Ernest Judet, 'did the wheels of justice turn more swiftly.'[1]

This was in March 1892. It was believed in New York that Mary had divorced her husband for his own misconduct, and much sympathy was felt with her. She was penniless when she returned to America, but she was able to make some money by giving lectures. The posters described her as 'the ex-wife of M. Clemenceau'.

It was not, as can be seen, an incident which did Clemenceau any credit. The threat of imprisonment, the imposed divorce and the despatch of Mary to America without resources are far removed from the kindness and understanding that he could so often show in his relations with women. Perhaps the only excuses for him are that he was deeply moved by his wife's infidelity, and that he really believed in the 'double standard', by which it is right for married men to have mistresses but infamous for married women to deceive their husbands. This, indeed, was the accepted moral code in France of the late nineteenth century, when husbands flaunted their *petites amies* in public, but no mercy was shown to the woman who took a lover.

Clemenceau was certainly upset by Mary's behaviour. On the day of her departure he sent a message to a woman-friend, asking her to come

---

[1] In addition to Goncourt's account (*Journal*, IV, pp. 528–9) the episode is described by Georges Gatineau-Clemenceau, the Tiger's grandson, in *Des Pattes du Tigre aux Griffes du Destin* (pp. 27–8). The two accounts are in general agreement, but the Daudet-Goncourt version is preferred, since it was written soon after the events described and came from a member of a family which was in close touch with Clemenceau.

round to his house. She found him 'pale, tragic, terrible'. He asked her to pack his wife's clothes and other possessions in two trunks which were in the drawing-room. While she was doing so he picked up a hammer and attacked a splendid bust of Mary which stood on a plinth in a corner. When it was reduced to rubble he said curtly '*Fini!*' and left the room.

Yet it was not quite finished. The marriage was ended, but he was to see Mary again in later years.

[6]

It was later in 1892 that the affairs of the Panama canal company were again brought to public attention. In September Quesnay de Beaurepaire, the public prosecutor, proposed that the directors should be put on trial for swindling and breach of trust, and it was arranged that they should be tried in the *Cour de Cassation* (the appeal court), since Ferdinand de Lesseps held the Grand Cross of the Legion of Honour and could not be tried in a court of the first instance. But neither ministers nor deputies were anxious to see the opening of a trial in which, as they knew or guessed, there were likely to be damaging disclosures concerning themselves or their colleagues.

In the end the damaging disclosures preceded the trial, for earlier in the year Drumont had launched a new antisemitic newspaper, *La Libre Parole*. The Jewish share in the scandal was now to be fully examined.

La Libre Parole carried on the work of Drumont's books. In June, for example, it published articles on the growing number of Jewish officers in the French army. Then in September it shook the political world by publishing a series of articles on the Panama canal company, accusing both the press and members of the Chamber of Deputies of corruptly accepting bribes to secure the passing of the act legalising the lottery bond issue. The agents of the corruption were said to be three Jews. These, who were not named, were Baron Reinach, Herz and their assistant Arton.

Reinach did not at first appreciate the power of *La Libre Parole*. In November he slipped away from Paris for a week in Monte Carlo, but he cut his holiday short on hearing that the deputy Jules Delahaye was to make an interpellation on the Panama affair in the Chamber on 21 November. On returning to Paris he found that *La Libre Parole* had mentioned a list of some 150 parliamentarians who were said to have taken bribes, and that another scandal-sheet, the Boulangist *La Cocarde*, had boldly announced that Charles Floquet, the former prime minister, had been given 300,000 francs by the company in 1888, to be used in fighting Boulanger's candidature in the Nord department. It seemed clear that the baron's 'fixing' activities would soon be exposed. Quesnay de Beaurepaire warned Joseph Reinach, the baron's nephew, that 'a name which was very dear to him' would appear in the list of those to be put on trial for complicity in the Panama affair.

Clemenceau was now drawn into the growing scandal. In imminent danger of trial and imprisonment, Baron Reinach felt sure that Herz had sufficient influence to stop the press disclosures, but he had no confidence in his own ability to win Herz's support. He asked his friend Rouvier, then minister of finance, to help him, and Rouvier agreed to go with him to Herz's house, but only if they took a witness. Clemenceau went with them, but they could get no comfort from Herz, who said he had no influence with either *La Libre Parole* or *La Cocarde*.

As a last hope Reinach asked Clemenceau to take him to see the ex-minister Ernest Constans, who was believed to have a hand in *La Cocarde*'s campaign. It took Constans only five minutes to tell his visitors he could do nothing for them. 'I am lost!' cried Reinach, as he entered a cab to drive to his home. A few hours later he was dead, presumably by suicide, though an autopsy at a much later date did not reveal any traces of poison. Clemenceau's share in these events was made public by the journalist Gaston Calmette in *Le Figaro*, which was followed by a corrected version in *La Justice* from Clemenceau's own hand.

Up to this time it seemed unlikely that Clemenceau would be harmed in any way by the Panama scandal. He was not named in Delahaye's interpellation in the Chamber on 21 November, when the speaker asserted that Baron Reinach had been given 5m. francs by the Panama company 'to buy all the consciences which were for sale in parliament', and that 3m. francs were distributed to more than 150 members of parliament, whose names he declined to give. After the debate the Chamber appointed a commission of enquiry into the charges of corruption, and the public prosecutor at last indicted Ferdinand and Charles de Lesseps, Gustave Eiffel and two other directors of the company on charges of fraud and breach of faith.

But Clemenceau's enemies were waiting to attack him. Among them was Déroulède, who on 20 December made an interpellation in the Chamber, ostensibly on the rôle of Cornelius Herz in the Panama affair, though it was soon clear that he was aiming at Clemenceau. How, he asked, did the little German Jew make so much headway in France? He must have had a powerful protector, and the name of that protector was on every deputy's lips, but none of them dared to mention it. 'For there are three things about him which you fear—his rapier, his pistol, his tongue. I am prepared to face all three, and I name the man. It is M. Clemenceau!'

After this forthright statement, which won great applause from the

Right and from some deputies on the Left, Déroulède went on to accuse Clemenceau of having received large sums from Herz. He mentioned a figure of 2m. francs, which, he asserted, Rochefort had heard from Herz himself. Why, he asked, should a clever financier have thrown so much money away, if, as Clemenceau had said, he had done nothing for Herz in *La Justice*? Déroulède asserted that Herz was a German agent and that Clemenceau was working for him, and against the interests of France, when he overturned governments or stirred up political trouble.

The enemies whom Clemenceau had made during his long dominance of the Chamber were delighted by his public castigation. There was an icy silence when he rose to reply. To some extent he was on shaky ground, for he had certainly had financial dealings with Herz in the early years of *La Justice*; but those were share transactions, and he flatly denied having received gifts of money from the financier.

He denied also that he had ever supported Herz's business interests, or recommended him for promotion in the Legion of Honour, or been influenced by him in the policies advocated by *La Justice*. To the final charge that he had served Germany by his conduct in the Chamber, he retorted that there was no evidence to show that he had ever betrayed or tried to harm France, and there was only one answer he could give: 'Monsieur Paul Déroulède, you have lied!'

The official report of the debate said that the speaker, on resuming his seat, was warmly congratulated by his friends. But the friends were few. Déroulède's attack had done its work; though the slanders had been answered they would not be forgotten. Clemenceau's opponents— Opportunists, monarchists and the surviving Boulangists—now had weapons which they could use against him at the appropriate time.

Since Clemenceau had called Déroulède a liar, a duel was inevitable. It took place on Saint-Ouen racecourse, in the presence of about three hundred people, with many others waiting outside the gates. Public sympathy was with Déroulède, the professional patriot; Clemenceau was already suspect because of the mud thrown at him in the Chamber. Each duellist was to fire three shots at a distance of twenty-five metres, but as so often happened, the duel was an anti-climax.

Some thought that the 'director' of the duel deliberately put the contestants off by leaving a long gap between 'Are you ready?' and 'Fire!', and then giving the second and third orders to fire in rapid succession; others said that he had reduced the charges of powder to a point which made the shots ineffective. Whatever the reason may have been, neither man was hit, and it may have been just as well for Clemenceau that his legendary skill with the pistol was lacking on this occasion. Maurice Barrès, the Right wing deputy who was one of Déroulède's seconds, thought that Clemenceau would have been torn to pieces by the crowd if Déroulède had been killed or wounded.

The duel can be regarded as the end of Clemenceau's direct involvement in the Panama affair, though he was still to suffer heavily for his friendship with Herz, who had fled to England and declined to come back to give evidence to a commission of enquiry. The list of the parliamentarians who had accepted bribes from the canal company—the *chéquards*, as they came to be known—was produced and was found to contain 104 names; Clemenceau's was not among them, and he was not concerned in the criminal proceedings against the canal company's directors and a handful of bribed deputies. For a variety of legal reasons few penalties were imposed, and the final stages of the scandal aroused little public interest.[1]

The Panama revelations did no lasting damage to the Republic. Politically the chief beneficiaries were the Socialists, who claimed that they stood for a social revolution which would make such scandals impossible; in the 1893 general election their strength in the Chamber rose from twelve to fifty seats. Several ex-ministers lost their seats in this election, and comparatively new deputies, such as Raymond Poincaré, Théophile Delcassé and Louis Barthou, suddenly found themselves potential ministers; as Jacques Bainville puts it, 'the Panama affair served to promote a generation.' Thanks to the prominent parts played by Reinach, Herz and Arton, it gave further impetus to the revival of antisemitism; and in combination with much personal enmity and a clumsy but well publicised forgery it helped to drive Clemenceau out of parliament for nearly ten years.

[7]

A fantastic forgery by a negro employed at the British embassy in Paris was one of the causes of Clemenceau's unexpected defeat at Draguignan in September 1893. The negro, a man called Louis-Alfred Varon who went by the name of Norton, forged a number of documents, apparently signed by one of the embassy secretaries, giving imaginary details of the

[1] Some years later, in 1902, Maurice Barrès revived interest in the Panama affair by publishing an account of it in *Leurs Figures*, the third volume of his trilogy, *Roman de l'Energie Nationale*, of which the two earlier books were *Les Déracinés* and *L'Appel au Soldat. Leurs Figures* is a curious and often brilliant blend of fact and fiction, which grossly exaggerates Clemenceau's connection with the scandal and describes him, without evidence, as being 'sold to Herz' and 'Herz's man'. During the First World War Barrès became one of Clemenceau's warmest admirers, and he then told a friend that it was 'the greatest regret of his life' that he had written *Leurs Figures*. But he never publicly disavowed it. (*See* Martet, *Le Silence de M. Clemenceau*, pp. 217–20.)

British government's secret service payments to its French agents. Among them were payments of £20,000 to Clemenceau, £3,600 to Rochefort, and various sums to other deputies and newspapers.

Norton took his papers to Edouard Ducret, director of *La Cocarde*, who was delighted to have another opportunity of smearing Clemenceau, though he must surely have suspected that the papers were forged. On 21 June, 1893, he published a statement, signed by himself, saying that important documents had been taken from a foreign embassy, irrefutably establishing the anti-patriotic and treasonable attitude of several French politicians and journalists. He was too cautious to give the names mentioned in Norton's papers, but on the following day Lucien Millevoye, a Boulangist deputy and close associate of Déroulède, borrowed the documents and took them to the Chamber of Deputies.

The plan to exploit Norton's forgeries misfired. The Chamber listened impatiently while Millevoye made generalised statements on the villainy of certain unnamed persons; to hold its attention he unwisely read out the list of the alleged recipients of British gold. It was greeted with loud laughter; the inclusion of Rochefort's name was enough to show that the list was a fake, for no one could have believed that the stoutly nationalist editor of *L'Intransigeant* was in England's pay. Clemenceau called out 'Liar!', and Barrès and other nationalist deputies hastened to disavow their too credulous colleague. A motion regretting the odious and ridiculous slanders was carried by 348 votes to two. The minority consisted of Millevoye and Déroulède, who resigned their seats after the debate.

Ducret and Norton appeared in court in August on forgery charges; Millevoye was not with them, for his slanders were protected by the privilege of the Chamber. Both defendants were sentenced to terms of imprisonment. Clemenceau was given the one franc damages which was all that he claimed, but he had not heard the last of the forgeries. More mud had been thrown at him, and some of it always stuck. The allegation that he was an English agent was too attractive to be discarded by his enemies.

Because of the Norton trial Clemenceau had to spend the whole of July in Paris, where he helped to draw up the Radical Socialist manifesto for the general election. It declared that a new situation had arisen, since the monarchists were no longer a danger to the Republic; France could look forward to a period of progress and social justice. Once again he put forward his fixed political views—separation of Church and State, revision of the constitution, freedom for trade unions, guarantees of civil liberties, and a tax on wealth, both income and capital.

As a diversion from politics he enjoyed many meetings with Violet

Maxse, who had returned to Paris to continue her study of drawing. She was now twenty-one, and was soon to marry Lord Edward Cecil, son of Lord Salisbury. In this last July of her spinsterhood she used to look in at the house in rue Clément-Marot every evening for a few minutes' chat with Clemenceau and his unmarried daughter Thérèse; one Sunday he took her to the Louvre for three hours in the morning, and then took both girls to Rodin's studio in the afternoon. It was a gay and happy relationship; they were still to be friends in the last years of his life.

It was not until 8 August that he could escape from Paris to the Var to begin his election campaign. The first count was due to take place twelve days later, and after his successes in 1885 and 1889 he would ordinarily have been certain of re-election. He was popular with the voters, who liked being represented by a strong personality. He was backed by the prefect of the Var. He had his own newspaper, *La Justice du Var*, which appeared at irregular intervals, and he was supported by another local paper, *Le Petit Varois*. But twelve days were not long enough for him to overthrow two separate attacks which were mounted against him.

The first of these was organised by a number of local politicians who had turned against him and were taking the line that only natives of the Var should represent the department in the Chamber. They had on their side an important paper, *Le Petit Draçenois*, which proclaimed: 'The Var for the Varois; no more foreign candidates.' Their plan was to form the opposing candidates, ranging from reactionary to Socialist, into an anti-Clemenceau league, whose members would be able to visit even the smallest villages and to use their personal influence to win voters away from Clemenceau.

The other attack was directed from Paris, principally by Ernest Judet, one of the editors of *Le Petit Journal*, and the Marquis de Morès, the founder of a nationalist and antisemitic organisation who has the un-enviable distinction of being Europe's first National Socialist. Judet, who for some years had spread the rumour that Clemenceau was 'sold to England', now used the discredited Norton forgeries as the basis for violent onslaughts in his newspaper. A cartoon in *Le Petit Journal Illustré* showed Clemenceau dancing a jig and juggling with bags of English sovereigns; on the day before the first count in the election a long set of scurrilous verses appeared in *Le Petit Journal* under the heading, 'M. Clemenceau's Litany.' The 'response' to every 'prayer' was 'Aoh, yes!'[1]

[1] It is ironical that Judet, who unjustly asserted that Clemenceau was 'sold to England', was himself 'sold to Germany' in the years preceding the First World War, and also during the war. German diplomatic documents discovered after 1945 show that he received considerable sums from the German government for his efforts to hinder Franco-British rapprochement. (*See* Jean-Baptiste Duroselle, '*Face à la Montée des Perils*', in Chastenet and others, *Clemenceau*, p. 157.)

This phrase became the anti-Clemenceau slogan in the Draguignan election. Thousands of copies of the cartoon were distributed in the constituency, and satirical references were made to 'Sir Georges Clemenceau'. The Parisian plotters hired a gang of hecklers, mostly Piedmontese, in Marseilles, and sent them to disrupt Clemenceau's meetings with cries of 'Aoh, yes!' He was rarely able to make himself heard, but one meeting at which he silenced the hecklers was at Salernes, one of the three townships in the constituency, where he eloquently defended himself against his enemies.

In a striking justification of his political career he made special reference to the millions of francs he was supposed to have received from Herz. He asked repeatedly what had happened to them:

> Shall I speak of my personal situation? I settled the debts of my youth with a loan from a lawyer at Nantes. You can go and see it, the debt is still there. Where are the millions? My daughter was married without a dowry. Where are the millions? I have lived in my present home for six years. The furniture dealer and the upholsterer have been paid gradually by instalments. I have not yet finished paying them. Where are the millions?

These, he added, were the avowals to which disinterested servants of the Republic were reduced. 'May the shame of this humiliation be upon those who have made this confession necessary.'

Only a small part of his speech was concerned with his personal affairs. For thirty years, he said, he had been an embattled Republican, serving the cause of the people and fighting monarchists, clericals and reactionaries under every name and every disguise. He was reproached for overthrowing ministries, but it was always the same men, and the same policy of procrastination, which he attacked. Conservatives and Boulangists accused him of having practised 'hidden government': how could he have done so, when he was always in the minority?

He went on to speak of Déroulède, who would have had no hesitation in unleashing civil war in the name of patriotism; and of *Le Petit Journal*, which he denounced for having accepted bribes from the Panama company. He claimed his place in a renewed struggle against the enemies of the Republic. 'The whole country,' he declared, 'wishes to keep the Republic. The question at issue is whether it shall be an instrument for preserving the old monarchical laws, or one of social and political regeneration. The Republic and the Republicans must make their choice.'

It was a rousing speech, but those who heard it were only a few among the consituency's electors; many of the others were swayed by the sharp practices of his opponents. On the first count he had the highest number of votes—6,334—but he did not achieve the overall majority that would have given him the seat. Jourdan, a reactionary, clerical, anti-Socialist candidate, was second with 4,686.

Had this been an ordinary election, the other Republican candidates would have stood down, advising their supporters to transfer their votes to Clemenceau on the second count. But the local politicians were resolved to keep Clemenceau out, and they therefore arranged that the other candidates should advise their supporters to vote for Jourdan, the clerical reactionary whom all true Republicans should have fought to the death. These discreditable tactics were successful. Jourdan was elected by 9,503 votes to Clemenceau's 8,600.

Clemenceau left Draguignan on the next day. The paid hecklers followed him to the station with cries of 'Cornelius! Cornelius! Aoh, yes! Aoh, yes!', but other onlookers raised counter-cries of '*Vive Clemenceau! Vive la République!*' His political enemies exulted in his downfall, and claimed that 'the extreme Left is decapitated.' He felt hurt and resentful, and for some days he avoided his friends. It needed Pelletan's kindly injunction, 'Don't play Hamlet', to shake him out of his moodiness.

So in September 1893, at the age of fifty-two, Georges Clemenceau came to the great turning-point of his life. His career, as it seemed, was in ruins. The spell had been broken, his years of consummate mastery of the Chamber of Deputies brought to an end. Even if he regained his seat at the next election, he could hardly hope to wield his old authority over his fellow deputies.

It had been good while it lasted. 'From the creation of the Chamber,' wrote J. E. C. Bodley in 1899, 'no other deputy had been so often and so rapturously applauded by his colleagues as this relentless justiciary, when he mounted the tribune and proceeded to pass sentence on the quaking culprits of the ministerial benches below him.' He would always be remembered as a passionate defender of the principles of the French Revolution and as one who had taken a great part in making the Third Republic. Yet Drumont had once called him *un homme fini*, and in his changed situation the words seemed sadly true. It is the measure of his character and determination that he built a new and greater career on the ruins of the old.

PART TWO

THE NEW CAREER

CHAPTER EIGHT

THE WRITER'S CRAFT

1. Industrious apprentice. 2. A versatile pen. 3. Blind alleys.

[1]

THOSE who hoped that Clemenceau was finished were soon disillusioned. Within a month of his defeat at Draguignan his hat was in the ring, he was again a menace to politicians and even to presidents of the Republic. He had become a journalist.

Up to this time he had little claim to be regarded as a writer. Nearly a quarter-of-a-century had gone by since the last of his letters from America appeared in *Le Temps*. Since then he had been the active political director of his own newspaper, but he had allowed others to put his ideas into print; his own contributions had consisted of only a few articles and occasional short notes. It was apparently Pelletan who suggested that he should now start to write, and after some hesitation he took his editor's advice.

The first of his regular articles appeared in *La Justice* on 3 October, 1893, under the challenging title, '*En avant!*' This was the beginning of a prodigious output of several million words between 1893 and 1906 and between 1913 and 1917, principally in *La Justice, La Dépêche de Toulouse* (the most influential of French provincial newspapers), *L'Aurore, Le Bloc, L'Homme Libre* and *L'Homme Enchaîné* (the new name given to *L'Homme Libre* after a brush with the war-time censorship).[1]

Jean Ajalbert, who had been on the staff of *La Justice* since 1885, was impressed by *le patron's* determined efforts to make himself an efficient journalist. He noticed that at first Clemenceau found writing difficult,

---

[1] Other papers to which he contributed regularly for shorter periods were *Le Journal, L'Echo de Paris, Le Français* and the *Neue Freie Presse* of Vienna. Statistical details of his work are given in Gustave Geffroy's *Georges Clemenceau, sa vie, son oeuvre* (p. 189) and supplemented in Georges Wormser's *La République de Clemenceau* (pp. 512–18). His articles usually ran to about 2,000 words. The major items in the list are 688 articles in *La Justice*, 1,643 in *L'Aurore*, 746 in *La Dépêche de Toulouse*, 506 in *L'Homme Libre* and 1,070 in *L'Homme Enchaîné*. Geffroy calculated that Clemenceau's entire journalistic work would have filled more than a hundred octavo volumes of 350 pages each.

because he had so much to say and wanted to say it all at once; but he was able to discipline himself, and his articles gradually shed their early blunders. Gone were the days when he arrived at the office at midnight in full evening dress, 'like a lion-tamer with a whip'; now he was up at five in the morning to start writing, sustained only by a roll and a glass of water. Few apprentices to the writer's craft can have been more industrious than was Georges Clemenceau.

Dr. Johnson's dictum that 'No man but a blockhead ever wrote, except for money' partly explains Clemenceau's remarkable productivity. Certainly he needed money. He was no longer drawing a deputy's salary, he was in debt, and though *La Justice* had its faithful readers they were too few to make the paper a really profitable venture. By writing himself he saved on payments to contributors; by cutting down the staff, moving to smaller offices and making new contracts with printers and newsprint suppliers he improved the paper's financial position; but even so, he had to dispose of some of his personal possessions, including Japanese prints and paintings by Pissarro, Raffaelli, Manet and others, to meet his domestic expenses. One thing he would not sell was a much-prized collection of Japanese ornaments. Berta Szeps believed that his collection of *netsuke*—the beautifully carved buttons worn on Japanese dresses—was unequalled in Europe.

Financial relief came when editors of other newspapers realised that he had become a formidable journalist and paid him to write in their columns. His long connection with *La Dépêche de Toulouse* began as early as April 1894, and he wrote for it twice a week until he was elected to the Senate in 1902. Assignments from other papers followed, and in 1897 he was at last able to close down the always precarious *La Justice*, as he had found another platform for his views in *L'Aurore*. This was a new paper whose director, Ernest Vaughan, invited him to become the senior member of the editorial staff, though without the authority of an editor-in-chief.

With assured incomes from *L'Aurore* and *La Dépêche de Toulouse*, payments from publishers for books in which he collected the best of his newspaper articles, and no expensive *La Justice* to worry about, Clemenceau was probably in a better financial position in 1897 than he had been for many years. Perhaps it was a feeling of euphoria resulting from his comparative affluence which helped him to fall in love with a young American, or Swedish-American, girl called Selma Everdon, who was a pupil of Rodin's and lived with her mother and sister in an old house in the place des Vosges.

Léon Daudet tells this curious story in *La Vie Orageuse de Clemenceau*. He gives no exact date, but says it happened when Clemenceau was over fifty, which places it in the 1890s. We know that young girls found Clemenceau a most agreeable companion, and Selma, like Berta and Violet before her, was flattered by the attentions of such a distinguished and entertaining escort. She allowed him to take her to the Comédie-Française and to supper at Paillard's, and to give her a beautiful ring. She even agreed to join him in Carlsbad and to stay in the same hotel, with Admiral Maxse as chaperon. But she was in love with a Bavarian officer and never had any idea of giving him up for her elderly admirer. After a few months Clemenceau himself realised that it was absurd for him to pursue such a beautiful young woman, and he decided to settle for her friendship, without hoping for her love.

[2]

Besides its practical value as a source of income, journalism fulfilled the very important function of giving Clemenceau a forum for his criticisms of successive governments and for statements of his own views on many matters of current interest. Such a forum was all the more necessary because of a significant change in the composition of the Chamber of Deputies. The Socialists, with the fifty seats they had won in the 1893 election, had taken over the rôle of the extreme Left; Clemenceau's Radical Socialists had been edged in nearer the Centre, though they were still to the Left of the Progressists (as the Opportunists now optimistically called themselves) and of those Radicals who were willing to support Progressist governments. If he wished to remain a political force, it was important that he should explain his attitude towards the new alignment in the Chamber.

He did so in an article in *La Justice* on 15 November, when he said that he did not expect social and political reform to come either from the Right, which wished to keep as much monarchy in the Republic as it could, or from the revolutionary Socialists of the Left. Reform, he believed, would come rather from the various groups, representing infinite shades of opinion, between the two extremes. 'This is the grand common reservoir of our Republican strength.'

Having given this general advice to his former Radical Socialist colleagues, Clemenceau took up a wide variety of causes in his early years as a full-time journalist. He did not, it seems, set particular store by his political writings at this time, for his first collections of articles to be published in book-form—*La Mêlée Sociale* (1895) and *Le Grand Pan* (1896)—were concerned mainly with social and industrial matters, together with criticism of the arts and descriptive reporting.

A foreword to *La Mêlée Sociale* explained that the title was chosen because the book illustrated the vital conflict pervading the world, the ceaseless struggle between living organisms. Poverty, trade unions, the right to strike, the eight-hour day (as illustrated by the experiments of the English firm of Mather and Platt at its Salford iron works), anarchism and capital punishment are among the subjects discussed. The English critic Sir Edmund Gosse wrote of the book:

> M. Clemenceau shows himself interpenetrated by the sorrows rather than sustained by the possibilities of the tormented inhabitants of earth. Recent events, in his own life and in the history of the French nation, had impressed on his consciousness the inherent cruelty of human beings to one another.

Gosse also observes of Clemenceau's journalism that 'nothing came amiss to the pen of a man whose curiosity about life was boundless, and whose facility in expression was volcanic'. It is, in fact, the versatility of his writing which gives these old newspaper articles their principal interest for a modern reader.

But he was anxious to be something more than an armchair theorist. After writing a number of articles condemning capital punishment, he was asked to provide a first-hand description of an execution, for the benefit of those who thought there was nothing wrong with the guillotine. With some reluctance, and after conquering an impulse to find an excuse for not going, he went to see an execution in the place de la Roquette, and duly described it in *La Justice*. At the end of an excellent piece of reporting, he remarked that he felt, as he came away, 'an inexpressible disgust at this administrative murder'.[1]

His contract with *La Dépêche de Toulouse*, which engaged him to write four political and four non-political articles a month, accounts for the even greater variety of the articles collected in his second book, *Le Grand Pan*, a rather fantastic title chosen in the belief that Pan was the symbol of human activity. 'Pan,' he wrote in his foreword, 'commands us to act. Action is the basic principle, action is the means, action is the end.'

In this book he touched on many aspects of life, turning from descriptions of a Montmartre soup-kitchen, the 'Red Mass' (the religious service for high legal officials) and the gaiety of Paris at the time of *mi-Carême* to essays on animals ('our poor relations'), prostitution and

---

[1] Violet Maxse did not agree with his views on this subject, and insisted that capital punishment was the right penalty for the anarchists who were then terrorising Paris. When she went back to England at the end of January 1894 Clemenceau wrote to her: 'I should like to scold you for your "speech" on capital punishment. Even if you were right, you would be wrong. It is not towards that side that one should lean at your age.' (*See* Milner, *My Picture Gallery*, p. 48.)

Lugné-Pöe's production of Ibsen's *An Enemy of the People*. He wrote a glowing review of Goncourt's new book, *L'Italie d'Hier*, which made the author, who was never a great admirer of Clemenceau, comment ruefully in his journal that he would now be condemned never to say anything unkind about his adulator. His dry humour was often in evidence, not least in his diverting account of a strip-tease *revue* at the café-concert des Ambassadeurs, in which, he reported, a girl appeared in a very short chemise, showing everything that could be shown '*à part les réserves les plus strictement obligatoires*', and at another moment in the show, '*Phryné enlève tout, en ayant soin seulement de tourner le dos au public.*'

The articles reprinted in these two volumes show how quickly Clemenceau made himself into a writer. Geoffrey Bruun says of *Le Grand Pan*: 'The volume reflects his self-education in literary style.' By the time it appeared its author had an assured place among the leading journalists of the day.

The early years were not a vintage period for Clemenceau's political writings, but one subject on which he kept a close watch was the project for a Franco-Russian alliance. Many Frenchmen thought that such an alliance would be a valuable contribution to French security, but Clemenceau had been sceptical about it since the days when the French fleet went to Kronstadt and the Grand Duke Alexis came to Paris. In 1894 he angered the government by revealing, in five signed articles in *Le Figaro*, that secret talks between representatives of the two countries had been held in Copenhagen.

The French ambassador to Denmark was the Comte d'Aunay, whose wife had once been Clemenceau's mistress. Both husband and wife were still his friends, and the details of the secret talks had been passed on to him in letters from the Comtesse. When the government discovered where the information had come from, d'Aunay was dismissed from his post, greatly to Clemenceau's annoyance. In an attempt to get his friend reinstated he appealed both to Casimir-Périer, who had become President of the Republic after Sadi Carnot's assassination earlier in the year, and to Théophile Delcassé, minister for the colonies. Neither could save the indiscreet ambassador. If Georges Suarez is right, Clemenceau's long feud with Delcassé had its origin in the minister's failure to help his friend.

Clemenceau soon realised that a Franco-Russian alliance was inevitable, and for a time he hoped that France might use it as a means of recovering Alsace-Lorraine. 'It must be our aim,' he wrote in *La Dépêche de Toulouse* on 25 August, 1896, 'to make Russia, who was an accomplice in our overthrow, the instrument of our complete rehabilitation, that is to say— to call a spade a spade—of our revenge.'

His hopes faded when it became clear that the alliance would be based on the preservation of existing frontiers in Europe, and that the Treaty of Frankfort would not be challenged. In *L'Echo de Paris* on 1 September, 1897, he commented sadly: 'Russia needs peace, and the unfortunate thing for us, as I have often pointed out, is that the peace she requires to maintain is called the Peace of Frankfort. . . . It is not clear why the two countries should enter into a close compact if they wish to maintain the same peace as the Triple Alliance. They might just as well, for this purpose, combine with the three allies.'

He had taken his stand. France had been warned to put no faith in the Russian alliance. But the winter of 1897–8 was to bring him a new subject which would take up the greater part of his journalistic energies. For four years he had dazzled his readers with his remarkable display of versatility. Now he was to write article after article on one question—that of justice for the Jewish officer, Captain Alfred Dreyfus.

[3]

Journalism did not fully satisfy Clemenceau's new-found thirst for writing. He told Goncourt in 1894 that he would like to write a novel and a play, if he were not so busy with his articles for *La Justice* and *La Dépêche de Toulouse*. Seven years later he had written them both, as well as two volumes of essays, country sketches, Jewish studies and short stories—*Au Fil des Jours* and *Aux Embuscades de la Vie*, from which selections were reprinted in two further books—*Au pied de Sinaï*, illustrated by Toulouse-Lautrec, and *Figures de Vendée*. Add to these the first nine volumes of his collected newspaper articles (including seven dealing solely with the Dreyfus affair), and it will be seen that the output of his first ten years as a writer was on a grand scale.

His novel was *Les Plus Forts*, published in 1898. Its theme is explained by his sombre hero, the Marquis de Puymaufray, who says that the world is *le syndicat des plus forts*. Apart from the force of arms, the greatest power is that of wealth, which includes all other powers: 'the richest are the strongest; that is the brutal fact.' Another character in the book observes that 'the world today belongs to the bourgeois dynasties. They also are a nobility.'[1]

---

[1] This assertion was elaborated half-a-century later by E. Beau de Loménie in his three-volume work, *Les Responsabilités des Dynasties Bourgeoises*, a trenchant criticism of the harmful influence exerted on French life by a number of wealthy bourgeois families. The author was unaware, until he had completed his first volume, that the striking phrase, 'bourgeois dynasties', had already been used by Clemenceau in *Les Plus Forts*.

The scene of the novel alternates between Paris and Puymaufray's gloomy chateau in Poitou, which is a faithful picture of L'Aubraie, the Clemenceaus' family home. A rather mechanical plot turns on the fact that Puymaufray knows himself to be the father of Claude, supposedly the daughter of his friend and neighbour, a wealthy paper manufacturer. His consciousness of paternity makes him anxious to give her moral guidance, and he tries, but ultimately fails, to prevent her from marrying a slick young deputy and so committing herself to a life of wealth and power '*dans le camp des plus forts*'. Even Sir Edmund Gosse, who was favourably disposed towards much of Clemenceau's writing, had to admit that in *Les Plus Forts* 'All the characters preach' and 'The episodes, the conversations, are little more than a series of irregular theses on various aspects of the struggle for life.'

When the book appeared in 1898 its author was already advocating the re-trial of Dreyfus, which was opposed by the bulk of the French press. His espousal of an unpopular cause may have been one reason for the cold reception of *Les Plus Forts* by the critics, who almost unanimously ignored it; but even in more favourable circumstances it could hardly have found many admirers. Clemenceau must have realised that he had no talent for writing novels, though in 1909 he told Berta Szeps that he would like to write a novel which had nothing to do with politics. It remained unwritten.

Drama was also beyond his grasp. He had originally planned *Les Plus Forts* as a play, and he completed the dramatic version after the novel had been published; but it was never produced. His one play which was actually seen by Parisian audiences was a long one-act piece, *Le Voile de Bonheur*, which was performed at the Renaissance theatre in November 1901, with incidental music by Gabriel Fauré and a distinguished actor, Firmin Gémier, in the leading rôle. It had only a short run.

The play is a parable about a Chinese mandarin who has been blind for ten years and regards himself as entirely happy with a faithful wife, a dutiful son and two devoted friends. A foreigner gives him some drops to restore his sight, though warning him that if he uses too many he will become blind again and will stay so for ever. The mandarin takes the drops and his sight is restored, but before anyone else knows that he can see he discovers that his wife is deceiving him with one of his two friends, that the other friend has put his own name as joint author on a volume of 17,000 poems written by the mandarin in praise of his wife, and that his son is ridiculing him. He decides to escape from the ugly truth by taking the rest of the drops, and so retreats for ever behind his 'veil of happiness'.

The story is worked out neatly, but Clemenceau had not enough technical skill to keep the audience guessing, and the plot becomes painfully obvious as the play goes on. It was a bold attempt in a new medium, but it was no more than a *jeu d'esprit*. As Geffroy points out, the philosophy it advocates—one of withdrawal from life to avoid unhappiness—is entirely contrary to Clemenceau's own belief in the importance of action and the unflinching pursuit of truth. It was an achievement to have a play produced and a novel published, but these were blind alleys. As a writer Clemenceau had found his true *métier* in journalism, and he did well to keep to it.

CHAPTER NINE

DREYFUS

1. First reactions. 2. Call for 'revision'. 3. Zola's J'Accuse. 4. Progress of the 'Affair'. 5. Re-trial and pardon.

[1]

THOUGH IT was only at the end of 1897 that Clemenceau became closely concerned with the Dreyfus case, his first comments on it had appeared in *La Justice* in December 1894. This was the month in which Captain Alfred Dreyfus, a staff officer in the French army and a member of a Jewish family well known in Alsace, was condemned by a court-martial to lifelong deportation to a fortified place and to military degradation for the offences of treason and espionage. Details of the supposed offences were not given, but before the case was heard a newspaper had alleged that letters written by Dreyfus to Colonel Schwartzkoppen, the German military attaché in Paris, had been found by the French army's intelligence department.

Like most Frenchmen at the time, Clemenceau saw no reason to distrust the court-martial's verdict. During five years in which Freycinet had been minister of war in successive governments the French army had been successfully reorganised. It was now a military instrument capable of facing Germany, and it was not surprising that the Germans should be anxious to learn the secrets of French armaments and military planning. Their espionage system made full use of French agents, and several French officers and technicians had been arrested and sentenced for betraying their country. Dreyfus, it seemed, was only another traitor, though a very regrettable one because of his access to staff papers. His deportation to Devil's Island, off the coast of Guiana, could hardly be regarded as excessive punishment.

In an article that he later described as 'cruel' Clemenceau expressed his horror at the thought that a French officer could help a foreign country to prepare for a new invasion of France. He even suggested that Dreyfus's sentence was inadequate; although he opposed capital punishment he found it extraordinary that soldiers could be shot for comparatively trivial acts of insubordination, while a man who was helping an enemy to invade

France should be exiled to a peaceful life, devoted to the pleasures of growing coconut palms. If the death penalty were to be preserved for anything, should it not be for the greatest crime of all, that of treason?

There, for Clemenceau, the matter rested. He was not involved in the developments of the next two-and-a-half years, in which, thanks to the faith and persistence of Dreyfus's brother Mathieu, the honesty and determination of Colonel Picquart, the new head of military information at the war ministry, and the espousal of the prisoner's cause by a young Jewish journalist, Bernard Lazare, the Dreyfus case began to be transformed into a confrontation between the pursuit of truth and justice and the preservation of the army's honour.

The fact that Dreyfus was a Jew had no bearing on his arrest and sentence. He was arrested because he had access to the papers mentioned in the *bordereau*, a list of French military documents offered to Germany which had been found by a French agent in a wastepaper basket at the German embassy, and because it was possible to trace a resemblance between his handwriting and that of the writer of the *bordereau*. With the help of Colonel Picquart, who carefully re-examined the documents used in the Dreyfus trial, Dreyfus's friends discovered that certain papers (later acknowledged to be forgeries) had been shown to the court-martial as proof of his guilt but had not been disclosed to himself or his counsel, and that the handwriting of the *bordereau* was not Dreyfus's, but more probably that of a Major Esterhazy. These discoveries proved that the case against Dreyfus was by no means as convincing as people had at first imagined. 'In fact,' writes Douglas Johnson, 'there was no case against Dreyfus. There were only assumptions, rumours, coincidences and misinterpretations. But the belief that he was guilty was persistent and proofs were manufactured so that he would not escape.'

The public at first knew nothing of the results of Colonel Picquart's investigations at the war ministry, but in 1896 they were used by Bernard Lazare in his pamphlet, *Une erreur judiciaire: la verité sur l'affaire Dreyfus*, which drew attention to inconsistencies in the supposed facts on which Dreyfus was convicted, and reached the firm conclusion that he was innocent. Though Lazare sent copies of the pamphlet to deputies and other prominent persons, it made little impression in high places. Clemenceau would not read it, Jaurès was not interested, and Lazare's intervention did more to rally the forces of antisemitism than to win friends for Dreyfus. In the Socialist *La Petite République* Alexandre Zévaès described the brochure as 'a new manoeuvre in the underhand campaign being waged by financial and Jewish newspapers to cast doubt on the traitor's guilt'. To antisemites, Dreyfus appeared as both traitor and conspirator, two rôles traditionally associated with Jews.

At this time Clemenceau felt that a great deal of fuss was being made about very little. 'They are boring me with their Jew,' he grumbled. Yet it was indirectly through Bernard Lazare that the case at last began to arouse his professional interest.

[2]

On becoming chief editorial writer of *L'Aurore*, which made its first appearance on 19 October, 1897, Clemenceau found that Lazare was one of his colleagues, and he at once urged the director, Ernest Vaughan, not to allow the young man to continue his pro-Dreyfus campaign in the new paper. A few days later, on chancing to meet his old friend Ranc, now a senator, he mentioned that he was stopping Lazare from writing about Dreyfus in *L'Aurore*. Ranc was surprised. 'Don't you know that Dreyfus is innocent?' he asked. 'Scheurer-Kestner has the proofs and will show them to you.' 'If that is so,' said Clemenceau, 'it is the greatest crime of the age.'

Scheurer-Kestner was then vice-president of the Senate. As a prominent Alsatian he had been consulted by Mathieu Dreyfus soon after the court-martial, and had become interested in the case without believing that Dreyfus was innocent. In the summer of 1897 he met another Alsatian, the lawyer Louis Leblois, who was a friend of Colonel Picquart and had seen many of the secret documents. Leblois convinced Scheurer-Kestner that there had been a miscarriage of justice. Though taking no official action he told some of his fellow senators that he was sure Dreyfus was innocent and that he would see that justice was done.

Clemenceau always had a high regard for Scheurer-Kestner. After his talk with Ranc he paid several visits to his old friend, and saw documents which proved, not that Dreyfus was innocent, but that the court-martial had been grossly irregular. He was introduced to Mathieu Dreyfus and became so interested in his views that they continued to meet every evening for two years. It was Mathieu, as he once told Georges Wormser, who inspired him to campaign for 'revision' (i.e. a re-trial); on 2 November he wrote in *L'Aurore* the first of the many hundred articles he was to write on 'the Affair'.

It was mere coincidence that *L'Aurore* was founded, and Clemenceau invited to join its staff, at the time when the Dreyfus case became a burning subject for discussion. Vaughan did not found the paper to champion Dreyfus's cause; his life was in newspapers, and he had recently been director of *L'Intransigeant*, edited by his brother-in-law, the incalculable Rochefort, but had resigned in order to found a new paper with a definitely Republican programme. A few days after *L'Aurore's* first issue the grounds for Scheurer-Kestner's belief in Dreyfus's innocence were explained in a long article in *Le Figaro*; a fortnight later the same paper published a letter from Mathieu Dreyfus, directly accusing Major Esterhazy of having written the *bordereau* found in the German embassy. Every newspaper had now to be for or against the demand for revision of Dreyfus's trial.

When Clemenceau began to write about the case he did not share Scheurer-Kestner's faith in the prisoner's innocence. But the documents he had seen and Mathieu Dreyfus's eloquence had convinced him that the court-martial was illegally conducted, since Dreyfus was convicted on evidence of which he was not informed. That was good enough cause for demanding a re-trial, but many other suspicious facts were coming to light and were discussed in Clemenceau's articles. Why, for example, were the military authorities so reluctant to investigate Mathieu Dreyfus's charges against Esterhazy? Why had Colonel Picquart been removed from the war ministry and posted to Tunis? Was there a conspiracy among senior generals to keep Dreyfus on Devil's Island at all costs and to avoid any re-examination of the documents in the case?

All these and many other issues were raised by Clemenceau in his articles on the 'Affair', often five or six a week, in *L'Aurore* and *La Dépêche de Toulouse*. His work fills seven volumes, which provide a running commentary on developments from day to day, and amazingly he found new points to make in almost every article. He wrote about debates in the Chamber, the actions and statements of ministers and army leaders, the case against Esterhazy, the persecution of Colonel Picquart and eventually the second court-martial at Rennes; he reported conversations with deputies and senators; he gave relevant quotations from other newspapers; and he wrote always with great verve and in the trenchant style which he had now mastered. Publication of the articles in book form began with *L'Iniquité* in 1899 and ended with *La Honte* in 1903; both Gustave Geffroy and Daniel Halévy describe the seven volumes as Clemenceau's *chef d'oeuvre*.

He wrote his articles in his new home in Passy, to which he had moved from the rue Clément-Marot in 1896. This house in the rue Franklin, which was to be his Paris home for the rest of his life and is now the Musée Clemenceau, was not luxurious, but it was big enough for his needs. He was particularly proud of his small garden, which at one corner overlooked the boulevard Delessert, so that he could sit among the flowers and watch the passers-by moving beneath him. It was in this house, in a book-lined study with a large horseshoe-shaped desk, that he produced his daily article for *L'Aurore*, rising at dawn to do so and sending his manuscript by messenger to the office in the rue Montmartre.

He would then appear in the office about 5 p.m., to correct the proof and to make sure that what he had written was in accordance with the latest news. As time went on, and France became split between Dreyfusards and anti-Dreyfusards, there were occasional demonstrations outside the office, and once a window was broken by a revolver shot. Clemenceau was not intimidated. When his work was done he walked back to the rue Franklin, to begin again on the following morning.

He had been writing about the case for two months when Emile Zola came to the office with 'a letter to the President of the Republic'.

[3]

At the end of the nineteenth century Emile Zola's realistic studies of French life had made him the best-selling novelist in France. He had many enemies, not least among his fellow writers, who disliked his lack of taste and his turgid style; but he was an important contemporary figure, and Dreyfus's friends, whom the anti-Dreyfusards jeeringly called 'the syndicate', made great efforts to win his support. The case for Dreyfus was forcefully put before him by Scheurer-Kestner, Leblois, Lazare, Joseph Reinach and Mathieu Dreyfus, and he became an enthusiastic convert. In December 1897 he wrote two pro-Dreyfus articles in *Le Figaro*, which had been calling for revision of the court-martial's verdict; but in the middle of the month the editor suddenly abandoned his revisionist campaign, and Zola was left to find another outlet for his views.

He was soon at his desk again. The case against Esterhazy had become so damning that he was brought before a court-martial, but he was acquitted after a trial in which the military witnesses and the handwriting experts gave evidence in secret. The acquittal shocked Zola, who believed that the army was shielding Esterhazy because a verdict of guilty would have established Dreyfus's innocence. He wrote all night on 11–12 January, and again during the day, intending at first to publish his article as a pamphlet; he then decided that a newspaper would give it wider circulation, and out of the few papers which were sympathetic towards Dreyfus he chose *L'Aurore*. In the early evening he took it to the rue Montmartre and read it aloud to Vaughan, Clemenceau, Reinach and Lazare. It was entitled *Lettre au Président de la République*.

It was a long article, which examined the trials of Dreyfus and Esterhazy, the conduct of the respective ministers of war (Generals Mercier and Billot) in 1894 and 1898 and of other generals involved in 'the Affair', the machinations of Colonel du Paty de Clam, who was responsible for Dreyfus's arrest and for the handing of secret documents to the court-martial, the evidence of so-called expert witnesses and other aspects of the case. It ended with eight shattering paragraphs, each beginning with the words, '*J'accuse*', and explaining the reasons for the particular accusation. Zola accused Colonel du Paty de Clam, Generals Mercier, Billot, de Boisdeffre and other senior officers, three handwriting experts, the war ministry (for encouraging the anti-Dreyfus press campaign), and the members of the two courts-martial, the first for having broken the law by convicting an accused man on evidence which had been kept secret from him, the second for having committed the juridical crime of knowingly acquitting a guilty man. He was aware, he wrote, that these accusations might expose him to a charge of defamation. He challenged the authorities to take him to the assize court, so that an inquiry might take place in the light of day.

It was at once agreed to publish the article. Clemenceau made only one objection. 'I don't like the title, Zola,' he said. 'It hasn't enough bite.' The pedestrian *Lettre au Président de la République* was kept as a subheading; above it, with Vaughan's approval, Clemenceau wrote boldly, '*J'ACCUSE. . . .*' It was under this heading that the article appeared on the next morning, covering all six columns of the front page of *L'Aurore*. More than 300,000 copies of the issue were sold.

Clemenceau did not write in *L'Aurore* on the day when Zola's letter was published. He gave it his warm approval in his next article, but he declared that his own position was unchanged: he was not yet convinced of Dreyfus's innocence, he was solely concerned with the illegality of the court-martial. He was still, in fact, a revisionist, calling only for Dreyfus's re-trial, and not yet a whole-hearted Dreyfusard.

Zola's challenge was accepted. He was summoned to appear in court, but only in respect of his comments on the Esterhazy court-martial; the government did not wish to re-open the entire Dreyfus case. Perrenx, the manager of *L'Aurore*, was also charged.

The trial aroused Clemenceau's fighting spirit. Zola was to be defended by Maître Labori, Perrenx by Clemenceau's brother Albert, who had become a successful advocate; and Clemenceau himself was allowed to join the defence on behalf of *L'Aurore*. He was thus one of Zola's party which descended from a carriage outside the Palais de Justice on 7 February, to be greeted with cries of 'Down with Zola! Down with the crook!' from a mob of hired demonstrators. 'Well orchestrated,' he observed.

Much of Zola's trial was a legal battle on technical points. The prosecution wanted to keep the Dreyfus court-martial out of it, the defence wanted to bring it in, since its illegality was the cornerstone of Zola's accusations. The presiding judge took the side of the prosecution, monotonously ordering, 'The question will not be put,' when the defence tried to widen the scope of the trial.

Even so, it was impossible to avoid all mention of Dreyfus. Colonel Picquart, who had come from a military prison, where he was serving a sentence for showing secret papers to civilians, described his amazement on finding that the Dreyfus file contained no proofs of his guilt; and Maître Demange, who had been defending counsel in the Dreyfus court-martial, was too quick for the judge in answering 'Yes, certainly' to Albert Clemenceau's question whether it was true that a secret document, of which Dreyfus had not been told, was shown to the judges. Generals and staff officers upheld the honour of the army and refused to answer incriminating questions; General de Boisdeffre, chief of the general staff, told the jury that he and his colleagues would resign if its verdict showed that it had no confidence in the army's leaders. Long and confusing, the trial dragged on for nearly three weeks. It was not until 22 February that Clemenceau spoke for the defence.

It was a curious scene. Since Clemenceau was not a member of the Bar he had no legal gown, and his dark blue suit looked out of place among the black gowns of the advocates and the red robes of the judges. For this occasion he changed his oratorical style: instead of browbeating his opponents, as he did in the old days at the Palais-Bourbon, he exercised rigid self-control and presented his arguments calmly and persuasively.

He was not, he said, an anti-militarist, but he believed in the supremacy of civil society over military power; indeed, the only reason for the soldier's existence was to defend the principles that civilian society represented. He therefore condemned General de Boisdeffre's threat that the general staff would resign if the verdict went against the army, and he rejected the claim that Dreyfus's sentence should no longer be discussed because the issue had already been decided. Developing the theme of the *chose jugée*, he pointed to the tall crucifix on the wall behind the presiding judge:

> The *chose jugée*? Look there, gentlemen, look at Christ on the Cross. There it is, the *chose jugée*. It has been put above the judge so that he will not be disturbed by looking at it. It should have been placed at the other end of the court, so that before pronouncing sentence the judge would have before his eyes this example of judicial error, which our civilisation regards as the shame of humanity.[1]

[1] Though always an unbeliever, Clemenceau was well versed in the Bible, and could make effective use of it. During the discussions of the Big Four at the Peace Conference of 1919, President Woodrow Wilson once remarked that he struggled constantly against emotion in order to preserve the accuracy of his judgements. Clemenceau retorted: 'Nothing is done except by emotion. Was not Christ carried away by passion when he drove the money-changers out of the Temple?' Other Biblical references occur in his newspaper articles, and there is also the story, told by Sir Denis Brogan,

In his peroration he reminded the jury that France had lived through a century of terrible experiences, and had known all kinds of glory and all kinds of disaster. This was a moment in history when they stood before the unknown, poised between fears and hopes. 'Your verdict, gentlemen, will be less upon us than upon yourselves. We appear before you. You appear before history.'

As was only to be expected in France at that time, the jury was more impressed by the generals and staff officers, who testified to the integrity of the Esterhazy court-martial, than by Zola, his defending counsel, and the literary and political notabilities, including Anatole France, the distinguished author, and Jean Jaurès, who bore witness to Zola's character. Zola and Perrenx were found guilty of defamation and were sentenced to terms of imprisonment—a year for Zola, four months for Perrenx—together with a fine of 3,000 francs each. The verdict and sentences were received with shouts of joy in the court room and in the corridors of the Palais de Justice, where Déroulède was waiting with a gang of rowdy supporters and Zola's defenders were jeered as they left the building. Clemenceau said later that he had not expected such a display of hatred. He believed that, if Zola had been acquitted, he and his friends would not have left the Palais de Justice alive.

Zola and Perrenx appealed against the verdict. Their appeal was allowed on technical grounds, but a new indictment was brought against Zola, who faced a second trial at Versailles in July. He was again found guilty, and the original sentences were re-imposed.

On the advice of Clemenceau, Labori and others, but against his own inclinations, Zola left France before the police came for him. He went to London, there to await an amnesty or the re-opening of his case when the revisionists secured a new court-martial for Dreyfus. Clemenceau resumed his daily articles in *L'Aurore* with greater fervour than ever. After hearing the equivocations of the army officers in the Zola trial, he was coming to believe that the Jewish captain on Devil's Island was really innocent.

[4]

An immediate sequel to the first Zola trial was a duel between Clemenceau and Drumont, editor of *La Libre Parole*. Angered by Drumont's attacks on Zola, Clemenceau wrote a paragraph in *L'Aurore* inviting him to say

of Clemenceau's remark when he withdrew from the presidential election in 1920 after his defeat in the preliminary vote. As 'the great man's cabinet clustered round him to assure him of their loyalty', he 'put his hand to his ear and asked, *"Did I hear a cock crow?"*' (*See* Mantoux, *Les Délibérations des Quatre*, I, p. 124; Brogan, *The French Nation*, p. 250.)

where he was in 1870, to which regiment he belonged and in which actions he had taken part. Drumont ignored the questions, but retaliated with a ferocious article headed '*A vous, Clemenceau!*', in which he recalled Montmartre in 1871 and asserted that it was due to Clemenceau's cowardice, or rather to his complicity, that the two generals were assassinated. As a deputy, wrote Drumont, Clemenceau had been partner and factotum of the German Jew, Cornelius Herz; as a journalist ('having been vomited forth by his constituents') he had made himself the defender of the traitor Dreyfus. 'You are a wretch, evidently,' the article concluded, 'but, of your kind, you have at least the merit of being a complete one.'

Drumont's admirer, Georges Bernanos, explains that he never issued a challenge, even when grossly insulted, since he was anxious not to transgress the laws of the Church unless he were obliged to do so; his tactics were to attack his enemies in *La Libre Parole* and wait for their challenges, which honour would compel him to accept. On this occasion Clemenceau at once demanded satisfaction for Drumont's insults, but the duel had to wait until the end of Zola's first trial. The two men met in the parc des Princes on 26 February. Pistols were the chosen weapons, three bullets to be fired at a distance of twenty paces.

Albert Monniot, who worked on *La Libre Parole*, warned his colleagues that Clemenceau was in great form with his pistol. 'Drumont is dead,' he said. But the duel was no more lethal than Clemenceau's twenty-one others. All the bullets missed; he looked at his pistol, smiled and murmured 'Astonishing!' Once again, it seems remarkable that such an expert shot as Clemenceau should not even have hit his man; possibly this was one of the duels in which, by tacit agreement, both contestants deliberately fired into the air, to avoid the embarrassment that would have been caused if either had been killed or seriously wounded.

For the rest of 1898 Clemenceau continued his campaign for Dreyfus's re-trial. In the spring a deputation from Draguignan asked him to stand for his old seat in the forthcoming general election; he prudently refused, knowing that public opinion was not yet on Dreyfus's side, and surmising that, as the sponsor of an unpopular cause, he would encounter new animosities in the Var. He was probably right. Jaurès, who became an ardent Dreyfusard after the Zola trial and wrote a series of full-page articles in *La Petite République* calling for revision, lost his seat at Carmaux because the anti-Dreyfusards closed their ranks against him.

But the Dreyfusards were gaining ground. In an article written shortly before Zola's second trial Clemenceau said that a deputy, who was a hunting friend of the President, Felix Faure, had told him that at least five ministers were on the Dreyfusards' side, though they would not admit it publicly. Further scrutiny of the documents convinced a new war minister that at least two of the papers had been forged by Colonel Henry, a senior officer in the intelligence department. Henry was arrested and committed suicide in prison. Esterhazy was dismissed the service, not for treason, but for private misconduct. The Dreyfusards felt that their case was proved. In October Clemenceau discarded the last of his doubts and for the first time declared in *L'Aurore* that Dreyfus was innocent.

The 'Affair' (as it is known to history) was now at its height. In the drawing-rooms of Paris, as in the columns of the press, France was divided between those who believed that justice must be done, no matter what the cost might be, and those who maintained that the honour of the army (as represented by the members of the first court-martial and the high officers who gave evidence at the Zola trial) must not be impugned for the sake of redressing some problematical injustice. Families were split in two, old friendships ended, engagements broken. The division was acute in the fashionable society of the Faubourg Saint-Germain, as can be seen in many chapters of Proust's epic novel; and it ran right through the literary and academic worlds, though most of the leading writers and professors were on Dreyfus's side and several hundred of them signed a Dreyfusard manifesto, which Clemenceau called 'the protest of the intellectuals'. Yet for all the heat it engendered, 'the Affair' affected only the educated classes. It seems to have had little interest for the masses.

Even after the discovery that part of the case against Dreyfus had been based on forged documents neither the anti-Dreyfusard President Faure nor the government was willing to order Dreyfus's re-trial. But the situation was suddenly changed on that embarrassing afternoon in February 1899 when the President of the French Republic was found in his private drawing-room, undressed, unconscious, and holding firmly in his clenched fist the long hair of a sobbing and entirely naked young woman. President Faure never recovered from the cerebral haemorrhage brought on by over-exertion. He died at 10 p.m., and later that night a journalist from *L'Aurore* went to the rue Franklin to ask Clemenceau for a short note on the President's death.

Clemenceau was in bed, reading Homer's *Odyssey* in Greek. His first thought was that Faure's death opened the way for a new president who might give Dreyfus his long-awaited re-trial. Such a man was Emile Loubet, president of the Senate and a sound Republican.

'Felix Faure has just died. It means not a man less in France,' Clemenceau wrote. 'At all events here is a fine place to fill. There will be no lack of claimants . . . I vote for Loubet.' He had chosen the right man. Loubet was elected by an overall majority on the first count, and the machinery for re-trying Dreyfus was at last put into motion.

In the previous year Madame Dreyfus had lodged an appeal against her husband's sentence. The case was now heard by the united appeal courts, whose judgement, ordering a second court-martial, was given in June. A boat was sent to Devil's Island to bring Dreyfus home.

[5]

It was arranged that the court-martial should be held at Rennes, in Brittany, which was too far from Paris for the use of the hireling crowds engaged for the Zola trial. It was at Rennes, therefore, that counsel, witnesses and many of the world's leading journalists, together with a fair sprinkling of publicity-seeking women whom Maurice Barrès described as '*nos snobinettes les plus connues*', assembled on 7 August, 1899, for the second court-martial of Captain Alfred Dreyfus.

The members of the court were in a dilemma. The new facts which had come to light made it virtually certain that Dreyfus had been improperly convicted; but how could a court composed of relatively junior officers cast a slur on the army's honour by implying that the members of the first court-martial and the generals who had given evidence were all at fault? Clemenceau, whose articles in *L'Aurore* provided a close study of each day's proceedings, noted the way in which the case was being conducted, and soon realised that the verdict would be against Dreyfus.

Yet even he was hardly expecting the remarkable verdict on 9 September that Dreyfus was guilty, but 'with extenuating circumstances'. If he was guilty, he was a traitor, and what circumstances could possibly extenuate the crime of treason? In his article in *L'Aurore* Clemenceau quoted a current remark that the extenuating circumstances were not for the accused but for the judges.

One feature of the Rennes court-martial was the poor impression made by Dreyfus. Even allowing for the hardships he had suffered on Devil's Island, he seemed unduly stiff and cold, and was loath to defend himself with any fervour against General Mercier, the one-time minister of war, and his other military accusers. Clemenceau was deeply disappointed. 'The imbecile!' he raged, when Zola asked him what he had against Dreyfus. 'Some signs of revolt on his part would have soothed the public. . . . His attitude to Mercier, above all, should have been violent. All the world would have heard the words which fell from his lips. Believe me, he alone had the right to overstep the bounds, and he ought to have overstepped them. He has let us down.'

Clemenceau's comments were in keeping with the opinions expressed later by many of Dreyfus's supporters. 'If he had not been Dreyfus, would he even have been a Dreyfusard?' asked Léon Blum. Charles Péguy said regretfully, 'We might have died for Dreyfus, but Dreyfus has not died for Dreyfus'; and retrospectively Clemenceau observed that Dreyfus 'was the only person who understood nothing about the Dreyfus Affair'. The man whom Clemenceau and others had built up into a test-case for truth and justice was concerned only about the opinion of his brother officers and cared nothing for the support of his partisans. He believed in authority, hated the enemies of order, and might well have condemned another Dreyfus for the sake of the army.

Clearly the Rennes verdict was not the end of the road. Waldeck-Rousseau, who had become prime minister in June, wished to find a solution which would satisfy the Dreyfusards without offending the army. A successful appeal, followed by yet another court-martial, would probably have produced another verdict of 'guilty' and would have benefited no one. Only a presidential pardon could provide a method of setting Dreyfus free without causing further unrest. This was Waldeck-Rousseau's solution; a condition of the pardon was that Dreyfus would not try to re-open the case by appealing against the Rennes verdict.

The offer caused dissension among Dreyfus's supporters. Clemenceau thought that a pardon would be an immoral ending to a great public campaign for justice, and Jaurès agreed with him; but Reinach, Mathieu Dreyfus and Lazare welcomed it as a means of saving Dreyfus from further suffering. Dreyfus himself at first opposed the pardon, not, like Clemenceau, in the interests of justice, but because he feared it would bar the way to full recovery of his military honour. But the arguments in favour of accepting the pardon were stronger. Reluctantly, and with mental reservations, Clemenceau said to Mathieu: 'If I were your brother, I should accept.' Dreyfus did so, and was pardoned by President Loubet in September. Nearly seven years were to pass before the court of appeal pronounced him not guilty of the original charge, and he was reinstated in the army with promotion to the rank of major.

Dreyfus's pardon did not end 'the Affair', which had a lasting influence on the life of France. Though the prisoner was pardoned, Frenchmen remained Dreyfusard and anti-Dreyfusard; long after the second trial the mere name of Dreyfus made Proust's Duc de Guermantes 'knit his Jupiterian brows'; fanatical supporters of each side were still to be encountered during the First World War. 'The Affair' had also an unfortunate effect on relations between the army and the nation. On the one side, it awakened public distrust of army leaders, though happily there was sufficient cooperation between army and government to allow France to regain her military reputation by 1914; on the other side, it deepened the officer class's feeling of forming a separate caste and its consciousness that the army was older than the Republic. This division in French life was to persist through the twentieth century.

A recent French historian of 'the Affair' names three 'great defenders' of Dreyfus—Clemenceau first, then Jaurès and Péguy. Yet there is still argument over his motive for giving years of his life to the defence of Dreyfus. When he began to write his articles, he is said to have told a journalist: 'I do not yet know what there is in it, but I see an admirable weapon for party warfare.' That may have been his view at the time, but it is surely wrong to assume, as some writers do, that his tremendous crusade was undertaken for political advantage.

There was never, in fact, much political capital to be made out of supporting Dreyfus. The Dreyfusards were always in the minority; even at the height of 'the Affair' they were backed by only seventeen daily papers in all France, representing from eleven to fifteen per cent. of French newspaper readership. Though *L'Aurore* had a dazzling circulation of 150,000 for some weeks after the publication of Zola's *J'Accuse*, the figure soon fell to 25,000 and then to 15,000, as readers showed their distaste for the strongly anti-militarist articles by one of its staff writers, Urbain Gohier. The falling circulation of the most ardently Dreyfusard newspaper shows that backing Dreyfus was never a good way of winning popularity.

It is true that Clemenceau's powerful articles re-established him as a leading public figure after his momentary eclipse, but they had deeper roots than political opportunism. Their inspiration came from his lifelong devotion to truth and justice and from his fear that the Republic would be doomed if military authority were to take precedence over the Revolutionary ideals of liberty, equality and fraternity. For it is in the clash between authority and freedom, far more than in the racial conflict between Jews and antisemites, that the real meaning of 'the Affair' is to be found.

CHAPTER TEN

APPROACH TO POWER

1. *Uneasy France.* 2. Le Bloc. 3. *Senator and editor.* 4. *Defender of liberty.*
5. Coup de Tanger. 6. *Church and State.*

[1]

'**M**Y POOR child, you ask me to tell you about France. I have not
the courage to speak of it. I struggle inch by inch, day by day.
The weakness of those who are in my camp is a more sinister
sign than even the audacity of our enemies. . . . I believe that Dreyfus will
soon ask for the revision of his trial with the almost certainty of obtaining
it. But what is Dreyfus in all this? It is France that must be saved.'

So wrote Clemenceau to Lady Edward Cecil (the former Violet Maxse)
on 10 December, 1899. He was wrong in forecasting that the Dreyfus
case would soon be heard for a third time, but he was right to complain
of the weakness of his companions in the Republican 'camp'. France had
a strong prime minister in Waldeck-Rousseau, but there was no effective
leader in the Chamber of Deputies. 'Apart from Waldeck, there is no one,'
said Pelletan.

And yet, as Clemenceau saw, this was a time when firm leadership was
needed, for throughout the year there had been portents of a coming
nationalist *coup d'état*. On the day of President Faure's funeral the always
explosive Déroulède had made an unsuccessful attempt to persuade
General Roget, commander of the troops attending the ceremony, to
lead them to the Elysée to overthrow the parliamentary Republic; and
when the ensuing trial ended with his acquittal, Clemenceau warned his
readers: 'M. Déroulède has promised to begin again, and I am sure he
will do his utmost to keep his word. This beginning again has only one
name—civil war.'

His warning was timely. At the beginning of August Déroulède and
sixty-six others, chiefly monarchists and Bonapartists, were arrested and
charged with conspiracy against the State. Many were released, but
Déroulède and fourteen fellow conspirators, who had been plotting to
seize power and had already nominated a provisional government, were
tried and sentenced to varying periods of exile. Rumours of a *coup d'état*

were again current in October, and warning paragraphs appeared in
L'Aurore and two or three Left wing newspapers; but it remained un-
certain whether or not there had actually been a plot. Yet even if
Clemenceau and his friends may have over-reacted on this occasion,
many believed that France was drifting towards civil war.

It was the new kind of nationalism sponsored by Maurice Barrès which
was mainly responsible for the unsettled state of France. Barrès was a
patriot, but his patriotism was authoritarian rather than sentimental. As
the American writer Michael Curtis observes, 'The spirit of militarism, the
hostility to foreign nations, the economic and political protectionism,
the denial of individual rights in the interests of the nation State, and
the proscription of internal opposition and dissent, signified a radical departure from nationalism in its liberal period.' This creed, which other
countries would develop into Fascism and National Socialism, was one
that Clemenceau could never accept. He had good reason for feeling
anxious for France in the face of this new nationalism and the continuing
activities of what he called 'the clerico-military syndicate'.

Yet it was at this critical time that he gave up his post on *L'Aurore*
and restricted his work to his twice-weekly articles for *La Dépêche de
Toulouse*. Differing reasons have been given for his decision to leave
L'Aurore. Georges Michon asserts that it was because he refused to take
a salary cut when the paper was going through a difficult period; but
although money may have been a contributory factor, the real cause of his
departure was an article by Urbain Gohier, who claimed that he alone had
dealt in *L'Aurore* with the general principles of the 'Affair', while the
other staff writers had concerned themselves only with personal issues.

This presumptuous claim was too much for Clemenceau. He refused to
remain on the same paper with Gohier, and he submitted his resignation.
Vaughan was distressed by his decision; apart from his wish to keep a
valued writer, he knew that Clemenceau needed money and still had
debts to pay. But his resignation was final. On 17 December he wrote to
Vaughan: 'In leaving you, as well as the colleagues who were my friends,
I take with me the regret of leaving unfinished the common campaign for
justice in which I have been proud to claim my part.' At his own request,
the letter was published in *L'Aurore*.

[2]

Clemenceau's last article in *L'Aurore* appeared on 16 December, 1899;
a year and six weeks went by before the first issue of his own weekly
paper, *Le Bloc*, on 27 January, 1901. When we remember his resilience in
starting to write for *La Justice* only a few days after his defeat at

Draguignan, it seems surprising that he had no place in Parisian journalism for more than a year.[1]

One reason for his lack of a journalistic post in Paris can be found in a letter he wrote on 3 January, 1900, to the Danish author, Georg Brandes, whose acquaintance he had made in the previous year. He wrote from England, where he was convalescing at Maxse's country house at Dunley Hill, Dorking, after what he described as 'an influenza crisis'. He told Brandes that he was continuing his Dreyfus campaign in *La Dépêche de Toulouse*, while waiting to be able to use his pen in Paris again, 'which I hope will be soon, though it will not be very easy for me to find a place among the existing papers.'

That was his difficulty. The bulk of the Parisian press was still anti-Dreyfusard, and was therefore closed to him. He would not have written for a Socialist newspaper, and non-Socialist Dreyfusard papers were few indeed. Evidently he found no opening, for on 26 March he wrote to Brandes: 'I am trying to start a paper. I hope I shall soon be successful.' He was hoping, in fact, to found a new daily newspaper, but plans moved very slowly, and at the end of the year he decided to take the easier course of starting a weekly paper which would be all his own work.

Ill-health was another reason for his comparative idleness in 1900. Throughout his life he frequently suffered from liver and stomach troubles, which he tried to alleviate by an annual visit to Carlsbad (a place, as he once wrote in *Le Journal*, where people drank the same three daily glasses of salty water for all kinds of different ailments). Vaughan had noticed how ill he was looking when he left *L'Aurore*, and the 'influenza crisis' he mentioned to Brandes was evidently the beginning of a longer bout of ill-health. Admiral Maxse died in July, and Clemenceau was well enough to go to England for the funeral. But at some later stage in the year he went through the physical crisis which he described to Rosny *aîné*:

> I thought I was dead. Every part of me seemed to be giving up. I felt a bitter distaste for everything, my will-power was plunging into the darkness. . . . And then, that little flame which was watching in the depths of the sanctuary began to grow bigger . . . there was warmth and light . . . I was at the helm again, and here I am—for a few years more.

The illness must have been both long and debilitating, for as late as May

---

[1] Most of Clemenceau's biographers pass lightly over this curious gap in his journalistic career, and some do not seem to have noticed its existence. Both Alexandre Zévaès and Gaston Monnerville, for example, incorrectly assert that he started *Le Bloc* a few weeks after leaving *L'Aurore*. (*See* Zévaès, *Clemenceau*, pp. 173–4; Monnerville, *Clemenceau*, p. 255.)

1902 he was writing to Brandes: 'I am in full convalescence and my strength is coming back only very slowly.'

The gravity of Clemenceau's condition at this time is also suggested by the fact that his three children joined in urging their divorced mother to come back to France towards the end of 1900. It was remarkable that they should have taken this action nearly nine years after the divorce, and no less remarkable that Madame Clemenceau, who had been treated so badly, should have agreed to return; presumably they all thought that Clemenceau was dying, and that Mary should be on hand in case he showed any wish for a last-minute reconciliation. There appears to be no record of any meeting at this time between the former husband and wife, but Mary Clemenceau stayed in France and met Clemenceau at least twice in later years.[1] (She died at Sèvres in 1923.)

By January 1901 Clemenceau was sufficiently recovered to be able to launch his own paper, *Le Bloc*, described on its front page as 'M. Clemenceau's weekly gazette'. The title recalled his assertion that the French Revolution was a *bloc*, and he explained in his first issue that the Republic was also a *bloc*. It was the government's duty, he said, to set the Revolutionary *bloc* of justice and liberty against the *bloc* of the theocratic Church. 'The two *blocs* are in collision; one must necessarily destroy the other. This one will kill that one.'

Le Bloc was cheap to run, because Clemenceau wrote all the articles himself, sitting at the famous horseshoe-shaped desk, littered with papers and press cuttings, at his house in the rue Franklin; but it was not a financial success. Most of its readers took out a two years' subscription, and Stock, the publisher, thought that only a quarter of them would have renewed their subscriptions if *Le Bloc* had continued beyond that period. Yet it served the useful purpose of bringing its editor back from his preoccupation with Dreyfus to the wider political arena. Nearly three-quarters of the articles in *Le Bloc*'s sixty issues dealt with home politics, and about a quarter with foreign or colonial affairs. The readers were regaled with a great variety of topics, extending from workers' pensions, the eight-hour day, the Anglo-Japanese Treaty and the possibilities of submarine warfare to Poincarism, divorce and the rules of the Comédie-Française.

The article on Poincarism is an early indication of the antipathy between

---

[1] The evidence for their later meetings can be found in Georges Louis's *Carnets*. Louis, who was on Clemenceau's personal staff during his first ministry, records that Mary once called at the ministry of the interior to see her ex-husband (probably about 1909) and remarks that 'they had not seen each other for four years'. The meeting at the ministry was not a happy one: two of the staff who were present heard 'a dialogue of terrible reproaches lasting for two hours'. (*See* Louis, *Carnets*, I, pp. 43-4.)

Clemenceau and Poincaré which marred their relationship in the closing years of the First World War. Poincaré, who was twenty years younger than Clemenceau, came from Lorraine and was one of the new men who had become prominent after the Panama scandal; he had been minister of education when he was only thirty-three and finance minister soon afterwards. Politically, he was always to Clemenceau's Right, though remaining a staunch Republican. Both he and Clemenceau moved in literary circles: they had often met at Alphonse Daudet's house and more recently in the *salon* of Madame Arman de Caillavet, who had the distinction of being 'Anatole France's Egeria'. Yet there was never much real sympathy between the dry and logical Lorrainer and the impulsive, temperamental Vendean.

In 1899, when Poincaré tried and failed to form a government, Clemenceau wrote caustically in *L'Aurore*: 'Deschanel, Poincaré, Barthou, triple symbol of our bourgeois youth. Each of them has his gifts. Poincaré's gift is not to be despised—it is intelligence. He would do remarkably well beside someone who could provide character. But neither Deschanel nor Barthou can be that person.' Now in 1902 Poincaré's speech at the congress of the Democratic Republican Alliance— a group of Republicans who were firmly anticlerical but distrusted the Radical Socialists' collectivist tendencies—produced a sharp criticism of 'Poincarism' in *Le Bloc*.

Poincaré, Clemenceau observed, was one of the young prodigies of the Republic, 'but like most young prodigies he has done nothing prodigious'. As minister of finance he had done nothing to reform France's bad tax system; he had taken no steps to introduce an income tax and he was a resolute enemy of progressive taxation; he was indifferent to the encroachments of the Church; and there was nothing to praise in his new-found zeal for resisting Socialism. This attack on the negative aspects of Poincarism helped the Radicals to reduce Poincaré's majority in the Meuse department at the next general election; but he gained in prestige through being singled out for Clemenceau's criticism.

While *Le Bloc* was a useful medium for Clemenceau during his convalescence, it was not enough to keep him fully occupied when he had overcome his temporary lassitude. But before he had time to revive his plans for a new daily paper a deputation of mayors and councillors from the Var came to Paris to see him. They asked him to be their candidate for the Senate in an approaching by-election.

[3]

Under the constitution of 1875 seventy-five of the three hundred seats in the Senate were to be held for life. This provision had been abolished in 1884; existing life senators were allowed to retain their seats, but as each one died, his seat was re-allocated for election in one of the departments, chosen by lot. Clemenceau had had his share of ill fortune. Now he was to profit literally from 'the luck of the draw'. The vacancy caused by the death of a life senator early in 1902 was allotted to the Var, which he had served as a deputy for eight years.

His first impulse was to decline the invitation to stand for election. For years he had campaigned for the abolition of the Senate. How could he sit in the assembly he had so often condemned? When the deputation approached him he refused to stand. The Var worthies withdrew, but sensibly decided to stay in Paris another day.

News of Clemenceau's refusal was spread about by his faithful secretary, Etienne Winter. His brother Albert, his daughter Madeleine, Gustave Geffroy and Winter himself all pleaded with him to accept the offer. When he still refused, Winter appealed to Stock, publisher of *Le Bloc*, who asked Clemenceau to come to see him.

Clemenceau told Stock that he was disgusted with politics and he could not enter a body which he had so often attacked. The publisher insisted that people were entitled to change their opinions, and reminded him of the poor state of his finances, which were unlikely to improve; but everything would change for the better if he became a minister and subsequently prime minister.

The publisher was persuasive. So was Winter. When the Var deputation returned to the rue Franklin on the following day, Clemenceau agreed to stand for the Senate; and on 25 March he announced in *Le Bloc* that its publication must be temporarily suspended as he was going to the Var for the senatorial election. It never appeared again.

Fifteen names were put before the congress of Republican groups which chose the candidate for the Var by-election, but there was no doubt of the result when it was known that Clemenceau was standing. After his nomination by the congress he was duly elected senator by a clear majority on the first count. He was to hold his seat until his retirement from politics in 1920.

So once again, after a lapse of nearly nine years, he had a platform for his oratorical talents; but he did not abandon his new profession of journalism. He wrote for *La Dépêche de Toulouse* until the end of the year, and in the following June he returned to *L'Aurore* as editor-in-chief. Vaughan, who had lost money and readers by supporting Dreyfus, had sold the paper to Valentine Simond, who was glad to invite Clemenceau to take charge.

As editor-in-chief he followed the prevailing practice of taking clever young men on to his staff at little or no salary; their office training and the prestige of having their names in print were regarded as adequate returns for their services. The most notable of his apprentices was a young Jew who had a letter of introduction from Joseph Reinach. His real surname was Rothschild, but since he wished to become a Left wing journalist he had decided that such a name was inappropriate, and instead he had taken his mother's maiden name. So it was under the name of Georges Mandel that he came to ask Clemenceau for a job, thus beginning a memorable association which was to be especially close during the First World War.

Clemenceau's reception of Mandel was typical of his rather equivocal attitude towards his very much younger colleague. Mandel was not yet twenty, and he had already written a few articles in *Le Siècle*. At the end of their interview Clemenceau led him into the writers' room and said: 'Gentlemen, I present to you your new colleague, Georges Mandel. From now on he will write for our paper a column on foreign affairs. I have just assured myself, after an hour's talk with him, that he knows nothing about them. That was what I wanted; one should not have prejudices in these matters.'

In fact, Mandel was remarkably well-informed and knew the whole history of the Third Republic, including every relevant fact and date. His articles were clear, competent and well-balanced, but Clemenceau persisted in making the new recruit the butt of his humour. The young man was slight and pale: Clemenceau called him 'the shrimp' and 'my friend Pierrot', and once observed that 'Mandel would know everything if he knew how to write'. Another of his witty but wounding comments was, 'Mandel has no ideas, but he would defend them to the death.'

One of the more experienced young writers on *L'Aurore* was Emile Buré, who later became editor of *L'Ordre*. Buré took due note of the editor-in-chief's biting criticisms of his staff, and it was he who said, as he heard Clemenceau's step on the staircase, 'Look out! Here comes the tiger!' It was thus from the offices of *L'Aurore*, between 1903 and 1906, that an unforgettable nickname passed into history.[1]

---

[1] When the origin of Clemenceau's nickname was discussed by correspondents of *L'Intermédiaire des Chercheurs et des Curieux* (the French *Notes and Queries*) in 1930, Buré's claim to have invented it was put forward and finally accepted as authentic. But there are other theories. Gustave Geffroy surprisingly asserts that Clemenceau was already called the Tiger *'par blague Parisienne'* when he founded *La Justice* in 1880, and others believe that the name originated when he was the dreaded *tombeur de ministères*; yet there appears to be no direct nineteenth-century reference to it, and (which is surely significant) it was never used or alluded to in the invective and satire directed against Clemenceau by Drumont, Déroulède and Barrès. One would imagine, then, that the name was not brought into use until the twentieth century; it was certainly current in 1909, for Barrès, who frequently mentions Clemenceau in his private

Clemenceau was sixty-one when he became editor-in-chief of *L'Aurore*. In addition to controlling its editorial policy he wrote a daily article for it, and he contributed occasionally to the *Neue Freie Presse* of Vienna. He had also his senatorial duties, and he rightly told Georg Brandes that he had not much leisure. '*A mon age, c'est probablement le dernier coup de feu,*' he added.

In that, at least, he was wrong.

[4]

In the year when Clemenceau became a senator Waldeck-Rousseau resigned from the premiership and a new Chamber of Deputies was elected. The election of 1902 was notable for the successful campaign of a new *bloc des Gauches*, including Socialists, Radical Socialists, Radicals and the moderates of Poincaré's Democratic Republic Alliance. Against it was a coalition of Right wing groups—monarchists, nationalists and Catholic *ralliés*, i.e. Catholics who had obeyed the Pope's injunction that they should come to terms with the Republic. Favoured by *scrutin d'arrondissement*, the Left *bloc* won 321 seats against its rivals' 268, but the close vote confirmed the sharp post-Dreyfus division between the two Frances—one hierarchic, clerical, traditionalist, heir to the *ancien régime*, the other egalitarian, laic, individualist, heir to the Revolution. This conflict was now being exacerbated by the factious manoeuvres of a new Right wing group known as the *Action Française*, which was founded as a nationalist organisation in 1899 and was soon to become royalist.

The Radicals had undergone an important change during Clemenceau's absence from parliament. In 1901 their various groups had been merged in the new Radical and Radical Socialist party—the great French national party of the early twentieth century. Clemenceau was not consulted about this development, and he would not, in any case, have been sympathetic towards it, for he did not believe in parties in the English or American sense, and he never belonged to one. 'One travels with a colleague as long as one agrees with him,' he wrote in *Le Bloc*, 'One separates from him at

Cahiers, calls him Tiger for the first time on 21 July of that year. Apart from Buré, others who claim to have invented the name are the journalist Etienne Chichet, who asserts that it originated during Clemenceau's first ministry, when he (Chichet) and his friends told a deputy that Clemenceau had 'sprung like a tiger' against an opponent, and Urbain Gohier, on the rather weak ground that he used the phrase, '*Le tigre s'éveillait*', in an article in *Fantasio* in 1908. The Buré version is surely the right one. (*See L'Intermédiaire des Chercheurs et des Curieux*, 15 December, 1930; Geffroy, *Georges Clemenceau, sa vie, son oeuvre*, p. 56; Barrès, *Cahiers*, VII, pp. 256, 362; Chichet, *Feuilles Volantes*, pp. 217–18; Wormser, *La République de Clemenceau*, p. 9n.)

the first sign of marked differences of opinion.' His views could hardly commend themselves to men who were anxious to form the Radicals into a closely-knit party, and he had no share in the new Radical leadership, which was in the hands of Pelletan, Goblet, Léon Bourgeois and Ferdinand Buisson.

He remained, however, a Radical elder statesman, and since Radicals were now included in every government he could expect to be offered a ministerial post when he was fully re-established in politics. But this could not happen while Loubet was President of the Republic, for Loubet regarded his name as a synonym for excess and violence. 'As long as I am at the Elysée, Clemenceau will not be a minister,' he told his friends.

Clemenceau's return to active politics was made under a new prime minister. Emile Combes, whom Waldeck-Rousseau had named as his successor, was a Radical senator who had studied for the priesthood before becoming a doctor of medicine. He was a fanatical anti-clerical, and regarded himself, in Sir Denis Brogan's words, as 'a delegate of the majority for a special purpose, the extirpation of the clerical menace'.

Though Clemenceau shared Combes's desire for the separation of Church and State, he had reservations about the prime minister's particular brand of anti-clericalism, which did not accord with his own belief in the freedom of the individual. He was now less certain than he had been as a young man about the necessity of compulsory lay education for all. In his maiden speech in the Senate, which was not made until October, he proclaimed the fundamental opposition between the French Revolution and the counter-Revolution of the Roman Catholic Church, but argued that the Church should not be deprived of the right to teach its young; there should be liberty for everyone, and a father should be free to choose the kind of education he thought best for his child. 'If there were ever a conflict between the Republic and liberty,' he said, 'the Republic would be on the wrong side, and I should choose liberty.'

His powerful speech showed that he was still an orator to be reckoned with. When he returned to the subject of educational freedom in 1903, he did so in a way which caused the enraptured Charles Péguy to place him in line with Montaigne, Rabelais, Descartes, Molière, Pascal and Rousseau as a champion of the plain man against the doctrinaires. His speech turned both on Combes's attempts to prohibit teaching by members of religious communities and on other Radicals' desire to bring all teaching under State control. He saw a dangerous monopoly in this proposal: 'I reject the omnipotence of the secular State,' he said, 'because I see it as a tyranny.' In a gallant defence of his liberal creed, in which authority was justified only for the protection of the individual, and should never be allowed to grow into oppression and tyranny, he declared:

We made the French Revolution. Our fathers thought it was to win freedom; not at all, it was to change our master. We have guillotined the King; long live the State-King! We have dethroned the Pope; long live the State-Pope! We are casting out God, as these gentlemen on the Right say; long live the State-God!

Péguy tells us that Lintilhac, the senator whose indiscreet speech had brought Clemenceau to his feet, sat miserably in his place, trying vainly to repel the first attacks and finally sitting back dumbfounded until the onslaught was over.

Though commenting daily on both home and foreign affairs in *L'Aurore*, Clemenceau made few important speeches in the Senate under Combes's ministry, which lasted two years and seven months. Combes at first thought that the new senator's interventions 'rivalled the wisdom of the wise', but the two men quarrelled over a question of patronage. Clemenceau wanted his secretary Winter to be made director of a public institution, but Combes gave the post to a prefect whom he wished to move. 'Henceforth,' he wrote in his memoirs, 'I had him [Clemenceau] as a determined enemy, and I am sorry to say that, in the last five months of my ministry, I found his hand in all the intrigues hatched against me.'

But the Combes ministry was not brought down by intrigues, whether by Clemenceau or by anyone else. It fell because of its own failings and misdeeds. Socialist deputies deserted Combes because they found his government too reactionary. Others objected to his excessive concentration on anti-clerical legislation to the exclusion of social reform. Finally a storm of protest was aroused by the revelation that General André, minister of war, was using secret files, compiled by freemasons, on army officers' religious affiliations, so that practising Catholics found themselves barred from promotion. It was the files scandal which drove Combes out of office in 1905, leaving the next government to be formed by Rouvier, who had re-established himself in politics after being one of the Panama *chéquards*. He brought members of leading finance houses into the cabinet, and Clemenceau grumbled: 'It isn't a ministry, it's a board of directors.'

[5]

Théophile Delcassé, who had been foreign minister since 1899, was one of the previous ministers whom Rouvier kept in his cabinet. It was under his guidance, and with the eager cooperation of King Edward VII, that the statesmen of France and Britain had begun the bargaining which led to the Anglo-French *entente* of 1904. The bargain provided that France would support British policy in Egypt in return for British support of French policy in Morocco. Nothing was arranged about Anglo-French military cooperation in Europe.

The Franco-Russian alliance was another corner-stone of Delcassé's foreign policy. His devotion to it brought him a sharp rebuke from Clemenceau early in 1905.

It was on 22 January of this year that an unarmed procession of Russian workers, on its way to petition the Tsar, was shot down by troops in front of the Winter Palace in St. Petersburg. Socialists in the French Chamber denounced the massacre, but Delcassé, fearful of anything that might imperil the Russian alliance, told them not to interfere. 'You are not judges,' he said, 'and even if you were, there are not sufficient data on which to arrive at an impartial judgement.' Clemenceau was shocked by the minister's remarks. 'Nothing,' he wrote in *L'Aurore* on 31 January, 'can excuse M. Delcassé for having attempted to justify the massacre in the face of humanity's world-wide condemnation. This misguided man is still beglamoured by his visits to St. Petersburg.'

The Tsar's misdeeds were of less importance to France than the Moroccan crisis which burst upon Europe in March. France had a long-standing interest in Moroccan affairs because of her possession of the neighbouring country of Algeria; after a period of anarchy in Morocco at the end of the nineteenth century she had acquired suzerainty over certain 'zones of influence', in return for which she agreed to help the Sultan to preserve order and maintain his authority. By the end of 1904 Delcassé was making plans for the economic, military and financial reconstruction of Morocco, which would have turned it into a French protectorate. He secured the approval of the three most interested European countries—Britain, Spain and Italy—but did not trouble to consult Germany, which had no rights in Morocco.

This was a mistake. Count von Bülow, the German Chancellor, felt that it was time for Germany to declare her interest in north Africa. On Bülow's advice, Kaiser Wilhelm II landed at Tangier, on the north coast of Morocco, during his annual spring cruise in the Mediterranean, and informed the French *chargé d'affaires* that Germany claimed equal rights in Morocco and recognised the Sultan as the ruler of an independent country. It was the gesture known in French history as the *coup de Tanger*.

French reactions were mixed. Rouvier saw the gesture as a threat of war. Delcassé was convinced that Germany was bluffing. Clemenceau, who still opposed colonial expansion, thought that the Kaiser's remarks should be taken seriously and that France should discuss the Moroccan problem with Germany. 'We should be mad,' he wrote, 'to persist in this game of china dogs.[1] . . . We have certain explanations to ask of Germany.

---

[1] '*jeu de chiens de faïence*': i.e. glaring at one another with fixed expressions.

Nothing is simpler than to ask for them, since we are certain in advance that the conversation will be most courteous and that an understanding is inevitable.'

Delcassé was unshaken. Apart from his confidence that Germany would not make war over Morocco, he believed that Britain would come to France's aid if Germany attacked her; he was also hoping to act as a mediator in the Russo-Japanese War, which had been in progress since February 1904, and he felt that success in this task would increase France's prestige and indirectly strengthen her position in Morocco. Rouvier did not share his foreign minister's views. He knew that the morale of the French army had not yet recovered from the Dreyfus Affair; he was told by the service chiefs that frontier defences were inadequate and that there were shortages of ammunition and equipment. For two months he lived in fear of invasion, and he had private information from Germany that there was no hope of Franco-German reconciliation as long as Delcassé was at the Quai d'Orsay.

Early in June he decided to dismiss Delcassé, and it is noteworthy that he consulted Clemenceau before doing so. Clemenceau raised no objection: he knew of France's military weakness, and though he regarded war with Germany as almost inevitable he did not think that the Moroccan issue was a good occasion for it. Most of the newspapers took the same line; apart from the nationalist press, there was a chorus of approval when Delcassé's resignation was announced. But Clemenceau now shared Rouvier's view that a serious threat lay behind the *coup de Tanger*. On 19 June he wrote in *L'Aurore*: 'To be or not to be, that is the problem now raised for us for the first time since the Hundred Years' War.' And a week later, at a reception at the British embassy, he said: 'From now on we cannot draw back. . . . If Germany wants war, very well then, we will fight.'

[6]

The year of the Tangier crisis was also the year in which Aristide Briand made his reputation as *rapporteur* of the parliamentary commission dealing with the separation of Church and State. Briand, who was then forty-three, was a Socialist lawyer who had once supported militant trade unionism and advocated the use of the general strike, but had modified his views as the prospect of ministerial office drew nearer. He was a fine speaker, with a magnificent voice, but he was indolent and often ill-informed; Jaurès once said of him that he had 'an encyclopaedic ignorance'. He was essentially a negotiator, and in 1905 he was so anxious to make the separation law acceptable to the Church that he reminded Pelletan of the eleventh-century Emperor Henry IV submitting to Pope Gregory VII at Canossa. 'Is the road to Canossa beautiful?' Pelletan asked Clemenceau. 'I don't know,' Clemenceau answered. 'Briand is taking us there in a closed carriage!'

The separation law was passed in July, though it was not promulgated until December. It made the State completely neutral in religious matters, assuring liberty of conscience and freedom of worship but neither recognising nor subsidising any religion. The salaries paid by the State to clergy under the Napoleonic Concordat were to cease, and the buildings used for worship or for ministers' residences would remain the property of the State, the departments and the communes. But it was not intended that such buildings should be confiscated: local congregations were invited to form religious associations (*associations cultuelles*), which would take charge of the property, both movable and immovable. To facilitate this procedure, inventories of all Church property were to be made by State officials within a year.

In the long run separation was a good thing for both Church and State, but there were difficulties at the beginning. The Pope condemned the proposal to form *associations cultuelles*, and very few were set up. The taking of inventories was bitterly resented by local congregations, who feared that it might be the first step towards expropriation of the Church's goods, and the unrest was exploited by members of the *Action Française*, who seized the opportunity of staging anti-government demonstrations. Priests and army officers stood at church doors to prevent government officials from entering; the police were attacked with stones and chair-legs at two Paris churches, and in the country men guarded churches with shot-guns and pitchforks, wolf-traps were set for the police, and wild bears were chained in church porches. Two demonstrators were killed in the riots; it would be Clemenceau's task to restore order.

His long wait for office was ending at last. The two major events of 1905—the *coup de Tanger* and the separation law—helped to bring down the government. Rouvier had prudently agreed that Moroccan problems should be discussed at an international conference, but many deputies felt that French prestige was affronted when the conference opened at Algeciras, in southern Spain, in January 1906. Rouvier was also blamed for the rioting and unrest which accompanied the taking of church inventories, and his ministry fell in February. By that time, ironically enough, the Algeciras conference had swung in France's favour, since all the participating countries, except Germany and Austria-Hungary, were ready to recognise her special interests in Morocco.

With Rouvier's fall the road to ministerial office was open at last to Clemenceau. President Loubet, who would never have allowed him to become a minister, had completed his seven-year term in January; it was the task of a new president—the genial Armand Fallières—to appoint the next prime minister and to approve his cabinet. After his successful return to parliament Senator Clemenceau was an automatic choice for a government post.

CHAPTER ELEVEN

MINISTER OF THE INTERIOR

1. 'The old beginner'. 2. Workers' challenge. 3. 'Duel' with Jaurès.

[1]

FALLIÈRES WAS an easy-going president who had no wish to encroach upon ministers' powers. To succeed Rouvier as prime minister he chose Ferdinand Sarrien, the influential leader of the moderate Radicals who supported all governments. He was regarded as a sphinx because he spoke little in the corridors of the Palais-Bourbon and not at all in the debating chamber, but Clemenceau maliciously called him 'a sphinx with a calf's head'. He knew the Chamber well, and had been, like Clemenceau, one of the 363 who had opposed President MacMahon nearly thirty years earlier.

His cabinet, which was formed on 15 March, 1906, included a number of former ministers like Léon Bourgeois, Gaston Doumergue, Raymond Poincaré (finance) and Louis Barthou (public works), but the two appointments which aroused the greatest interest were those of Clemenceau to the ministry of the interior and Aristide Briand to the ministry of education and public worship (a reward for his patient work as *rapporteur* of the commission dealing with separation of Church and State).

Before announcing the names of his ministers Sarrien invited his future colleagues to a reception at his house in the rue de l'Observatoire, and it was there, as glasses of anisette and orangeade were being offered to the guests, that he genially remarked to Clemenceau, 'What will you have, dear friend?' 'The interior!' said Clemenceau, deliberately misunderstanding the question, and the ministry of the interior was the office he duly received. It had all, of course, been arranged beforehand; Clemenceau's smart rejoinder had no effect on the cabinet-making; and Poincaré, for one, was displeased by the appointment. He wrote in his diary: 'I insisted that Clemenceau, if he entered the ministry, should not be placed at the interior.' This insistence had not affected Sarrien's decision.

So in his sixty-fifth year Clemenceau was at last in charge of a government department, and characteristically he had chosen to be placed in 'the hot seat'. At the time when he took office the inventory riots were

7 'Le pas du commandité' ('The partner's dance') (1893)

8 Back to politics:
Clemenceau as senator
talking to Adolphe Aderer,
parliamentary corresponden
of *Le Temps* (1903):
drawing by Noël Dorville

9 Clemenceau saying
good-bye to a woman
delegate after the
conference at the Ministry
of the Interior which
ended the postal workers'
strike, 1909

10 The first issue of *L'Homme Libre*, 5 May 1913 (Musée Clemenceau)

11 The first issue of *L'Homme Enchaîné*, 30 September 1914 (Musée Clemenceau)

12 Editor and elder statesman, Clemenceau before the First World War

continuing, and the Confédération Générale du Travail had called a nation-wide general strike for the first of May. No government post would be more onerous than that of the minister of the interior.

Clemenceau's translation to the ministry's headquarters in the place Beauvau caused a temporary break in his journalistic career. His last article appeared in *L'Aurore* on 11 March, but he took some of his staff to the ministry with him. At first he refused to find a place for Georges Mandel, but he soon relented, and Mandel was allowed to work for Albert Sarraut, a member of the family which owned *La Dépêche de Toulouse*, who was appointed under-secretary for the interior when Clemenceau became prime minister. In time Mandel was transferred to the Tiger's own staff, and he showed great ability in keeping his master informed about the contents of the day's papers and the whispers in the corridors of the Palais-Bourbon. Though he often infuriated Clemenceau, he gradually made himself indispensable, and so paved the way towards the important position he was to hold in the First World War.

Clemenceau was pleasantly epigrammatic about his late assumption of power. 'In life,' he said, 'one is always beginning. I am an old beginner.' But he was not impressed by his first contacts with his department. With his secretary Winter he made a tour of the ministry to see his staff at work. The first two rooms were empty; the occupant of the third was asleep, with his elbows on the table. Winter stepped forward to awaken the sleeper, but Clemenceau stopped him. 'Don't wake him,' he said. 'He'd go away!'

He soon found that senior bureaucrats took their duties lightly. When Berta Szeps called on him at the ministry she saw a pile of notices on his desk, reading 'Gentlemen are requested not to leave the office before they arrive.' He told her that the ministry was a desert when he got there at nine o'clock, and his colleagues assured him that he had no chance of seeing one of the bureaucratic pillars of the State before 10.30. Since other sanctions had failed to make them mend their ways, he was going, he said, to see what could be done by ridicule.[1]

Besides dealing with the civil servants of the place Beauvau, the minister of the interior controlled the prefects of France's ninety-four departments. They found him a stern taskmaster, who kept them firmly in their place, frequently asked them to submit written reports or summoned them peremptorily to Paris for oral questioning, and sometimes played off one

[1] Georges Wormser says that these notices were issued to the editorial staff of *L'Aurore*, not to the staff at the place Beauvau (*La République de Clemenceau*, p. 206). Since Berta Szeps claims that she actually saw the notices at the ministry of the interior (*Clemenceau tel que je l'ai connu*, p. 153), Clemenceau may have been repeating with the civil servants a ploy he had first tried out on the journalists.

prefect against another. According to Léon Daudet, he was particularly angry with prefects who slept with their subordinates' wives. Yet he could be generous when he was in the mood, as can be seen from a story current in 1908 about a visit from a prefect who, he had been told in advance, was incredibly ugly. The Tiger took one look at him, exclaimed '*Ah, nom de Dieu!*' and hurried from the room to his *chef de cabinet's* office.[1] '*Ah, nom de Dieu,*' he repeated, 'give him some promotion. He really *is* ugly.'

One can well imagine that both the higher civil servants and the prefects were suspicious of their new minister's intentions; certainly Louis Lépine, the very conservative prefect of police, greeted Clemenceau without enthusiasm. Yet even a brief spell of working together brought about a remarkable change in Lépine's opinion of the minister. 'Six months later,' he wrote in his memoirs, 'no one would have recognised us. In the interval, to my great surprise, I had discovered that a man of government lay behind the trouble-maker.'

Clemenceau had barely arrived in the place Beauvau before he was called on to show his qualities as 'a man of government'. Though most of the church inventories had now been completed without serious trouble, the remainder included many which were likely to cause a revival of serious rioting. As an anticlerical, Clemenceau was not usually disposed to give in to the clergy, but as a minister he saw no point in exacerbating a difficult situation. He therefore prevented further rioting by telling prefects only to take inventories in churches where there was no likelihood of resistance. 'The question of knowing whether or not one should count the number of candlesticks in a church is not worth a single human life,' he told the Senate.

His action was doubly effective, for besides maintaining order it robbed his Catholic opponents of the chance of exploiting the inventories trouble in the coming general election. But the unrest on the industrial front would not be disposed of so easily.

[2]

The merging in 1902 of the trade union movement's two big industrial organisations—the Confédération Générale du Travail and the Fédération

---

[1] A minister's *chef de cabinet* is his principal private secretary, the other members of the *cabinet* being secretaries or assistants recruited by the minister on assuming office. Winter, who was Clemenceau's *chef de cabinet* at the ministry of the interior, had been his secretary for some years. In certain circumstances the *chef de cabinet* may become virtually an under-secretary of state. This was to happen in 1917–18, when Georges Mandel was Clemenceau's right-hand man at the war ministry.

des Bourses du Travail—was the first sign of a concerted challenge by workers to established authority. The name of the larger body, the CGT, was retained, but the Fédération des Bourses imbued the combined organisations with its own syndicalist doctrine. Thus the trade union movement was committed to a revolutionary syndicalist programme aimed at emancipating the proletariat by expropriating the capitalists and putting the workers in full possession and control of factories and workshops. These changes were to be brought about by a general strike, not by political action, since syndicalists were opposed to the State as well as to employers, and denounced 'the danger and sterility of government institutions'. At its congress at Bourges in 1904 the CGT chose 1906 as a year for action; the general strike arranged to begin on 1 May was designed to secure an eight-hour day for all workers.

By chance the strike wave began nearly two months before May Day. Early in March the biggest mining disaster in French history occurred in five pits near Courrières, in the Pas-de-Calais department, where more than 1,200 men were killed. The surviving miners, who blamed their employers for lack of adequate safety measures, went on strike for higher pay.[1] Two unions were involved—the old miners' union, which was autonomous and covered about seven-tenths of the work-force, and a younger, anarchist union which was affiliated to the CGT. In a short time 61,000 miners in the Pas-de-Calais and Nord departments were on strike.

On taking office Clemenceau had told Emile Buré, 'As a minister I shall try to put into practice my ideas as a journalist.' One of these ideas, which he had aired in *La Justice* a dozen years earlier, was that a minister should himself go to the scene of an industrial dispute and discuss the situation with the strikers. He went to Lens on 26 March.

His actions in connection with the miners' strike have been described as tactless and brutal—tactless, because he saw the leader of the 'young' union as well as the leader of the old one, and brutal because he eventually sent in troops to keep order. Such criticism may not be entirely fair. It is true that Basly, leader of the old union, grumbled about Clemenceau's visit to Monatte, acting leader of the rival body, but as a minister he would hardly have been doing his duty if he had heard the arguments of only one section of the strikers and had ignored the other. Moreover, his desire to avoid violence was genuine; for a short time he must really have believed that he was opening a new era in industrial relations. As he told the members of Monatte's union:

I have not come here to take part in discussions between the two

---

[1] 'Miners invariably translate protests about the ghastliness of their situation into demands for pay increases.' (Shorter and Tilley, *Strikes in France, 1830–1968*, p. 385.)

unions. I have come here as a member of the government which is
responsible for allowing you to exercise freely your rights and your
liberties. The right to strike is absolute. I can promise you that it will
be fully maintained as long as you respect the law. . . . But there is
another right—that of persons and property. . . . For the first time in a
strike you do not see troops intervening. . . . Show yourselves worthy
of our confidence.

And he promised to keep the troops quartered inside the mining company's
premises so long as there was no violence in the streets.

His hopes were not fulfilled. Acts of violence began to occur in the
middle of April, when there were demonstrations against the prefect and
an attack on the house of the mining company's managing director.
Clemenceau returned to Lens to see what was happening, decided that he
was no longer bound by his promise and sent in the cavalry. An officer
was mortally wounded by a stone thrown by a striker, but the mob in the
streets quickly dispersed when the soldiers loaded their guns. So the old
French formula of troops *versus* strikers was repeated, after all, but
Clemenceau had at least tried to change it. The strike dragged on for
another fortnight, and ended with a compromise worked out between the
company and the old union.

The first of May provided the next major industrial challenge to the
minister of the interior. Many people believed that the CGT's call for a
general strike was a cover for the beginning of a workers' revolution.
Ominous stories went the rounds, like that of the woman who was
supposed to have said: 'My husband's still very ill, and I'm afraid he won't
be better by the first of May. It's annoying, he won't be able to do any
looting.' The general strike was not, in fact, intended to be an immediate
bid for workers' power, but Parisians grimly awaited a day of massacre,
looting and arson, to be followed, perhaps, by a new Reign of Terror.
For fear of food shortages, cows were brought in from the country and
put into stables, hens, rabbits and even sheep were to be seen in the gardens
of Parisian houses. Some of the more credulous citizens, remembering the
Tiger's stormy past, wondered if the minister of the interior might not
have secretly come to terms with the revolutionaries.

In view of public fears and the uncertainty of the CGT's aims,
Clemenceau concentrated 60,000 troops in Paris at the end of April. He
also prohibited all assemblies and processions on the first of May, and he
claimed to have discovered a plot against the Republic, linking the CGT
with the extreme Right. This 'discovery' must have been based, at best, on
flimsy evidence, but it gave him an excuse for arresting Griffuelhes and
Lévy, respectively secretary and treasurer of the CGT, together with

Monatte, the anarchist miners' leader. They were released in a few days for lack of evidence.

Fears of a revolution were soon dispelled. Sporadic rioting occurred in Paris on May Day, and a number of men were arrested; but no one succeeded in putting up barricades in the streets, and the day ended quietly enough. The provinces, too, were calm. Yet the first attempt at a centrally directed national strike had not been a total failure; many workers had responded to it, and in Paris alone 128,000 men, including 72,000 construction workers, were on strike in May. Though the eight-hour-day campaign yielded no results, syndicalism had given an impressive demonstration of its strength.

So, too, had the government, and the outcome of 1 May must have warned the unions that the new minister of the interior might be more than a match for them. In the following months Clemenceau made his position clear. He told a CGT deputation: 'You are behind the barricade; I am in front of it. Your method of action is disorder; my duty is to make order supreme'; and addressing the Chamber, he said, 'I am accused of being in favour of order, and I willingly admit it.'

His words indicated a perceptible change in his attitude since his assumption of power. In the great French division between parties of movement and parties of order he had always been on the side of movement; now, as a man of government, he realised that at all costs order must be maintained. But the new champion of order still retained his impish sense of humour. At the end of May there were rumours of division in the cabinet, and a journalist asked Clemenceau if the difficulties had been settled. 'Yes, all the ministers are agreed on one thing,' he replied. 'They all want to keep their portfolios!' And he turned on his heel and went off, laughing at his own wit.

[3]

The *bloc des Gauches*, which had defeated the monarchists and the nationalists in 1902, was again successful in the election held in May 1906, but its composition had undergone an important change. The Socialists had split up: the orthodox Socialists, now known as the unified Socialists, had broken with the Radicals and were on their own, but some twenty dissident Socialists, most notably Alexandre Millerand and René Viviani, were faithful to the *bloc*, in which, however, there were so many moderate deputies that it was Left wing only in name. The strength of the moderates under a Radical ministry helps to explain the occasionally incoherent government for which Clemenceau was blamed during his period as prime minister.

This summer Clemenceau's biggest parliamentary success was his oratorical 'duel' with Jaurès, the unified Socialists' leader, in the Chamber of Deputies. As a minister, Clemenceau was entitled to speak in either Chamber or Senate if challenged to explain his actions; on this occasion Jaurès's condemnation of Clemenceau's use of troops in the miners' strike led to a lively dialogue on the respective merits of collectivism and individualism.

Jaurès, who was really addressing the nation over the heads of the deputies, gave a clear account of collectivist principles, and asked what use the Republicans were going to make of their victory at the polls. Socialisation, he claimed, was essential; great public works could be undertaken with resources obtained from the wealthy, but there was nothing in the government's programme which would promote social reform.

Clemenceau enjoyed the chance of attacking Socialism. On the strike issue he said that Jaurès was confusing *le droit de grève* and *le droit de matraque*—the right to strike and the right to use a bludgeon, and he declared that Jaurès himself would have to preserve order if he were ever a minister. It was absurd, he added, to say that workers could loot and steal and one must not check them; and when a deputy tried to interrupt him, he cried: 'No! Outside Charenton [the mental institution on the outskirts of Paris] there is no one who could support such a theory.'

In a general attack on collectivism he derided the Socialist leader's 'fairy palaces', which would dissolve in mist at their first contact with reality, and contrasted them with 'the great Republican cathedral', in the making of which he was only a humble artisan. His speech was both serious and satirical, proclaiming his faith in individualism and frequently setting the deputies laughing. One of his sallies was his retort to Jaurès's demand that the government should announce its programme of social reform. To this demand, he observed drily, he had found it hard not to answer, 'My programme? It is in your pocket, you have taken it from me.'

The government had a comfortable majority at the end of the 'duel'. The deputies also voted that Clemenceau's speech should have the honour of *affichage*, i.e. that a copy should be displayed in the town hall or *mairie* in every commune in France, where it might or might not be read by passers-by. Barrès thought at the time that Jaurès had the better of the argument, but that Clemenceau pleased the deputies infinitely more because of his sallies and witticisms. The arguments on both sides seem old-fashioned now, and indeed, two clever young men thought them already out of date in 1906. On 3 July Jacques Rivière wrote to his friend Alain-Fournier, the future author of *Le Grand Meaulnes*: 'You are right; the Jaurès-Clemenceau spouting is grotesque.'

It was significant that Clemenceau made official tours of both the Vendée and the Var during the parliamentary recess. He probably knew that he would soon be prime minister, and it was good publicity to show himself outside Paris. In the Vendée he spoke of his boyhood and the influence of his father, 'to whom I owe everything'; his speech at La Roche-sur-Yon, glorifying the Vendean way of life, amazed Albert de Mun, a Catholic deputy, who had always pictured Clemenceau as entirely Parisian and had never imagined that he shared Barrès's devotion to the soil of France. 'For a moment,' de Mun wrote, 'one thought that national- ism had triumphed and that Maurice Barrès was prime minister.'

A speech at Draguignan showed how far the Tiger had moved since his old days on the extreme Left. After four years as a senator he warmly defended the Senate because it provided an opportunity for the recon- sideration of reckless decisions. The art of government, he further declared, lay in the mixture of reform and conservation, and the spirit of timidity was no less dangerous than the spirit of adventure. Here, indeed, was a more pacific side of the Tiger's nature.

Parliament was due to meet for a special session in October. A few days before the appointed date Sarrien resigned on account of ill-health and advised Fallières to send for Clemenceau. Unlike most of his predecessors, Fallières had no objection to having a strong man as prime minister. He invited Clemenceau to form the next government.

CHAPTER TWELVE

PRIME MINISTER

1. *Cabinet-making.* 2. *Strikes and protests.* 3. *The Villeneuve 'massacre'.*
4. Entente cordiale. 5. *Germany and Morocco.* 6. *The poisoned arrow.*

[1]

AT SIXTY-FIVE Clemenceau looked young for his years. Everyone knew that round-shouldered, squarish figure, the bald head, the grey moustache, the sallow complexion and the bushy eyebrows; and though 'the Tiger' was becoming his usual nickname, some called him 'the Kalmuck' because of his Mongolian appearance.

With his top hat still on the side of his head, and carrying a walking-stick wherever he went, he looked more like a *boulevardier* than a prime minister. He brought, it seemed, some of the fragrance of the Second Empire to the sober Third Republic. Yet the nonchalant exterior was in some ways deceptive, for he was no longer a connoisseur of Parisian night-life. He was more likely to be in bed at midnight and up again at four o'clock, thus making time for a formidable working day.

Though for some months the opposition press usually referred to him as 'the former destroyer of ministries', his appointment was generally well received. Even Jaurès, writing in the Socialist paper, *L'Humanité*, approved of it, on the ground that he was the real leader of the Radical Socialists in parliament and should therefore bear the responsibility for their actions.

Only two days were needed for the formation of his ministry. Two well-known names were missing from it: Léon Bourgeois, foreign minister in Sarrien's cabinet, made ill-health his excuse for not serving under Clemenceau; and Poincaré stood down from the ministry of finance because the Chamber's budget commission did not agree with his views. The vacancies were easily filled: the foreign ministry was an appropriate haven for Clemenceau's old friend Stephen Pichon, who had worked in the diplomatic service since the death of *La Justice*, and the brilliant but unprincipled Joseph Caillaux, financial expert and *grand bourgeois*, was given his chance at the ministry of finance. From the old ministry Barthou (public works) and Briand (education and public worship) kept their posts. Clemenceau stayed at the ministry of the interior, since it was customary for a French prime minister also to hold one of the principal ministries.

Two new appointments caused some surprise. General Picquart, who as Colonel Picquart had done much to establish Dreyfus's innocence, became minister of war; René Viviani, independent Socialist, was given the new post of minister of labour.

Picquart had been a close friend of Clemenceau since the critical years of 'the Affair'. His appointment was clearly a reward for past services, but Clemenceau's loyalty to a friend seems to have outweighed his good judgement. Picquart was admired in intellectual circles as a music-lover, a man of letters and a linguist, but he had no great military reputation; Barrès thought he would have been better as a professor of philosophy than as a soldier.

Even the Tiger found it hard to give a rational explanation of his choice of Picquart as war minister and, a year or two later, of the undistinguished Alfred Picard as minister of marine. When Charles Benoist suggested that his real motive was 'Because no one but you would have thought of appointing them', he could only reply, 'There is something in that.'

A more enterprising feature of his cabinet-making was the establishment of a ministry of labour. The idea was not new. As far back as 1848 Louis Blanc had aired it in the National Assembly, it had been discussed in the 1880s and 1890s, and in 1903 the Senate's finance commission had approved it in principle. But it was left to Clemenceau to carry it out, by forming a ministry authorised to examine the principles of workers' contracts with their employers, to ensure that conditions of work should not compromise health or safety, and to find ways of providing means of subsistence for those who were temporarily or permanently unable to work. It was presumably because of this last objective that the words 'and of social insurance' were added to the ministry's title.

Clemenceau's inclusion of a Socialist in his government may seem inconsistent with his denunciations of Socialism in his 'duel' with Jaurès, but it was a sound tactical move, designed to win trade union approval for the new ministry. The ministry of labour was, in fact, one of the durable results of Clemenceau's first term of office as prime minister. Viviani held the post for four years, and had the satisfaction of seeing the ministry firmly based before he left it in 1910. It is a pleasant paradox that this creation of the great strike-breaking prime minister was soon to be regarded by trade unionists as 'their' ministry.

When Clemenceau formed his second administration in 1917 he was criticised for filling it with henchmen and mediocrities. No one could have brought that charge against his 1906 cabinet, which contained most of the ministerial talent available in the middle period of the Third Republic. Among its members Briand, Caillaux, Barthou, Viviani and Doumergue were future prime ministers, and the last-named was also a future president.

Many of the ministers and under-secretaries were given nicknames by Clemenceau. Caillaux and Barthou became '*Les deux gosses*', Thomson (minister of marine) '*le petit Mousse*', Millies-Lacroix (minister for the colonies) '*le Nègre*' and Chéron (Picquart's under-secretary) '*le Cid de Normandie*'. Clemenceau's fondness for giving nicknames became known outside the cabinet room and was mentioned in a popular farce.[1]

With his new ministry established, Clemenceau put forward a legislative programme which included many of the social changes he had been advocating for a quarter-of-a-century. He promised a total of seventeen reforms, among them the long overdue introduction of income tax (which had always been fiercely opposed by progressists and Right wing parties), a ten-hour working day, retirement pensions for workers, better compensation for industrial accidents, new civil rights for trade unions, increased State control of mines and the State purchase of the Western railway company. After this hopeful start it was unfortunate that the first measure which the new parliament actually passed, in circumstances that Goguel describes as 'strangely rapid and surreptitious', was one increasing the salaries of deputies and senators from 9,000 francs (£360) to 15,000 francs (£600) a year. The workers were not pleased.

[2]

The main business in the first winter of Clemenceau's government was the introduction of the measure for the State purchase of the Western railway. Here, too, he may seem to have been acting inconsistently in sponsoring a piece of apparently Socialist legislation, but the Western railway, though an essential part of the national transport system, was uneconomic, and the private company which ran it already owed the government 400m. francs. Since so much State money was at stake, there was a strong case for taking the railway over and setting an example to private companies of how railways should be run. After being passed by

---

[1] In Georges Feydeau's farce, *Mais n'te promène donc pas toute nue*, produced in 1911, a deputy reproves his wife for walking about the house in her night-gown and taking baths without drawing the curtain, so that she can be seen by anyone looking through the window, for example, by Clemenceau, who lives in the house opposite. The wife makes light of it ('*Bah! il en a vu bien d'autres, Clemenceau!*'), but the husband insists that it is a serious matter, because Clemenceau is 'our leading comic'. 'If he makes a joke about me or gives me a nickname, he can ruin me!' (*See* Feydeau, *Théâtre Complet*, VIII, p. 249.)

the Chamber of Deputies, the railway bill was roughly handled in the Senate, and Clemenceau had to make it a matter of confidence before it was passed into law with a tiny majority. This was the only one of his proposed seventeen reforms which was actually carried out.

On the religious front Briand continued his task of separating Church and State without unduly antagonising the clergy; but here the government was taken aback by the Church's almost universal refusal to form religious associations to look after its goods and property. It was this unexpected refusal which inspired Clemenceau's tactless remark in the Chamber on 39 January, 1907, that 'The separation law provided for everything except what has happened. . . . We are in full incoherence.'

The remark sounded like a snub for Briand, who had largely shaped the measure; he angrily left the Chamber after Clemenceau had spoken. It was an awkward moment, for Briand's resignation might easily have brought down the government. To avert danger, Clemenceau hurried after the outraged minister and brought him back to the Chamber amid general applause.

The episode was a reminder that, even as prime minister, Clemenceau could not resist the temptation to make his famous sallies. Madame Arman de Caillavet, who heard all the political gossip in her *salon*, joked about it in a letter to their common friend, Georg Brandes. 'The other day,' she wrote, 'Clemenceau, with one of his sallies, nearly brought down the government, of which he had forgotten that he was a member.'

A wave of strikes and protests was now to put anti-clericalism into the background and to show France that she had a strong man at the head of the government. This was the period in which Clemenceau gaily called himself *'le premier flic de France'*—'France's number one cop'.

The first industrial challenge came from the electricity workers, who began a strike which blacked out many houses and other buildings in Paris for two nights. Clemenceau took it in his stride. He simultaneously encouraged the electricity company to come to terms with the strikers and announced that, if the strike went on, he would bring in army engineers to run the central services. Work was soon resumed.

It was then the turn of the *fonctionnaires*—France's vast army of civil servants—to stake their claim for the right to form unions. At the end of March 1907 an open letter to the prime minister appeared as a poster in the streets of Paris. It was signed by teachers, sub-postmasters, prison wardens, customs officers and others, and declared that they would continue to fight 'for a right which was an essential attribute of human personality.' Clemenceau was unmoved. The signatories of the letter were brought before disciplinary councils, and six were dismissed.

Clemenceau's attitude was that civil servants could form themselves into professional associations, but they could not become affiliated to the revolutionary CGT, because they were servants of the State. 'One is not obliged to become a public servant,' he said in the Chamber of Deputies on 7 May, 'but if one does, one has certain obligations to fulfil. . . . No government will ever accept that people in public service should be assimilated to industrial workers. A contract binds them to the nation. Their place is neither at the labour exchange nor at the CGT.'

In the same debate he explained that he believed in a strong trade union movement, but he would not tolerate anarchy and anti-patriotism. 'The present government,' he said, 'offers a policy which combines the repression of disorder with reform and conciliation,' and he took the opportunity of lecturing those Radicals who still looked to Combes as their leader and attacked the government in their newspapers, though they would not dare to do so in the Chamber. 'I have had enough,' he declared. 'I do not wish to be strangled by the mutes of the harem.' If they had charges to bring against him, let them do so openly. 'Speak up! The rostrum is here for you. *Messieurs les Radicaux, je vous attend!*'

It was the wine-growers' protest which caused the gravest trouble in 1907. Since the planting of new vines to make good the havoc caused by phylloxera in the nineteenth century, the French wine-growing industry had begun to suffer from over-production, particularly in the southern departments of Aude, Hérault, Gard and Pyrenées-Orientales, where the price of wine had fallen by more than fifty per cent in two years. The crisis was due to over-plantation of new vines, but the wine-growers, who in those areas were mostly peasants, blamed everything on the competition of 'fraudulent' wine produced by *sucrage* and *mouillage*—i.e. sugaring to make it stronger and watering to increase its quantity.

The growers asked the government to find a remedy before 10 June, and as the day grew nearer huge demonstrations were held in the four departments. The leader of the protests was a peasant called Marcellin Albert, who was grandly known as 'the Redeemer'. When no action had been taken by the appointed day the organising committee called for a strike and the resignation of all the mayors and municipal councils.

At first Clemenceau did not take the protests seriously. When Caillaux reproached him for allowing the railway to run special trains for people attending the demonstrations, he said airily, 'You don't understand, Caillaux. You don't know the south. It will all end with a banquet.' But the new moves called for his intervention, and as minister of the interior he wrote to all the local mayors, promising action against fraudulent practices and asking them to resume their posts, but adding that force would be used if necessary. This threat caused the resignation of his under-secretary Albert Sarraut, who was deputy for Narbonne, in the department of Aude, and felt that he could not cooperate with the government in using force against his own constituents. But the wine-growers' rebellion continued.

Clemenceau now acted vigorously. Three members of the organising committee were arrested, but three others, including Marcellin Albert, could not be found. One of those arrested was the former mayor of Narbonne; that evening barricades went up in the Narbonne streets, and the sub-prefecture was burnt down. The prefecture at Perpignan was also burnt by demonstrators, and troops sent to restore order had to fire live cartridges, since they were attacked and suffered casualties while they were firing blank. Most of the 17th infantry regiment, which was sent from Béziers to the worst affected area, mutinied and joined the rioters—an action which Jaurès described as 'the greatest social fact of the last thirty-five years.'

Clemenceau also acted in parliament. A law to prevent wine frauds was passed by the Chamber on 22 June, by the Senate a few days later, and promulgated on 29 June. It was at this point that Marcellin Albert un-expectedly turned up in Paris and asked to see Clemenceau. He apparently hoped to put everything straight by a personal appeal, but Clemenceau told him to go home and surrender to his arrest. Astutely he gave Albert a hundred francs for his railway fare, and told the press that he had done so; 'the Redeemer's' acceptance of government money shattered his prestige, and he never regained his former influence. As July went on, the strikers wanted to return to normal conditions. Since the law against wine frauds had made a good impression in the south, they resumed work by the end of the month.

It was generally thought that Clemenceau's clever handling of 'the Redeemer' had been a decisive factor in securing a settlement. Yet the simplest solution of all would have been an offer of economic assistance to the small wine-grower, taking account of the problems raised by mono-culture and seeking to reconcile the interests of growers and merchants. It is unlikely that Clemenceau even thought of this solution. Robert Dell was hardly exaggerating when he wrote of Clemenceau in 1920: 'His greatest admirer would not venture to say that he ever grasped even the elementary data of an economic problem or ever thought it worth while to do so.'

[3]

The outskirts of Paris, where labourers had come from all over France to work on Métro extensions, were the scene of the worst industrial trouble in 1908. In June the quarrymen at Draveil-Vigneux came out on strike, and two of them were killed in clashes with the gendarmerie. A month later there were even uglier incidents at Villeneuve-Saint-Georges, where building workers, masons and navvies formed a closely-knit group, isolated from the ordinary life of Paris. The builders' trade union was then the spearhead of the syndicalist movement, and its members readily acted on the advice of an extremist Left wing paper, *La Guerre Sociale*, that they should use sabotage and violence to secure better pay.

When the Villeneuve workers went on strike with CGT support and put up barricades in the streets, their action seemed to presage a syndicalist revolution. But once again, as had happened in so many strikes before, the government was able to make use of the considerable standing army which the system of compulsory military service always placed at its disposal. Clemenceau ordered troops to disperse the strikers, and something like a pitched battle ensued. Four workers were killed, and a large number wounded, while the troops suffered sixty-nine casualties.

This bloody clash showed that Clemenceau could be ruthless in breaking what he regarded as revolutionary strikes. It also gave him an excuse for arresting the three leaders of the CGT, and it quelled the strikers. At the beginning of August they went back to work on much less favourable terms than they had demanded.

Most of the Parisian newspapers blamed the CGT, which had encouraged the strikers to make provocative demonstrations, for the loss of life; but the Socialist press accused Clemenceau of 'Machiavellian' preparation of 'the massacre'. Significantly a new daily paper of the extreme Right took the same line. This was *L'Action Française*, formerly a monthly revue for café intellectuals run by the nationalist organisation of the same name, but now embarking on a formidable career as a Catholic and monarchist daily newspaper committed to virulent attacks on parliamentary government, Jews, Freemasons, Protestants and foreign residents in France. Its editor was the brilliant Charles Maurras, who now accused Clemenceau of having 'willed the carnage' and called him 'this bloodstained old man'. This was the beginning of a long feud between *L'Action Francaise* and the Tiger, which was temporarily checked in 1917–18, when Maurras and his principal lieutenant, Léon Daudet, sank their enmity towards him in sincere appreciation of his efforts to win the war.

The charge that Clemenceau had 'willed the carnage' cannot be sustained; though he may have expected there would be fighting when he sent in the troops, the strikers themselves were to blame for the defiance which led to the rioting and shooting. But another charge against him in connection with the Villeneuve strike must be taken more seriously.

In the first decade of the twentieth century the French police used what Robert Dell described as a 'detestable method of manufacturing crime in order to have the credit of suppressing it', i.e. the method of planting their own men as *agents provocateurs* in industrial upheavals or criminal situations. Two men arrested in the Métro workers' strikes— Ricordeau, leader of the largely anarchist building workers' union, and Métivier, secretary of the gingerbread-makers' union—were suspected at the time of being *agents provocateurs*; but nothing was proved against them, and when Clemenceau was questioned in the Chamber about their arrest he roundly denounced Métivier and said that he had been the chief instigator of the troubles.

Ricordeau may or may not have been a police spy, but three years later *La Guerre Sociale* published documentary evidence that Métivier had not only been paid by the police but had even insisted on seeing Clemenceau before agreeing to act in the Villeneuve strike. When these revelations were made Clemenceau was no longer in office and could not be questioned in the Chamber about them; but the facts seemed clear, and we are left to conclude that he tolerated the use of an *agent provocateur*, whose function was to stir up trouble and so provide a reason for the arrest of the CGT leaders. This is certainly the shadier side of his strike-breaking.

These strikes were the last major confrontations with the CGT during Clemenceau's first ministry. The arrested leaders were released without trial in October, but they had lost much of their influence, and the CGT no longer presented the revolutionary threat which had looked so alarming earlier in the year.

There was still, however, to be another show-down with the *fonction-naires*. In March 1909 postal workers came out on strike for better pay and conditions of service, in defiance of the government's ban on strikes by public servants. The effects were impressive; postal, telegraph and tele-phone services were reduced to chaos, but on Clemenceau's orders Lépine engaged temporary postmen in both Paris and the provinces and re-opened mail services in all directions. But this time Clemenceau agreed to open negotiations with the strikers, and they returned to work on the assurance that their grievances would be met.

France's *premier flic* had earned his reputation as a strike-breaker. In 1906 there had been a record total of 438,466 strikers; in 1908 the number dropped to 99,042—the lowest total in any peace-time year. This was a considerable achievement, which goes far to answer Jaurès's complaint that Clemenceau was 'unnecessarily provocative'.

[4]

Though strikes and protests, with their accompanying interpellations in the Chamber, occupied so much of the government's time, Clemenceau was able to claim that he had not neglected his social objectives. In one of the last speeches of his ministry he mentioned the nationalisation of the Western railway, the implementation of the law (introduced by a previous government) entitling workers to a weekly day of rest, the passing of an income tax bill through the Chamber (but not through the Senate) and the preliminary discussions of a plan for introducing old age pensions. 'I have been inadequate, I admit,' he said, 'but my intentions have been to serve the Republic, liberty, justice and the cause of the poor.'

He had found time, too, to show that France had a prime minister who was interested in art and literature. His patronage had made Rodin a semi-official sculptor to the Third Republic; he had arranged for the transfer of Manet's 'Olympia', which had scandalised art-lovers in 1865 and had been presented to the nation by a group of artists in 1890, from the relative obscurity of the Musée du Luxembourg to the Louvre; and Zola's ashes, which had been placed in Montmartre cemetery, were transferred to the Panthéon.

Throughout his term of office he was closely concerned with foreign affairs, and in Pichon, his old friend and newspaper colleague, he had a foreign minister who would faithfully follow whatever policies he suggested. But though he had told Buré that he meant, as a minister, to carry out the policies he had advocated as a journalist, he did not regard it as his duty to reverse policies adopted by previous governments. He had never approved of the Franco-Russian alliance, but as prime minister he did nothing to undermine it; he was still anti-colonialist, but he maintained the continuity of French colonial policy, and he now realised that the French presence in Morocco gave additional strength to the *entente cordiale* created by the Franco-British agreement of 1904.

This agreement, concluded when a Conservative government was in power in Britain, was equally acceptable to its Liberal successor; but it was not a military treaty, and it gave France no assurance that British troops would come to her aid if she were attacked by Germany. Clemenceau's great objective was to obtain such an assurance, which he discussed in conversations with British statesmen and their king.

His first attempt to strengthen the *entente cordiale* was made in April 1907, when Sir Henry Campbell-Bannerman, the British prime minister, visited Paris. It was a somewhat frustrating episode.

Meeting alone and in strict secrecy, the two prime ministers discussed possible Anglo-French cooperation against Germany, and Clemenceau spoke of the recent reduction of Britain's armed strength. The British army had been reconstructed as a 'new model' army of only 100,000 men; naval expenditure had also been cut; and when Bannerman defended the reductions on grounds of economy, Clemenceau retorted, 'Pardon me, I could economise on the price of my shoes and catch pneumonia, but that would not be economy!'

More disturbing still were Bannerman's remarks on military co-operation. Clemenceau understood him to say that 'The sentiment of the English people would be totally averse to *any* troops being landed by England on the continent under any circumstances', and that Britain's contribution to a war with Germany must be exclusively naval. He was so upset by Bannerman's attitude that he broke his pledge of secrecy and described the whole interview to Lord Milner, a friend of the Maxse family and an opponent of the British Liberal government, with whom he went to a theatre and dined at the café Anglais on the following evening. He even suggested that Milner should telegraph to London to ask Leo Maxse, Violet's brother and editor of the Imperialist *National Review*, to come over to Paris and take a private message back to Sir Edward Grey, the foreign Secretary.

His fears were exaggerated. He had misunderstood the British prime minister. When he asked Sir Francis Bertie, the British ambassador, for further enlightenment, the matter was referred to Grey, who assured Clemenceau that Bannerman had *not* meant that there were no circumstances in which Britain would send an army to France. So the upshot of the interview was that military cooperation was not ruled out, though there was no certainty of immediate assistance by the British army in the event of war.[1]

Clemenceau was not satisfied. When Campbell-Bannerman died in 1908, he went to London for the funeral and had a talk with Sir Edward Grey. But the position had not changed. He was given no definite answer when he asked how many hundred thousand men, fully equipped for war, Britain could land within a fortnight in north-eastern France, should a sudden and unprovoked attack be made.

In addition to his talks with British statesmen the Tiger had a number of meetings with King Edward VII, with whom he was soon on excellent terms. They shared a devotion to Anglo-French friendship and a liking for beautiful women. Their first meeting was early in 1907, when the King came to Paris with Queen Alexandra for a week's private visit; they appear to have met again on less formal occasions, for Clemenceau recalled in later life that King Edward once invited him to a party at which there were twelve women, all of whom had been the King's mistresses. (More boastfully, but possibly describing the same party, he

---

[1] Presumably Campbell-Bannerman had not made himself clear. When the incident was reported to King Edward VII he accepted his prime minister's version, but said privately: 'Clemenceau could hardly have invented such a statement.' (*See* Hardinge, *Old Diplomacy*, p. 140.)

told his grandson Georges Gatineau-Clemenceau that he once dined with the King at the café de Paris, where the guests included 'a number of his former mistresses, of whom several had also been mine.')

Their best opportunity for discussing the *entente* came in the summer, when both men went to central Europe for cures—the King to Marienbad, Clemenceau to his inevitable Carlsbad. In 1907 King Edward had brief meetings with both Kaiser Wilhelm II and the aged Emperor Franz Josef of Austria on his way to the spa. Fearing that his French friends might be upset by his talks with the German and Austrian rulers, he invited Clemenceau to come over from Carlsbad for lunch at the hotel Weimar, Marienbad.

The meeting had not been suggested by the British foreign office. 'The idea,' the King wrote to his friend Charles Hardinge, 'emanated from my fertile brain!!!' Clemenceau was able to give his views on Morocco and other international issues, and the King thought that the lunch was very successful. Hardinge assured him that his action had given great satisfaction in France and had 'allayed any susceptibilities or suspicions to which the French are too prone'.

A second meeting at Marienbad followed in August 1908. Clemenceau had had a trying summer. His daughter Madeleine had had typhoid fever, and though she recovered he feared at one time that she was going to die; at home there had been the strikes at Draveil-Vigneux and Villeneuve-Saint-Georges; in foreign affairs he felt that the whole European situation was deteriorating. Shortly before leaving for Carlsbad he told his assistant Georges Louis: 'I believe there will be war. I regard it as inevitable.' He was prepared to speak frankly when he met King Edward again.

This time the lunch was a 'triple *entente*' affair, for Isvolsky, the Russian ambassador to Vienna, was also present. Clemenceau expressed his fears for the future of international relations and his belief that war must come. England, he reminded the King, trusted to the strength of her fleet, but France had to face the real danger of invasion. Yet 'it was not at Trafalgar, even though it was a brilliant naval victory, but at Waterloo, which was a little battle, that England smashed Napoleon', he told his royal host.

King Edward was impressed by this plain speaking. 'Clemenceau is a true friend of our own country and of France,' he said to Wickham Steed, the British journalist, a day or two after the lunch.

It is impossible to say how far British policy was influenced by Clemenceau's continued pressure for a promise of military assistance in the event of war. It should be noted, however, that in 1909, when he was just concluding his period of nearly three years as prime minister, the British government conditionally approved a plan by the general staff for sending a British force to France if war broke out; and in the following year Major-General Sir Henry Wilson, as director of military operations, became responsible for arrangements to send a British expeditionary force to France if it were needed. In this way, at least, the *entente cordiale* was strengthened during Clemenceau's first period as prime minister of France.

[5]

Though Clemenceau had complained to Campbell-Bannerman about the run-down of British military and naval power, he had no reason for complacency about the state of France's own defences. Under Combes's government the period of compulsory military service had been reduced from three years to two, and the army was weaker than it had been at any time during the previous twenty years; yet the Chamber refused to vote increased military credits, and Clemenceau did not try to force them through by making the vote a question of confidence. The navy, too, was suffering from a shortage of guns and of dry docks for the largest cruisers, and an explosion which destroyed the cruiser *Iéna* caused a great outcry about naval inefficiency. Yet neither Clemenceau nor his successive ministers of marine, Thomson and Picard, were prepared to initiate radical changes.

On the credit side Clemenceau made useful contacts with Basil Zaharoff, Paris representative of Vickers, the British arms manufacturers, and of the German arms firm of Loewe-Gontard. It is sometimes regarded as sinister that he should have been on good terms with a 'merchant of death', and that much later his son Michel should have worked for one of Zaharoff's firms; but Geoffrey Bruun rightly points out that 'The evidence, as evidence, proves nothing more than Clemenceau's desire to win the services of an indispensable agent for the army of the Republic, and there can be little doubt that Zaharoff's aid contributed in no small measure to the *Entente* preparation for war.' He was also responsible for the appointment of Colonel Ferdinand Foch as commandant of the Ecole de Guerre (the French Staff College) after an often quoted interview in which he replied that he 'didn't give a damn' when Foch said that he was a Roman Catholic and had a brother who was a Jesuit priest.

The relative weakness of French defences had its effect on Clemenceau's foreign policy. Though he regarded war with Germany as inevitable, he had no wish to rush blindly into such a conflict. It was thus his policy to conciliate the Germans over Morocco, and to prevent the occurrence of another *coup de Tanger*. Unfortunately a minor incident at Casablanca brought about a renewal of Franco-German friction.

One day in September 1908 an official of the German consulate in

Morocco brought a number of intending travellers to Casablanca, equipped with papers signed by the consul. Before they could sail, French naval police identified four of them—three Germans and one Austrian—as deserters from the French Foreign Legion, and arrested them in spite of the German official's protests. Inquiries showed that the consul was running an agency for helping German deserters from the Legion to leave the country.

German newspapers were indignant about the arrests, and the German government demanded an apology and the prisoners' release. The matter was taken up in Paris by Prince Radolin, the German ambassador, but Clemenceau and Pichon, feeling sure that Germany would not make such a trivial incident an excuse for war, refused to give way. Radolin was told that the German consul ought to be reprimanded for his illegal conduct, and that France was ready to submit the case to the International Court at The Hague. The French tactics were successful. The German government agreed to accept the International Court's verdict, and the judgement given in May 1909 was substantially in France's favour.[1]

Though the Casablanca affair was a technical victory for France, the worsening situation in eastern Europe, where Austria had antagonised both Russia and Serbia by annexing the former Turkish provinces of Bosnia and Herzegovina, made Clemenceau particularly anxious to avoid trouble in the west. He therefore acceded to a German request for talks about the economic development of Morocco, and Pichon and Kiderlen-Waechter, the German foreign minister, together worked out details of the Franco-German agreement of January 1909. (Caillaux asserts in his memoirs that Pichon initiated the agreement, and did not tell Clemenceau about it until the terms had been settled; but everything we know of the relationship between Clemenceau and Pichon proves that the foreign minister could never have been guilty of such an act of insubordination.)

[1] The Casablanca incident gave rise to an amusing if basically improbable story. As told, for example, by Georges Suarez, Prince Radolin made his protest to Clemenceau in person, and said: 'You do not wish to put me in the sad position of having to ask you for my passports.' Clemenceau replied: 'Your Excellency, the train for Cologne leaves at nine. It is now seven. You will have to hurry if you don't want to miss it.' Radolin then gave way.

In 1928 Jean Martet asked the Tiger about this incident, and was told that the dialogue had actually been in the conditional tense. Radolin had said that he might be forced to ask for his passports, and Clemenceau had replied: 'If you took that decision, I would ask for the time of your train, so that I could come to the station to say good-bye.' But Clemenceau's memory may have been at fault, for it seems doubtful whether the meeting with Radolin occurred at all. David Watson comments: 'The published documents do not mention any personal interview. The affair was carried on through regular diplomatic channels.' (*See* Suarez, *Clemenceau*, II, p. 121; Martet, *Clemenceau peint par lui-même*, pp. 77–9; Watson, *Clemenceau*, p. 229.)

The agreement provided for German political disengagement in Morocco in return for economic advantages: Franco-German industrial *consortia* were to be set up for Moroccan development, so that great firms like the German Krupps and the French Schneider-Creusot could share industrial power. Another purpose of the agreement was to strengthen the French government's authority in Morocco, so as to prevent reckless adventures by ambitious civilians or soldiers; but as a means of conciliating Germany its success was only temporary. Trouble in Morocco would produce a new Franco-German crisis in 1911.

[6]

In January 1909 Clemenceau was re-elected as one of the senators for the Var. He had then been prime minister for two-and-a-quarter years, an uncommonly long term of office in the Third Republic, and the position of his government still seemed unassailable, since it was unlikely that any combination of his opponents could be strong enough to defeat him. His firmness in dealing with strikes and his conclusion of the Moroccan agreement had raised his prestige with the French people. He also had admirers in other countries: a writer in the British *Fortnightly Review* said that 'His decision and resource, the clear steel of his temperament, and the dry light of his mind are such that France in a crisis would probably find him one of the greatest war ministers she has ever had.' He had not, however, fulfilled the prophecy of old Princess Metternich, widow of a former Austrian ambassador to Paris, who ironically commented, after reading a eulogistic article about him in a Viennese newspaper, 'They'll be giving him an archduchess next!'

Yet signs of discontent could already be seen among the Radicals, whose support was essential for the maintenance of his government. On some occasions, indeed, many of his nominal supporters voted with the Socialists against the government, which was kept in power only with the assistance of votes from the Right. Briand, who had become minister of justice, had his own eye on the office of prime minister and intrigued against Clemenceau in the lobbies. In May the executive committee of the Radical party passed a resolution expressing its regret 'that M. Clemenceau's government, by its successive and contradictory attitudes, had disappointed the hopes of democracy and aggravated the misunderstandings between its different sections'. The writing, it seemed, was already on the wall.

Yet it was, in the end, Clemenceau's own impulsiveness which destroyed his first ministry. And it was an apparently innocuous debate on the naval estimates which led to his downfall.

Several debates on the army and navy took place in the early part of 1909, and in March Delcassé, who had remained a deputy after his dismissal from the foreign ministry, called for a parliamentary commission to examine some inconsistencies in ministers' statements regarding naval credits. The government was obliged to appoint the commission. Its report produced damaging evidence about the condition of naval armaments, but Clemenceau was not unduly perturbed. When the report came up for debate on 1 July he thought he could persuade the Chamber to accept a motion expressing confidence in the government and calling upon it to take the necessary action indicated in the report.

This was not good enough for Delcassé, who proposed an alternative motion regretting that the government had taken no rigorous measures to check inefficiency in naval administration and to make public expenditure productive. Since Picard, the minister of marine, had been in office only a few months, the motion was clearly aimed at the prime minister.

If the motion had come from anyone but Delcassé, Clemenceau might have handled it tactfully and won the Chamber round to his side. But he still bore his old grudge against the ex-minister for his refusal to help the Comte d'Aunay in time of need, and he used the debate as a means of viciously attacking Delcassé's policy at the Quai d'Orsay, which, he said, had led France to Algeciras. 'Remember that time,' he thundered, 'and say whether it is tolerable that the man who led us to Algeciras should attack ministers and accuse them of carelessness in organising national defence.'

It was a confused and self-contradictory diatribe. The Algeciras conference was not really a strong debating-point, for although it had been viewed in advance as a national humiliation, its results had been quite satisfactory for France, and in any case Delcassé had accepted dismissal rather than agree to it. In reply Delcassé accused the prime minister of abusing the privileges of his office by speaking and acting as he chose, without fear of punishment, but even after this rebuke Clemenceau would not restrain himself. At a later stage in the debate he returned to the crisis of 1905. 'You were a minister, and you led us to the gates of war, and you had made no military preparations,' he told Delcassé. 'You know very well, everyone knows, all Europe knows, that the ministers of war and marine, questioned at that time, replied that we were not ready!'

He had gone too far. Both his personal attack on Delcassé and his public disclosure of cabinet secrets shocked the Chamber. By 212 votes (including those of 62 Radical-Socialists) to 192 it refused to give priority to the motion expressing confidence in the government. This, in effect, was a vote of no confidence, and Clemenceau was obliged to resign. He had been heard to say insultingly, 'What's this gentleman's name?' when

Delcassé had opened the debate. As the result of the vote was announced, a usually taciturn deputy called out, 'His name's Delcassé!'[1]

Clemenceau had only himself to blame for his defeat. It was unfortunate for him that 176 deputies, including many who could have been expected to vote for him, were not present, since no danger to the government had been foreseen at the end of the parliamentary session; but even without their votes he could have won the day by a sober and reasonable reply to Delcassé's charges. His old grudge led him to self-destruction. 'He was a bowman,' Barrès wrote in his *Cahiers*. 'He ascended the tribune and wished to shoot his poisoned arrow once again, but he let it fall on his foot.'

He behaved with great dignity after his resignation. He told President Fallières that the hostile vote was against himself alone, and that there was no need for his ministers to resign; Briand, he suggested, was the minister best suited to take his place. Fallières took his advice. Briand formed the first of his many ministries. It was the only one that he formed with Clemenceau's approval.

The Tiger's first government is often described as incoherent, but the final balance is more in his favour than his critics allow. He had inherited a dangerous industrial situation, which might have become a revolutionary one; by standing firm he had countered the syndicalist threat and maintained the authority of the Republic. If his social programme was largely unfulfilled, it must be remembered that he had to deal with a difficult Chamber, in which he often needed support from the Right to counterbalance the Radical dissidents, and it was not easy to make progress with social reform.

Yet he had made headway. He had nationalised the Western railway, he had set France on the way towards the introduction of old age pensions, he had persuaded the Chamber to pass a measure providing for a graduated income tax; but the deep-rooted French suspicions of this tax found their champions in the Senate, and the measure did not become law. (It was not until 1917 that France, under the stress of war, at last fell into line with other countries and took income tax into her fiscal system.) For all his reputation as a 'priest-eater' there was little trouble between Church and

[1] Though Clemenceau dug his own pit and walked into it, it is possible that Briand's intrigues had predisposed many Radicals to voting against the government when the right moment came. H. M. Hyndman writes in *Clemenceau, the Man and his Time* (p. 232n.): 'It was said at the time that M. Briand's intrigues in the lobbies were the real cause of Clemenceau's defeat and resignation. Lately this has been confirmed to me on good authority.' It is true that Hyndman is not always a reliable witness, and in this instance he may only have been repeating café gossip; yet it is interesting that his book, containing this reference to Briand's alleged actions in 1909, was published in 1919, i.e., the year *before* similar intrigues by Briand were considered to be responsible for Clemenceau's defeat in the election for the presidency.

State under his government, and his contributions towards the strengthening of the *entente cordiale* and the easing of Franco-German tension were useful achievements in the field of foreign affairs. His ministry lasted for two years and nine months, and was the third longest in the history of the Third Republic. Its record was certainly better than that of any of the eight short-lived ministries which governed France between his fall and the outbreak of the First World War.

How had his first experience of power affected him? There were some, like Madame Arman de Caillavet, who felt that he had lost his *mystique* by taking office and showing himself to have as many weaknesses and faults as other people had. It was ironical, she wrote to Brandes, that 'the intrepid hero, before whom reaction trembled', had himself ordered troops to fire on civilians, just as reactionary generals used to do. And later, when it was clear that Clemenceau's faith in authority and order was drawing him apart from many of his former Radical Socialist colleagues, she wrote again: 'He who was the terror and horror of the bourgeoisie has become its rampart, its hope and its salvation.'

That, indeed, was the paradox of Clemenceau's first ministry. The social reformer had shown himself to be also a champion of authority and social order; the *bloc des Gauches* disintegrated under the rule of one who had once been the acknowledged leader of the Left wing; his autocratic government, particularly in its relation to strikers, seemed to have borne out once more the truth of Acton's dictum that 'Power tends to corrupt, absolute power corrupts absolutely.' He remained, as ever, a true Republican. But he had no party behind him, and when Combes, who was still the nominal leader of the Radical party, at last resigned, it was Caillaux, not Clemenceau, who was chosen to succeed him. It was unlikely that any future prime minister would want the Tiger in his government. Once again it seemed that his political career was ended.

CHAPTER THIRTEEN

BEFORE THE WAR

1. *Peaceful interlude.* 2. *A democrat in South America.* 3. *Caillaux's fall.*
4. *Rifts with Poincaré.* 5. L'Homme Libre. 6. *1914.*

[1]

O N THE evening of his defeat and resignation Clemenceau dined at
the Chateaubriant restaurant with Claude Debussy, Gabriel Fauré
and other friends. He was in high spirits. 'You know, music is
better than politics,' he said. 'I have been prime minister for two years and
eight months, which makes nearly 970 days. During this time I have seen
about ten members of parliament a day, say 9,700 in all. Well, of these
9,700 elected representatives of the people, not one came to see me to
talk about State affairs. They were all concerned with personal matters.
What a system!'

He was nearly sixty-eight. After his long stint in the place Beauvau it
was pleasant to relax a little and see more of his non-political friends. In
August his visit to Carlsbad was more leisurely than it had been when he
was prime minister. Brandes, who had taken Maxse's place as his Carlsbad
companion, had complained in 1908 that Clemenceau was so busy with
politics that they hardly ever had time for a good talk. Now he had plenty
of time for both talking and walking.

One day he went for a long walk with Berta Szeps and a young artist.
Berta praised the work of Paul Poiret, the leading Parisian dress designer,
and said that his models were being hissed in Vienna when they appeared
in the new divided skirts. 'How stupid,' cried Clemenceau. 'Poiret deserves
to be decorated for his brave innovation. Woman liberated! Not only from
the abominable corset, that instrument of torture, but also, and this is
essential, from all the hypocrisy which demeans this delightful being. . . . I
hope that twentieth-century woman will free herself from our tutelage.
But Heaven preserve me if the Senate hears me saying so! It's still at the
cave-woman stage.'[1]

[1] Though favouring women's liberation half-a-century before the phrase passed into
general use, Clemenceau was concerned mainly with social liberation and had no
sympathy with the French 'votes for women' movement. He felt it would be wrong to

Yet even now he could not entirely escape from politics. King Edward VII was again at Marienbad, and though Clemenceau was no longer prime minister he was invited to lunch. They discussed, as always, the German menace, and they agreed that Germany was returning to Bismarck's 'piratical methods'; they both regretted Austria's fatal error in making Russia her irreconcilable enemy by annexing Bosnia and Herzegovina. It was their last meeting. Nine months later the King was dead.

These months after his fall from power were a peaceful interlude in Clemenceau's stormy life. He paid his usual September visit to the Var, where he kept in touch with local problems by meeting electors in a score of different villages every year. This time he had a special matter to talk about—a project for launching his own daily newspaper in the department.

His financial position had improved during his years as editor-in-chief of *L'Aurore* and subsequently as prime minister. Though he had not cleared off all his debts, he could now afford to have two houses—the one in the rue Franklin and another at Bernouville, in the department of Eure, some forty-five miles north-west of Paris and only twenty miles away from Claude Monet's house at Giverny. The two old friends would often visit each other's houses; Geffroy was a frequent visitor at Bernouville; but there were probably no visits from Rodin, with whom the Tiger had quarrelled over a bust that the sculptor had made of him. He complained that Rodin had turned him into a Mongolian general, but Rodin saw no harm in that, since in his opinion Clemenceau *was* Tamerlane and Genghis Khan. Clemenceau wanted him to destroy the bust and start again, and when Rodin refused to do so he said he would never speak to him again.

It was in the winter of 1909–10 that Georges Mandel, who had been only a minor figure in the place Beauvau, definitely established himself as Clemenceau's right hand man. Though two other friends—Winter, his former secretary, and Coussol, an official at the ministry of health—helped him with his correspondence in their spare time, it was Mandel who was chiefly consulted over the launching of a new *Journal du Var* in April 1910.

The paper, which replaced the *Justice du Var* of earlier years, was intended to be a Radical voice in the Var, where most of the local papers were either reactionary or Socialist. Clemenceau was its general director,

give Frenchwomen the vote, because the Church played so great a part in their education: 'to entrust the destiny of government to the votes of women *tout impregnées de sacristie* would be a return to the middle ages.' But he saw no objection to women's suffrage in Britain, where the educational system was different. He wished the British suffragettes well, if they could achieve their aim without burning down the British Museum, the National Gallery or the Wallace Collection. (*See* 'Toutes ces dames au scrutin', *L'Homme Libre*, 13 May, 1913, reprinted in Clemenceau, *'Dans les champs du pouvoir'*, pp. 48–55.)

but the practical control was in the hands of Mandel, who was also the journal's Paris correspondent, and Francisque Varenne, the editor.

Clemenceau soon showed that he meant to keep a watchful eye on his new venture. He was taking a spring cure at Carlsbad when publication began, and the first issues were sent to him there. In a long letter to Mandel he complained of the commonplace make-up, the faulty printing, the faintness of the ink and the poor quality of the newsprint; he also objected to the choice of articles, some of which were written by his political opponents. Even the impassive Mandel must have been slightly shaken by such damning and detailed criticism. It was fortunate for his peace of mind, and for that of the local editorial staff, that the Tiger had arranged to spend the summer in South America.

[2]

Gabriel Astruc tells an odd story about the origin of Clemenceau's South American tour. He says that he was asked by the management of the Teatro Colon in Buenos Aires to book the violinist Kubelik for a series of concerts in the principal cities of South America; but Kubelik was ill and unable to go. New instructions came from Buenos Aires: 'If Kubelik impossible, book Jaurès.' But Jaurès, too, could not go, because there was a general election for the Chamber of Deputies in 1910. Knowing that this election did not concern the Senate, Astruc cabled back: 'Jaurès unavailable, do you want Clemenceau?' The Argentinians liked the idea, the Tiger accepted their offer, and South American audiences heard lectures on democracy instead of violin solos.

The Tiger sailed for South America in June, choosing the Italian liner *Regina Elena* in preference to a slower and less comfortable French vessel. His round trip took four months. He visited Argentina, Uruguay and Brazil; he gave nine different lectures, eight in Buenos Aires and one in Sao Paulo, and repeated some of them at Rosario, Tucuman, Montevideo and Rio de Janeiro. Everywhere, according to Maurice Ségard, a young doctor who accompanied him and afterwards made the lectures into a book, his reception was enthusiastic.

Though Clemenceau wrote a series of articles in *L'Illustration* describing his tour (later published in book-form as *Notes de Voyage dans l'Amérique du Sud*) he truthfully said that he had discovered nothing new about South America. Apart from his lectures, he was only a sightseer. He admired the window-dressing in Buenos Aires's Avenida del Mayo (which reminded him of London's Oxford Street). He met members of the French colony in Argentina. He was surprised, at a Franco-Argentinian school at Tucuman, to hear the Marseillaise sung in French, with an

Argentinian accent, by children who did not know a single word of the French language. ('Yet, after all,' he reflected, 'what do our beautiful ladies know of the Latin in their Mass books?')

In his lectures he spoke always as 'a soldier of democracy', which he defined as the only regime that enabled equality to be established for all and allowed men to approach the ultimate aim of liberty and justice. It was the *régime*, he said, which offered the greatest opportunities to the individual and gave government its true strength in the consent of the people. He defended the parliamentary system in spite of its imperfections, and he explained why his experience of the French Senate had brought him round to a firm belief in two-chamber government. 'At one stage of my life,' he said, 'when I was closer to theory than to reality, I had faith in the single chamber, the direct representation of popular feeling. Events have taught me that the people must be given time to reflect; the time for reflection is provided by the Senate.'

These were the principles which lay at the heart of his South American lectures. Sometimes his enthusiasm ran away with him. When he declared that democracy alone had 'the magnificent rôle of reconciling all citizens in a common effort of solidarity', he must have forgotten that the interplay of group and party interests does not, as David Thomson points out, automatically produce the harmony in which he believed. But no one could doubt the sincerity of his belief in the virtues of organised democracy, based on order, and in the need for action to strengthen and defend it. In words that foreshadowed the events of later years he affirmed that 'In peace, as in war, the last word is with those who never give in.' And in one of his perorations he appealed to his listeners: 'Have the courage to act, the courage to debate. Do not be afraid of making enemies. If you have none, it is because you have done nothing. You wanted democracy. You have written it into your laws. Live it!'

In October he was back in Paris, where Mandel now came to the rue Franklin every morning to discuss the latest issue of *Le Journal du Var*. At this time an outsider might have thought that the tempo of Clemenceau's life was slowing down. Supervision of a small provincial paper was a trifling matter compared with his former editorship of an important Parisian daily. His contribution of a preface to a French edition of Lord Byron's letters seemed to suggest that at last, in his seventieth year, he was settling cosily down with the books he loved so much.

But if he had ever thought of withdrawing from public life, a new threat from Germany was enough to bring him back to it. This was provided in June 1911 by the dispatch of the German gunboat *Panther* to Agadir, in the south-west of Morocco.

[3]

After Clemenceau's defeat Briand held office until February 1911. A few months of weak government under Jean Monis were then followed by the appointment of the formidable Joseph Caillaux as prime minister.

Like Jaurès, Caillaux was 'a European'. Both men believed that war with Germany could be avoided, and that some kind of Franco-German reconciliation was possible. But Caillaux thought that peace was a matter for private negotiation by statesmen and diplomats, while Jaurès's hopes rested on the international solidarity of the working class.

Caillaux's theories were soon tested by the Agadir crisis. Earlier in the year France had sent troops to Morocco, at the Sultan's request, to recover Fez, the capital, from the rebellious tribes which had seized it; but when the rebels were expelled the French troops stayed in Morocco, ostensibly to prevent further unrest. This military occupation was in breach of the Algeciras agreement, which had limited French control of Morocco to police supervision at the ports; and Germany demanded compensation. On the advice of Caillaux, who was then finance minister, the Monis government announced that it was ready to open negotiations; but the Germans would not wait for a conference, and a few days after Caillaux had become prime minister, the *Panther* was sent to Agadir 'to assure the defence of menaced German interests' (which did not, in fact, exist).

Confronted by an apparently warlike Germany, the French government felt obliged to make concessions. The negotiations were conducted on two levels; while Selves, the French foreign minister, was dealing with his German counterpart, Kiderlen-Waechter, Caillaux was secretly in contact with Baron von Lancken, counsellor at the German embassy in Paris. A bargain was struck. By an agreement signed on 4 November France was allowed to assume the protectorate of Morocco in return for the cession to Germany of 275,000 square kilometres of French Congo.

The agreement had now to be ratified by the Senate and the Chamber of Deputies. It was at this stage that Clemenceau came into conflict with Caillaux.

The Tiger was still an anti-colonialist. Though he had supported France's Moroccan interests while he was prime minister, he had done so only because he regarded the French presence in north-west Africa as a useful contribution to the *entente cordiale*. He had never approved of French colonisation in more distant countries, and he might have been expected to welcome the French withdrawal from part of the Congo. But his distrust of Germany outweighed his anti-colonial feelings. He was angry about Caillaux's surrender to German pressure, and when the agreement was discussed in parliament he joined the empire-builders in defending the integrity of France's African empire.

His opportunity of punishing Caillaux came in January 1912, when he sat, with Poincaré, Bourgeois, Pichon and others on the Senate commission of twenty-six members appointed to examine the Franco-German agreement. It was Caillaux himself who made the mistake which allowed the Tiger to pounce on him.

Caillaux was well aware that his private talks with Lancken were open to criticism, and he did not want them to be brought out into the open. Unfortunately for him, some of Lancken's telegrams to Berlin had been decoded at the Quai d'Orsay, where high officials disliked the prime minister's pro-German attitude and were angered by the discovery of his secret negotiations. Hoping to be able to hush things up, Caillaux asked Poincaré, as *rapporteur* of the Senate commission, if he would ignore any decoded telegrams coming from the Quai d'Orsay. Poincaré agreed that such telegrams could be overlooked. He advised Caillaux to brush them aside by saying that, as head of the government, he was responsible for the outcome of the Franco-German negotiations, and that he had used whatever agents it seemed helpful to employ.

When the commission met the prime minister duly put up this face-saving formula, but then, to Poincaré's surprise, he rashly elaborated it by saying: 'There have been attempts in the press and elsewhere to prove that negotiations have been conducted outside the foreign ministry. I pledge my word that there were no political or financial dealings of any kind, other than the diplomatic and official negotiations.'

This foolish prevarication gave the Tiger his chance. Knowing that Selves and his *cabinet* at the Quai d'Orsay resented Caillaux's interference, he asked coolly: 'Can the foreign minister confirm the prime minister's statement?' The embarrassed Selves asked if the commission would allow him not to answer that question, but Clemenceau said that he was not satisfied with the foreign minister's attitude.

No more was needed. Selves, whose refusal to speak had shown that Caillaux was lying, resigned after the meeting. Caillaux offered his post to Delcassé, who was then minister of marine, but met with two refusals when he tried to name Delcassé's successor. Realising that he had lost his backing, he also resigned.

Even at the height of his fame as an overthrower of ministries the Tiger had never before turned a prime minister out of office with so few words. But though he had thus signalised his return to active politics, he was not offered a portfolio in the next ministry. Poincaré, who succeeded Caillaux, prudently decided that Clemenceau had too strong a personality to allow him to submit to a governmental discipline which did not depend on his own authority.

The last words on the Franco-German agreement were spoken in the Senate in February. Poincaré defended it because of the importance of Morocco to France; Clemenceau continued to oppose it, and used the occasion for a general denunciation of Germany's menacing attitude towards France. 'We desire peace in all good faith,' he said, 'but if war is imposed on us, we shall be ready.' Germany, he declared, wished to dominate, but France was not willing to submit. 'We come from a great history, and we mean to preserve it. The dead have made the living, the living will remain faithful to the dead!'

His speech was applauded, but the Senate and Chamber ratified the agreement, which was supported by most of the Radicals in both houses. Clemenceau's opposition was a further sign of his increasing separation from his old parliamentary colleagues.

[4]

He was in great pain when he spoke in the Senate. Almost immediately afterwards he went into a nursing home, staffed by nuns, in the rue Georges Bizet for the removal of his prostate gland. The operation gave no trouble; the Tiger was a surprisingly good patient, and was soon on excellent terms with his nurse, Sister Théoneste. Though he often teased her about her religion, he was grateful for her attentions. Once he took her hand and said gently: 'Ah, what would become of the old Republicans without the Little Sisters of Charity?' (In later years the operation inspired him to make his much-quoted saying that 'There are two things one can do without—the prostate gland and the President of the Republic!')

On returning to the Senate after his convalescence he was soon at loggerheads with Poincaré. Though both were great Frenchmen, the contrast in their characters made it difficult for them to work together. As Vladimir d'Ormesson has observed, Clemenceau 'symbolised the powerful, individualist and heroic side of the French character', whereas Poincaré's dry, legalistic manner made him the personification of the economical, unadventurous French bourgeoisie. In 1912 it was his desire for electoral reform which set the Tiger against him.

Since the Boulanger era the Chamber of Deputies had been elected by single-member constituencies under the system of *scrutin d'arrondissement*. Poincaré wanted to go back to *scrutin de liste*, combined with a rather unwieldy system of proportional representation. The intention was to produce a Chamber consisting of substantial bodies of members agreeing on particular policies instead of a heterogeneous collection of individuals, who might claim to belong to a party but were largely representative of local interests.

Clemenceau had supported *scrutin de liste* in the 1880s, mainly as a means of 'dishing' Boulanger, but he now opposed it because it involved the introduction of proportional representation, which he regarded as a distortion of the voting system. His attack on the bill in the Senate was backed by Caillaux in the Chamber of Deputies—an unexpected alliance in view of the events of the previous January.

Another rift with Poincaré occurred over the presidential election of January 1913. The veteran Ribot had been mentioned as a possible successor to Fallières, and it was said that Poincaré had promised to support him; but at the end of December Poincaré announced that he would stand for election himself.

His decision was surprising. For some years it had been the practice to elect relatively weak presidents, like Faure, Loubet and Fallières; but Poincaré was a strong man, and there was no knowing what he might make of the presidency. Clemenceau thought there would be a risk of a Poincaré dictatorship, and he decided to find someone to defeat him, just as he had put up Sadi Carnot to beat Ferry.

But who should it be? Apart from Ribot, the strongest challengers were Antonin Dubost, president of the Senate, and Paul Deschanel, president of the Chamber, but none of these seemed likely to beat Poincaré. Clemenceau at first decided to take a chance with Dubost.[1] Then he changed his mind and dropped Dubost in favour of Pams, the Radical Socialist minister of agriculture.

Pams was a light-weight in comparison with Poincaré, but he had all the Radicals behind him, and Clemenceau's plan nearly succeeded. As in previous years a preliminary vote was taken among the Republican deputies and senators. After three ballots no candidate had an overall majority, but Pams had a definite lead, with 323 votes against Poincaré's 309. Clemenceau and Combes then led a Radical deputation to Poincaré, asking him to withdraw his candidature as a matter of Republican discipline.

Poincaré declined to give way. He did not see why he should stand down in favour of a minor member of his own cabinet. His obstinacy won him the presidency. When the full vote was taken he had further support from the Right wing senators and deputies who had been excluded from the Republicans' meeting, and on the second ballot he had an overall

[1] According to Caillaux, Clemenceau's recommendation of Dubost was hardly enthusiastic. To those who objected that Dubost was insignificant, he retorted: '*Oh, je sais bien que c'est un c . . , mais qu'est-ce que vous voulez? Nous n'avons personne.*' (*See* Caillaux, *Mes Mémoires*, III, p. 28.)

majority of 483 votes (out of 870) against Pams's 296. France was to have a strong man as president of the Republic.

Clemenceau's first reaction to Poincaré's election was one of intense anger. When his friend Benoist approached him during the second ballot and said pleasantly, 'Ah, well, it's all over now,' the Tiger looked at him furiously and replied, 'Oh, you think it's over? No, it's beginning.' Later he cooled down, and Benoist ventured to congratulate him on the fighting spirit he had shown on Pams's behalf. 'You weren't afraid of the Tiger?' asked Clemenceau. 'Good Lord, no,' said Benoist, 'and as for tigers, you know what happens to them when they grow old?' 'No, what?' 'They are made into bedside rugs!' said Benoist, and both men laughed.

But no one would ever make a bedside rug out of France's Tiger. A few months after Poincaré's election he launched a new daily paper in Paris, and at seventy-one he resumed his busy double life as senator and working journalist.

[5]

The newspaper which Clemenceau founded in 1913 was no semi-amateur sheet like *Le Bloc*, but a full-fledged Parisian daily. Preparations for launching it had been made by Mandel, who looked after the financial and business side of the new venture, from capital-raising and printing arrangements to engaging staff and making agreements with distributors and news and advertising agencies. But he was disappointed when Clemenceau decided to wind up *Le Journal du Var* in view of the launching of the new paper. Mandel had hoped to stand for the Var in the next election for the Chamber, and he had felt that his connection with a local paper was a strong point in his favour.

The new paper was called *L'Homme Libre*. Its staff included Mandel, Georges Gombault, Jean Martet, Emil Buré, Etienne Chichet and François Albert, the editor. Clemenceau was named on the front page as editor-in-chief.

Though *L'Homme Libre* covered all the topics generally dealt with by its rivals, it was essentially a vehicle for the Tiger's opinions. He wrote a long article, usually from 1,500 to 2,000 words, every day, following his old routine of choosing his subject at night in the office, writing at home in the early morning and sending the manuscript to the printers before noon. Then, as in the old days of *La Justice* and *L'Aurore*, the proof would be waiting when he arrived at the office at 4 p.m., or later if he were kept at the Senate. Even on holiday in the Vendée he still posted his daily article to the printers.

The first issue of *L'Homme Libre* appeared on 5 May. From the beginning Clemenceau's overriding concern was with the German menace.

For more than a year France had been racked by controversy over the length of compulsory military service. Briand, who succeeded Poincaré as prime minister, introduced a bill for raising the term of service from two years (to which it had been reduced in 1905) to three. The compelling argument for the increase was that because of the low French birth-rate a two-year term of service would not provide enough men for essential defences, but the measure was hotly opposed by Caillaux and Jaurès, who for their different reasons believed that war with Germany was avoidable.

In March Briand resigned, after being defeated in the Senate on the electoral reform bill, which he had inherited from Poincaré; a powerful speech by Clemenceau, deriding the complications of proportional representation, played a big part in bringing him down. He was succeeded by Barthou, and the three years' service bill continued its stormy passage through parliament.

Clemenceau had once opposed standing armies, and even in 1905 he had voted for the reduced period of military service, on the ground that three years' absence from civilian life caused too much interference with young men's careers. But now he was convinced that France must deploy her maximum military strength, and in article after article in *L'Homme Libre* he explained the need for an extra year's service. At the same time he commented wryly on Britain's blindness in putting her faith in 'the silver belt' of the sea and ignoring Lord Roberts's call for conscription.

The controversy took a new and dangerous turn in May 1913, when agitators persuaded soldiers in Nancy and other eastern garrisons to mutiny against the year's extension in their period of service. The mutinies inspired Clemenceau to write an impressive article entitled *Vouloir ou mourir*, which was reprinted as a pamphlet. It was at once a warning that a failure of national will-power would mean the end of France, and an exposure of the futility of those who thought that war was impossible. Rhetorically he asked the mutineers: 'While you throw away your arms, do you not hear the clatter of field-guns on the other side of the Vosges?' In a fine peroration he said he was sure that when the time came for action they would go gladly to fight for their cause and their country.

It may be doubted whether his arguments had much effect on the soldiery, for there were more mutinies later in the summer; but the attitude of *L'Homme Libre* must have helped to persuade many Radicals to support the government, rather than Caillaux, when the vote on the three years' service bill was taken in the Chamber of Deputies on 18 July.

The bill was carried by 358 votes to 204, and a few days later the Senate gave it the big majority of 244 votes to 36. Clemenceau's first major campaign in his new paper had ended on the winning side.

[6]

Though many Frenchmen thought that the risk of war had been averted by the Moroccan settlement, Clemenceau did not share this popular illusion. His articles continued to warn his countrymen of the German menace, and when he unveiled a statue to Scheurer-Kestner at Metz on 11 March, 1914, he said of Germany: 'Her fury for the leadership of Europe decrees for her a policy of extermination against France. Therefore, prepare, prepare, prepare.' To Berta Szeps, who came to Paris in May, he declared that the Franco-German agreement of 1912 threw dust in the eyes of the French, and he berated her own country for bullying Serbia. 'I regard Austria as so guilty that she deserves to disappear,' he said. 'And I hope she will.'

It was a year of short-lived governments. Barthou was succeeded by Doumergue, Doumergue by Ribot, and in June Viviani, the independent Socialist, formed a weak cabinet without politicians of the first rank. He was thus prime minister when Archduke Franz Ferdinand of Austria was assassinated at Sarajevo.

During the few weeks between Franz Ferdinand's death and the outbreak of war Clemenceau took part in a grave debate in the Senate on the state of French armaments. Senator Charles Humbert, who presented a report by the Senate's army commission, called attention to alarming gaps in military equipment, particularly in heavy artillery, and was supported by Clemenceau, who asked: 'What will happen to the morale of an army which finds itself within range of the enemy's guns, though its own guns cannot reach the enemy?' When General Messimy, minister of war, tried to excuse the deficiencies by saying that military credits were restricted by the minister of finance, Clemenceau asked why he did not appeal directly to the prime minister. 'The truth is,' he said bitterly, 'we are neither defended nor governed.' Since 1871, he declared, he had never taken part in such a moving, agonising and painful sitting of parliament.

On the next day, 15 July, he used the phrase, 'Neither defended nor governed' as the heading of his article in *L'Homme Libre*. Moral force, he wrote, would not be enough to conquer the enemy's material strength; arms, guns and munitions were needed. He recalled the heroism of those who had fought for France in 1870, and pointedly added: 'It is not enough to be heroes. We wish to be conquerors.'

Yet at this time, when half Europe stood poised on the brink of war, the French press gave more space to an approaching trial than to either the murder at Sarajevo or the army's shortage of heavy guns. It was the trial of Caillaux's second wife, who had shot and killed Gaston Calmette, editor of *Le Figaro*, for publishing private letters which damaged Caillaux's reputation. She was acquitted in the last week of July, but few papers agreed with the verdict; Caillaux, who had resigned from Doumergue's cabinet after the shooting, was left in the political wilderness, with no hope of an early recall to office.

Another important figure disappeared from the French political scene on the last day of July, when Jaurès, the Socialist leader and apostle of international brotherhood, was murdered by a fanatic in a Paris café. Clemenceau's tribute to him was sympathetic, but tinged with irony. 'It was his fate,' he wrote, 'to preach the brotherhood of peoples and to have so firm a faith in this great idea that he could not be discouraged even by the brutal evidence of facts.' But towards the end of his life, in a day-long talk with René Benjamin, Clemenceau declared that Jaurès's death was a happy deliverance for France. 'I can never think without a shiver,' he said, 'of the first, the very first, cause of victory. The murder of Jaurès!' He believed, and his belief was justified by his knowledge of the Socialist leader's character, that if Jaurès had been in the Chamber in 1917–18 he would have been calling for peace instead of the prosecution of the war, and sooner or later would have overthrown Clemenceau's government.

Already in eastern Europe Germany and Austria were aligned against Russia and Serbia. As France awaited the inevitable declaration of war, President Poincaré said that there were no more parties, only eternal France, and called for a *union sacrée*. Clemenceau wrote in *L'Homme Libre*: 'Today there must not be two Frenchmen who hate each other. It is time for us to know the joy of loving each other, of loving each other through what is greatest in us, the duty of bearing witness before men that we are no less worthy than our fathers, and that our children will not have to lower their eyes when our names are spoken.'

It was his last peace-time article. On the next day, 3 August, France and Germany were at war.

PART THREE

WAR AND PEACE

CHAPTER FOURTEEN

LEADER IN WAITING

*1. The bad beginning. 2. L'Homme Enchaîné. 3. Parliamentary commissioner.
4. The changing war. 5. Malvy indicted. 6. Peace moves. 7. The call.*

[1]

FROM AUGUST 1914 TO NOVEMBER 1917 Georges Clemenceau watched other men directing the policies of France at war. As senator, chairman of the Senate's army and foreign affairs commissions and editor of his own newspaper, he had ample opportunity for expressing his opinions, but it was galling for a man of action to have to confine himself to the critic's rôle.

Though not a minister, he was still an important figure in French life, and before the declaration of war one member of Viviani's cabinet thought it advisable to consult him about a crucial decision which had to be made. Jean Malvy, minister of the interior, was a rising young Radical who was closely associated with Caillaux; it was his duty to decide what should be done about the 2,500 men named in Carnet B, a list compiled by the secret police of suspected spies, anarchists, syndicalists, members of anti-militarist groups and others who might be expected to endanger national defence when war broke out. In theory they were all to be arrested as soon as general mobilisation was ordered, but Malvy hesitated, telling the cabinet that he was afraid of a general strike if he arrested trade union leaders. In the hope of finding support for inaction, he went to the office of *L'Homme Libre* to see Clemenceau. But the Tiger was not impressed by his arguments, and earnestly advised him to put all the Carnet B men in gaol.

Malvy had other advisers to consult. One was the prefect of police, who shared Clemenceau's opinion; another was the head of the secret service, who thought it would be safe to leave the men at liberty; a third adviser was a strange character originally called Jean-Baptiste Vigo, 'part thug, part blackmailer, part revolutionary, part newspaper editor', who had taken the name of Almereyda (an anagram of *y a la merde*) and was editor of a Left wing, revolutionary and anti-militarist paper called *Le Bonnet Rouge*. Almereyda, whose own name was in Carnet B, not surprisingly advised Malvy to make no arrests; he promised to act as mediator between the government and the militant Left, and the grateful Malvy agreed to subsidise *Le Bonnet Rouge* out of government funds.

In the end all the Frenchmen in Carnet B were left at liberty, and only known or suspected foreign spies were taken into custody. The smoothness of the French mobilisation seemed to justify Malvy's policy, but his refusal to arrest potential saboteurs and defeatists was to expose him to the Tiger's wrath at a later stage of the war.

For the moment the Tiger was in an unusually conciliatory mood. He welcomed the *union sacrée*, and declared in *L'Homme Libre* that Poincaré's message to the Chamber 'says, in concise and forceful terms, everything that needs to be said'. When the President invited him to call at the Elysée he greeted his old opponent as 'dear friend'. He was delighted when Britain declared war on Germany on 4 August, and he anxiously awaited the landing of a British expeditionary force in France. In a letter to Violet Cecil he urged her to tell the British secretary for war that 'if he sends only three men, with a flag, to the Continent, it will have a good effect'.

His mood was soon changed by the bad news from the front. For many years the French military leaders had advocated, in the event of war with Germany, a defensive-offensive strategy of waiting for the enemy's attack and then counter-attacking; but more recently a younger school of staff officers had successfully expounded the rash doctrine of an offensive at all costs. Though the army had been skilfully remodelled by General Joffre, who became its commander-in-chief in 1911 and was now leading it in war, the offensive strategy, combined with inferiority in weapon-power and the lack of an adequate plan for resisting a German advance through Belgium, produced disastrous results for France in the first fortnight of August. The French army suffered a sequence of defeats which allowed the Germans to sweep round its left flank and advance as far as Chantilly, twenty-five miles from Paris.

As the situation began to show ominous similarities to that of 1870, Clemenceau adopted a more critical tone in his articles. His first target was the military censorship, which falsified war reports in order to minimise French reverses. In the view of *L'Homme Libre* this policy was mistaken, since the French people would be better able to go through difficult periods if they knew the truth about them.

Already, in the first month of the war, people were expecting Clemenceau to join the government. When Viviani decided to change his predominantly Radical government into one of national unity, Sir Francis Bertie, the British ambassador, wrote in his diary: 'There is talk of Clemenceau or Millerand taking the War Office.' In fact, it was Millerand who became war minister in the all-party government formed by Viviani on 28 August. The Tiger had been offered the post of minister of justice, but had angrily rejected it, making it quite clear that he would enter the cabinet only as prime minister or minister of war.

Viviani told Poincaré what the Tiger had said, and offered to resign in his favour; but Poincaré would not accept his resignation. He was not yet ready for a Clemenceau ministry.

His attitude was confirmed when Clemenceau paid another visit to the Elysée and stormily reproached him for surrounding himself with a ministry of nonentities. He was astonished by the violence of the Tiger's onslaught. 'The more I think about it,' he wrote in his journal, 'the more I tell myself, "So long as victory is possible, he is capable of spoiling everything." Perhaps a day will come when I shall add, "Now that everything seems lost, he is capable of saving everything." '

[2]

In view of the German threat to Paris General Joffre advised the President and the government to move to Bordeaux. Clemenceau and other leading journalists went with them, since the removal meant that Bordeaux would be the centre both for war news and for military censorship. Mandel accompanied him.

In Bordeaux he continued his daily articles for *L'Homme Libre*. He shared a small apartment with his widowed daughter, Madeleine Jacquemaire, who soon found work as a nurse in a big military hospital. Her experiences gave him part of the material for a vehement attack on the inefficiency of the army medical services.[1]

His attack was inspired by a chance visit to the railway station when a train-load of wounded soldiers was arriving from the front. A revolting stench arose from the stretchers on which they were carried away, and he was shocked to learn that they had been lying in horse-boxes which had not been disinfected, and had contracted tetanus. Further investigation revealed chaotic conditions throughout the hospital service: amputations were bungled, deaths were caused by incompetent treatment of minor wounds, medical students were employed on menial tasks and dentists were performing surgical operations.

[1] The elder of Clemenceau's two daughters, Madeleine, had married Numa Jacquemaire, a wealthy lawyer some twenty years older than herself. Her marriage ended tragically when her husband found her in a compromising situation with his best friend, and shot himself in their presence. She never remarried. In her middle years she wrote books under the name of Madeleine Clemenceau-Jacquemaire, contributed to *Le Figaro* and had a literary *salon* which her father did not attend. (*See* Gatineau-Clemenceau, *Des Pattes du Tigre aux Griffes du Destin*, p. 29.)

On 29 September he wrote a stinging article on military hospital inefficiency. It was passed by the Bordeaux censor, but the prefect of Haute-Garonne showed it to the military governor, who at once wired to all military regions to suppress that day's issue of *L'Homme Libre*. The matter was then discussed by the cabinet, and Malvy was instructed to suspend the paper for a week; but Clemenceau, feeling that 'free man' was being turned into 'shackled man' by the censorship, simply dropped the name of *L'Homme Libre* and at once brought out an exactly similar paper called *L'Homme Enchaîné*. The new name was used for the next three years.

September brought 'the miracle of the Marne', the battle in which the French and British armies forced the Germans back beyond Reims and converted the war of movement into the long stalemate of trench warfare. As the 'saviour of France', Joffre was now the nation's unchallenged leader. Parliament had been prorogued at the beginning of hostilities, and Joffre's headquarters, with its two hundred officers and scores of secretaries busy at typewriters and telephones, was the real seat of government. In the long struggle for power between generals, ministers and parliament, with which Clemenceau would be closely associated in 1917–18, the first round had gone to the military.

To Clemenceau the victory of the Marne was an occasion for honouring the *poilu*—the ordinary soldier of the French army. 'Unknown yesterday,' he wrote, 'these men will be unknown tomorrow. Today is their day.' And again: 'Go forward, great unknown Frenchmen, who will have no name in the glorious record of your country.' But he felt no complacency. When the Bordeaux exiles returned to Paris in December, his articles repeatedly ended with the warning phrase, 'The Germans are at Noyon'— only fifty miles from Paris.

At the beginning of 1915 both the Chamber and the Senate were in session again, and Clemenceau, besides being senator and newspaper editor, was now a member of the Senate's army and foreign affairs commissions. (He was subsequently chairman of both commissions.) He had begun to suffer from diabetes, but he never failed to carry out his manifold duties. In each aspect of his life he was helped by Mandel, who divided his time between the office of *L'Homme Enchaîné* in the rue Taitbout and the corridors of the Palais-Bourbon, where he knew all the deputies and flattered some of the clever young men, such as André Tardieu and Pierre Laval, by introducing them to Clemenceau. He reported to his master what was being said in other newspapers, in debates and in private conversation, and his information provided useful material for the Tiger's constant criticisms of the war leadership.

These criticisms were neither defeatist nor destructive. If he did not spare the President or the government or the high command, it was because he felt they were not showing enough energy in running the war. He wanted bold action and dynamic leadership, and he thought that military failures reflected the government's incompetence. The many white spaces on the front page of *L'Homme Enchaîné* showed where the censors thought that he had gone too far.

He was sometimes unfair. On 30 December, 1914, he accused Poincaré of wasting military resources by asking for a troop of cavalry to escort him on his New Year visits, and of increasing his official expense allowance while people were dying of hunger; but though the President wrote him a long letter, clearing himself of the charges, not a word of apology or correction appeared in the paper. He was on surer ground when he began a campaign against the *embusqués*—the officers and other ranks who had dug themselves into comfortable posts well behind the lines. Members of the Chamber of Deputies were not spared in this campaign: *L'Homme Enchaîné* published figures showing that of 220 deputies mobilised for military service only a handful were at the front and fewer still in the trenches.

The white spaces were not the only evidence of *L'Homme Enchaîné*'s friction with the censorship. In August 1915 the paper was suspended for four days for publishing a banned attack on Joffre; but in the following month no objection was raised to an article pleasantly entitled 'The illegality of the censorship.' The censors also tolerated the Tiger's sharp comments when Viviani resigned in October and was replaced by Briand; the rest of the press welcomed Briand's appointment, but Clemenceau accused him of having intrigued for 'this great day' since the flight to Bordeaux. At the same time he refused an invitation to join the new cabinet as minister of state. 'Do I look like a walker-on?' he asked scornfully.

In 1916 the changing fortunes of the long battle of Verdun bore out, in Clemenceau's opinion, the pre-war disclosures of the shortage of French heavy artillery; his comments on the battle caused the paper to be suspended again in March. When it reappeared he wrote a stirring article on the heroism of the ordinary soldier. Already he was forging those links between himself and the *poilu* which were to serve him well when he became prime minister.

Inevitably there were some who thought that his criticisms were unpatriotic. It was said that at least ten letters threatening him with death reached the office of *L'Homme Enchaîné* every day, and he was fiercely denounced in *L'Action Française*, which had suspended its royalist activities in the interests of the *union sacrée*. The editor, Charles Maurras, believed that Clemenceau's articles were damaging to the national cause.

He called their author 'a disastrous mountebank' and 'the anarchist Clemenceau', and sneeringly noted that extracts from *L'Homme Enchaîné* were reprinted in *La Gazette des Ardennes*, a propagandist French-language newspaper published by the Germans for the inhabitants of occupied territories. In later years Caillaux called the articles 'venomous diatribes' which no government should have tolerated for a moment.

Such onslaughts may be expected by any outspoken journalist who tries to keep a war-time government up to the mark. The purpose of Clemenceau's 'diatribes' was to secure a more vigorous and efficient prosecution of the war, and his daily articles were an honourable part of his service to France. Even the government was not always displeased with him, for in November 1915 the minister of finance wrote to thank him for a fine article supporting the latest war loan; and the public was certainly appreciative, for the circulation of *L'Homme Enchaîné* rose to the very respectable figure of 100,000. It was the soldiers' favourite paper.

[3]

Clemenceau's 'other hat' was worn in the Senate, where he was recognised as a fiery champion of war to the end. When General Galliéni, who had succeeded Millerand as war minister, told the Senate that the conflict would be ended only when France, in agreement with her Allies, could say, 'I have obtained full satisfaction; I stop fighting and I resume my work of peace,' the Tiger's roar of '*Jusqu'au bout!*' could be heard above the senators' loud applause.

He spoke too in the Senate's secret sessions, which had been introduced by Briand when deputies and senators wanted to question ministers about the inadequate defences in the Verdun area. The Senate held four secret sessions in 1916–17, the Chamber of Deputies eight; though some of the speakers aired fantastic ideas, much of the discussions was sensible and realistic.

But it was in the Senate's army commission, often meeting in joint session with the foreign affairs commission, that Clemenceau exerted his greatest political influence during his years as leader in waiting. The Chamber had a similar commission, and both bodies had important functions in war-time. They had the usual right of a French parliamentary commission to summon ministers, including the prime minister, to attend their meetings and answer questions about policy; they were also empowered to send representatives to inspect the fighting front and to discuss in secret the results of these inspections. In the early part of the war Joffre refused to allow the parliamentary commissioners to have unrestricted access to the front; Clemenceau's persistence in making his own contacts with all ranks of the army, from generals to *poilus*, was one of the factors which enabled parliament gradually to wrest authority from the army's GHQ.

On becoming chairman of the army commission Clemenceau made full use of its right to question ministers. Briand and Galliéni had to attend for eighteen long sessions, and shortcomings of various kinds were carefully examined; Clemenceau claimed that 'The reports of our meetings prove incontestably that by patient obstinacy we have often succeeded in making our voice heard.' One subject which came under close scrutiny was the army medical service. Though it had improved since it was first criticised in *L'Homme Libre*, its deficiencies were still, in Clemenceau's opinion, 'materially and morally deplorable'; the commission kept it constantly under review until the middle of 1917, and could take credit for the gradual improvement in the army's treatment of its sick and wounded.

Only a relatively few people knew what the Tiger was doing for the army behind the Senate commission's closed doors, but his visits to the front gave the *poilu* visible proof of his interest and concern. One of his earliest visits was made in September 1915, when preparations were being made for an offensive in Champagne. He returned to Paris full of praise for the soldiers' fighting spirit, but owing to Joffre's restrictions on the commissioners' movements, he had not been able to visit the British section of the line. When he became chairman of the commission he made his own contact with the British army by inviting Major-General Sir Henry Wilson to come to see him in Paris in December 1915.

Wilson, a tall Irishman, had been the British director of military operations for four years before the war, and now held the important post of principal liaison officer between the French and British armies. He was a born intriguer, and it was, indeed, for a proposed intrigue that the Tiger wanted to see him.

By this time the scope of the war had been greatly extended by the adherence of other countries to each side. The original Allies—Russia, Serbia, France, Britain and occupied Belgium—had been quickly joined by Japan, whose main objective was the seizure of German possessions in China and the Pacific, and later by Italy, who had been lured away from her *entente* with Germany and Austria by the promise of territorial gains after the war. On the other side Turkey and Bulgaria had joined Germany and Austria. This enlargement of the war opened up the possibility, approved by some Allied statesmen and deplored by others, of turning away from the stalemate on the western front and attacking the enemy in what came to be known as 'side-shows'.

One of these 'side-shows' was the Salonika front. Though Greece was neutral, a small Anglo-French force (more French than English) landed on Greek territory in October 1915 with the intention, which was not fulfilled, of protecting the Serbs when Bulgaria entered the war on Germany's side. As December approached Briand asked the British government to send more troops to Salonika, but Clemenceau, whose eyes were still on the blue line of the Vosges, regarded the whole affair as a criminal waste of man-power. He wanted Wilson to persuade the British government to refuse Briand's request, in the hope that this would lead to the withdrawal of the entire force from Salonika.

This attempt to go behind the French prime minister's back was no part of the official duties of the chairman of the Senate army commission. It was not, in fact, successful, for both the French and British governments had political reasons for maintaining the Allied force in Salonika. The French government was influenced by the personality of the commanding officer, General Sarrail, who was the only genuinely Republican and anti-clerical general in the French army. Sarrail had powerful friends, who would have regarded withdrawal from Salonika as a personal affront to him, and would certainly have overthrown a government which insulted their favourite soldier. For the British government, which was far from enthusiastic about Salonika, the deciding factor was the wish to show solidarity with Briand; its ministers feared that if Briand fell, the Tiger would take his place, and that France would be weakened by his clashes with Poincaré. It therefore agreed to Briand's request; more troops, both French and British, were sent to Salonika and stayed there till the end of the war.

Though Wilson's visit to Paris had no practical result, he enjoyed his first meeting with the Tiger. 'A real character and personality—one of the few I have ever met,' he wrote in his diary. 'He thought little of Poincaré, and thought he himself could perhaps just manage a year of strain, although he knew he was old and already "seriously ill", thought Joffre admirable as "figure-head" and "Buddha", but of no use otherwise.'

Revisiting the front in May 1916 with his new authority as chairman of the army commission, Clemenceau was able to visit both the French and British armies. General Joffre, smarting from the Tiger's attacks in *L'Homme Enchaîné*, refused to see him, but he made a good impression on Sir Douglas Haig, the British commander-in-chief.

Once again he was trying to influence the strategy of the war, for he urged Haig to restrain Joffre from any large-scale offensive until the Allied armies, both in France and on the Russian front, were at their maximum strength. Haig found his visitor 'most interesting' and 'wonderfully active', and felt that he had made a new friend. It would be useful in 1917–18 that Clemenceau could attract even hard-headed British generals by the vivacity of his conversation and the charm of his personality.

From Haig's headquarters Clemenceau went to see General Wilson, who had been removed from his post of liaison officer and sent back to the British front as a corps commander. The Tiger arrived by appointment at 7 a.m., and he astonished Wilson and his staff, who had expected him to 'toy with a cup of coffee and a rusk', by going right through a 'sumptuous breakfast' of porridge, kippers, bacon and eggs and finally, strawberries and cream. In a long talk after breakfast he again urged that there should be no offensive in the west until Russia was ready to attack in the east. Wilson thought he had never seen the Tiger so anxious about the future.

No one heeded his warnings against a large-scale offensive. This was the summer of the first battle of the Somme, in which the British lost 410,000 men, the French 190,000 and the Germans 500,000, and of the gallant French defence of Verdun, which turned the eyes of the world on the resolute French commander, General Philippe Pétain. In the autumn both French and British commanders-in-chief were criticised because of the immense human losses and small territorial gains of the battle of the Somme, and in each country there was a tendency to think that the other country's generals had done better. In a letter to King George V on 18 October Sir Douglas Haig described with some relish an encounter between Clemenceau and Field-Marshal Lord French, the former British commander-in-chief, who had come back to France to find out the truth about the Somme offensive. Haig's story begins with French's visit to General Foch's headquarters:

After lunch Gen. Foch handed over the F.M. [French] to one of his staff who took him to see some guns & incidentally called at the H.Q. of a Divisional General where (whether by chance or design I know not!) M. Clemenceau happened to be. The latter had recently been studying *British* tactics in the Somme Battles: he had spent a week on the ground and had gone into every detail. On being introduced to Lord French he at once *expatiated* on what the English had done: the skill of everyone & the accuracy of the artillery, etc., etc. I understand that it was quite amusing to see the critical Frenchman who had come to the British front to find arguments wherewith to chastise the French Higher Command, brought face to face with the British Field Marshal who had the exact contrary rôle! I expect that neither will succeed in doing much harm.[1]

Clemenceau's meetings with Foch at the front confirmed his high opinion of the general's abilities; he told Wilson that he meant to get rid of

[1] RA GV Q 832/127.

Joffre and that Foch would be the best man to succeed him. But Foch was not having an easy war. As commander of the French northern army group, he was made a scapegoat for the Somme failure, and at the end of the year he came to the rue Franklin in a state of great excitement, to tell Clemenceau that, on Poincaré's orders, Joffre had relieved him of his command. He had been given the trivial post of army inspector on the Swiss frontier, and he wanted to know what he should do.

Clemenceau gave him good advice: 'They cannot do without you. Obey without arguing or recrimination. Go back quietly to your own home. Lie low. Perhaps you will be called back inside a fortnight.' In fact, Foch's rehabilitation took much more than a fortnight, but in May 1917 he was given the important post of chief of the general staff under a new commander-in-chief, General Pétain.

[4]

By the beginning of 1917 Clemenceau was widely recognised as a potential war leader. Poincaré had observed in his diary that the time was coming when he would have to entrust the government to a man who would sacrifice everything for the sake of the war, whether it was Clemenceau or his own worst enemy. The censors, too, were more lenient with his articles in *L'Homme Enchaîné*, but they made heavy cuts in a rival paper's article attacking the Tiger as 'the always angry old man', and another paper was suspended for two months for a vicious onslaught entitled 'Mossieu Clemenceau'. Censored or uncensored, *L'Homme Enchaîné* continued its caustic comments on the conduct of the war. When Briand resigned in March, his successors—Ribot (March–October) and Paul Painlevé (October–November)—had to bear the full weight of the Tiger's criticisms.

In the early weeks of the year the continuing stalemate on the western front made it seem as if the war might go on for ever. Then suddenly, in March and April, the whole outlook was changed by events in other countries.

The first of these was the Russian revolution in March, when the Tsarist regime was overthrown by the Workers' and Soldiers' Soviet of Petrograd (as St. Petersburg had been renamed early in the war), rather half-heartedly supported by the Duma, the powerless Russian parliament. This momentous event was misunderstood in the French press. The Soviet's battle-cry was 'Peace and social revolution', but French newspapers (including *L'Homme Enchaîné*) at first portrayed the revolution as a movement designed to ensure a more vigorous prosecution of the war. Clemenceau went so far as to call it 'a first and decisive victory over

Germany', but as the summer went on he began to appreciate the menace of the Workers' and Soldiers' Soviet, which he denounced as 'a gang of scoundrels in the pay of the German secret service, a band of German Jews with a more or less plausible Russian veneer, repeating what they have been taught to say in Berlin'.

Barely a fortnight after the fall of the Tsarist regime the German policy of unrestricted submarine warfare brought the hitherto neutral United States into the war on the Allies' side. Whatever might happen in the east, the outlook on the western front was dramatically altered by the pledge that a great American army would be built up and sent to Europe. Victory now seemed certain in fifteen or eighteen months, provided that the Allies held firm in the meantime. In Clemenceau's view 'there was nothing for it but to wait for the Americans and meanwhile not to lose men'.

But men were still being lost in large numbers. Plans for an April offensive on the western front had been made before America's entry into the war, and for this Anglo-French attack it was agreed that both armies should be under the command of General Nivelle, who had succeeded Joffre as French commander-in-chief after doing well in the defence of Verdun.

Nivelle's plan was for a big French assault on German positions in the Craonne-Reims area, while the British drew off German reserves by an attack on Arras. The British attack succeeded in pushing the front some five miles forward, but only at the cost of 145,000 killed, wounded or missing; but the French assault failed, yielding only insignificant gains in return for a casualty list of 131,000. The French government was alarmed by the heavy losses. It called off the offensive and dismissed Nivelle, putting Pétain in his place. The first experiment in placing the Allied armies under a single command had been a regrettable failure.

This unlucky offensive had immediate effects on French morale. In the army it led to mutinies in May and June—mutinies which were partly caused by the distribution of pacifist pamphlets to soldiers on leave, but more essentially by the fighting men's practical grievances (such as suspension of leave periods, monotonous food, too little rest and too much drill between spells in the trenches) and by a loss of will-power due to the useless and life-wasting offensives into which their leaders drove them. Those who asked for peace did so because they had ceased to believe in war. Among civilians, too, there were signs of a moral crisis; pacifists and defeatists were active, and trade unionists began a series of strikes which made 100,000 workers idle in seventy-one industries.

The army crisis was settled in a few weeks. A score of the ringleaders were shot, and Pétain, who shared his men's distaste for reckless carnage and was genuinely concerned for their welfare, toured the whole of the

French front line and remedied most of the *poilus'* material grievances by giving them better food and accommodation behind the lines, and by ensuring that they were allowed to take their regular leave. He also won their confidence by modernising the technique of attack, so as to avoid heavy casualties. At the same time he sent a sharp report to the government, condemning the circulation of pacifist newspapers, inadequate press censorship, official tolerance of strikes and criticism of the high command by parliamentarians who visited the front.

[5]

Civilian morale presented a harder problem. The strikes were settled, but only after Malvy, who had remained minister of the interior in successive war-time governments, had aroused criticism by his personal negotiations with the strike leaders. Yet *Le Bonnet Rouge* and other anti-war papers were allowed to encourage defeatism, and found a ready response because of general dissatisfaction with shortages, restrictions and high living costs. It was in this summer of discontent that the Tiger dealt a heavy blow to defeatism by denouncing Malvy in the Senate.

The editor of *Discours de Guerre*, the collection of Clemenceau's wartime speeches, thinks that this tremendous onslaught, which took more than two hours to deliver, finally established him as France's destined leader. It was a remarkable oration, which was based on exact quotations from anti-patriotic newspapers and pamphlets and from communications between the ministry of the interior and the departmental prefects. The research must have been Mandel's work, but the speech itself was in the Tiger's most brilliant vein, turning from one grave charge to another with occasional flashes of humour or sarcasm that made the senators smile or laugh outright.

Malvy was a familiar target for Clemenceau's criticisms in *L'Homme Enchaîné*, and the two men had already had one clash in the Senate in the previous December, when Clemenceau challenged the minister to explain why he had forbidden a prefect to prosecute a disseminator of anti-patriotic propaganda. Now he returned to the attack in a public session which followed two days' secret debate on the failure of the April offensive.

His general charge was that Malvy had done nothing to stop the flow of anti-patriotic propaganda which was endangering the country's war effort. He dealt at length with the minister's failure to arrest any of the Frenchmen named in Carnet B, and contended that the arrest of only fifteen of them would have been enough to check the anti-patriotic movement. He reproached the minister for having consulted Almereyda about Carnet B, and observed that, while he had not seen the list, it would make God and man despair if Almereyda's name were not in it. He derided Malvy's explanation that he had not wished to offend the workers by arresting some of their leaders, and he blamed him for failing to track down the authors of seditious pamphlets distributed to the troops and for not keeping the army authorities informed about the circulation of pacifist propaganda. He also cited some disturbing cases of enemy aliens who, on Malvy's instructions, had been allowed to move freely about France, and even, in some instances, to travel to and from Switzerland.

Malvy made only a lame reply to most of these charges. He was on good ground in pointing out that mobilisation had proceeded smoothly after his decision not to arrest the men named in Carnet B, but he was less convincing when he claimed that his policy of conciliation and avoiding trouble had been no less successful than a policy of sanctions and repression would have been. When he declared, 'You have reproached me for not bringing you enough heads; I bring you results,' Clemenceau retorted: 'I reproach you for having betrayed the interests of France'.

These were strong words, and it must be conceded in Malvy's defence that he was not a traitor in the ordinary sense of the word. He was neither pacifist nor defeatist; his real offences were laziness, a fondness for taking the easy course rather than the hard one, and an untimely loyalty to his former leader, Joseph Caillaux, who was in temporary eclipse but would certainly have become prime minister again if there had been any serious question of a negotiated peace with Germany. It was in Malvy's interest to be as gentle as possible towards the appeasers, pacifists and pro-Germans who would be the ruling class if Caillaux returned to power; but this policy involved the loosening of control, so that the ministry of the interior under Malvy never became a genuine ministry of national security. His habit of playing poker until two o'clock in the morning suggests a certain levity in his approach to his very important job.

Clemenceau's indictment did not immediately drive Malvy out of the government. The speech was made on 22 July; it was not until 31 August that Malvy conceded defeat and resigned from the ministry. He was subsequently tried by the Senate, sitting as a high court; no charge of treason was brought against him, but he was convicted of having 'failed in, violated and betrayed the duties of his office' and was declared to be 'guilty of forfeiture'. He was sentenced to five years' banishment, but returned to politics after the war and became chairman of the Chamber of Deputies finance commission.

Malvy's trial took place in January 1918. By that time *Le Bonnet Rouge* had ceased to exist, Almereyda had been arrested and had committed suicide in prison, and action was being taken against other traitors, including the notorious German agent, Bolo Pasha. Besides removing an unsatisfactory minister from office, Clemenceau's speech had inspired a more vigorous approach to the problems of treachery and defeatism.

[6]

Socialist pacifism was another menace to France's war effort in 1917. Officially the *union sacrée* was still in being, but the Socialists had split into two groups, of which the more militant and doctrinaire group believed that nothing could justify the workers of one country killing the workers of another. An international workers' conference at Stockholm offered them a chance of meeting German Socialists and working out a formula for peace. The young Socialist deputy Pierre Laval set the pattern for Left wing appeasement by declaring in the Chamber: 'The way to give hope to the troops and confidence to the workers, whether you like it or not, is Stockholm. Stockholm is the star of the north!'

The Socialists' wish to attend the conference was discussed in the press and in parliament. Clemenceau persuaded the Senate to vote against the proposed journey, and from GHQ General Pétain told the government there would be a moral crisis in the French army if it were known that French Socialists were exchanging views with Germans. Ribot, who was then prime minister, saw the danger, and refused to allow the Socialists to go to Stockholm. They continued, however, to erode the national unity proclaimed by Poincaré.

But the French Socialists were not the only people who were thinking about a negotiated peace in 1917. Other efforts to begin peace talks were made unofficially, and though Clemenceau was not concerned in them, they were to have important repercussions after he had become prime minister.

The first of these attempts is generally called 'the Prince Sixtus affair', since the go-between was Prince Sixtus of Bourbon-Parma, brother of the Empress Zita of Austria, whose husband Karl had succeeded to the throne on the death of Emperor Franz Josef in November 1916. Prince Sixtus, who was a descendant of Louis XIV, had wished to join the French army, but had been rejected because of his Bourbon ancestry and had then joined the Belgian army. He was commissioned by Emperor Karl to sound out the French about the possibility of a negotiated peace, on the basis of the return of Alsace-Lorraine to France, the restoration of Belgium and the re-establishment of the kingdom of Serbia. The prince saw Poincaré and gave him, in strict confidence, a copy of the letter he had received from the Emperor. The offer was then studied by the French government, but the project collapsed when it became clear that Austria would not consider any Italian territorial claims as part of a general settlement.

After the war Prince Sixtus's approach was represented as the offer of a separate peace by Austria, and Ribot, who was prime minister at the time of the discussions, was accused of having wrecked a promising peace move. But the idea of a separate peace with Austria had been mentioned only by Prince Sixtus himself in conversation with Poincaré; it did not appear in the Austrian Emperor's letter, and in any case Count Czernin, the Austrian foreign minister, was consistently opposed to such a project. Moreover, Germany would not at that time have considered peace on the terms mentioned by the Emperor Karl; the minimum German terms for ending the war were the retention of Alsace-Lorraine, the cession by France of the Longwy-Briey area and the partition of Belgium. Since no French government could have yielded to such demands, there was no possibility of peace in 1917.

Briand was involved in another peace move, which was initiated by Baron von Lancken, the former counsellor at the German embassy in Paris, who had become director of the political section of the German government in Belgium. He proposed that Briand, who was then out of office, should meet him in Switzerland to work out the basis for a negotiated peace; but when Briand told the President and members of the government about Lancken's suggestion, they refused to sanction his journey to Switzerland. They were sure that Germany would not voluntarily give up Alsace-Lorraine, and they felt that the whole affair was a trap, designed to demoralise French public opinion by raising hopes which would not be fulfilled. In the following month Ribot, as foreign minister in Painlevé's government, made an oblique reference to the Lancken proposal in the Chamber; Clemenceau, who rarely missed an opportunity for scoring off Briand, at once picked it up and wrote in *L'Homme Enchaîné* that he found it hard to believe that a French politician could have been involved in a secret German peace manoeuvre. Briand observed in the Chamber that on this occasion *L'Homme Enchaîné* had been 'remarkably unchained'.

The French government agreed, however, to the holding of exploratory peace talks in Switzerland between Major Armand, an officer in the army reserve, and Count Revertera, an Austrian diplomat. They met in August, but their talks were sterile. A second meeting, in February 1918, was equally unproductive, and was important only because it was sanctioned by Clemenceau as prime minister.

[7]

At 10 a.m. on 2 November, 1917, Clemenceau unexpectedly presented himself at the headquarters of General Mordacq, commanding officer of the 24th division, whom he had met on several occasions during the war. He told the general that he was soon to be appointed prime minister, and that he intended to be his own minister of war. He invited Mordacq to come to Paris as his military *chef de cabinet*, and the general, who had high hopes of becoming a corps commander, accepted the invitation with some reluctance. It was the beginning of a happy and useful partnership.

The date of this meeting was twelve days before the Tiger was formally asked to form a ministry, but at last he was confident that the call was coming. Poincaré had thought of appointing him when Ribot resigned in October, but Marcel Sembat, a leading Socialist, warned the President that he would lose the support of the working class if he made Clemenceau prime minister. Poincaré allowed himself to be over-persuaded, and chose Painlevé instead.

Painlevé was not cut out to be a war-time prime minister. His government was weak, and pleased neither Left nor Right. His early fall was inevitable. Then there would be only two choices left for France—Clemenceau, and war to the limit, or Caillaux, and peace on the best terms available. For a patriotic Lorrainer like Raymond Poincaré only one of these choices was possible. On 18 October he wrote in his diary: 'At this time Clemenceau seems to me to be marked out by public opinion, because he wishes to go to the limit in war and in judicial matters, and in these conditions I have no right to put him aside simply because of his attitude towards me.'

The President had made up his mind. He told his friends that he was resolved to send for Clemenceau in the event of a new ministerial crisis. In October there were rumours that the Tiger had been to the Elysée, and they were not far short of the truth. In fact the faithful Pichon had gone as his emissary, and had assured Poincaré that Clemenceau would answer his call.

On 13 November Painlevé became the first (and only) war-time prime minister of France to lose his post through defeat in parliament. (His three predecessors had resigned.) After the vote which brought down his ministry there were cries of 'Down with Clemenceau! Long live the Republic!' from Socialist deputies. Poincaré went through the usual procedure of consulting the presidents of the Chamber and Senate, chairmen of parliamentary commissions, departing ministers and former prime ministers, but he paid no attention to those who advised him not to send for Clemenceau. On the afternoon of 14 November the Tiger was summoned to the Elysée and invited to form the next government.

In accordance with precedent, he said only that he would try to do so, but there was never any doubt of his success. 'He'll make his cabinet, even if he has to bring in his *valet de chambre*,' said one who knew him well. And on the morning of 16 November *L'Homme Enchaîné* announced: 'M. Clemenceau agrees to form a cabinet.'

The day of his access to power was also the last day of his long and distinguished journalistic career. His final article appeared in *L'Homme Enchaîné* on 15 November, but the paper had given a curious sign of impending change four days earlier, when the old line, 'Editor-in-chief, G. Clemenceau' was altered to 'Political director, G. Clemenceau'. After his assumption of power this in its turn was replaced by 'Founder, G. Clemenceau', and the newspaper's name reverted to *L'Homme Libre*. He was to write several books in the closing years of his life, but he was never again to be a journalist. He took Mandel with him to the war ministry, and he entrusted *L'Homme Libre* to Nicolas Piétri, a Corsican who had been the manager of *Paris-Journal* and would become the Tiger's friend and travelling companion after the war.

CHAPTER FIFTEEN

MAN OF WAR

*1. The daily round. 2. Settling with Caillaux. 3. The Fourteen Points. 4. Generals
and statesmen. 5. 'Je fais la guerre.'*

[1]

VICTORY SEEMED far away at the time when Clemenceau became
prime minister of France. There was little activity on the western
front: Pétain and Haig thought there should be only limited attacks
until 1919, when two million American troops would be massed for battle,
and only Foch believed that the war could be won in 1918. In other
theatres of war the Italians had been routed at Caporetto and would be on
the defensive for many months, Russia had virtually stopped fighting and
was believed to be on the point of making a separate peace with Germany,
and the Allied force at Salonika was still inactive. At home the government
had to be on its guard against defeatism, treason and espionage; workers
demonstrated against the war, bread was scarce, there were long queues
at food shops and air raids by German Gothas were causing great damage
to life and property in Paris; Poincaré believed that a third of the deputies
wanted peace without daring to avow it. It was a challenging situation for
the man who, after years of criticising other men's conduct of the war,
suddenly found himself entrusted with supreme power.

He had become, too, an isolated political figure. He was no longer a
man of the Left, and though he could draw support from the Centre and
the Right he had no close links with any of their parliamentary leaders;
in forming his government he had to rely on his own circle of friends
and followers. Keeping the war ministry for himself, he gave the ministry
of foreign affairs to Pichon and the ministry of the interior to Pams, whom
he had backed for the presidency in 1913. None of the leading ex-ministers
was offered a portfolio, and the Socialists declined to allow any of their
members to take office in a Clemenceau government.[1] His choice of

---

[1] It is an irony of history that one of the Socialists whom Clemenceau invited to
join his government for 'war to the limit' was Pierre Laval. (*See* Suarez, *Clemenceau*,
II, p. 215.)

ministers was thus severely restricted, but men like Loucheur (munitions), Klotz (finance) and Leygues (navy) were far from being nonentities, and the principal ministries were run with reasonable efficiency. Clemenceau was grossly unfair to his war-time colleagues when he once described them as 'the geese who saved the Capitol'.

At the heart of Clemenceau's system of government was his personal *cabinet*, the little group of men who worked closely with him at the war ministry in the rue Saint-Dominique, where he combined his posts of prime minister and minister of war. The appointment of General Mordacq as military *chef de cabinet* was a new departure: with an experienced general to advise him daily on war strategy, Clemenceau was in closer touch with military affairs than any of his predecessors had been. Another key figure of his inner group was Edouard Ignace, the loyal and capable under-secretary for military justice, who had the onerous tasks of fighting defeatism and rounding up the *embusqués* and 'indispensables' and sending them back to active service.

The most remarkable of Clemenceau's close associates was Mandel, rewarded at last, after his long political apprenticeship, with a post that gave full scope for his talents. Nominally he was the civil *chef de cabinet*, but in reality he was much more than that, for apart from the special functions devolved on Ignace, he was the prime minister's chief executive on the home front. He had complete responsibility for press censorship, and his nightly press conferences gave journalists an exact knowledge of what they might or might not say; he continued to provide Clemenceau with accurate press summaries and confidential reports on public and parliamentary opinion; he acted as liaison officer for the different ministries concerned with home affairs, and among other duties he kept a careful watch on the appointment of prefects, since Clemenceau attached great importance to the choice of suitable men for these posts. It was sometimes said that Mandel was the real minister of the interior, and that Pams was only a figure-head; but this was an exaggeration, for although Pams regularly consulted him, he never saw the ministry's departmental heads and never dealt with problems of administration.

Clemenceau, who was so often rude to him and grumbled about his being '*toujours au téléphone*', had to admit after the war: 'I could not have done my work successfully if I had not had Georges Mandel near me.' Mandel himself claimed that 'I was so used to working with M. Clemenceau that I knew all his ideas.' It was unfortunate that one who served his master and his country so loyally should have incurred so much enmity on his own behalf because of his brusque and arrogant manner.

These three—Mordacq, Ignace, Mandel—were the intimates who were in touch with the Tiger at various times during the day, and always came to his office at 8 p.m., together with Raux, prefect of police, and Jeanneney, under-secretary of state, for a final discussion of urgent matters. Clemenceau had a long day, rising at five or six o'clock for an hour or two of reading and writing before his gymnastic instructor came to take him through half-an-hour's physical exercise—a practice which he had adopted with advancing years and to which he attributed his vigorous old age. He arrived at the war ministry at 8.45 a.m., sometimes earlier, and after signing the previous day's letters and reading the latest war telegrams he would have consultations with Mordacq, Pichon and Mandel before going on to a council of ministers or a parliamentary commission. He went home for lunch, but was back at the office at 2 p.m., when he received visitors for an hour before spending the rest of the afternoon at the Chamber or the Senate or again with a parliamentary commission. At 5.30 or 6 p.m. he was again at his desk, ready to read and sign important documents, dictate letters and receive visitors on urgent business until eight o'clock brought the regular conference with his little group of intimates. Then for the last half-hour of his day he relaxed, and was willing to chat with unofficial callers, such as members of his family or journalists who were personal friends. At 9 p.m. he went home for a light dinner and an early bed-time, followed by a night in which he had little sleep. At this time he never accepted an invitation to lunch or dine with friends, and he attended official luncheons or dinners only when his presence was indispensable.

It will be observed that the President of the Republic had no place in Clemenceau's daily programme. On taking office he had promised that he would never make any decision without discussing it with Poincaré, but the President was soon complaining that he never heard anything from his prime minister. Certainly Poincaré presided at cabinet meetings, in accordance with constitutional practice, but whereas Clemenceau's predecessors had held such meetings daily, they were now called only occasionally, and important issues were not discussed at them. Crucial decisions were usually taken at private meetings between Clemenceau and the appropriate minister; Poincaré's diary from January 1918 onwards contains frequent laments about the impotence of the cabinet.

The Tiger's daily routine was varied only when he went to Versailles for meetings of the Supreme War Council, which had been set up after the Caporetto disaster to co-ordinate Allied strategy, or on the days, which became more and more frequent, when he went to the front. His accession to power meant little at first to the men in the trenches; to most of them he was 'just another politician', and the monthly assessment of soldiers' morale showed that only a small minority were encouraged by his appointment. Yet the confidence he inspired in a few was to grow from month to month, as the fighting men became accustomed to seeing a tough old civilian in their midst, wearing his chosen front-line attire of long great-coat trailing in the mud, wide-meshed muffler and helmet-like cap. (Poincaré, by contrast, was laughed at for visiting the front in a costume which greatly resembled a chauffeur's uniform.) And from the trenches the confidence spread to the home front, until, as Barrès put it, 'We believed in Clemenceau rather in the way that our ancestors believed in Joan of Arc.'

[2]

Clemenceau's ministry was well received in the press, though with a certain reserve in the more conservative newspapers. *Le Journal des Débats* thought there were risks in his appointment, but *L'Action Française*, which had been so bitter about his articles in *L'Homme Enchaîné*, now gave him whole-hearted support, as its leading writers, Charles Maurras and Léon Daudet, felt that the new government satisfied their desire for strong leadership. It was generally recognised that there were two great points in Clemenceau's favour: throughout the war he had never been discouraged, and he had never ceased to wish for and believe in total victory.

Scepticism about his staying power could be found, however, among experienced politicians on both sides of the Channel. At the end of November Lloyd George, the British prime minister, and Lord Reading, a prominent fellow Liberal, were in Paris for the first meeting of the Supreme War Council. Colonel Maurice Hankey, British secretary of the council, had breakfast with them and several French guests. He noted afterwards:

> Like everyone else they think that Clemenceau will not last long—only long enough to clean up the '*affaire* Bolo' and the '*affaire* Malvy'.

Another British visitor to Paris was equally convinced that Clemenceau would have only a short time in office. In a letter to Queen Mary on 27 December Lord Esher wrote:

> . . . during the past six months the War has descended into a lower plane in political circles. Everyone is absorbed by Caillautism. It killed Briand, Ribot and Painlevé, and now it is killing Clemenceau.
>
> Opinion is rapidly veering away from Clemenceau, and everyone in the Chamber seems convinced that his Government will *not last beyond the middle of February*.
>
> He has mismanaged the attack on Caillaux, who, from being a man

whom everyone shunned, has become, since his speech, a personage with whom men shake hands. It is an ominous business.[1]

Lord Esher's pessimism about the government was ill-founded, but in mentioning Caillaux and Caillautism he had put his finger on one of the danger-spots in French politics.

In announcing his government's policy on 20 November Clemenceau had said: 'We present ourselves before you with the single thought of a total war.' This was the speech of which Winston Churchill, who was present in the Chamber of Deputies, has left such a vivid impression in his *Great Contemporaries*:

> He looked like a wild animal pacing to and fro behind bars, growling and glaring; and all around him was an assembly which would have done anything to avoid having him there, but having put him there, felt they must obey. Indeed it was not a matter of words or reasoning. . . . The last desperate stake had to be played. France had resolved to unbar the cage and let her tiger loose upon all foes, beyond the trenches or in her midst. Language, eloquence, arguments were not needed to express the situation. With snarls and growls, the ferocious, aged, dauntless beast of prey went into action.

And the action he promised was victory with justice, loyalty to the fighting man, immediate punishment of crimes against France—the policy of war *jusqu'au bout*, which was opposed both by the Socialists and by Joseph Caillaux, the pro-German appeaser of pre-war days, and his followers. It was clear, therefore, that Caillautism must be challenged and overcome if France were to win the victory which, in Clemenceau's opinion, she deserved.

Caillaux claimed afterwards that he had practised 'patriotic self-effacement' during the war, for he had made few speeches and had written to the press only when he was attacked; but it was not the kind of self-effacement that any government could view with equanimity. He had begun the war as a paymaster with the army, but after a few weeks he gave up his post and spent the winter in South America, where he made contact with German diplomats. For a year after his return to France he stayed quietly at his country house at Mamers, where Malvy and Almereyda came to see him; but it was when he visited Italy in 1916—Florence in the autumn, Rome in December—that his actions became suspect to the French authorities, who feared that he was trying to imbue one of France's allies with his own brand of pro-German defeatism.

Their fears were justified. In Rome Caillaux made contact with Giolitti, a leading pro-German politician, and with other Italians of dubious

[1] RA GV Q 724/99.

loyalty. He was received by the Pope, and a few days later the Apostolic Nuncio in Vienna gave Count Czernin a peace programme said to have been drawn up unofficially by 'someone who could be regarded as an interpreter of the feelings of the Entente'. (This was obviously Caillaux's work.) He also told the Italian politician Ferdinando Martini that France would have to make peace, even without compensation, even without the recovery of Alsace-Lorraine.

News of these activities reached Paris, and Briand, who was then prime minister, told Camille Barrère, the French ambassador in Rome, to explain to the Italian foreign minister that Caillaux was not authorised to make any statement on behalf of the French government. Poincaré felt that this was not enough; he wanted to see Caillaux behind bars; but Briand thought it would be dangerous to arrest a former prime minister on charges of treason, and Ribot, who succeeded him, took the same view.

Clemenceau's appointment changed the situation. His policy of war to the end was diametrically opposed to Caillaux's advocacy of a negotiated peace, which could be achieved only by a virtual surrender to Germany. The national interest demanded the removal, not only of traitors, but of others who were potential dangers to security. On this subject, at least, he and Poincaré thought alike, and the machinery for putting Caillaux out of harm's way was set in motion on 11 December by a request from General Dubail, military governor of Paris, that the Chamber should agree to waive the parliamentary immunity of two deputies, of whom one was Joseph Caillaux.

Clemenceau himself appeared before the parliamentary committee which had to decide whether the military governor's request should go before the Chamber, and he candidly admitted that there was no absolute proof of any crime committed by Caillaux. The case was based on presumptions, but on presumptions which, if they concerned any ordinary French citizen, would already have caused the necessary measures to be taken. 'In any case,' he added, 'the government has done its duty. The Chamber will follow suit. If the waiving of parliamentary immunity is not voted, I shall not stay in office a minute longer.'

When the question was put to the Chamber, only a handful of deputies voted against it, though there were massive Socialist abstentions. This was the debate which Lord Esher thought to have been mismanaged, presumably because Caillaux, who was still a deputy, was given an opportunity of speaking in his own defence, and even making sarcastic comments about the Tiger's past association with Herz, while Clemenceau, as the man ultimately responsible for military justice, was not entitled to reply. But the debate did not rehabilitate Caillaux, as Lord Esher imagined; he had always had friends on the extreme Left, but he won no more by his defence; and a close observer of the political scene noted that there was general satisfaction when he was arrested on 14 January, 1918.

People at first expected that he would be court-martialled, but Clemenceau did not want an old colleague to be shot, and it was agreed that he should be treated as a political offender. Searches by the Deuxième Bureau (the military counter-espionage branch) after his arrest produced some interesting discoveries without proving that he was a traitor in the usual sense of the word. A particularly damning document, found in a safe which Caillaux had leased in an Italian bank, was headed 'Rubicon' and outlined a project for seizing power in France, proroguing parliament, purging the Senate and opening peace talks with Germany. Such a document was enough to show that Clemenceau and Poincaré were right in thinking that Caillaux was too dangerous a man to be left at liberty.

Clemenceau was not concerned with the lengthy investigations which followed Caillaux's arrest, and he had himself retired from public life when the case was heard in February 1920. The decision to have Caillaux arrested was then justified by his conviction and sentence to three years' imprisonment and ten years' banishment. In fact, both sentences were waived because he had already been in gaol for more than two years, and he was promptly liberated.

A few years after the war a diplomat who had served in Rome at this period discussed the Caillaux case with Clemenceau. 'I do not believe that Caillaux was actually a traitor,' Clemenceau said, and few would now disagree with him. Yet his offence was serious: Jean Ybarnégaray, a well-known deputy of the inter-war years, put the case neatly when he said of Caillaux: 'His crime was not to have believed in victory; to have gambled on his nation's defeat.' That was a gamble which neither Poincaré nor Clemenceau was prepared to tolerate.

In some circles the arrest of Caillaux and the various treason trials held in the winter and spring were taken as signs that the new government had begun a 'reign of terror'. The idea was fostered by aggrieved 'indispensables', who felt they were being victimised when they were chased out of their safe and comfortable jobs and packed off to the front. One such incident was mentioned by Brigadier Edward Spears, British liaison officer with the French army, to Colonel Hankey early in May, and was absurdly adduced as evidence that 'Clemenceau has created a regular reign of terror in France'.

The charge was exaggerated. Caillaux's case was exceptional. The ordinary citizen had nothing to fear from the Clemenceau government; the men who were arrested and put on trial were generally traitors, or associates of traitors, who should have been dealt with by previous governments. Certainly the arrests aroused great public excitement: one newspaper said ironically, 'The war must be over, for no one is talking about it any more.' But the 'reign of terror' existed only in the minds of Clemenceau's enemies and embittered 'indispensables'. Abel Ferry, a clear-thinking deputy, presented a different picture when he wrote that the treason trials 'exalted national feeling'; they let people know that action was being taken at last and that, for the first time in the war, they were being firmly governed.

It is sometimes said that Clemenceau's firm government was virtually a dictatorship, but this, again, is an accusation which is not supported by facts. It is true that political power, which had been seized by GHQ in the early months of the war and then slowly recaptured by parliament, was now assumed by the chief executive, but without the denial of parliamentary rights that can be expected under a dictatorship. Parliamentary forms were still respected; the law permitting the government to legislate by decree applied only to economic matters; but Clemenceau had still to justify his actions before parliament, and his government could at any time have been overthrown.

A slight relaxation of the press censorship was another proof that Clemenceau's government was not a dictatorship. Remembering the angry protests of *L'Homme Enchaîné*, the chief censor had wondered if the new prime minister would abolish the censorship; 'I am not a complete idiot,' Clemenceau observed acidly, and gave orders that military and diplomatic directives must be carefully followed, pacifist articles severely handled, but greater freedom given to political articles, since newspapers were entitled to criticise the prime minister and other members of the government. As he once rather nicely phrased it, 'The right to insult members of the government is inviolable.' One cannot imagine a dictator giving such a ruling.

Pierre Renouvin says of Clemenceau's government that 'Authority, but in the framework of the constitution, was the special feature of this system.' The country's political organisation was not tampered with; the big change was a shift in the balance of power from parliament to the government, which allowed Clemenceau to initiate an authoritarian government without infringing the constitutional rules. The only powers he assumed were those that he thought necessary for the tasks of suppressing treason and defeatism and winning the war.

[3]

At 3 a.m. on 9 January, 1918, a cable from Washington, addressed to the

Havas press agency, reached the French press censors' office in Paris. It reported an address by President Woodrow Wilson to Congress, outlining the necessary conditions for a satisfactory conclusion of the war. These were the Fourteen Points, of which more would be heard before and after the end of hostilities.

The censor who received the message realised its importance and at once rang up Mandel, who had given orders: 'Don't be afraid of waking me up. Besides, I hardly ever sleep.' After having the report read to him Mandel said he would go to the rue Franklin and tell Clemenceau, and that nothing must be done until he rang again.[1] His final instructions were to hold up the message for the night and release it to the news agency in the morning. It was spread over five or six columns in the next day's papers.

The Fourteen Points, which included detailed territorial proposals as well as more general provisions, such as open diplomacy, freedom of the seas, the removal of economic barriers and the formation of a League of Nations, at once became an article of faith with the French Left. Clemenceau felt that some of President Wilson's ideas were Utopian, but that it was no time for haggling with America and that France should accept the proposals as a whole. An important reason for supporting them was that one of the Fourteen Points called for the return of Alsace-Lorraine to France. Since Lloyd George had pledged Britain's support of France's claim (though rather cagily speaking of 'reconsideration', rather than 'revision', of the great injustice done to France in 1871), Clemenceau could now feel sure that victory would fulfil the one war aim consistently upheld by every French government. He asked Pichon to present Wilson's Fourteen Points to the Chamber of Deputies, which expressed its confidence in the government by 377 votes to 113.

It can be imagined that the sceptical Tiger had grave doubts about Wilson's advocacy of a League of Nations. People had often brought out plans for uniting the world, but Clemenceau's distrust of men made him feel that such a proposal was unrealistic; he had never believed that world peace was anything more than a dream.[2] But in view of the need to keep on good terms with Wilson it was hardly statesmanlike of him to say to a Dutch journalist, in an interview reprinted in *Le Matin* on 1 February: 'The League of Nations? Do *you* believe in it? In a world built upon violence?'

[1] It was unusual for Mandel to disturb his master in the middle of the night. He said after the war that he did not remember having awakened Clemenceau more than three times in twenty months. (*See* Berger and Allard, *Les Secrets de la Censure pendant la Guerre*, p. 276.)

[2] Some years earlier Maurice Barrès was present when a deputy was expounding to

[4]

Clemenceau had no time for visiting the front during his first weeks in office. There was too much to do in Paris, too many callers who wanted to see him. General Sir Henry Wilson looked in, and recorded afterwards that 'Clemenceau talked about Unity of Command, but did not seem to know quite what he wanted'. Another caller, to whom he was soon talking like an old friend, was General John Pershing, the chosen commander of the future American army; and he was greatly impressed by Colonel Edward House, close friend and European representative of President Woodrow Wilson, whom he found to be cultured, calm, thoughtful and well informed, with a good knowledge of Europe and a sincere friendship for France.

At the same time an important question of military command urgently called for his attention. General Sarrail, commander of the French 'army of the Orient' at Salonika, was also commander-in-chief of the mixed force of French, British, Italians, Serbs and Greeks assembled on the Macedonian front; but France's Allies had become irritated by his tactless manner and his concentration on political matters at the expense of military activity. The British government had been demanding his recall for months, but Painlevé, as war minister in Ribot's cabinet and subsequently as prime minister, had been too timid to dismiss the man who was known as 'France's only Republican general'.

Clemenceau had no such inhibitions. Just as he had not 'given a damn' about Foch's brother being a Jesuit, so too he did not 'give a damn' about Sarrail being a Republican; what mattered was to get the right man in the right place, and since Sarrail had lost the confidence of his Allied colleagues and their governments he was clearly the wrong man for Salonika. Early in December Clemenceau dismissed him (ostensibly on the ground that he had reached retiring age), and put in his place the distinguished and entirely acceptable General Guillaumat. The political storm feared by Painlevé did not arise. Clemenceau had shown what could be done when a strong man was at the head of affairs.

So, at last, with Salonika straightened out, his ministry organised and the Fourteen Points placed squarely in front of the French people, he was able to resume his visits to the front, which was only a few hours' journey from Paris, either by train or by road.

For his first visit in 1918 he left Paris by train in the evening of 18

Clemenceau and others 'his dreams of disarmament and universal peace'. Suddenly a whimpering was heard under the table at which they were sitting, and Clemenceau, lifting the tablecloth, found a dog there, asleep. 'Dogs have their dreams too,' he said. (*See* Barrès, *Cahiers*, VIII, pp. 248–9.)

January. Thereafter there was never a week in which he did not go to the front, and sometimes, especially during the great German offensives of March and July, he would make two visits in the same week. Mordacq was always with him.

There were two reasons for his visits. He wanted to meet the generals and discuss strategy with them, and to see for himself how they were carrying out the decisions of the Supreme War Council. He also wanted to see the *poilus*, to go into their trenches and talk to them, so that they could be assured that the government was watching over them. The *poilus*, for their part, gave an enthusiastic welcome to the little old man in the funny hat, and they admired his disregard of danger which alarmed the general staff. On one occasion, when he visited a part of the line where the German trenches were only about two hundred yards away, he insisted on going forward to shake hands with the two French soldiers who were nearest the enemy.

The Tiger's days in the trenches played no small part in winning him the title of 'Father of victory'; his appearances at GHQ were not always so happy. In principle, it was a good thing that the prime minister, who was also war minister, should be in close touch with his generals, but when the prime minister was accompanied by his own military adviser, who could supply him with good technical arguments, there were drawbacks as well as advantages in such contacts.

In January, for example, Clemenceau was presumptuous enough to set up his own military opinion against the commander-in-chief's. Pétain was a great believer in training, and was reluctant to take the risk of putting raw troops into the battle-line; he could show that his faith in training had been justified by results. To Clemenceau it seemed that the defensive works behind the lines were not yet strong enough, and he urged Pétain to hurry up with them, even at the cost of training. Pétain defended his policy with his usual stolidity, but appears in the end to have compromised, so that part of the precious training was sacrificed in the interests of building defensive works.

General Tournès, in his book *Foch et la Victoire des Alliés*, rightly claims that Clemenceau's interference was regrettable, since it meant that untrained troops, worn out by digging, were put under fire. 'The example is worth considering,' he writes. 'It shows the fatal effects which are constantly produced by the intrusion of the civil power into purely military questions where it has neither the knowledge nor the competence to intervene.' Fortunately for the Tiger's reputation, such interference with the commander-in-chief's use of his troops was exceptional; the later quarrel with Foch over the use of American troops was of a different character.

His visits to the British sector of the front were more in the nature of courtesy calls and were appreciated as such by Sir Douglas Haig, who retained his high opinion of the Tiger. ('He is most active and alert in mind and body, though 76 years of age,' he noted. 'He has always drunk water, but eats well . . . Clemenceau and I parted great friends.') But he was on his dignity in January when Clemenceau mentioned his theory of unity of command, which implied that all the Allied forces would serve under a French generalissimo. They were breakfasting at Haig's headquarters, and Clemenceau recalled in 1929 that

> . . . the soldier jumped up like a jack-in-the-box, and, with both hands shot up to heaven, exclaimed: 'Monsieur Clemenceau, I have only one chief, and I can have no other. My King!'

Time was to show that this was not a final decision; the moment would come when Haig would find it to his advantage that the British and French armies should be under a single command.

Clemenceau met other British war leaders in the Supreme War Council. He thought that Lloyd George was greatly gifted, remarkably intelligent and very clever, but also *un peu léger*, since he dealt with serious questions without having studied them beforehand. But he was soon at loggerheads with the British premier, for Britain, as it seemed to France, was not sending sufficient reinforcements to the western front, though she was anxious to increase the Allied forces in the Near East for a decisive offensive against Turkey.

To Clemenceau, who believed that the war must be won on the western front, the British proposal seemed heretical; he did not know that the British government was reluctant to send more troops to France for fear that they would be uselessly slaughtered by Haig. At a meeting of the council on 30 January he rounded on Lloyd George, and sharply declared that 'the Allies could not really afford to go on looking for victory on the Euphrates'.

Haig was delighted by the Tiger's use of his claws. 'He gave L.G. a real dressing-down,' he wrote to his wife, 'but unfortunately L.G. does not understand French, and the translator missed a good deal of the force of the speech though he gave its general meaning all right.'

At the same meeting the council discussed the formation of a general reserve of thirty divisions, whose movements would be controlled by the council's own executive war committee, headed by the French and British chiefs of staff, Foch and General Sir William Robertson. Essentially this was a plan for transferring control of part of the French and British armies from Pétain and Haig to Foch and Robertson. Haig would have nothing to do with it, and Pétain refused to contribute French divisions if no

British troops could be expected from Haig. In this argument Clemenceau sided with Pétain, and was thus in direct opposition to Foch, who favoured the creation of a reserve.

In a statement after the meeting the British government said that it would use its forces in the eastern theatre of war in the most effective way without diverting forces from the western front; but this did not satisfy Clemenceau, who now showed that, even as prime minister, he was prepared to use devious means to get his own way. In the previous October, when he had no ministerial responsibilities, he had discussed the man-power question with Colonel Repington, the military correspondent of the *The Times*, and Repington had duly expounded the Tiger's views in one of his articles. He decided to repeat the process, even though it meant going behind the backs of his colleagues on the Supreme War Council.

He had invited Repington to come to Paris while the council was sitting; after the meeting he told him what had been said and asked him 'to stop the side-shows and send us men'. Repington needed no further encouragement. Since their last meeting he had resigned from *The Times* and joined the *Morning Post*; on 11 February he summarised the council's discussions and echoed Clemenceau's views in a savage article in his new paper, accusing Lloyd George of poltroonery, of starving British armies in the field and of advocating adventures contrary to the advice of his legitimate military advisers, and declaring that 'Mr. Lloyd George has clearly and finally proved his incapacity to govern England in a great war.'

Certainly Repington made good use of the information Clemenceau had given him. But the British censor had marked the article 'Not to be published', and both the writer and the editor of the *Morning Post* were prosecuted and fined for defying the ban. All that can be said in defence of Clemenceau's 'leak' is that he was concerned only with the most advantageous use of Britain's man-power and had not intended to provoke a personal attack on Lloyd George; but few are likely to dispute the verdict of an historian of war strategy that 'It is not easy to remember a parallel "indiscretion" in the long and acrid history of civil-military relations.'

Those who had expected an early end of Clemenceau's government were proved to be wrong. He remained firmly in power as the months went by, though he had to revise some of the opinions he had expressed so freely in *L'Homme Enchaîné*. Salonika, for example, no longer seemed a complete waste of effort when he realised that it kept fifteen or twenty enemy divisions away from the western front; and when he discovered in February that the eastern army had become completely disorganised, it was due to his own insistence that more officers, men and armaments were sent to Salonika.

One subject on which he never changed his mind was that the restoration of Alsace-Lorraine was France's basic war aim. It must have been an unpleasant surprise for him when Winston Churchill, the British minister of munitions, arrived in Paris in cantankerous mood and showed himself to be out of sympathy with French aspirations.

The story of Churchill's visit was told in a letter from the British ambassador in Paris (who had been raised to the peerage as Lord Bertie of Thame) to Lord Stamfordham, King George V's private secretary, on 28 February. Churchill, Lord Bertie wrote, had dined at the embassy and 'talked a lot of rot after and at dinner to the effect that we did not go to war to obtain Alsace-Lorraine for France'; the war, Churchill had said, should not be continued if we could obtain from Germany the evacuation of Belgium and the occupied French territory and the restoration of some *portion* of Alsace-Lorraine.

Lord Bertie continued:

> Clemenceau told me that W. Churchill paid him a visit and had talked nonsense, and he, Clemenceau, had told him '*tout court*' that England is fighting for France and France fighting for England and that their interests are inseparable. I suppose that W. Churchill had dilated on our sacrifices for French interests which are not entirely British ones. If so, it was foolish to use such language to Clemenceau.[1]

It should be added that the Tiger seems to have borne no grudge against Churchill for his unwelcome views, which were, indeed, the views of many British people. The two men were on good terms when they toured the front together at the end of March.

[5]

By this time, as Geffroy remembered later, the crowds which strolled along the darkened boulevards at night were accustomed to seeing 'the rapid passing of the lighted car of the minister of war coming back from the front line, covered with mud, sometimes with windows broken'. Coming back from one such visit on 3 March, Clemenceau was anxious to return to the front as soon as possible, so that he could examine the aircraft position; but he was kept in Paris to answer interpellations in the Chamber of Deputies. He found it exasperating to have to make speeches when there was so much else that he wanted to do; and he complained to Mordacq about the fools who, for matters of infinitesimal importance,

[1] RA GV P 1273/7.

took a malicious pleasure in making him lose time that was precious for the country.

Yet the 'fools' had their uses. On the very day when he was growling about their 'malicious pleasure' an interpellation about the Bolo trial gave him the opportunity for expounding his war policy more simply and more strikingly than he had ever done before.

The subject of the interpellation was quickly brushed aside: Bolo had been arrested, and his acts of treason had been committed, under previous governments, and Clemenceau had no responsibility for matters of which he had no knowledge. From this beginning he went on to explain his war policy, and declared that his only maxim was the eastern saying, 'The victor is he who can believe a quarter-of-an-hour longer than his enemy that he has not been vanquished.'

His policy, the Tiger said, was to maintain the morale of the French people in a crisis which was the worst in their history. Like everyone else, he wanted peace as soon as possible, but one could not silence Prussian militarism by bleating for peace. Then came the whip-crack sentences which won applause from the whole Chamber, apart from the Socialists. One of the speakers, he said, had chided him for his silence about foreign policy:

> My foreign policy and my home policy are all one. Home policy, *je fais la guerre*. Foreign policy, *je fais toujours la guerre. Je fais toujours la guerre. . . .*
> I seek to retain the confidence of our Allies. Russia betrays us, I continue to make war. Unhappy Rumania is forced to capitulate: I continue to make war, and I shall continue to the last quarter-of-an-hour.

In his closing sentences he promised that France would go on to the end in the suppression of treachery, on to the end in the field of military action. Nothing would stop her, nothing would make her turn aside.

After this clear statement of the doctrine of *jusqu'au bout* the Tiger hurried to the front to see the air squadrons near Château-Thierry and to discuss the strategy of aerial war with the commanding general; then on 14 March he was in London for a meeting of the Supreme War Council, which decided to postpone the formation of a general reserve until a number of British and French units would be set free by the arrival of American troops. It was this decision which caused an open clash between Clemenceau and Foch, who was present as chief of the French general staff. Foch, who had strongly advocated the immediate formation of a general reserve, said he objected to the council's decision, but Clemenceau shouted him down with a brusque: 'Be quiet! It is I who represent France here.'

Clemenceau's pledge that France would fight to the end had been given at the right moment. A week after the London meeting of the Supreme War Council sixty-three German divisions launched an attack north and south of the Somme.

CHAPTER SIXTEEN

FATHER OF VICTORY

1. Unity of command. 2. 'Count Czernin is lying.' 3. Chemin des Dames. 4. The turning point. 5. Nearing the end. 6. Armistice. 7. 'Soldier of the ideal.'

[1]

THOUGH IT was nearly a year since the United States had joined the Allies as 'an associated power', only a small number of trained American soldiers—fewer than 300,000, including supply troops—were in France by the spring of 1918. These troops had been fighting as divisions or occasionally at corps strength since the end of 1917, but they were not yet a determining factor in the war. It was left, therefore, to the British and French to face the great German offensive of 21 March, which was the first of five sledgehammer blows spread over a period of four months, when at one time the Germans had more than 200 divisions against the Allies' 162. Two of the offensives were on the British section of the front, three on the French; between them they brought the Allies nearer to defeat than they had been at any time since 1914. They also gave the Allies an incentive for unifying the command of their forces on the western front.

Clemenceau had long believed in the need for unity of command. He often discussed it with Mordacq, he spoke to Henry Wilson about it in January, he tried to enlist Italian and American support for it, he raised the issue with Lloyd George at the Supreme War Council; but Britain's insular reluctance to entrust her armies to a foreign generalissimo had remained unchanged since the beginning of the war, when the commander-in-chief of the British Expeditionary Force had been assured that 'you will in no way come in any sense under the orders of any Allied general'. It was only when the March offensive brought the Germans almost up to the outworks of Amiens, and it was feared that Haig might soon be racing for the coast while Pétain fell back towards Paris, that unity of command was recognised as a vital necessity.

It was now clear that the existing system of Allied co-partnership could never achieve the concentration of effort and economy of force which were possible under a single control; even Haig, who had once boasted that he would have no commander except 'my King', began to discover previously unsuspected virtues in the appointment of a French general-issimo. He was alarmed by the opening of a gap between the British and French forces, and dismayed by Pétain's reluctance to send his reserves to rescue the British army. He felt that a French generalissimo would be bound to give him the help he needed, and in the hope of forcing Pétain's hand he telegraphed to London, asking Lord Milner (a member of the small British war cabinet) and General Wilson (now chief of the imperial general staff) to come to France at once.

In Paris the need for action was underlined by the impact of a new German weapon of war. In the morning of 22 March Parisians were surprised to hear a sound like that of bombs exploding, though no German bombers could be seen or heard. Clemenceau and Poincaré drove to a site where one of the supposed bombs had fallen, and found the director of the Paris municipal laboratory examining the fragments of a projectile. 'It's from a cannon,' he declared. 'From Charenton,' said Clemenceau, sceptically, but two hours later it was confirmed that the projectiles were shells from a long-range gun—the famous Big Bertha, taking its name from Bertha Krupp of the German armaments firm, which could lob shells into Paris from a distance of seventy-five miles.

The emergence of Big Bertha was a warning of what might happen to Paris if the Germans came even nearer the city, as seemed ominously likely to happen; for by 24 March, only three days after the launching of the German offensive, it was known that the British Fifth Army had been routed and that its retreat was opening the dreaded gap between the British and French lines. Clemenceau went to Pétain's headquarters at Compiègne, and found little comfort in the commander-in-chief's pessimistic comment, 'If we are beaten, we shall owe it to the English.' On the following morning he saw Poincaré at the Elysée, and they decided to summon a full Anglo-French conference at Compiègne that afternoon. Both men were convinced that the Allied command must be unified, but it is not clear whether they saw Foch or Pétain as the man for the job.[1]

---

[1] It is often claimed that Clemenceau was resolved to make Foch the allied general-issimo, but the claim is distinctly doubtful. The principal evidence for it is supplied by André Tardieu, who asserted, in a book written soon after the war, that on being appointed French high commissioner in the United States in 1917, he had said to Clemenceau: 'They are going to talk to me again over there about unity of command. And no doubt they will ask "Who ?". What shall I say ?'; and Clemenceau had answered 'Foch'. But Guy Pedroncini points out that there is no other important proof of his wish to nominate Foch to the unified command, or of his having taken any firm decision before the Doullens meeting on 26 March. When the matter was discussed in military circles Pétain was named as the man most likely to be appointed. (*See* Tardieu, *The Truth about the Treaty*, p. 37; Pedroncini, *Le Haut Commandement*, p. 1255.)

By this time Milner and Wilson had arrived in France, and Milner attended the Compiègne meeting, at which Poincaré, Clemenceau, Loucheur (minister of munitions), Pétain and Foch were also present. Haig and Wilson had been unable to attend at such short notice, and no important decisions could be reached in their absence. It was decided to hold a further meeting, at which the British generals would be present, at Doullens, only a few miles behind the new and precarious front line, on the following day.

Unity of command was certainly the topic of the hour. Lloyd George claimed afterwards that he had sent Milner to France 'to put Foch in command of both armies'; but it is unlikely that such clear instructions were given, for Milner seemed to be making up his mind as he went along, and made no mention at Compiègne of any new appointment for Foch. In conversation he gained the impression that Clemenceau wanted Pétain to be Allied commander-in-chief, but this would have been unacceptable to the British government. Another idea, springing from Wilson's fertile mind, was that Clemenceau should become commander-in-chief, with Foch as his technical adviser; but Foch would have nothing to do with this proposal, pointing out that the Tiger knew nothing about leading an army, and would be pulled in opposite directions if he and Pétain made different recommendations. Clemenceau joked about this proposal after the war. 'I even had a uniform made—and a marvellous hat!', he said.

The German attack was less than a week old, and showed no sign of coming to a halt, when the Allied civil and military leaders met at Doullens —Clemenceau, Poincaré, Loucheur, Pétain, Foch and General Weygand for France, Milner, Wilson, Haig and General H. Lawrence, Haig's chief of staff, for Britain. Wilson and Milner, who drove to the conference from Versailles, agreed on the way that Foch should become the co-ordinating authority for the Allied armies. Milner said that he would put the idea before the conference, though he felt (in contradiction of Lloyd George's claim to have nominated Foch) that he had not been empowered by the British cabinet to take such a decision.

The conference was short but decisive. Foch was asked for his view of the military situation, and said firmly: 'My plan is not complicated. I want to fight. I would fight without a break. I would fight in front of Amiens. I would fight in Amiens. I would fight behind Amiens. I would fight all the time. . . . In any case, for the moment it is like 1914 on the Marne: we must dig in and die where we stand if need be; to withdraw a foot will be an act of treason.' His statement drew from Clemenceau the admiring comment, '*Quel bougre!*' ('That's a tough nut!') More constructively, Haig said that if General Foch would be willing to give him advice, he would be glad to take it.

This was Milner's cue. He called Clemenceau away from the table, and they agreed that, if Pétain and Haig raised no objections, Foch should be appointed to co-ordinate the Allies' use of their forces before Amiens. According to Milner in 1921, 'Clemenceau *simply jumped* at my proposal to put all our money on Foch right away'; and after separate talks between Clemenceau and Pétain, and between Milner and Haig, it was decided to make Foch the co-ordinating authority for the Allied forces, not only before Amiens, but also, at Haig's request, on the whole of the western front.

The members of the conference were pleased with their decision. Poincaré declared, 'I think, gentlemen, that we have done good work for victory.' Wilson wrote in his diary: 'Both Lawrence and Haig are delighted with this new arrangement about Foch. So is Foch, and so really is Clemenceau, who patted me on the head and said I was *un bon garçon*.'[1] Haig, he added, 'is ten years younger than he was yesterday afternoon'— not surprisingly, since his whole aim in agreeing to Foch's appointment had been, says one of his biographers, 'to override Pétain and get the French to send reinforcements to prevent the British and French armies being separated'.

The appointment of Foch to the supreme command was a joint achievement, in which Clemenceau and several others had a share, and possibly Milner had the biggest share of all; but it is to Clemenceau's credit that unity of command was achieved at all, for it was he who repeatedly called for it at times when both Haig and Lloyd George regarded it as incompatible with Britain's honour. Yet he was curiously brusque in congratulating Foch on his appointment. 'Well, you've got it at last, your high command,' he said. And when Foch retorted, 'It is a fine present you are making me; you give me a lost battle and you tell me to win it,' he could only repeat lamely, 'Anyway, you've got what you wanted.' But he was certainly delighted by the result of the conference. On their return to Paris Mordacq thought he had never seen the Tiger looking so calm.

As for Pétain, the commander-in-chief who had been passed over for the top job, he accepted Foch's elevation like the good soldier he was, and when Clemenceau asked him to give up part of his staff to Foch, he said simply: 'Take it all and give me an army corps; I assure you that I will lead it with all my heart and will ask for nothing more.' He remained a loyal and efficient commander-in-chief until the end of the war, and strange as it may seem to those who remember him as the defeatist old man of Vichy, there was much justice, in the context of the First World

---

[1] Since Wilson was at least a foot taller than Clemenceau, one presumes that Wilson was sitting down and Clemenceau standing up. Otherwise the gesture would have been grotesque.

War, in Clemenceau's final verdict on Philippe Pétain: 'He did not believe in victory, but he was a different man from Foch. . . . He had more moral grandeur.'

[2]

Two days after the Doullens conference, on Good Friday morning, Clemenceau hurried from his office to the church of Saint-Gervais, near the Hôtel de Ville, to see the havoc caused by a shell from Big Bertha which had brought down the roof during a service, killing seventy-five worshippers and injuring ninety. The dangers of this new form of attack, combined with the advance of the German armies, had already caused the cabinet to discuss the possible removal of the government to Tours, but Poincaré had made it clear that he would not leave the Elysée, and Clemenceau told his intimates that he would join the armies if the government left Paris. In the meantime he bolstered up the deputies' confidence by showing himself in the corridors of the Palais-Bourbon, smiling serenely as though all were well; and though there was neither radio nor television to keep ministers in touch with the public, the people of France, and of Paris in particular, were reassured to know that Clemenceau was in charge. How often, says Léon Daudet, one heard people saying in the Métro, on the buses, in the streets: 'The old man's there. We'll beat them!'

In the months of crisis which followed the launching of the German offensive Clemenceau's constant aim was to get away from Paris and follow the fortunes of war in the midst of the Allied armies. Sometimes he had to be content with a day trip, but a day trip lasted a good many hours, as can be seen from Winston Churchill's account of the day in the middle of the March offensive when he and the Duke of Westminster (who had come to France with him as his military aide-de-camp) went to the front with the Tiger.

They left Paris at 8 a.m., stopped at Beauvais for a talk with Foch and Weygand (now his chief of staff), and went on to General Rawlinson's headquarters, where they met Haig. Clemenceau, who was in high spirits, then announced: 'I wish to pass the river and see the battle,' and in spite of Rawlinson's protests he took his companions over the river Luce to a point about 300 yards behind the British front line. A shell burst not far away while they stopped their cars to look at the scene. They returned by Amiens, dining with Pétain in the French headquarters train at Beauvais; as they drove back to Paris, Churchill said seriously to Clemenceau: 'This sort of excursion is all right for a single day; but you ought not to go under fire too often.' 'It is my great pleasure,' the Tiger replied. They reached Paris at one in the morning, after seventeen hours on the road, at the front and in important conversation with generals; Clemenceau, wrote Churchill, was 'alert and fresh as when we started'.

The Tiger was back at Beauvais on 3 April, when the March offensive was gradually dying out. This time it was for a conference with Lloyd George and the senior French, British and American generals.

The reason for the conference was that Foch had learned by experience that co-ordination was not command; with two commanders-in-chief and a dozen or more army corps commanders to deal with, it was not easy for him, in Liddell Hart's words, 'to be more, or less, than an officially appointed Busybody-in-Chief'. Clemenceau, too, saw that the arrangement was not what he had meant when he asked for unity of command, and at Beauvais he secured a significant strengthening of Foch's position.

It was now agreed that Foch should be in command of the Allied armies (including the American army), though their commanders-in-chief would still be responsible for tactics and would have a right of appeal to their governments if they disagreed with any of Foch's orders. This, in effect, made him the Allied commander-in-chief in France, though Lloyd George would not at first allow him to use the title. He conceded the point a few days later, when the British front was endangered by the second German offensive; Foch then became generalissimo in name as well as in fact, so that at last, thanks to Clemenceau's initiative at Beauvais, the Allies had an entirely unified command.

The Tiger was not so happy in his handling of a diplomatic issue which arose on the morning of the Beauvais conference. A telephone call from Mandel told him that Count Czernin, the Austrian foreign minister, had said in a speech that Austria had never made proposals for a separate peace, but that she had received proposals to that effect from Clemenceau. After holding up the report for twelve hours, Mandel was now prepared to release it, but the censors were asking for an official comment. The Tiger gave them one: 'Just say, "Count Czernin is lying", that's all.' The speech was published in France with this curt rejoinder attached to it.

Count Czernin was not to be put down so easily. He repeated his statement, which was based on the French government's authorisation of renewed talks in Switzerland between Major Armand and Count Revertera. These negotiations were trifles compared with the compromising remarks by the Austrian emperor in the letter given to Poincaré by Prince Sixtus, but Czernin had been kept in the dark about the Prince Sixtus affair and did not know how far Emperor Karl had committed himself.

He was soon enlightened. The Prince Sixtus correspondence was confidential, but Clemenceau had it taken from the files and released for publication. Now it could be seen that Emperor Karl had been angling for peace in 1917, and had promised to support France's 'legitimate claims' to Alsace-Lorraine. Czernin at once resigned, and the unfortunate Karl was left to explain the letter away to the German Emperor. Many Frenchmen were amused to think that the old Tiger, who had demolished so many French governments, had overthrown the foreign minister of an enemy country in war-time.

But Clemenceau was not at his best in his handling of the Czernin incident. Since he had sanctioned the resumption of the Armand-Revertera talks, which could fairly be regarded as a French approach to a separate peace, it was a mistake for him to say that Count Czernin was lying. He was wrong again to have published a letter which Poincaré had given his word of honour not to reveal. As an officer-deputy saw it, 'The President of the Republic's word of honour is France's word of honour. . . . The French public feels confused and is troubled.'

Both Poincaré and Ribot felt that Clemenceau's conduct had been frivolous, and Paul Cambon, the French ambassador in London, could excuse it only by referring to the prime minister's previous career. ('As a journalist,' Cambon told a censorious lady, 'he could not resist the temptation of scoring off people.') Others again took the Austrian Emperor's offer at its face value, and thought, though quite mistakenly, that Clemenceau had wrecked a genuine chance of peace on honourable terms. In fact, as had been clear in 1917, Austria could never have made a separate peace while the issue of the war was undecided, but a less impulsive man than Clemenceau would not have exposed himself to the charge, unjust though it was, that he had thrown away a chance of peace.

[3]

The spring and early summer of 1918 were a disastrous time for the Allies. Though the first German offensive had come to a halt without the loss of Amiens, the British front had to face a second attack in April, the attack which caused Haig to issue his historic order of the day: 'With our backs to the wall and believing in the justice of our cause, each one of us must fight on to the end.' In three weeks of desperate fighting the British line was pushed back ten miles, the Allies had 350,000 casualties and the Germans nearly as many; but Ypres and the Hazebrouck railway junction were still in British hands when Ludendorff, the German commander-in-chief, halted the second offensive at the end of the month.

At the end of May it was the French turn to suffer the third of Ludendorff's hammer-blows, and to suffer it, moreover, in a part of the line where no attack was expected by the French or British high commands. In after years Clemenceau remembered that only three days before the

Germans struck, 'a staff officer, who was not by any means a nobody, said to me, "At any rate, there is one place we are comfortable about, and that is the Chemin des Dames!" '

This was a quiet and supposedly impregnable section of the front line between Reims and Soissons, the Chemin des Dames being the long ridge north of the Aisne which formed the backbone of the river's defences. The sector, originally held by the French, was so quiet that four weary British divisions were sent there for a rest. When the American intelligence service warned the British and French commanders that the next German attack would be launched there between 25 and 30 May, its warning was disregarded.

The Americans were right. It was here that the Germans began a tremendous bombardment in the early hours of 27 May, to be followed by a massive attack which led to the capture of the Chemin des Dames and the crossing of the Aisne. In the next four days the Germans crossed the Vesle, took Soissons and finally occupied Château-Thierry, on the north bank of the Marne; here the offensive lost momentum and was halted by resolute defence, in which two American divisions, assigned by Pershing to help the French, fought gallantly and had a 40 per cent. casualty rate in some of their combat units. Château-Thierry is fewer than fifty miles from Paris. The Germans had achieved another menacing advance by an attack which, as was later revealed, had been intended only as a diversion from a major offensive in Flanders.

Clemenceau was at Foch's headquarters on the day after the battle had begun. In the ensuing days he visited all the French commanders in the area, and had two meetings with General Duchesne, who had largely caused the disaster by concentrating his troops in the front line and ignoring Pétain's orders for an elastic defence in depth. At this time the Tiger felt that the fall of Paris could not be ruled out. 'Yes,' he admitted to Mordacq on 31 May, 'the Germans can take Paris, but that will not stop me making war. We shall fight on the Loire, then on the Garonne if necessary, and even on the Pyrenees. If, at last, we are driven out of the Pyrenees, we shall continue the war at sea. But as for making peace, never! Don't ask me to do that!'

From the front he returned to face a scared and indignant Chamber of Deputies. Intriguers were saying privately that France would be lost if the Tiger stayed in power even for another week; he must be overthrown in favour of a broader government, headed by Briand, who would soon make peace on advantageous terms. Pétain and Duchesne were also on the intriguers' black list, and some would have liked to get rid of Foch.

A weaker man might have sacrificed Foch and Pétain to appease the opposition. But the Tiger was in no yielding mood when he addressed the Chamber on 4 June. He declined to discuss in public the conduct of a battle which was still in progress, and he refused requests for a secret session. In the early part of his speech there were so many Socialist interruptions that he left the tribune. When he returned, he threw the whole weight of his powerful oratory into the defence of the high command.

He spoke of the million German soldiers previously fighting in the east and now released for the western front by the defection of Russia; no one, he said, could have failed to understand that the Allies would have to give way in one place or another because of these massive German reinforcements, but in this terrible battle French soldiers had fought, one against five, without sleep for three or four days. 'These soldiers, these great soldiers, have leaders, good leaders, great leaders, worthy of them at every point,' he declared amid cheers from the Right and the Centre. He named Foch and Pétain as great soldiers and said he was not going to put them on trial or to demand explanations from a general exhausted by the strain of battle. 'Overthrow me if that is what you are asking for,' he said, 'for I will not do it.'

Point after point was driven home. The government would make no peace except a victorious one. The coming of the Americans would decide the issue of the war. Victory depended on the civil power rising to the height of its duty; there was no need to tell the soldiers to do so. 'It remains for the living,' he concluded, 'to complete the magnificent work of the dead.'

The Chamber gave him its confidence by 377 votes to 110, but it had needed all his strength to save Foch and Pétain. In his own judgement, 'Had I faltered for a single moment, the high command would have been swept away.'

Clemenceau had spoken highly of the soldiers and their leaders, but the defeat at the Chemin des Dames had convinced him that some of the generals were either too old or too tired for their posts. When the front was temporarily stabilised he went to Foch's new headquarters at Bombon, a château hidden in the forest a few miles from the main road between Provins and Melun, and presented a list of generals to be removed from their commands in favour of younger and more energetic men. At certain names the generalissimo murmured sadly, 'An old friend,' but he agreed that most of them must go. The list was then shown to Pétain, who also gave it his reluctant approval.

One of the generals who rightly disappeared was the blundering Duchesne. Another was one of the army commanders, Franchet d'Esperey, but Clemenceau gave him a new appointment as commander of the Allied forces at Salonika only a few days later. He succeeded General Guillaumat, who had been making plans for an autumn offensive on the Bulgarian front, and it was Franchet d'Esperey's good fortune to be able to carry out these plans in September, and with great success. Guillaumat, for whom Clemenceau had a high regard, was brought home to take up the important post of military governor of Paris.

[4]

Of Clemenceau's many visits to the front in the summer of 1918 one which he always remembered was in the Champagne sector in July. He had seen Pétain and other generals, and at Les Monts de Champagne a *poilu* approached him and gave him a small bouquet of wild flowers picked by the roadside. He was deeply touched and promised to keep them all his life.

The war in France was approaching its turning-point. The fourth German offensive, aimed at the capture of the Montdidier-Compiègne-Soissons railway, had been broken off after a gain of only six miles; and on 15 July Ludendorff made his final attack east and west of Reims. Clemenceau hurried to the front to urge Foch and Pétain to launch a counter-offensive, but his advice was unnecessary. The German attack had been contained by Pétain's skilful use of elastic defence; Foch had already planned an offensive against the Marne salient created by the previous German advance. It began on 18 July, when the successful use of light tanks forced the Germans to retreat and to straighten their battle-line.

The initiative on the western front had passed to Foch. He arranged with Pétain, Haig and Pershing for a series of local offensives on different parts of the German lines. On 8 August, which Ludendorff was later to call 'the black day of the German army', British, French, Australian and Canadian forces made a surprise attack in the Somme area, driving back the German forward divisions and taking 21,000 prisoners; in succeeding weeks pressure was kept up all along the line; and in a battle beginning on 12 September an American army, operating for the first time as an independent unit, successfully eliminated the German salient at Saint-Mihiel. Clemenceau had a personal interest in this engagement, for his son Michel was a captain in a French colonial unit which assisted the Americans.

The German army had now been pushed back to the defensive position known as the Hindenburg line to the Allies and as the Siegfried line to the Germans. Clemenceau was radiant. When once Foch had launched his great counter-offensive he was sure that victory was near; General Wilson, who saw him in Paris on 22 July, noted that 'He was looking well and said our politicians were fools, but I was a good boy. He was well pleased with the turn of events, but not boasting.' It was about this time that the troops began to speak of him as '*Père-la-Victoire*'—Father of Victory—and the name spread from the front line to the towns and villages of France.

In these weeks he was often at Bombon, and it must surely have been in this period (and not in the gloomy spring, as Raymond Recouly suggests) that he arrived at GHQ unexpectedly on a Sunday morning and was told that Foch was at Mass. An officer said he would let the general know that Clemenceau was waiting for him, but the Tiger said gaily: 'Don't disturb him at Mass. It's done so well for him! I'll wait.' And it was certainly in August that he had the happy task of reading to Foch the decree appointing him a marshal of France—a promotion which was made not only for meritorious services, but also because the rank would give Foch more authority over Haig, who had been made a field-marshal, and Pershing, who had been promoted to be full general. After reading the decree Clemenceau opened his arms and held Foch in a long embrace.[1]

Always, whether going to Dunkirk for a friendly talk with King Albert of the Belgians or to Pershing's headquarters to congratulate him on the American victory at Saint-Mihiel, he was happier at the front than in Paris, where his enemies—the Socialists, the Caillautists and to some extent the ex-ministers of previous war-time governments—were giving freer rein to their opposition, now that France seemed no longer in danger. He was disheartened when he came back to the rue Saint-Dominique after a trying session at the Palais-Bourbon. 'Don't you think one must love France to carry on with a job like this?', he asked Mordacq.

For the war was not yet over, and he was becoming nervously exasperated over everything that stood in the way of an early victory. One day he was angry about Lloyd George, who was raising difficulties about transport for the American troops; the British prime minister, he said, was 'more and more unbearable'. At a cabinet meeting he upbraided two of his ministers because harbour and transport congestion had caused a shortage of bread in Breton ports; he would not listen to explanations and seemed, in Poincaré's opinion, to think that economic

---

[1] It was in August, too, that Clemenceau was involved in one of his front-line escapades which so much alarmed the officers who had to look after him. While visiting Rawlinson's headquarters he heard that a neighbouring French division was attacking, and he at once said he must see how they were getting on. All went well on the outward journey; after leaving his car he was able to talk to soldiers who were actually engaged with the enemy. But German artillery observers had noticed the cars approaching the front line, and Clemenceau's party was under heavy fire on its way back. Officers were shocked by his imprudence, but he brushed their protests aside. 'These damned generals are always scared about something,' he said to Mordacq as they drove back to Paris. 'It's only civilians (*pékins*) who have courage.' (*See* Mordacq, *Clemenceau*, pp. 148–9.)

miracles could be achieved by vehement talk. He was always impatient with the Italians, who kept on postponing an offensive which should have begun in May. He said angrily to Poincaré: 'Oh, these Italians! We shan't finish the war without fighting them, or we'll fight them afterwards.'

The Italians had irritated him throughout the summer. Their first reason for not attacking was that they expected an Austrian offensive and thought it advisable to wait. At the beginning of September General Diaz, the Italian commander-in-chief, came to France to see Clemenceau and Foch, and said he was not yet ready to move for fear of provoking an Austrian counter-offensive.

When Clemenceau pointed out that the Austrians were exhausted and there could be no danger in launching an offensive against them, Diaz protested, 'But they are lions, they are lions!' Unfortunately for Diaz's credibility, several thousand Austrians had been fighting on the western front. Clemenceau retorted scornfully: 'Lions, indeed! We have just taken five thousand of them prisoners at one go!' But Diaz still refused to move, and it was not until the end of October that the Italians vindicated themselves by knocking Austria out of the war at Vittorio Veneto.

[5]

By the time of the Italian offensive the Allies' victory was certain. The first decisive blow had been struck on the Macedonian front, where Franchet d'Esperey, with the Tiger's encouragement and support, carried out Guillaumat's plans for an attack on Bulgaria. It was entirely successful. The Bulgarians were driven out of Serbia, their retreating soldiers threw away their arms, and their government had to sue for an armistice. The road to Constantinople was open.

This notable success by a French general led to angry exchanges between the Tiger and Lloyd George. They had always been at loggerheads over Salonika, and Lloyd George was indignant when Franchet d'Esperey proposed to make a triumphal march into Constantinople, with French troops in the van. When the plan was discussed by the Supreme War Council on 7 October, Clemenceau and Lloyd George (in the words of a British representative) 'spat at each other like angry cats'. The British case for calling off the march was upheld.

It was then Britain's turn to annoy France by her conduct in the Near East. The Turks, who had been routed by the British in Palestine and Mesopotamia, asked for an armistice, which the British Admiral Calthorpe conceded to them at Mudros on 30 October, without consulting France. This unilateral action led to further squabbling between the British and

French prime ministers. 'They bandied words like fishwives,' wrote Colonel House. 'At least George did. Clemenceau was more moderate.' But again Lloyd George had his way. Clemenceau, with the greater question of Germany on his mind, agreed to accept the Turkish armistice as a *fait accompli*.

At this time he was also involved in one of many disputes with Foch. A general Allied offensive had begun on 26 September, and while progress had been made on all sectors of the front, it was slowest in the Argonne, where the American First Army had been expected to advance thirty miles. After a good beginning it had been held up by skilful German defence; by mid-October it was obliged to pause for rest and reorganisation. Clemenceau thought that Foch was not exerting sufficient authority over Pershing, and he drafted a strong letter to the marshal, which Poincaré, to whom he prudently showed it, advised him not to send. The President rightly observed that Clemenceau was not entitled to criticise Foch in his capacity as overall commander-in-chief of the American army.

In the end Clemenceau wrote Foch a reproachful letter, praising him for having conducted the battle 'in such a way as to place you in the front rank of the great captains', but complaining that the Americans had been marking time since their first forward move. 'Nobody,' he wrote, 'can maintain that these fine troops are unusable; they are merely unused.' Foch, who knew that the Americans had fought well and needed their short respite, was unmoved by Clemenceau's protests; he sent a tactful reply, mentioning the magnitude of the Americans' effort and the heavy casualties they had sustained. In due course he ordered Pershing to resume the attack, which continued successfully until it was stopped by the armistice.

The temporary American setback did not impair the effectiveness of Foch's September offensive. The Hindenburg line was breached, the Germans were on the run, and on 29 September Ludendorff told the German chancellor that the military situation called for an immediate armistice, without which a catastrophe might be expected. Five days later Prince Max of Baden, who had been appointed chancellor to wind up the war, sent a note to President Wilson asking for an armistice and agreeing to make peace on the basis of the Fourteen Points and the President's subsequent declarations. Clemenceau saw the note as an admission of defeat.

[6]

In the weeks between the sending of the German note and the signing of the armistice Clemenceau had two memorable quarrels—the first with

Poincaré, the second with Foch. The first was caused by the President's use of a tactless phrase, and had no lasting effect; the second was the opening shot in the long quarrel over peace terms which would continue until the end of both men's lives.

Poincaré viewed the German request for an armistice with deep suspicion. He distrusted the Germans, and he wrote in his diary: 'I continue to think that an armistice should certainly be accompanied by the most serious guarantees, and that we must not leave to the enemy the possiblity of hiding the gravity of his defeat from German opinion.' He was afraid that Germany might be trying to confuse the Allies by asking for an armistice she intended to reject, and that the disappointment caused by the sudden withdrawal of hopes of peace would have a harmful effect on the morale of the French army. It was in this mood that he sent a letter to Clemenceau expressing the hope that 'no one would hamstring our troops'.

He could hardly have put his point more tactlessly. Since the two men rarely met, the President had begun to send Clemenceau frequent letters, which would often have been thrown away unread if the watchful Mandel had not retrieved them from the waste-paper basket. A junior minister, Henry Lémery, who happened to be at the war ministry when one of Poincaré's notes arrived, never forgot Clemenceau's outburst: 'That's the fourth one! I've had enough of them! . . . I am going to the Elysée to inform M. Poincaré that I forbid him to write to me. He's a maniac. He's building up files for history. I've other things to do!'

The 'hamstring' letter was the last straw. Clemenceau wrote back to say that he did not recognise Poincaré's right to tell him not to hamstring the troops: 'If you do not withdraw this letter written for the history you wish to make, I have the honour to hand you my resignation.'

It was a shattering threat at such a moment. Poincaré replied that Clemenceau's resignation would be disastrous for the country, but the Tiger was adamant. He not only demanded that Poincaré should withdraw the letter, but he also insisted that future communications between them should be oral and before witnesses. Poincaré gave in and withdrew the letter. When they met two days later Clemenceau was as gay and smiling as if nothing had happened.

But Poincaré was not alone in thinking that there were dangers in an immediate armistice. Both Pershing and General Tasker Bliss, the American military representative on the Supreme War Council, thought that the war should go on until the Germans surrendered unconditionally; several leading diplomats, including the experienced Camille Barrère, the French ambassador in Rome, were afraid that a premature armistice would allow Germany to dispute the reality of her military defeat.

Barrère's view was that the armistice terms should be so severe that no German government could accept them, and then the Allies would be able to enter Germany, sword in hand.

It was an impressive argument, which was often discussed in the early post-war years, when even the faithful Mordacq maintained that the armistice should have been signed in Berlin. Certainly Barrère was right in suggesting that Germany, whose homeland had not been invaded, would later pretend that her armies had never been beaten. But in 1918 Foch himself took the humanitarian view, which won greater support. As he told Colonel House, 'One makes war only for the results; when these results are achieved, no one has the right to shed another drop of blood.'

This was also Clemenceau's opinion. When Foch declared that enough blood had been shed already, the Tiger said: 'Marshal, I am entirely of the same opinion.' He therefore invited Foch to draw up the technical military conditions on which an armistice could be granted.

It was during the preliminary discussions of these conditions that Foch staked out the claim which opened his long political feud with Clemenceau. In a letter which the Tiger found waiting for him on his return from a tour of the liberated areas in mid-October, the marshal complained that he was not being kept sufficiently informed about the inter-Allied negotiations concerning the proposed armistice. He wanted to know what were the French government's intentions regarding the left bank of the Rhine, and he asked that a high official of the foreign ministry should be appointed to keep him in touch with political developments.

The letter displeased Clemenceau, who saw it as an attempt to encroach on the government's authority; he replied to it sharply, and enclosed an equally sharp letter from Pichon, the foreign minister, reminding Foch that war was his business, but that Rhineland policy and everything pertaining to peace belonged to the government exclusively. 'We will not suffer you to interfere in these matters,' Pichon wrote. The request for a liaison officer between the Quai d'Orsay and GHQ was also rejected.

Foch was deeply offended by this rebuff. In later years he said that from this time 'M. Clemenceau showed himself extremely jealous of his prerogatives and his authority. . . . He became more and more authoritarian and dominating, less and less willing to have anyone about him who would dare to challenge his views even for a moment.' These were exaggerated charges, but they indicate the gravity of the rift between the marshal and the prime minister.

Their disagreement, however, was to show itself more over the peace treaty than over the armistice, for Foch generally agreed with Clemenceau's view that 'the armistice has no other purpose than that of maintaining

Allied military supremacy during the peace negotiations'. They agreed, too, that the terms must be severe enough to make it impossible for Germany to resume the war, and this was achieved in spite of protests by Lloyd George and Colonel House, who were afraid that Germany might refuse the armistice if the conditions were too stiff. (At this time none of the Allied soldiers and statesmen had any idea of the extent of Germany's collapse.) The crucial points finally included in the armistice were the evacuation of all German troops from France, Belgium and Alsace-Lorraine, Allied occupation of all German territory west of the Rhine and of bridgeheads on the east bank of the river, the internment of most of the German fleet and the surrender of submarines, guns and aircraft. Though the armistice was not intended to foreshadow the peace terms, Clemenceau took care to include a clause which established the Allies' claim to reparations.

The British and American fears proved to be groundless. Before the armistice terms were presented Germany's three allies—Bulgaria, Turkey and Austria-Hungary—were all out of the war; with her armies routed and demoralised, mutiny in the navy and fear of a Bolshevik revolution, she had no option but to accept the Allies' terms.

Soon after six o'clock on the morning of 11 November General Mordacq drove to the rue Franklin to tell the Tiger that the armistice had been signed and would come into force at eleven o'clock. 'The task is accomplished at last,' said the general solemnly. 'It is a great one, and France will know what it owes to you.' 'To me and others,' Clemenceau replied, and one of his first actions was to send a note to his American friend Colonel House. 'My very dear Friend,' he wrote, 'In this solemn moment of great events in which your noble country and its worthy chief have played so fine a rôle, I cannot restrain the desire to open my arms to you and press you against my heart. Your sincere Georges Clemenceau.'

[7]

The golden hours of the 'Father of Victory' had begun earlier in the month, when he had read out in the Chamber the terms of the armistice granted to Austria-Hungary, and had recalled that he was the last survivor of those members of the National Assembly in 1871 who had signed a protest against the German seizure of Alsace-Lorraine. In his speech he asserted both his faith in Allied solidarity and his intense pride in France. 'Certainly one must be humanitarian,' he said, 'but one must be French first, for France represents an idealistic conception of humanity which has prevailed in the world, and one cannot serve humanity at the expense of

France.' Yet none of the Allies could have won, he declared, without the help of the others: 'I see here a new hope for humanity, and we must preserve that hope. Alliance in war must be followed by unbreakable alliance in peace.' His moving words were punctuated by frequent bursts of applause, and at the end the deputies rose to their feet and gave him a great ovation.

On the following day the Senate joined in the general feeling of euphoria, and passed a resolution stating that 'The armies and their leaders, the government of the Republic, citizen Georges Clemenceau, prime minister and minister of war, and Marshal Foch, generalissimo of the Allied armies, have deserved well of the fatherland,' and ordering that the declaration should be inscribed for permanent preservation in every town hall and school of France. Poincaré wrote ruefully in his diary: 'The press lauds him [Clemenceau] to the skies this morning. To everyone he is the liberator of occupied territory, the organiser of the victory. He alone personifies France. Foch has disappeared; the army has disappeared. And for myself, naturally I don't exist. The four years of war, during which I presided over the State and which Clemenceau consecrated to a merciless opposition to the successive governments, are entirely forgotten.'

For all their personal bitterness, Poincaré's words give a good idea of the Tiger's place in the minds and hearts of the French people on 11 November, 1918. It was amazing how he had borne the strain. He was diabetic: 'No one knows,' he once remarked, 'that I made war with forty grammes of sugar in my urine.' He suffered from eczema, and always wore grey silk gloves to protect his hands from irritation. He was expecting to have a throat operation later in the month. Yet after a night in which he had little sleep he was happy to be acclaimed by excited crowds as he drove from the rue Franklin to the war ministry, and later to the Elysée, the Palais-Bourbon and the Palais du Luxembourg. Léon Daudet, who was walking along the boulevard Saint-Germain as the Tiger's car raced by, thought that he looked 'pink and plump, sure of himself, just as he had looked thirty-four years earlier in the office of *La Justice*'.

At the war ministry his children had assembled to see him receive the signed armistice from Marshal Foch. Later there was a cabinet meeting at the Elysée; when Poincaré embraced him, he said gaily, 'I've been kissed by more than five hundred girls since this morning!' From the Elysée he drove to the Chamber of Deputies, where he read out the armistice terms, welcomed the return of Alsace-Lorraine and expressed the nation's thanks to the dead who had made victory possible. As for the living, he said, the nation was waiting to applaud them when they passed under the Arc de Triomphe. 'Through them France will find again her place in the world, to continue her splendid advance in the infinity of human progress, yesterday the soldier of God, today the soldier of humanity, always the soldier of the ideal.' Friends who were watching him knew how hard he was finding it to hold back his tears.

The last words of his short speech were accompanied by the booming of cannons from the esplanade des Invalides, and the deputies rose to sing the Marseillaise. From the Palais-Bourbon he went to the Palais du Luxembourg, where he repeated his speech and the Senate voted unanimously that his bust should be placed by the side of those of other great Frenchmen who had given lustre to the Senate. That was the last public event in an exciting but exhausting day. In a long talk with Mordacq that evening he said reflectively: 'Yes, we have won the war, and not without difficulty. But now we must win the peace, and perhaps that will be harder.'[1]

Two days later the 'Father of Victory' strolled along the boulevards with his two daughters. He was almost suffocated by the admiring crowds which surrounded them.

What had he done to deserve the acclamations he was now receiving? On the technical side he had been an impressive minister of war. He had reorganised the ministry, creating new sub-directorates for tanks and motor transport, and had given close attention to the problems of munitions, aircraft manufacture and manpower. Helped by Mandel and Ignace, he had restored the national morale by prosecuting defeatists and traitors, and had encouraged the fighting men by chasing shirkers out of their safe jobs and making them take their turn at the front. He had worked hard to make unity of command a reality.

But Clemenceau's contribution to victory cannot be measured only in men, munitions, tanks and aeroplanes. It was will-power which made the difference between victory and defeat, and the Tiger had it in abundance. When once he had announced his programme—to make war until victory was won—he never wavered. His speeches were few, but each one confirmed his determination to hold on until the last quarter-of-an-hour; he radiated confidence as he walked in the corridors of the Palais-Bourbon; his visits to the front were a constant reminder to the troops that the government had not forgotten them. His enemy Ludendorff admitted that he was 'the most energetic man in France'.

Moreover, victory had been won without recourse to dictatorship. He kept France's democratic institutions intact, and it was thanks to his work

---

[1] In conversation with Sacha Guitry Clemenceau said that he went to see Claude Monet on Armistice Day, but it is hard to see how a visit to Giverny could possibly have been fitted into his crowded programme. More probably he went on the previous day (a Sunday) to tell Monet that the armistice was on the point of being signed. (*See* Sacha Guitry, *If I Remember Right*, pp. 238–9.)

and example that France never turned to a 'man on horseback' during her various post-war crises. The tributes of Armistice Day were well deserved by one who, largely by the strength of his personality, had kept France in the war and enabled her to play her full part in the Allies' victory.

CHAPTER SEVENTEEN

MAKING THE PEACE

1. Before the conference. 2. Council of Ten. 3. The way of an invalid. 4. Rhineland argument. 5. Council of Four. 6. Reparations. 7. The Treaty of Versailles.

[1]

ON THE day after the signing of the armistice Clemenceau took a decision which would be remembered months later. A Te Deum was to be sung at Notre Dame in thanksgiving for the Allied victory, and President Poincaré wished to be present. To Clemenceau the separation of Church and State meant that there could be no official recognition of any religious ceremony. He ruled that neither the President nor any member of the government should attend the service, and to avoid a constitutional clash Poincaré obeyed his order.

The Tiger was riding high after the armistice. He was reluctant to accept honours or gifts for his war services, but he allowed the members of his cabinet to give him a picture—a magnificent Daumier—and he agreed to receive an honorary degree from Oxford university. He was elected a member of the Académie Française, though he never took his seat among 'the Immortals', as he declined to make the traditional speech in honour of the dead member whose place he was taking. He was also asked if he would like to be a member of the Académie de Médecine, but he smilingly refused. 'Which section would you put me in?', he asked. 'Invalids?'

At this time his mind was chiefly occupied with arrangements for the peace conference, which it was proposed to hold as soon as possible. From Washington President Wilson at first opposed Clemenceau's wish to hold it in Paris; he thought that neutral Switzerland would be more appropriate, but he changed his mind when he heard that the Swiss Social Democratic party was arranging mass rallies for the first anniversary of the Bolshevik revolution in Russia. He was afraid that Switzerland might have gone Communist before the conference met, and he soon came round to the idea that it should be held in France. The official meeting-place was Versailles, but the real work was done in Paris.

It was now known that President Wilson was coming to Europe for the conference, and Clemenceau thought it advisable that the British, French and Italian prime ministers should have a preliminary meeting before the President's arrival. Since Lloyd George could not come to Paris, because of the imminence of a British general election, the meeting was held in London, where the Tiger and Foch were given a great welcome. Colonel Repington thought he had 'never heard such cheering in staid old London before'.

The meeting passed a number of resolutions about the implementation of the armistice and procedure for the peace conference, but Clemenceau stored up trouble for himself by one of his impulsive remarks in a private conversation with Lloyd George about the future of Mesopotamia and Palestine, which were now freed from Turkish suzerainty. Lloyd George said that Britain wanted all Palestine and the important oil district of Mosul, and Clemenceau readily agreed, though he feared that Pichon would make difficulties about Mosul. No one else was present at their meeting, but Lloyd George gave an account of it to Maurice Hankey, secretary to the British war cabinet and the Supreme War Council, who noted it in his diary. But what Hankey did not mention (presumably because Lloyd George had not told him) was that French support for British interests in Mosul was a *quid pro quo* for British backing of France in Syria and Cilicia. A few weeks later Clemenceau complained to Colonel House that Lloyd George had not kept his promises about Syria.

On 14 December President Woodrow Wilson arrived in Paris, where his tumultuous welcome was in marked contrast to the indifference which greeted statesmen from other nations. The Fourteen Points and the concept of the League of Nations had made a great impression on the war-weary French, and the American President had become the hero of the Left wing. At their first meeting Clemenceau realised that Wilson was a man of principle and a man with a conscience, though he feared that it was 'a conscience in blinkers' and that the President did not perceive 'the abyss that lies between theory and practice'. Further acquaintance was to convince him that 'President Wilson, the inspired prophet of a noble ideological venture, to which he was unfortunately destined to become a slave, had insufficient knowledge of Europe lying torn to pieces at his feet. . . . He acted to the very best of his abilities in circumstances the origins of which had escaped him and whose ulterior developments lay beyond his ken.'

Yet in spite of their ideological differences, which it would be Lloyd George's task to attempt to reconcile, the two men had some things in common. Both were sincere democrats with a steady faith in progress; both believed in humanity but mistrusted men as individuals. They were thus able to be on good terms during the peace conference, and it was only on rare occasions that the Tiger became enraged by Wilson's naïve belief that the Fourteen Points would inaugurate a reign of peace and justice on earth. (The contrast between Wilson's idealism and Lloyd George's Machiavellian grasp of power politics once made him say to a friend who asked him how he was getting on at the conference: 'What can I do? I find myself between Jesus Christ on one side and Napoleon Bonaparte on the other.')

Since Clemenceau had no wish to antagonise Wilson it was unfortunate that a phrase he used in the Chamber of Deputies on 29 December should have been interpreted in some quarters as a slur on the American President. A debate on estimated expenditure in 1919 had begun two days earlier, and had given deputies a chance of raising issues of foreign policy. Clemenceau spoke at a later stage, with the object of answering Left wing critics who thought that he would be incapable of negotiating the peace and should give way to the subtler Briand.

Part of his speech was devoted to Russia, for Allied diplomacy was then bedevilled by the problem of possible intervention in force to assist the White Russians (heirs of the Tsarist regime) in their attempt to overthrow the Bolshevik government. Clemenceau was anxious to prevent the spread of Bolshevism (as Communism was then generally known), but he was not prepared to use French arms against it on any large scale. He told the Chamber that Allied policy in Russia was purely defensive, and was designed to contain Bolshevik Russia by establishing a *cordon sanitaire*.

When he turned to the peace conference he soon showed that he had no intention of making way for Briand. He had read in the papers, he said, that he was not 'a man of peace'. The same thing had been insinuated in the Chamber, and he regarded it as an insult to his dignity; but if, for political reasons, the Chamber wanted a change of government, he would retire, and no one would ever hear him utter a word of recrimination. Of President Wilson he said: 'He is a man who inspires respect by the simplicity of his words and the noble candour of his mind.'

The deputies quickly showed that they did not dare to overthrow the government; a hostile amendment was defeated by 386 votes to 88. But the Tiger was in trouble because of his double-edged remark about Wilson. What had he meant by 'candour'? He said he had meant honesty, and had intended it as high praise; but the Left wing press interpreted 'candour' in the more usual French sense of ingenuousness or naïveté, and condemned the phrase as a jeer at Wilson. Newspapers of the Right and Centre accepted Clemenceau's explanation, but the Left wing comments were not lost on Wilson and his confidant, Colonel House. The latter wrote in his diary on 1 January: '. . . we discussed Clemenceau's speech in the Chamber of Deputies. In my opinion it is the greatest diplomatic blunder that Clemenceau has made since the famous Prince Sixtus letter.'

On the day after his speech Clemenceau was able to leave Paris for a short holiday in the Vendée. Whenever he felt run down, he told Mordacq, he went back to breathe his native air, and then he was fully restored and ready to take up the fight again. He could be sure that there was a hard fight ahead in 1919.

[2]

Since the conference was being held in France the Allied statesmen agreed that Clemenceau should be its president. 'That was an admirable decision,' said Maurice Hankey, who became secretary to the British delegation, 'for Clemenceau was one of the best chairmen I have ever known—firm to the point of "tigerishness" when necessary, understanding, conciliatory, witty and a tremendous driver. His leadership never failed from first to last, and was never questioned.' He had also the advantage, which was not shared by his principal colleagues, of speaking both French and English, which were the official languages of the conference.

As originally planned, the prime ministers and foreign ministers of France, Britain, the United States, Italy and Japan were to meet regularly in what became known as the Council of Ten; there were to be occasional plenary sessions, at which the delegates of the great powers would be joined by those of the smaller powers invited to the conference; five commissions were to examine special subjects of major importance, such as the League of Nations, war guilt and reparations; and as many as fifty-eight technical commissions were to examine and report on particular issues. Looking back on this elaborate organisation, André Tardieu rightly poured scorn on the legend that the Treaty of Versailles was a document 'hurriedly improvised and thrown together by four fallible and ill-informed men, closeted in a dark room, imposing on the world their whim as law'.

Tardieu, a journalist and deputy who had recently been high commissioner to the United States, was one of the members of the French peace delegation, and virtually acted as Clemenceau's chief of staff; the other delegates were Clemenceau, Pichon, Klotz, the finance minister, and Jules Cambon, former French ambassador in Berlin, with Marshal Foch as their military adviser, though not a delegate. The Tiger had picked his men carefully. Three former prime ministers—Briand, Ribot and Bourgeois—had hoped to be chosen and were aggrieved when they were passed over.

The Council of Ten held its first meeting on 12 January, 1919. Its principal members were Clemenceau, Wilson, Lloyd George and Orlando, the Italian prime minister, for the Japanese prime minister played only a minor part. On arriving in Europe Wilson had been doubtful whether, as head of a State, he could properly sit at a conference table with the Allied prime ministers; he had been persuaded to do so, though his position was in some ways anomalous. Since the signing of the armistice Clemenceau had been given a decisive vote of confidence by the Chamber of Deputies and Lloyd George had won a great victory in the British general election; but in the United States the mid-term Congressional elections had left Wilson, a Democrat, opposed by Republican majorities in both the Senate and the House of Representatives. His power had gone, but he still represented the United States in Paris, where his word carried far more weight than it did in his own country.

The dilemma facing the leading delegates became obvious as soon as the conference was launched. Unlike the autocratic statesmen and diplomats who reshaped Europe after the Napoleonic wars, the men who met in Paris were not free agents; all had to take account of public and parliamentary opinion in their own countries, and in 1919 this opinion was violently anti-German. Even Clemenceau, who had distrusted Germany since 1870 and would continue to hate and distrust her until the end of his life, did not share the desire for ruthless vengeance felt by the French Right wing and fostered by Foch and Poincaré. Moreover, the three principals had essentially different peace aims. In Sir Denis Brogan's words, 'Wilson was trying to create a world that had never existed. . . . Lloyd George was trying to justify the rash promises he had made to the British people. Clemenceau was trying to secure the military safety of France. In these cross-purposes none of the victors attained his ends.'

In accordance with Wilson's wishes, it was decided to deal first with the proposal for a League of Nations, in which the cynical Clemenceau never really believed; but other problems soon pressed on the Council of Ten. One of these concerned the conference's relations with Russia, which would certainly have sent a delegation to Paris if Tsardom had not been overthrown.

What should be done in the new circumstances? Lloyd George suggested that the Bolshevik government and the White Russians should be invited to call a truce in their civil war and to send representatives to a meeting in Paris; but Clemenceau, who was more anti-Communist than his colleagues in the Council of Ten, refused to allow Bolshevik delegates to come to Paris and threatened to resign from the conference if they were invited. It was then proposed that the rival Russian groups should meet at Prinkipo, on the Princes Islands in the Sea of Marmora, but the Russians declined to go there, and the idea of ascertaining Russian opinion on the peace settlement came to nothing. The Russian problem remained unsolved; the Allies had refused to grasp the nettle of either beginning normal diplomatic relations with the Russian government or sending sufficient military forces to crush Bolshevism.

One of the problems on which the Allied leaders were divided was that of bringing Kaiser Wilhelm II to trial. The Kaiser had abdicated and fled to Holland before the armistice; it had been widely assumed that he would be put to trial as the man chiefly responsible for the war, and 'Hang the Kaiser' had been a British election slogan. Wilson was doubtful whether the Kaiser's personal guilt could be established, and thought that there was a risk of making him a martyr; but Clemenceau argued that the principle of responsibility, which was the basis of domestic law, should also be introduced into international law. His view prevailed, and the decision to try the Kaiser was written into the treaty. It was never put into effect, as the Dutch government refused to extradite him.

The early weeks of the conference were less productive than had been expected. The Council of Ten worked hard. It had morning and afternoon sessions every weekday in Pichon's elegant office at the Quai d'Orsay, but the work went slowly, mainly because it was too broadly based. Delegates from smaller powers, ministers and experts all came before the council to give evidence; in the opinion of Charles Seymour, an expert attached to the American delegation, 'there were too many people in the room', and André Tardieu thought that 'Little by little everybody had got into the habit of making speeches. Matters were constantly being adjourned.'

It was probably the slow pace of the conference which induced Clemenceau to give a tempestuous interview to an American journalist. France, he told the Associated Press, had won only a Pyrrhic victory. Industrially and commercially, he said, Germany had won the war; her factories were intact, her war debts were internal and could easily be liquidated by financial manipulation, and in a short time the German economy would be stronger and healthier than that of France.

This remarkably prophetic interview was probably intended to justify stern treatment of Germany. A few days after its publication the Council of Ten became inhibited from taking major decisions through the temporary absence of two of its leading figures. On 14 February the covenant of the League of Nations was approved at a plenary session of the conference, and President Wilson left for a short visit to the United States. Five days later a would-be assassin shot and wounded Clemenceau.

13 At the front: a 'Sem' cartoon

14 With Foch and Haig

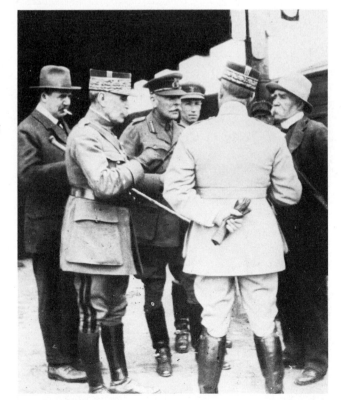

15 With Poincaré at Strasbourg after its liberation (1918)

16 With President Wilson and Lloyd George after the signing
of the peace treaty (1919)

17 'The one with the gun': at an Indian tiger-shoot with the
Maharajahs of Gwalior and Bikanir (1921)

18 At the horseshoe desk, rue Franklin (Musée Clemenceau)

19 'In the evening of my thought': at Belébat, Saint Vincent-sur-Jard

A. J. Balfour, the tall and distinguished British foreign secretary, was sitting in Colonel House's office in Paris when news was brought that Clemenceau had been shot. Balfour was always reluctant to commit himself: once, in the Council of Ten, after he had discussed every aspect of an urgent problem in a most erudite way, Clemenceau had turned to Lloyd George in bewilderment, asking 'But is he *for* or is he *against*?' Even the news of an attempted assassination could not disturb his calm. 'Dear, dear,' he said, 'I wonder what that portends.' 'I don't know,' said House, 'but we must find out.' He hurried Balfour into his car and drove to the rue Franklin.

Clemenceau was shot at 8.40 a.m. on 19 February by a twenty-two-year-old anarchist called Emile Cottin. He said at his trial that he had decided to kill Clemenceau for taking 'sanctions' against anarchists, who had been forbidden to hold meetings and had been attacked by municipal guards during a strike. Cottin was standing near a public urinal at the corner of the rue Franklin and the boulevard Delessert when the Tiger entered his car to go to the war ministry. Running behind it, he fired seven shots through the back panel; one bullet lodged in Clemenceau's chest, others went through his clothes.

The car turned back to his house. The war ministry was at once informed, and Mordacq told the duty officer to take a cab, pick up two doctors and take them to the rue Franklin. He then drove there himself, and found Clemenceau sitting in a chair, looking very pale but perfectly calm. 'They attacked me from behind,' he said. 'They shot me in the back. They didn't dare attack me from the front.' And on noticing the general's distress, he added comfortingly: 'Come now, don't get upset. I'm not dead yet!'

Mandel was the next to arrive, followed by the two doctors, who thought that the bullet had not touched any vital spot, but decided to postpone an X-ray examination till the following day. Sister Théoneste, who had looked after Clemenceau when he had his prostate operation and was said to be the only person who could handle him, was then summoned to take charge of the invalid.

It was not an easy task; on the next morning Sister Théoneste was shocked to find that the Tiger had got out of bed at four o'clock and moved into an armchair. Later in the day, when the X-ray confirmed the doctors' opinion but showed that the wound would have been fatal if it had been a few millimetres to the right or the left, Clemenceau looked at his nurse and said impishly, 'That simply proves that I am well in with the good Lord.' 'That is quite possible,' Sister Théoneste replied, 'but it's no use your being well in with the good Lord if you are going to be as imprudent as you were last night.'

During his convalescence he had many visitors and many messages of sympathy, including a warm tribute from the great actress Sarah Bernhardt; the Pope sent his blessing by telegram, and Clemenceau returned the compliment by sending his own blessing to the Pope. And he was always ready to crack a joke, even about the attempt to kill him. Stephen Bonsal, the former journalist who was now an expert attached to the American delegation, was present when the prosecutor in the Cottin trial and several other lawyers came in to discuss the appropriate sentence for the criminal. He always remembered the Tiger's jesting comments on Cottin's bad marksmanship:

> We have just won the most terrible war in history, yet here is a French-man who misses his target six times out of seven at point-blank range. Of course the fellow must be punished for the careless use of a dangerous weapon and for poor marksmanship. I suggest that he be locked up for about eight years, with intensive training in a shooting gallery.

Cottin was actually sentenced to ten years' imprisonment, but was released when he had served about half his sentence.

With the help of Sister Théoneste, the Tiger joked and talked his way to recovery. The doctors decided not to operate to remove the bullet; it remained lodged in his chest, and since he was to live for another ten years, it cannot have done him much harm. One of his eccentricities during his convalescence was to sleep from 9 p.m. till midnight and then be ready to receive visitors, who thronged his sick-room in spite of the doctors' protests. In one of these midnight sessions he made a brief but significant comment on his attitude to the peace conference:

> I must make a peace based upon my belief and upon my own experience of the world in which we have to live. My responsibility is personal and non-transferable. When called to the bar of history, I cannot say, 'Well, I made these arrangements to conform to Mr. Wilson's stand-point.'

It was in this mood that he returned to the Council of Ten on 1 March, ready to face, among much else, the two crucial problems of France's eastern frontier and reparations.

[4]

The central point of the long dispute over France's eastern frontier was the sovereignty of the Rhineland, the area of about 10,000 square miles with some 5½m. inhabitants lying west of the Rhine between Alsace-Lorraine and the Dutch frontier. Germany's possession of this territory left France without a natural frontier in the east and simplified the task of an invading army. Before and during the war many books had been written in France about the need to detach the Rhineland from Germany. The French now believed that the peace treaty should make it impossible for the Rhineland to be used again as the springboard for an invasion of France.

Annexation was never possible. Neither Wilson nor Lloyd George would have agreed to the creation of 'a German Alsace-Lorraine'. But Foch was convinced that the Rhine must become Germany's western frontier, and in principle Clemenceau agreed with him, as did most Frenchmen, except the Socialists. A favoured solution was the establishment of an autonomous republic or republics in the Rhineland, though Tardieu, for one, thought that this would be 'annexation in disguise'.

From the beginning of the conference the Tiger had to steer a middle course between the two opposing viewpoints. Foch, supported by Poincaré and the Right wing press, and prompted by his shrewd chief of staff, General Weygand, argued that 'Any other solution than making the Rhine the Allies' frontier is a bad one'; Wilson and Lloyd George insisted that the Rhineland must remain German. During his convalescence Clemenceau asked Tardieu to prepare a memorandum disclaiming all thought of annexing the Rhineland, but proposing that the left bank of the Rhine should be made into a free State, possibly in customs union with France and Belgium. He must have known that this would be unacceptable to Wilson and Lloyd George, but he may well have thought that by asking for something which was bound to be refused, he would be in a good position for demanding some other concession as compensation.

President Wilson came back from America on 13 March to find his colleagues still deadlocked on the issue of the Franco-German boundary. It was left to the ingenious Lloyd George to suggest a way out of the difficulty. On condition that the Rhineland autonomy proposal was dropped, he persuaded Wilson to join him in offering France a guarantee of immediate military assistance if Germany should attack her without provocation. With Welsh exuberance he even promised to build a Channel tunnel to bring troops more rapidly to France in time of need.

It was a brilliant stroke, which undermined the French demand for an autonomous Rhineland. Clemenceau discussed the offer with Tardieu and Loucheur; the choice, as he saw it, lay between pursuing French policy in the Rhineland without allies and maintaining the war-time alliance. They agreed that it would be impossible to refuse the Anglo-American offer, and Pichon, too, favoured acceptance, though wondering whether the alliance would really endure, and fearing that they might be throwing away the substance for the shadow.

It can be argued that Clemenceau was being too naïve in imagining that the American guarantee would be ratified by the United States Congress. Early in March a resolution hostile to the League of Nations, which Wilson insisted on making part of the peace treaty, was presented to the United Senate over the signatures of thirty-nine Republican senators or senators-elect. Since treaties required a two-thirds majority in the Senate, which had ninety-six members, the opposition of thirty-nine senators was more than enough to block the approval of the peace treaty; and if the treaty were not ratified, the guarantee would also be lost. This, of course, is what actually happened: should not Clemenceau and the other French delegates have foreseen the danger?

Certainly they had been told by the French *chargé d'affaires* in Washington that the constitution of the League of Nations would not pass the Senate as it stood; but Wilson assured them that, when the time came, his personal authority and a direct appeal to public opinion would win him enough votes in the Senate to ratify the treaty. We cannot be sure that Clemenceau was convinced by the President, but he may have been, since his experience as *tombeur de ministères* had taught him a great deal about whipping up votes in times of emergency.

In any case it was not for a Frenchman to tell the President of the United States that he was in danger of being disowned by his own countrymen. After discussion Clemenceau accepted the guarantee in principle, but he insisted that the Rhineland must be occupied for a number of years, that it must be demilitarised and that France must be given the Saar. The bargain would not be such a simple one as Lloyd George and Wilson may have hoped.

[5]

The Rhineland issue was not to be fought out in the Council of Ten. Though the council was still holding its twice-daily meetings, there was increasing discontent about its slow progress and the leakages of secret information to the press, which were inevitable when so many people attended the sessions at the Quai d'Orsay. Ten days after Wilson's return from America the four principals of the peace conference decided that in future they would meet separately and privately in what became known as the Council of Four. They often met in the study of Wilson's house in the place des États-Unis, sometimes at Lloyd George's flat in the rue Nitôt or in Clemenceau's office at the war ministry, but never at the Quai d'Orsay.

The Council of Four was a perfect setting for the Tiger's persuasiveness. He had spoken comparatively little in the Council of Ten; more often, as Lloyd George recalled, he had sought out members of the British and American delegations and in separate personal conversations had 'tirelessly reiterated the French demand for a Rhine frontier as a guarantee of peace', pointing out again and again that France, with a population of only 40m., could not be left to face a hostile Germany with 65m. inhabitants and territory on both sides of the Rhine. He was happier to be alone with Wilson, Lloyd George and Orlando in the Council of Four, though here too they were joined from time to time by ministers, expert advisers and members of other delegations. 'Within the council chamber,' wrote Robert Lansing, who was frequently present in his capacity as U.S. secretary of state, 'his domineering manner, his brusqueness of speech and his driving methods of conducting business disappeared. He showed patience and consideration towards his colleagues, and seldom spoke until the others had expressed their views. It was only on rare occasions that he abandoned his suavity of address and allowed his emotions to affect his utterances.'

It was in these surroundings that he made his last stand for the French claim to a Rhine frontier and the Saar, and won substantial concessions for which Foch was never to give him credit. Chief among these was the agreement for the Allied military occupation of the Rhineland for fifteen years.

Both Wilson and Lloyd George had, as usual, their reservations about this proposal by the French delegation. They realised, however, that the Tiger had resisted great pressure from Foch and Poincaré in abandoning the idea of an independent Rhineland, and they were persuaded to concede the more moderate claims which he now advanced. It was agreed that the Allies should occupy German territories west of the Rhine and the three bridgeheads of Cologne, Coblenz and Mainz, which would be vacated in three five-year stages (or earlier, in the unlikely event of Germany having paid her reparations in full before the fifteen years expired); that the Rhineland would then be permanently demilitarised; and that Germany must have no military installations in a zone extending some thirty miles on the east bank of the river.

Clemenceau was sharply criticised in France for this agreement, on the ground that Germany would be too impoverished to make war again in the next fifteen years; the treaty provisions meant, therefore, that the Rhineland would be occupied while Germany was weak and vacated when she became strong again. But Clemenceau's point was that France needed a period of complete security for reconstruction and the strengthening of her defences; at the end of fifteen years she should have made herself impregnable against a shock invasion, and the treaty would allow her to return to the Rhineland if Germany made any attempt to remilitarise it. As far as could be seen, he was giving France security. He was not to blame for the failure of post-war French governments to keep pace with German rearmament, or with Anglo-French inaction when Hitler re-militarised the Rhineland in defiance of the Treaty of Versailles.

The return of Alsace-Lorraine to France was provided for in the Fourteen Points, but the destiny of the neighbouring Saar basin caused sharp controversy. The Saar had been French for a few years during the Napoleonic era, but had become German again under the 1815 settlement. France now felt that she had a legitimate claim to the area, since the Germans had deliberately wrecked the coal mines of northern France and Saar coal was needed for the working of Lorraine iron.

It was during an early discussion of the Saar that Clemenceau told his colleagues: 'I am old. In a few months I shall have left politics for ever. My disinterestedness is complete.' At the same time he warned President Wilson that the Germans' idea of justice was different from that of the Allies. 'You wish to do justice to the Germans,' he said. 'Do not believe that they will ever forgive us. They will seek only the chance of revenge. Nothing will suppress the fury of those who hoped to dominate the world and believed success so near.' But Wilson still thought it would be unjust to detach the Saar from Germany. He resisted the French claim so firmly that after a particularly stormy session the Tiger called him 'a pro-German'.

Lloyd George acted as conciliator. Thanks to his intervention the Saar coal mines were given to France, and the territory was placed under French administration for fifteen years; at the end of that time the in-habitants would decide their future by plebiscite, and if they placed themselves under German rule Germany would be allowed to buy the mines back from France. It was a compromise settlement, which left each side confident of success in the plebiscite. In the end the Saar voted enthusiastically for incorporation in Nazi Germany.

While bargaining with Wilson and Lloyd George over these complex issues Clemenceau had to hold at arm's length the over-demanding Foch and his *éminence grise*, General Weygand. He maintained his view that peace-making was a matter for politicians, not for soldiers, and he regarded the interference of Foch and Weygand as an attempt by the army to influence national policy. When Henry Wilson was in Paris at the end of April he found Foch complaining that 'the Tiger never sees him nor tells him anything'.

Yet Foch was not kept entirely in the background. He was allowed to address the Council of Four on 31 March, but he found no support for his renewed claim that the frontier of western Europe should be on the Rhine. He also spoke at a plenary session on 6 May, and astonished the delegates by saying that the military guarantee would be null at the end of five years, and that the Allies had no means of assuring the payment of German reparations. When the conference adjourned for tea, Clemenceau grumbled to him: 'You think the world revolves around you, *monsieur le Maréchal*. That was all right during the war, but it's finished now.'

In his talks with Raymond Recouly towards the end of his life Foch said it was extraordinary that Clemenceau did not make more use of his services to overcome Wilson and Lloyd George. He naïvely thought that the Tiger would have been able to secure a permanent Rhine frontier by telling his colleagues that he was obliged to take Foch's advice on these matters. These comments reveal the marshal's inability to grasp what was going on at the peace conference. His patriotism was never in doubt, but he did not understand politics. He did not realise how stubbornly Clemenceau had fought for the strategic frontier of the Rhine, but had been defeated by the firm resistance of Wilson and Lloyd George, backed by public opinion in their respective countries. Certainly Foch himself could have done no better, for Clemenceau's Rhineland settlement went as far as it was possible for him to carry his colleagues with him.

[6]

In 1919 it seemed to be common justice that Germany should pay reparations for the damage and losses caused by the war. The peace conference was expected to decide how big the bill should be.

Clemenceau was neither a financial expert nor an economist, and he was out of his depth in discussions of reparations. But both he and Lloyd George were under strong public and parliamentary pressure to make Germany's bill as big as possible. At the beginning of April 370 British Conservative M.P.s signed a telegram to Lloyd George urging that Germany must be made to pay the full financial claims of the British empire; their example was followed by a large group of French senators, supported by 300 deputies, who presented the French delegation with a manifesto insisting that 'the full cost of the war be charged to the enemy' and that Germany must be held responsible for 'the reparation of damage to persons as well as to property'. Clemenceau shared these views, but refused to commit himself to any specific claim. When Raoul Péret, chairman of the Chamber's budget committee, was rash enough to write to him asking for details of his reparations policy, his reply was a tart letter of only eight lines.

While there was general agreement that Germany should pay to the limits of her capacity, the experts produced widely differing estimates of what the amount should be, ranging from the comparatively modest figure of £2,000m. (which even the sceptical J. M. Keynes regarded as feasible) to a staggering £20,000m. proposed by the governor of the Bank of England. Some compromise might have been found, but Clemenceau, prompted by Klotz, pointed out that any such compromise would fall short of the expectations of the French people, and would endanger the government which accepted it. Lloyd George said that the same would be true of Great Britain, and it was decided to put no definite figure in the treaty, but to set up a reparations commission which would examine Germany's capacity to pay and would fix the appropriate sum.

To establish the claim the treaty stated in article 231 that 'The Allied and Associated governments affirm and Germany accepts the responsibility of Germany and her allies for causing all the loss and damage to which the Allied and Associated governments have been subjected as a consequence of the war imposed upon them by the aggression of Germany and her allies.' This 'well and carefully drafted article', as Keynes called it, was later to be bitterly attacked by Germany as 'the war guilt clause'. In fact, the affirmation of war guilt was only incidental; the purpose of the article was to establish once and for all the Allies' juridical right to reparations.

Clemenceau was not concerned with the later history of reparations, which proved almost impossible to collect from Germany and were finally written off at a Lausanne conference in 1932. ('It seems likely,' writes David Thomson, 'that on balance she paid no reparations at all, for her creditors and others sank and lost as much in investments in Germany as was ever paid out in reparations.') But Clemenceau must bear responsibility for allowing his finance minister to increase French debts in the hope that huge payments from Germany would soon balance the budget. The devaluation of the franc in 1926 was a direct consequence of unsound finances in 1919. Perhaps there was some justice in the Tiger's complaint that Klotz was the only Jew who could not count.

In these months of hard bargaining Clemenceau had little time to spare from his double duties as prime minister and peace negotiator, and he fully earned his occasional hours of relaxation. As a change from the wholly masculine environment of his working day, he liked to look in for afternoon tea at Lloyd George's flat in the rue Nitôt, where Frances Stevenson, Lloyd George's secretary and mistress, tempted him with chocolate *langues de chat* especially made by the cook in honour of his visit. ('He enjoyed them like a child,' she remembered.) Or again, after long sessions at the conference it was pleasant to put in an hour or two at the back of a box at the Opéra or the Opéra-Comique, listening to some elegant but undemanding work like *The Barber of Seville*, 'which', he observed to Mordacq, who accompanied him, 'does not require one to make the slightest cerebral effort'.

Yet even at the opera he could not entirely forget the peace conference. 'Figaro here . . . Figaro there . . . he's a kind of Lloyd George,' he murmured.

[7]

While much work had still to be done on the treaties with Austria, Hungary, Bulgaria and Turkey, the German treaty, which alone was to bear the name of Treaty of Versailles, was far enough advanced in April to be shown to the Germans. The first plan had been that the Paris talks should be a preliminary peace conference, after which the Germans would be invited to attend a full conference for the preparation of the final terms; but as time went on and so much detailed work was done, this plan was abandoned and the treaty was drawn up by the Allies alone. The German government did not at first realise that the peace terms had been prepared for acceptance rather than discussion. When it was told that the treaty was ready it replied that it would send a minister and two officials to Paris to bring the document back to Berlin for study. Clemenceau would not agree to such a procedure. The Germans were sharply told that they must send plenipotentiaries fully authorised to deal with the whole question of peace.

The plenipotentiaries duly arrived in Paris, and the treaty was handed to them at a meeting in the Trianon palace, Versailles, on 7 May. The Germans were sullen, Clemenceau stern. As president of the conference he gave the envoys their copies of the bulky and elaborate treaty, and curtly told them that they had two weeks in which to submit their comments, which must be written, not oral. He warned them that 'the peoples represented here' were unanimously resolved to use every means in their power to secure all the satisfaction due to them in 'this second peace of Versailles'. To one spectator he seemed to be 'announcing to prisoners in the dock the hour of their condemnation and punishment'; another was fascinated by 'his beetling brows, his magnetic eyes sunk in a face yellow with age like an old parchment', as he listened intently to a bitter speech by Count Brockdorff-Rantzau, the German foreign minister.

It took the Germans much longer than two weeks to study and make their observations on the treaty. In the meantime Clemenceau was infuriated by the actions of Generals Mangin and Gérard, senior French commanders in the Rhineland army of occupation, who connived at an attempt by German separatists to set up an independent Rhineland republic.

It was a delicate situation. Clemenceau knew that Rhineland separatism was a forlorn hope, which would not be supported by the majority of the inhabitants; but he also knew that many Frenchmen, and many deputies in particular, still cherished the dream of a Rhineland buffer state, which would never have been accepted by Britain and America. Indeed, the Rhenish separatists found favour with Poincaré, who wrote to Clemenceau, saying: 'In my opinion it would be very unfortunate if we were to take part against these as yet very shy dispositions towards independence.'

Realising that public opinion would have been against him if he had sacked the generals for their mischievous intrigues, Clemenceau merely reminded them that they must observe strict neutrality in everything concerning political affairs, which were the government's concern, not the army's. In the face of such clear instructions the generals felt obliged to sever their connections with the separatists, and the independence movement collapsed. Later in the year, when the treaty had been signed, Clemenceau gave the generals their deserts by reorganising the Rhineland army in such a way that Mangin and Gérard, as well as Fayolle, their army group commander, all lost their commands. By these actions, says Jere Clemens King, he 'demonstrated not only political cunning but a high order of statesmanship'.

Home politics also demanded the Tiger's attention while he waited for the Germans to sign the treaty. Mandel had been watching the home front in peace as he had in war, and had successfully handled a one-day general strike on 1 May; his activities had won him the title of *le deuxième flic de France*. But Clemenceau felt that repression was not enough; he thought it wise to make some concession to the workers, who were suffering from the high cost of living and the inadequacy of food supplies. So on 7 June he received a deputation from the CGT and promised to introduce the eight-hour day. This was one of the reforms included in the programme of his earlier government. It had taken a world war to achieve it.

Throughout June the Germans lodged protests about particular articles in the treaty, without securing any change in its general pattern. Their obstinacy raised doubts about whether they were likely to sign it. What should be done if they refused? The Allied statesmen's first proposal was that their armies should march to Berlin and impose a settlement by force; but both Foch and Pétain felt that such a march would be very difficult, and Foch saw little hope of advancing further than the Weser, about sixty miles beyond the Rhine. This dubious half-measure was never put to the test. The Germans agreed to sign.

On 28 June the delegates of the Allied and Associated powers, the German plenipotentiaries and a crowd of privileged onlookers assembled in the great Galerie des Glaces at Versailles for the signing of the treaty. To one observer, at least, the presence of so many spectators seemed inappropriate. General Sir Henry Wilson described the scene in his diary:

> About 1,000 people, of whom I daresay 150 were ladies, which I thought all wrong. . . . I have never seen a less impressive ceremony. The room was much too full, a crowd of smart ladies, a constant buzz of conversation, the whole thing unreal, shoddy, poor to a degree. . . .

Even the crowds outside the palace seemed to this jaundiced general 'very undemonstrative'.

Clemenceau, who presided, deliberately made the ceremony as short as possible. The massive Treaty of Versailles, providing, among hundreds of clauses, for the restoration of Alsace-Lorraine, the fifteen-year occupation of the Rhineland, the transfer of the Saar mines to French ownership, reparations, German disarmament and the dismemberment of Germany's colonial empire, was signed by the Allied representatives and the German plenipotentiaries, headed by Count Brockdorff-Rantzau. Then Clemenceau coldly informed the Germans that the engagements undertaken in the treaty must be fully implemented, and it was all over.

If the crowds had been undemonstrative before the ceremony, they made up for it afterwards. Clemenceau, President Wilson and Lloyd George had great difficulty in forcing a way to their cars through the masses of cheering and excited people. Throughout the day and night every city, town and village in France kept up the rejoicing.

Two days later the Palais-Bourbon was overflowing with deputies and spectators when Clemenceau presented the treaty to the Chamber. Knowing that it was already being criticised from the Right, and that many deputies resented their having been kept in the dark during the negotiations, he made no attempt to defend the treaty, but simply introduced it for later debate. But he warned the deputies that peace was not assured merely by its signature; the important thing was to establish it and make it succeed, and all who had posts of responsibility in the nation should commit themselves to that task. As representatives of the people, he said, the deputies would give their verdict in complete independence; it was the law of democracy that the country itself must give judgement in the last resort.

His tactful reference to the deputies' authority was duly rewarded. His speech was greeted with loud applause.

Much work had still to be done on the other peace treaties, particularly in connection with Italy's territorial claims and the creation of new nation-States in eastern Europe out of the now dismembered Austro-Hungarian Empire. In Clemenceau's opinion the eastern European settlement was 'the keynote' of the peace-making. It represented, he wrote in *Grandeurs et Misères d'une Victoire*, '*the liberation of the peoples*, the independence of nationalities, whereas the keynote of the policy of Marshal Foch and M. Poincaré was the *occupation* of a territory by force of arms against the will of its inhabitants.'

After the signing of the treaty Wilson went back to America, to await both the rejection by Congress of all that he had done in Europe and his own physical collapse. The 'Big Four' were separated, the old Council of Four no longer existed. Clemenceau continued to work for a few weeks on the remaining treaties, and as late as October he was wrangling bitterly with Lloyd George over France's claims to special rights in Syria (which eventually became a French mandated territory); but he gradually left most of the negotiations in Pichon's hands and devoted himself to his ministerial duties and the organisation of the coming general election. In spite of the pressure of other work he remained minister of war, because as he told Mordacq, he did not think anyone else could run the ministry as well as he could.

Clemenceau has rarely been given much credit for his work as a peace-maker. Keynes set the fashion in denigration by calling the Treaty of Versailles 'a Carthaginian peace', in which, he asserted, little had been overlooked that might impoverish Germany or obstruct her development in future.[1] But while in Britain and the United States the treaty was condemned for its severity, in France it was criticised for its mildness. The truth lies between the two extremes, and is probably best expressed in the Right wing view of Jacques Bainville that the peace was 'too gentle for its harshness' (*trop douce pour ce qu'elle a de dur*). Or in Pierre Renouvin's words, 'the most serious criticism of the solutions adopted by the Four underlined the contrast between the rigour of certain clauses and the weakness of the guarantees of their execution'.

Looking back on the treaty nine years later, Clemenceau said there were

[1] Almost at the exact time when Keynes was drafting his fallacious *Economic Consequences of the Peace*, General Groener, quartermaster-general of the German army, was commenting on the likely effects of the treaty: 'I do not see why we should not forge ahead again, especially in the economic field.' (*See* Nowak, *Versailles*, p. 281.) And this, indeed, is what Germany did, in defiance of Keynes's arguments. The huge sums which she spent on rearmament in the 1930s disproved his contention that heavy reparations would have crippled her; his claim that 'Those who sign this treaty will sign the death warrant of millions of German men, women and children' was not borne out by events. Keynes was at fault both in under-estimating Germany's capacity for recovery and in ignoring the necessity for French security; the widespread acceptance of his views had an unfortunate effect on British public opinion between the wars and made it easier for Germany to break the Treaty of Versailles without fear of reprisal. (For a critical examination of Keynes's arguments, *see* Étienne Mantoux, *The Carthaginian Peace, or the Economic Consequences of Mr. Keynes*.)

two things to consider—what *he* had got out of it and what his successors had got out of it. 'When I resigned,' he said, 'Alsace and Lorraine had been restored to us; French troops occupied the left bank of the Rhine and the bridgeheads; Poland and Bohemia had been brought back to life, Rumania and Serbia had been enlarged; we had recovered Morocco, put our hand on the Cameroons, and so on. Then came Millerand and others —and that was the end of the treaty.' His comment is fair. The failure of the Treaty of Versailles was due as much to the unwillingness of later governments to enforce its provisions as to its own defects.

One of these defects had its roots in the Tiger's character. To Jacques Chastenet the treaty's principal error is that it took no account of the profound post-war lassitude of the French people, who were presented with a peace which demanded continuous effort for its implementation. Yet such an error, he adds, is excusable in a man who, though almost an octogenarian, remained the personification of combativeness.

To have been effective, the treaty would have required a spirit of resolute determination in all the victor nations, as well as the maintenance of the war-time alliance between Britain, France and the United States—the alliance which the Tiger had fought to preserve during the months of peace-making. But the will-power was missing, the alliance collapsed. In the remaining years of his life Clemenceau watched the progressive weakening or abandonment of the provisions of the Treaty of Versailles.

CHAPTER EIGHTEEN

DEFEAT

1. Ratifying the Treaty. 2. 'Horizon blue' Chamber. 3. The presidential election.

[1]

AFTER HIS five months' work on the Treaty of Versailles the Tiger had again to turn his attention to social and industrial matters. A ban on processions and demonstrations, which was enforced even when a procession was sent out with war widows at its head, had prevented any possibility of a revolutionary outbreak because of continuing food shortages and the rising cost of living; Mandel had shown skill and coolness in handling a dangerous situation on 1 May; but now there were threats of graver trouble on 21 July, when the CGT proposed to call a general strike.

Clemenceau was used to dealing with the CGT. On 18 July he asked its leaders to come to see him, and urged them to call off the strike in return for an increased rate of demobilisation, a partial amnesty for political prisoners and immediate action to reduce the cost of living; but he warned them that if they wanted a fight the government would reply with all the forces at its disposal. The CGT leaders were almost won over, but feared that they would lose face if they called off the strike at this late moment. Mandel obligingly got them 'off the hook' by arranging for the defeat of the minister of supply in the Chamber of Deputies; the appointment of a new minister, pledged to reduce the cost of living, gave the CGT an excuse for saying that a new situation had been created and that there was no need for a general strike. This was one of the many occasions on which Mandel served Clemenceau well, though his ruthless manoeuvres won him a reputation for hardness and arrogance which harmed his career when he became a deputy.

As autumn approached the strain of the Tiger's arduous two years as prime minister began to tell on him. At the end of September he admitted to Mordacq that he had been feeling very tired for some time, and that there were some nights when he did not sleep for more than an hour. Friends and colleagues noticed his fatigue and his curious way of treating it. 'He has a mania for taking medicine,' Tardieu told Barrès. 'How *does* he avoid poisoning himself? He has remedies in his drawer and helps himself by the handful. You know valerianate? You take a spoonful of it. *He* swallows the whole bottle!'

But neither tiredness nor too much medicine prevented him from spiritedly defending the treaty in both the Chamber and the Senate, when the question of ratification was debated. The result of the debates was never in doubt, but they allowed the opponents of the treaty to complain that it did not provide adequate security, that the amount to be paid in reparations would be inadequate, and that Clemenceau should not have negotiated the peace without the collaboration of parliament.

The debate in the Chamber lasted more than a month, but Clemenceau did not intervene until the closing stages, speaking briefly on 24 September and at greater length on the following day. He pointed out that parliament could not amend the treaty, since it was an international agreement and must be taken as a *bloc* ('to use an old word', he added reminiscently). He defended the work of the Council of Four and dismissed much of the Rhineland argument by reminding deputies that every apparently secure frontier had been crossed at some time by an invader. The treaty, he admitted, was necessarily imperfect; life, as he saw it, was a perpetual struggle in war and peace, and France would need vigilance, much vigilance, for years, or even for ages, to come. 'Make of this treaty what it ought to be; if you do what you should, France and the whole world will join in thanking you.'

In the Senate, where he spoke on 11 October, he again dwelt on the need for vigilance, and he warned his hearers that the mentality of the defeated Germans would be just as it would have been if they had been victorious. 'The German is a man who becomes a slave in order to enslave others. We are men who wish to be free in order to liberate others.' When the royalist Delahaye asserted that the treaty irritated and humiliated Germany, but left her the instruments of power and vengeance, he replied that the German army had been reduced from 5m. to 100,000, and that it was necessary to allow her some form of defence if she were not to become a second centre of Bolshevism in Europe.

These were Clemenceau's last parliamentary speeches; each was followed by a decisive vote for ratification. In the Chamber it was carried by 372 votes to 53; in the Senate the vote was unanimous. The press in general approved of ratification, but something of the magical aura surrounding Clemenceau had disappeared during the peace conference. The concessions he had been obliged to make to Wilson and Lloyd George had shown that he was no longer invincible. As Pierre Miquel observes, victory had come as a miracle largely due to the Tiger's energy, but there had been no miracle of the peace. Possibly it was the best peace that could be made, but it was not the French peace which the French people had dreamed of after four years of a bitter and destructive war largely fought on their own soil.

[2]

Unlike Britain, where a 'khaki election' was held a month after the armistice, France retained its wartime Chamber of Deputies until November 1919, when Clemenceau found himself presiding over an election conducted under the system of proportional representation which he had vigorously opposed before the war. It was a curious and unsatisfactory system, under which lists of like-minded candidates were presented for multi-member constituencies, and if a list won an absolute majority its members took all the seats. Proportional representation came into operation when there was no overall majority.

The keynote of the election was given by Clemenceau in a speech at Strasbourg on 4 November. He outlined a programme of action to be accepted by candidates who wanted his backing, and made an appeal for national unity, which was especially needed to counter the Bolshevik danger. The supporters who rallied to his call came from Right and Centre and went to the poll as the *bloc national républicain*; it included royalists and Catholics, as well as the former independent Socialist, Alexandre Millerand, who became its leading figure. Radicals and Socialists stood aloof, but since they refused to work together and presented separate lists of candidates they stood little chance against the big battalions of the anti-Socialist *bloc*. Minority parties suffered under the curious electoral system, and the triumphant *bloc national* won 437 out of 613 seats.

Clemenceau was invited by the Alsatian Radicals to head their list for the department of Bas-Rhin; he replied that he was touched at being invited to stand for Gambetta's old seat, but his age and the state of his health obliged him to retire from political life. Mandel was elected for the Gironde, and gave up his post as Clemenceau's civil *chef de cabinet*. He was succeeded by Georges Wormser, a young man who had written for *L'Homme Libre* before the war, and had served in the army as a private soldier before winning a commission on the battle-field.

Some 360 outgoing deputies were defeated in the election, and the new men were mostly ex-soldiers who had worn the horizon blue uniform of the French army. The 'horizon blue Chamber', as it came to be called, was the most Right wing Chamber which France had had since 1871; it seemed that an unusually large number of voters had been alarmed by the attitude of the extreme Left and had moved back to the Centre or the Right. Yet although the deputies of the *bloc* had won their seats as Clemenceau's supporters, many were hostile to him. They disliked his authoritarianism, his concessions to the British and Americans in his treaty-making, and the repressive measures which Mandel had carried out in his name; and now that the war was won the Catholic deputies could safely resume their opposition to his anticlericalism. These feelings of animosity were soon to have a surprising result.

One by-product of the election was a temporary coolness between Clemenceau and the faithful Mandel. During his campaign in the Gironde Mandel had replied to criticisms of the government by saying: 'You can blame me for any mistakes the government may have made.' Clemenceau thought that his former *chef de cabinet* was being much too presumptuous, and resented his open claim to have been the power behind the throne.

After his triumphs in the ratification debates and the general election the Tiger was back in his old exuberant form. His old friend Charles Benoist was appointed minister plenipotentiary to the Hague, and before leaving Paris he asked Clemenceau if he had any special instructions for him. 'None at all,' was the answer. 'Oh, yes! Tell your daughter, when she goes to the Amsterdam museum, to take down the Night Watch [Rembrandt's masterpiece], roll it up and send it to me in the diplomatic bag!' And in December, when he went to London for a conference about the treaty with Turkey, he gaily slandered contemporary French politicians in conversation with Lloyd George. 'Barthou,' he said, 'would murder his own mother. Briand would not murder his own mother, but he would murder someone else's mother!'

Yet already he was thinking about retirement from politics, and about finding a summer home in the Vendée. In November he went there with Mordacq to look for a suitable property, and found a pleasant cottage at Saint Vincent-sur-Jard, not far from the coastal resort of Les Sables d'Olonne. Perched on a small cliff, with views of the sea and the country and with no other building close by, it was just what he wanted, and he offered to buy it; but the owner, who lived in a château not far away, preferred to lease it to him at a modest rent, after Clemenceau had rejected a proposal that he should live in it rent-free. This was the cottage called Belébat, which became his summer residence for the rest of his life and is now a Clemenceau museum.

[3]

Raymond Poincaré's seven-year term of office as President of the French

Republic was coming to an end; his successor was to be elected in January 1920. For the greater part of 1919 Clemenceau had no idea of becoming a candidate for the presidency, and he more than once announced that he would soon be retiring from political life. Yet when he came back to Paris in November, refreshed by his holiday in the Vendée, he found that some of his friends wanted him to stand in the coming election.

His first reaction was a flat refusal. When Wormser said that everyone was sure he would be elected, he retorted: 'But they want to kill me! It would be another shot in the back!' It was only after the London conference in December that he began to take the idea seriously, and on Tardieu's insistence (not Mandel's, as has sometimes been said), he agreed to sign a paper saying he would stand for election to the presidency if his friends chose to put his name forward. At the same time he made it clear that he would do nothing to solicit votes and that no campaign should be organised on his behalf. He was too proud to fight for the presidency, though he was beginning to feel that the country owed it to him for his successful prosecution of the war.

This hesitant approach to the election was a tactical error. While the Tiger declined to make use of publicity, his enemies were able to intrigue against him and to mobilise all those who, for one reason or another, might be expected to oppose a Clemenceau presidency.

It was soon clear that his one serious rival would be Paul Deschanel, a shallow intriguer whose father had been exiled after the *coup d'état* in 1851. He had been an impartial president of the Chamber of Deputies for many years; he was well known in Paris society, where he was much admired for his perfect manners and faultless dress; he was also the son-in-law of a senator, and could expect the votes of many of his father-in-law's colleagues as a gesture of friendship. Moreover, though his father had been an anticlerical free-thinker and he himself had not been baptised, he took steps to win Catholic support by sending a friend to Rome to ask Cardinal Gasparri, the Vatican secretary, if he would tell French Catholics not to vote for Clemenceau. After consulting the Pope, Gasparri sent the required message to Paris, with the result that the parliamentary Catholics voted for Deschanel.

Briand, too, was busily at work to prevent Clemenceau's election. He had many old scores to pay off, including the most recent one of his omission from the French peace delegation. Unwisely the Tiger had told his friends that, when he became president, Briand would have to kick his heels for seven years before he became prime minister again; and the remark had gone the parliamentary rounds. Briand must certainly have been thinking of it as he buttonholed deputies in the corridors of the Palais-Bourbon and dropped remarks best calculated to turn them against

Clemenceau. He warned the Radicals against the Tiger's authoritarianism and insinuated that his election might imperil democracy; he reminded Socialists of Clemenceau's harsh measures against strikes and workers' demonstrations; and he shocked the Catholics by observing that there would have to be a civil funeral from the Elysée if Clemenceau died in office.

While the subtle Briand, with his usual cigarette drooping from the corner of his mouth, was dropping his insidious words in deputies' ears, Clemenceau himself was further antagonising the Catholics by his honest but obstinate attitude towards France's relations with the Vatican. His refusal to allow the President or the government to attend the victory thanksgiving service at Notre Dame was still remembered; he now told a Catholic deputation that he was opposed both to the re-establishment of the French embassy to the Vatican and to the presence of a Papal nuncio in Paris. Deputies and senators from Alsace-Lorraine, which had been German when Church and State were separated in France and was still linked with the Holy See by the old Concordat, were particularly anxious for the reinstatement of the embassy to the Vatican, but Clemenceau would not give way, though he must have known that his obstinacy was losing him votes in the coming election.

While the intrigues continued at the Palais-Bourbon the press was fairly evenly divided for and against Clemenceau. For example, Alfred Capus warmly supported him in *Le Figaro*; *Le Temps* thought that perhaps there had never been such an embarrassing choice; and in *L'Action Française* the two principal writers took up opposing attitudes. Léon Daudet declared that he would vote for Clemenceau through gratitude, but Charles Maurras used his considerable skill to explain why he was the wrong man for the Elysée. Since Maurras was the most prestigious journalist of the epoch, the Right took his advice and decided that an apparently able man like Deschanel, who had sound views on European equilibrium, was preferable to an impulsive and unpredictable politician with a disturbing past.

Even without Briand's intrigues, the forces opposing Clemenceau's election were formidable; yet it still seemed impossible that the senators and deputies would refuse to elect the 'Father of Victory' to the presidency of the Republic. Lloyd George was in Paris on the day when, in accordance with custom, the Republican groups of both Chamber and Senate held their preliminary meeting to agree on a presidential candidate; and he went with Lord Derby, who had succeeded Lord Bertie as British ambassador, to call on Poincaré and ask him what the result of the election was likely to be. Poincaré told them: 'Clemenceau will have an overwhelming majority. Indeed, the result of today's preliminary voting will probably be so overwhelming that Deschanel may not even present himself.'[1]

Poincaré was wrong. Clemenceau had too much running against him. He had enemies Right, Left and Centre, who for different reasons were unwilling to see him as President. At the Republicans' meeting Deschanel received 408 votes, Clemenceau 389.

It would still have been possible for Clemenceau to have stood as a candidate in the next day's election by the full National Assembly, consisting of all senators and deputies, just as Poincaré had done in 1913 after his narrow defeat by Pams in the preliminary count; and like Poincaré, he would probably have been elected. But he would not humiliate himself by asking for a second chance. Shocked and disgusted by the parliamentarians' ingratitude, Maurice Barrès hurried to the war ministry, where he found Clemenceau in his office among a group of friends and sympathisers. What, asked Barrès, was he going to do? For answer the Tiger showed him the letter he was sending to the president of the National Assembly. It said: 'I beg to inform you that I am withdrawing from my friends the authorisation to put forward my candidature.'

On the following day he went to his house at Bernouville, and then to Giverny to see Monet. By the time he returned to Paris Deschanel had been elected President of the French Republic without opposition. Rather tactlessly, the President-elect drove to the rue Saint-Dominique to call on Clemenceau, who declined to see him. The story that he said curtly, 'Tell the gentleman I am not here,' seems to be apocryphal. In fact he sent Mandel, Mordacq and another of his assistants to receive Deschanel, who had the effrontery to say that he had never asked to stand for the presidency and that he had been chosen almost without his knowledge. Later revelations about his envoy's mission to Cardinal Gasparri show that these remarks were utterly untrue; perhaps he was already on the verge of the mental breakdown which abruptly ended his presidency a few weeks later.

What kind of a president would Clemenceau have been? Poincaré could not understand how a man of action, whose reputation was built up on his strength and his energy, could have dreamed of taking up a post of 'obligatory inactivity'; but a remark attributed to Mandel—'We shall make of the presidency something which it has never been up till now'— suggests that Clemenceau may have hoped to deploy greater power than had been exercised by other presidents during the Third Republic.

Yet one doubts whether Mandel really understood Clemenceau's view of the presidency. Mordacq gathered that he would have held office for only a year or two, during which he would have paid a visit to America

[1] RA GV P 1273/38.

and attempted to prevent the United States from abandoning France. Two years were also the period he suggested in one of his many talks with Jean Martet towards the end of his life. The honour of being president, the hope of steering France through some of her early post-war difficulties —these, perhaps, were his real reasons for wanting to be elected. 'He was beaten,' thought Barrès, 'by the Catholics and Foch—the embassy to the Vatican and the left bank of the Rhine.' But Vladimir d'Ormesson may have been nearer the truth when he wrote, 'France cut off Clemenceau's head because he had become greater than himself.'

So France, through her senators and deputies, had refused to elect her war-time leader to the highest office in the State. It was not an incident in which Frenchmen could feel any pride, and people in other countries were amazed. Lloyd George said caustically, 'This time it's the French who are burning Joan of Arc'; and Lord Derby wrote in a memorandum drawn up for King George V:

> I think the general feeling—and it is one I must say that one feels oneself—is that he has been treated with base ingratitude. . . . The vast majority of the Chamber was elected because it claimed to support Clemenceau; and then to turn round on him and refuse to elect him to the highest office in the land seems to be unforgivable.[1]

And in the accompanying letter he told the King: 'I shall miss him very much—and I do not hesitate to say he was the best friend England had in this country.'[2]

Clemenceau showed great dignity in the closing days of his political life. In his farewell speech to the Supreme Council, in which the Allied statesmen still met, he urged the importance of preserving the understanding between France, Great Britain, the United States, Italy and Japan, and said prophetically: 'If one day these nations are separated, I do not dare to foresee the misfortunes which could follow.' To his personal staff his final words were 'And now, gentlemen, let us all return to our duties. France still has need of us.'

Defeated for the presidency, he had no wish to linger on as prime minister. His last visit to the Elysée was to submit his government's resignation; he never saw Poincaré again. Millerand, who was chosen to succeed him as prime minister, said airily, 'Don't bother,' when Clemenceau offered to tell him about current negotiations and other important matters. 'I turned over Europe and the government of France to him as casually as if I had given him a pebble,' he wrote later.

It was over. He was seventy-eight, he had deserved well of his country,

[1] RA GV P 1273/38.   [2] RA GV P 1273/37.

he had earned his retirement. But this was by no means the final curtain. He was to have a busy life, shared between the cottage at Saint Vincent-sur-Jard and the house in the rue Franklin, and occasionally venturing very much further afield, for more than nine years.

CHAPTER NINETEEN

PRIVATE CITIZEN

1. *Egypt and the East.* 2. *American pilgrimage.* 3. *Paris and the Vendée.*
4. *Friends and family.* 5. *Last writings.*

[1]

BEFORE SETTLING down into his new life as a private citizen
Clemenceau fulfilled an old ambition to see the wonders of Egypt
and India. He was off on the first of his travels little more than a
month after the presidential election.

His zest for antiquities was not shared by all Frenchmen. 'What
interest can you possibly have in going to Egypt?' asked a puzzled
senator. 'I should be discourteous to the English,' Clemenceau solemnly
assured him, 'if I refused their kind offer to organise a sphinx hunt round
the pyramids in my honour!' 'What, do they still do that?', said the
credulous senator, leaving the Tiger with a good story to tell to his
friends. In the event he was shocked, rather than impressed, by the
pyramids. 'Their pretensions are excessive,' he told Mordacq on his
return. 'How could men have flung this vainglorious challenge at Death
the great leveller?'

From Cairo and Alexandria he went to the Nile valley and the Egyptian
Sudan, tirelessly asking questions and amassing information wherever he
went. He was away for two months, and when he returned to Paris his
apparently robust health delighted his friends. 'He seems,' wrote Capus
in *Le Gaulois,* 'to have ripened to an age which is entirely his own,
protected from outside influences, and in which he can stay as long as he
wants to.'

After a cure at Vichy in July he set off for India and the East at the end
of September, accompanied by a new friend, Nicolas Piétri, the Corsican
who had taken over *L'Homme Libre.* Outward bound from Marseilles, they
called at Port Said, Djibouti, Colombo and Singapore, but the trip was
threatened with disaster when Clemenceau went down with fever soon
after his arrival in Calcutta.

What followed was a classic example of the Tiger's indomitable spirit.
His illness caused consternation in British official circles, and the Governor

of Bengal sent his personal physician to visit the distinguished invalid. When the doctor said that he must go back to France at once, as his health would not stand the Indian climate and only a sea voyage could save his life, he retorted that he wanted to be treated, not cured, and he refused to leave India. A second doctor also insisted that he should take the first boat home, but he again refused, and after much argument he signed a document absolving the doctors of all responsibility for what might happen to him. They then continued his medical treatment, which was so successful that he was out of bed within ten days.

From Calcutta he went to Benares, to Delhi, where he was received by the Viceroy and met an old war-time friend, General Rawlinson, and then to Rawalpindi, where he found another corps commander of the war years, the Australian General Sir William Birdwood. The postscript to a letter from Birdwood to Clive Wigram, King George V's assistant private secretary, gives a pleasant glimpse of the Tiger's visit:

> I have just had dear old Clemenceau staying with me for the last three or four days. I last saw him when I took him into Lille the day after we relieved it. He is certainly a wonderful old man, and quite seemed to enjoy his stay here, being especially interested in the excavations at Taxila, which the Archaeological Department have been at for the last ten years. . . .[1]

And it was characteristic of the Tiger's versatility that he passed contentedly from archaeological studies to the delights of tiger-shooting in the native States of Bikaner and Gwalior.

He had made up his mind to shoot a tiger while he was in India, and he told Piétri that he was ready to stay till the spring if he had not killed one before. Fortunately his chance came early in 1921, when he was able to kill two tigers at a shoot arranged by the Maharajah of Gwalior. He sent a delighted telegram to a friend in Paris: 'I am among the tigers, but I am the one with the gun.'

There was still more to be seen at Agra and Bombay, and in Hyderabad and Mysore, before he left India to return home by way of Burma, Java and Ceylon. He fished and hunted buffaloes, he looked in at Bali to see the dancing girls, and on visiting Boro Budur he insisted on taking Piétri to see the famous 'temple of a thousand Buddhas' before sunset, by moonlight and at dawn. The temperature was 40 degrees Centigrade; the temple was about an hour's walk, there and back, from their hotel. One suspects that the devoted Corsican may have felt a certain amount of relief when the six months' tour ended at Toulon on 21 March.

Once again Clemenceau's travels had done him good. When Colonel

[1] RA GV N 2556/1.

Repington called on him in the rue Franklin in April, he noticed 'the same old dirty woodwork on the walls, crying for coats of paint, the ordinary, almost lodging-house furniture, and the red carpet worn threadbare and in patches at the entrance', while the master of the house was 'dressed in the same old clothes and with a black half-turban cap on his head'; but the Tiger, he also observed, had 'all the old fire, the alert brain, the rapid thought, the clear word, the penetrating sarcasm'. He told Repington that he was not interested in controversies about the past, and that he was not going to say or write anything about the war.

He was travelling again in June, but only as far as Oxford, to receive the honorary degree of Doctor of Civil Law. The traditional Latin citation for such awards referred to him as 'a man old in years but young in spirit' (*senem annis animo juvenem*).

[2]

He had told Repington that he was not going to speak about the war, but there were times when he could not avoid speaking about the peace. At the end of August he went for the first time to Corsica, where Piétri was his host; and in replying to a speech of welcome by the mayor of Sartène he spoke proudly of his share in making the Treaty of Versailles. He made the point which he was to repeat for the rest of his life: the treaty, he said, allowed a lasting peace to be established, but it was not being applied in full and too many concessions were being made to Germany. Unless the Germans were made to fulfil all their obligations under the treaty, and all the agreed measures for guaranteeing France against future aggression were taken, 'everything', he warned his listeners, 'will begin all over again'. It was an impromptu speech, which won the hearts of the Corsicans. Clemenceau himself grew to admire the Corsican people and the beauties of the countryside during his brief stay on the island.

Again, he could hardly have kept silent in October, when he was asked to unveil his own statue, sculptured by Sicard and showing him among a group of *poilus*, at Sainte-Hermine, in the Vendée. This time his speech was a glowing tribute to the courage of the men in the trenches; it was the occasion on which he first publicly told the story of the bunch of flowers a *poilu* had given him close to the front line. He also spoke of the need for a close watch on French security: 'To equal our forefathers in valour and surpass to them in vigilance—that is what our children's future demands of us.'

In these early years after his retirement Clemenceau was still hovering on the fringe of politics. His old followers, Mandel and Tardieu, kept in touch with him, and with their help he started a new paper, for which Tardieu suggested the name of *L'Echo National*.

Georges Wormser, his last *chef de cabinet*, was asked to arrange the business details of the new venture, and had no difficulty in raising a capital sum of 1,200,000 francs, which Tardieu thought sufficient to finance the paper for a year; there were fourteen subscribers, of whom one put up 200,000 francs, seven 100,000 francs each and six 50,000 francs each. It was rumoured at the time, and was later repeated (for example, by Donald McCormick in *Pedlar of Death*), that *L'Echo National* was financed by Sir Basil Zaharoff, the armaments magnate, to further his own interests; but Georges Wormser states definitely that Zaharoff did not subscribe to it, since its founders were resolved that the paper should not be linked with big business.

But Clemenceau was not returning to active journalism. When the first issue of *L'Echo National* appeared on 10 January, 1922, it bore on its front page, in type of equal size, the names of André Tardieu as political director and Georges Clemenceau as founder. The declared aim of the new paper was 'to reawaken in France the spirit that led us to victory, and to support . . . the men capable of translating it into action'; it repudiated the policies of all French governments since Clemenceau had left office and described them as 'governments of abdication'. But though *L'Echo National* reflected the Tiger's attitude towards current politics, neither he nor Mandel ever wrote for it; Tardieu, a highly experienced journalist, was its leading writer. Perhaps its founder's silence was one reason why the new paper had only a short life; its chief importance was that for the time being it established Tardieu as the leader of the opposition and the upholder of Clemenceau's policies.

The Tiger was deeply affected by the successive international conferences which watered down the Treaty of Versailles and by the withdrawal of the United States from Europe. France, like Britain, was caught between the failure of Germany to pay genuine reparations and the insistence of the United States that the money she had lent her Allies for war purposes must be repaid in full; this tragic and mercenary collapse of the war-time alliance was a bitter blow to the 'Father of Victory'. He was therefore in the mood for speaking out when the British writer, Rudyard Kipling, gave an interview to the *New York World* attacking the United States for her late arrival in the war and for withdrawing from Europe while the tasks of peace-making were still unfinished.

The interview made headlines in the world's press, and the *New York World* invited Clemenceau to comment on it. In a telegram from Saint Vincent-sur-Jard he declined to associate himself with Kipling's attack, but admitted that it showed the dangers of the present situation. With a late flowering of his old impulsiveness he added that he was ready to go to the United States, on his own account and without a mission from anyone, to explain what, in his opinion, were the rights and duties of each country in the world crisis caused by the war.

His offer to cross the Atlantic was warmly received in the United States, and a series of meetings was quickly arranged for him; but at the Quai d'Orsay it was frigidly pointed out that the ex-prime minister would speak in America only as a private person. Foch also threw cold water on the proposed visit. To vent the spite he had felt ever since the peace conference, he told the *New York Tribune* that Clemenceau would be lachrymose and sentimental in the United States, and would give way to the inevitable symptoms of old age; since he had manifestly lost the peace the marshal urged him to stay at home instead of trying to win from the Americans the sympathy which he could not expect from the French.

He was far from being lachrymose or sentimental when he spoke to a *New York Times* reporter at Le Havre before sailing in the *Paris* on 11 November, 1922, six weeks after his eighty-first birthday. The American visit, he said, was likely to be his very last public appearance. 'My body is robust,' he declared, 'but when I went on my trip two years ago it tired me, and I know very well from a personal standpoint that this American journey is not advisable. But what would you have? I feel that I ought to go there and tell the truth, and for the rest I do not care.'

When the reporter spoke of the ingratitude shown in his defeat for the presidency, he said coolly: 'A politician who expects gratitude doesn't know his *métier*. He has gone into the wrong branch of business.' And one wonders what fleeting memories of a young Mary Plummer may have passed through his mind when a girl journalist asked him what he thought of American women. He answered gallantly: 'It is fifty-seven years since I first saw the American women. They all had lovely blue eyes, all had sweet smiles, and all were charming. I trust I shall find that the new generation—their daughters and grand-daughters—have the same looks, splendid qualities, courage and virtues.'

His brother Albert, Piétri and his chauffeur had driven from Paris to Le Havre with him; his two daughters had come to see him off; but only his valet, Albert Boulin, went with him to America. As the ship sailed, he murmured, '*Partir, c'est mourir un peu.*'

New York was delighted by the arrival of the dogged old man whose will-power had done so much for the war-time Allies. As he drove through the city it gave him a characteristic welcome of showers of ticker tape and torn-up telephone directories, accompanied by the din of motor horns and ships' sirens; and later he was received with great enthusiasm in Boston, Chicago, St. Louis, Philadelphia and Washington. He gave ten major addresses and made a score of other speeches, and he had to refuse invitations which came from as far away as California and Arizona.

Basically, he was asking America to emerge from her isolation and play her part in the post-war world, but he also defended France from charges of militarism and of unwillingness to pay her debts. His speeches conveyed his sense of the dangers again facing the world only four years after victory had been won. If France were enslaved, he said, America would not be able to go on living in peaceful prosperity. Were they so blind, he asked, that they could not perceive the new drama which was being prepared, as military organisations were growing all over Germany? 'Only your presence, only your return to Europe, will quell Germany and bring her back to reason.' Woodrow Wilson had said that America wanted to make the world safe for democracy. Were they now saying that they did not care whether democracy was saved or not?

During his visit Clemenceau saw President Harding, Woodrow Wilson's Republican successor, but since he had no authority to speak for the French government their conversation was only in general terms. When he reached Washington he had a message from Wilson, then stricken by the complete breakdown from which he never recovered. 'I would like to talk with you about our battles of not so long ago,' the ex-President wrote. 'You were a staunch friend as well as at times an open foe.' The Tiger went to see him, and was so much saddened by his condition that he asked to be excused from an evening engagement, and dined alone in his room.

Clemenceau's mission to America was essentially a goodwill mission. 'I do not deny,' he told a French journalist before sailing for France on 12 December, 'that there are a certain number of Americans who do not wish to be linked with France either for peace or for war. What I assert is that there exists in America a very lively and widespread feeling of affection for France. We must do everything we can to preserve that sentiment.'

His reception in the United States proved that he had made some contribution to a better Franco-American understanding, but it could not be claimed, either then or later, that the journey had any practical results. It was only a gesture, but a gesture which came from one who genuinely believed in world democracy. The earnings from his tour—his lecture fees and a payment of 15,000 dollars for publication rights—were given to war charities.

[3]

As the Tiger had told the *New York Times* reporter, his visit to America was his last public appearance. He was to make one further appeal to the

United States in a letter to President Coolidge, but with that exception his political life was over. When he was pressed to stand for the Vendée in the senatorial election of 1923 he replied that he had taken a definite resolve not to re-enter parliament, and even if he had wanted to, the state of his health would not have allowed it.

One by one, his political contacts were disappearing. After the failure of *L'Echo National* Tardieu remained a close friend for two or three years, but when he accepted office in a Poincaré ministry in 1926 Clemenceau would have nothing more to do with him. Apart from rare visits from Charles Benoist, Louis Lépine and one or two others, the break with his old political life was complete.

This separation from old friends of the Senate and Chamber has fostered the illusion that Clemenceau's last years were lonely and unhappy. It has been said, for example, that 'he shut himself up in meditation, among his books and a few rare friends, such as Geffroy and Monet', and that he retired to 'an obscure and poor old age'. Certainly he had amassed no fortune during his political career. Yet a man who had a house in Paris and a cottage by the sea, and commuted between them three or four times a year in a Rolls driven by his chauffeur, cannot really be described as poor; and the number of friends and acquaintances who lunched, dined or stayed with him at Saint Vincent-sur-Jard, as well as the visits paid to him by his son and daughters, show that he was neither lonely nor unfriended. 'I find that I am rather too much encumbered by visitors,' he wrote in the summer of 1925. They continued to arrive on his doorstep as the years went on.[1]

He had disposed of the house at Bernouville on his retirement, and he did not own either of the homes of his closing years. In Paris he had been a tenant of the house in the rue Franklin, with the horseshoe desk, simple furniture and worn carpets, since 1893; it was bought in 1926 by J. S. Douglas, a wealthy American friend and admirer, so that Clemenceau could live in it for the rest of his life and it could then be preserved as a museum. He insisted on continuing to pay rent, but one happy result of

---

[1] It is fair to point out that the full extent of Clemenceau's social activities in the last years of his life was not revealed until the publication in 1970 of the substantial volume of his *Lettres à une Amie*, which provides an almost day-to-day account of his life in the Vendée from 1924 until his death. Yet there were ample indications in the writings of Jean Martet and in General Mordacq's *Clemenceau au Soir de la Vie*, which were all published between 1929 and 1933, that he had many callers and visitors, and was not personally soured by his sense of France's political deterioration. Mordacq, indeed, was expressly concerned 'to destroy the legend of the embittered man'. That legend is finally shattered by his lively letters to his woman friend, Marguerite Baldensperger.

the transaction was that the new owner had the house completely redecorated. The Tiger stayed with Piétri while the work was being completed, and seemed rather surprised that such extensive repainting and recarpeting were considered necessary. 'They tell me it was dirty,' he remarked to his young friend Jean Martet, a former member of the staff of *L'Homme Libre* whom he saw frequently in these years. '*Was* it dirty?' 'It was a bit dirty,' Martet admitted.[1]

His other home was Belébat, the cottage at Saint Vincent-sur-Jard, which he leased from Luce de Trémont, who lived in the neighbouring château of Avrillé. Belébat was a long building, all on one floor and extended at one end by the conversion of a barn into a comfortable living-room; it had three bedrooms (though the two guest rooms were only big enough to take single beds), a pleasant kitchen-dining-room, pantry and servants' quarters; and though small by Parisian standards it was big enough for Clemenceau and his guests. There were sand-dunes at the side of the cottage, and in front only a large garden, filled with roses and other flowers, separated it from the sands and the sea. The village consisted of little but a couple of hotels, a shop or two, a few houses, a hall and a church; it had no railway station, and visitors who came by train descended at either La Roche-sur-Yon or Les Sables d'Olonne and completed the journey by road. Though Saint Vincent-sur-Jard was not in the Vendean *bocage*, which does not extend beyond La Roche-sur-Yon, Clemenceau was happy to feel that he was back in his own countryside.

As the prospect of a life divorced from public affairs opened before him, he had the good fortune to meet Marguerite Baldensperger, the forty-year-old wife of a professor of literature at the Sorbonne. The Baldenspergers, who had lost their elder daughter in tragic circumstances, divided their time between Paris and Saint-Die, in the Vosges; Marguerite had conceived the idea of producing a series of simply written books by leading authors for circulation in Alsace-Lorraine, as an introduction to the French language for French people who had been brought up to speak German, and she wrote to Clemenceau to ask if he would write a book for her. He was then engrossed in his massive scientific and philosophical work, *Au Soir de la Pensée*, and he could not accept her invitation; but he asked her to come and see him in Paris and discuss her project. Their first meeting was in April 1923; she returned in May to introduce her husband; she paid a third visit in June, when Clemenceau asked her why she was in mourning and was told of her daughter's death.

---

[1] While Clemenceau was staying with Piétri the actress Cécile Sorel sent him a splendid box of huge chrysanthemums. He wrote back to her: 'Thank you for the wonderful flowers by which it has pleased you to humiliate my old age.' (*See* Martet, *Le Silence de M. Clemenceau*, p. 49.)

He urged her to recapture the zest for living, and as they parted, he said: 'I will help you to live and you will help me to die. That is our pact.'

This was the beginning of a close and loving friendship between the octogenarian and a woman half his age—a friendship which was viewed sympathetically by Marguerite's husband, who thought that contact with Clemenceau's strong personality would help her to overcome her grief for her daughter. It was not, however, until the spring of 1924, after Marguerite had paid the first of her many visits to the cottage at Saint Vincent-sur-Jard, that they began their long correspondence, of which Clemenceau's share can be found in *Lettres à une Amie*. (At Marguerite's request, he destroyed her letters to him after he had read them.) In five-and-a-half years he wrote 668 letters to her. When he was in the Vendée they exchanged letters every day; when they were both in Paris there were few letters, because Marguerite paid a daily visit to the rue Franklin. In these fascinating letters we can see not only his attachment to Marguerite but also the pattern of his life in his final years.

[4]

Who, then, were the friends of Clemenceau the private citizen? There were many of them. In addition to Marguerite and her family there were Geffroy and Monet, whom he visited often at Giverny until the artist's death in 1926, and whose widow came more than once to stay at Belébat; former members of his *cabinet* like Mandel, Wormser, Ignace, Mordacq and Colonel Alerme; Jean Martet, who wrote valuable records of their many conversations; Georges Leroy, a *societaire* of the Comédie-Francaise and teacher at the Conservatoire, whose devotion was so great that he once waited with four of his girl students outside Clemenceau's Paris house, in order to give him bouquets and 'a crazy letter' when he left for the Vendée at four o'clock on a summer morning; the former Violet Maxse, who married Lord Milner after the death of her first husband, Lord Edward Cecil, and was widowed for the second time in 1925; and admiring Americans like J. S. Douglas, H. S. Bacon (Douglas's lawyer) and Colonel House. A few Englishmen, such as Lord Derby, Colonel Repington and Rudyard Kipling, came to see him once or twice; in the Vendée many local acquaintances were invited to lunch; and medical and academic friends like Dr. Florand (with whom he once went to Chantonnay races) and Professor and Madame Gennes were among his house guests. (The two last-named stayed for several days in 1928, and Clemenceau commented to Marguerite on Madame de Gennes's clothes: 'She knows nothing of stockings, and I do not think that her dress at dinner last night would have encumbered a soup-plate.') When he was in

Paris Sister Théoneste and her Mother Superior called, 'possibly to see', he told Marguerite, 'if I was ready for conversion'; Madame Edmond Rostand came to Belébat and wrote a charming poem in *Le Petit Journal* about her visit; and in September 1927 he greatly upset his beloved Marguerite by entertaining the smart Madame Callot, one of the heads of a leading fashion house, as a weekend guest.[1]

The episode of Madame Callot's visit is worth recalling as an indication of the intensity of the relationship between Clemenceau and Marguerite. One feels that the old man was rather carried away at finding his cottage honoured by the visit of an attractive and fashionable dress designer, who surprised him by descending from a first class carriage when he met her at Les Sables d'Olonne. Before her arrival he joked to Marguerite about the forthcoming 'twenty-four hours' visit from the *maison* Callot'; afterwards he was misguided enough to tell her that 'the reactions of the *maison* Callot were perfect—in her unaffectedness, her good humour and her good manners'.

His letter was written on Monday, 5 September. Evidently Marguerite was deeply hurt by his praise of another woman, and sent him a sharp reply; for on Wednesday he wrote again, reproving her rather too airily: 'You are misjudging the Callot business, which is quite understandable because you know nothing about it.' His nonchalance seems to have made Marguerite see red, for on Friday, after picking up another house guest, Violet Milner, at La Roche-sur-Yon, he found a further letter waiting for him, and one, as he wrote in reply, which 'made me very sad'. Cautiously he assured her that the widowed Lady Milner 'has come here in search of the consolation of an old friendship', and he countered her reproaches about Madame Callot by saying: 'When I said that Callot was *perfection* I meant to refer to her tact and her manners. Would it have been better if they had been different? It is raining in my head and in my heart.' But Marguerite was already repentant for having scolded her old friend; without waiting for a reply she had written again, and on the next day the Tiger thanked her for 'an excellent letter, which reassures me as much as the previous one upset me'. The lovers' quarrel was over. Thereafter their friendship was undisturbed, but though the '*maison* Callot' had spoken enthusiastically of paying a second visit to Belébat there is no record of her ever having stayed there again.

In addition to his wide circle of friends, Clemenceau was always in close touch with his two daughters and had occasional visits from his son and

---

[1] At the turn of the century Worth, Paquin and Callot were three of the greatest names in French *haute couture*. Since then all three had been overtaken by Paul Poiret, but they still had immense prestige in the 1920s.

from one or two of his grandchildren.[1] Madeleine was the one of whom he saw most. She was then in her middle fifties; she was talented and neurotic, and was always liable to work herself up into a state over some trifling matter. ('If the wretched child would decomplicate herself a little, everything would be perfect,' he once wrote to Marguerite.) She was herself a writer, and she spent long periods in the rue Franklin, and sometimes at Belébat, helping her father to sort out his notes and arrange his books for publication. One of Clemenceau's fears was that she would write his biography after his death; he knew she was thinking of doing so, and he asked Marguerite to dissuade her when the time came. Most regrettably Madeleine honoured his wishes, and a book which would have been of great interest was never written. Her volume of childhood reminiscences, *Le Pot de Basilic*, contains only a few references to her father; there had been more in the book as originally written, but most of them were deleted, on Clemenceau's orders, before it was published. He threatened to disown her if the offending passages appeared in print.

Apart from his friends and his family, and one or two favoured journalists and writers to whom he gave the occasional privilege of a few hours' conversation about the war and the peace, groups of casual visitors often came to look at his cottage at Saint Vincent-sur-Jard, hoping also to have a glimpse of the great man himself. One day the 150 children of a *colonie de vacances* arrived and were generously fed with cake; once a hundred people came while he was away and had to content themselves with talking to the gardener; and one evening in 1926 he found himself 'surrounded by tulip-shaped Dutch men and women of all ages and all known sexes who had chosen to pay me a visit at the hour when I was going to bed'.

Georges Wormser says that the last three years of Clemenceau's life were 'the most bitter years'. They were the years in which he was saddened by the weakness of French government, the revival of German militarism, the futility of the 'Kellogg pact' for the renunciation of war and the

---

[1] Of Clemenceau's children, Madeleine had not remarried since her husband's suicide; she had one son, René Jacquemaire, who became a doctor and died at the age of thirty-six. Thérèse was also a widow: she had divorced her first husband, Louis Gatineau, and had enjoyed a happy second marriage to Jules-René Jung, who had died in 1918. She had one son, Georges Gatineau-Clemenceau, who was involved in various scandals and was the 'black sheep' of the Clemenceau family. Clemenceau's only son, Michel, had a number of business interests, and at one time was the South American representative of the British armaments firm, Vickers Armstrong. He was married three times; Clemenceau took a close interest in the two sons of his first marriage, Georges and Pierre. (*See* Professor Jean Murard, 'Le docteur Georges Clemenceau', *Histoire de la Médecine*, April 1972, pp. 2–15; Georges Gatineau-Clemenceau, *Des Pattes du Tigre aux Griffes du Destin*, pp. 29–39.)

continued demand by the United States for the repayment of France's war debt. It was this last issue which caused him to write a letter in 1926 to Calvin Coolidge, the President of the United States, pointing out that the debt was not a commercial one and should not be treated as such. He spoke of France's sacrifices while she was waiting for America to enter the war: 'Three years of blood and money flowing from every pore. . . . Is not the living energy of all that lost youth itself a "banking account"?' His appeal brought him many letters of congratulation from both sides of the Atlantic, but it had no effect on Coolidge.

These were the years, also, in which death carried off his friends Geffroy and Monet, his brother Albert and his sisters Emma and Adrienne. Yet even at this time it would be wrong to depict him as a morose and embittered old man. His relationship with Marguerite continued to give him great happiness; he enjoyed the visits of his friends and his family, and he liked entertaining guests to the special Belébat luncheon of exquisite sole, *poulet Soubise*[1] and an excellent Vouvray, which he did not drink himself; and he was mobile up to the time of his last illness.

Indeed he was mobile. In 1928, when he was eighty-six, he was able, among other engagements, to help the curator of the Musée Guimet to receive the King and Queen of Afghanistan, and to stand for an hour in doing so; to go to Giverny to see Madame Monet; and to have tea with Colonel House at the Ritz, where he was scandalised by the dress and behaviour of some of the women he saw there. (But he was even more shocked by the short skirt of a salesgirl at the Marché des Fleurs, when he went shopping with Martet a few months later. 'One sees right up to her buttocks,' he grumbled.) He still did his physical training; when he was in Paris he always began the day with half-an-hour's gymnastic exercises, supervised by his instructor, Edouard Leroy, a practice he had now kept up for twenty-five years. Only in the last year of his life was the lesson curtailed, probably at Marguerite's request, for he wrote to her in April 1929: '*Je fais une toute petite gymnastique qui me convsient parfaitement.*'

Such was the pattern of Clemenceau's life as a private citizen from 1923 to 1929. But nearly every day, whether he was in Paris or in the Vendée, would also find him at his desk, quill pen in hand, covering sheet after sheet with the chapters of one or other of his books. In the last years of his life he was again an author.

---

[1] Clotilde, Clemenceau's cook at Belébat, had her own recipe for *poulet Soubise*, a dish named after the Prince de Soubise, a seventeenth-century Vendean marshal. The chicken was cooked with a thick onion sauce, and took forty-eight hours to prepare. Clemenceau used to say: 'I like the sauce better than the marshal.' (*See* Clemenceau, *Lettres à une Amie*, p. 323n.)

[5]

He wrote four books in this period—the two-volume *Au Soir de la Pensée* (translated into English as *In the Evening of my Thought*), a study of Demosthenes, an essay on Monet's great series of water and flower paintings, Les Nymphéas, and a defence of the Treaty of Versailles under the title, *Grandeurs et Misères d'une Victoire*, which was published after his death. With the exception of the last-named, which is a contribution to the history of the First World War and the subsequent peace-making, these books are important only because they were part of their author's life. One can hardly imagine their being read on their merits by anyone who knew nothing of Georges Clemenceau.

The book which meant most to him was *Au Soir de la Pensée*. This survey of the evolution of mind, matter and civilisation, based largely on the teachings of nineteenth-century materialism, though also extending as far as the work of Rutherford and Einstein, was intended to be 'a balance-sheet, such as a man of ordinary cultivation can today prepare, of our positive knowledge of the world and of ourselves, amply annotated with theories and even with hypotheses still undergoing verification.' But in Léon Daudet's opinion, Clemenceau's real aim in writing *Au Soir de la Pensée* was to prove that the existence of God and belief in the immortality of the soul are not needed for the fulfilment of one's duty on earth.

As might have been expected, he used typical nineteenth-century arguments to support his atheistic attitude. His rejection of religion was based on such statements as

The quite simple fact is that God and his angels have not yet been 'observed'.

What reasonable explanation can be offered to account for the fact that God, supposed to be absolute perfection, should have absurdly taken the trouble to create something imperfect, only to impose on us, poor mortals, the task of perfecting it, and then should have punished us with eternal damnation for not succeeding where he had failed?

In these and similar passages we feel that Clemenceau's view of the universe had not changed much since his student days; the more rewarding parts of the book are those in which he illustrates his arguments by references to his own experiences and to things seen in his travels in India, Ceylon, Java and the United States. Occasionally, too, he throws in unexpected scraps of information like

How generally is it known that mice sing? I have seen them and heard them sing both in the Vendée and in America. Their song was like that of birds. The fact is established beyond argument.

But one may doubt whether anyone's understanding of the universe would be much advanced by reading *Au Soir de la Pensée*.

This was the book on which Clemenceau set to work when he withdrew from the political scene, but owing to its great length it did not appear in print until 1927. In the meantime he had completed a small book on Demosthenes, which was published in the year before his larger work.

The subject was chosen almost by accident. When Marguerite had called on him in 1923, to discuss the series of books she was commissioning for the publishing house of Plon, she had asked him if he would write a short book on Abraham Lincoln or some comments on the war. He said he had no time to spare, but then he was struck by a sudden idea. There was a man, he said, to whom he owed some delightful hours—Demosthenes. 'Yes, indeed, a Demosthenes for the young. I should only need a month to write a few pages about him.'

In due course the book was written, and was the seventh volume in the Plon series, '*Nobles Vies—Grandes Oeuvres*,' which was not designed for Alsace-Lorraine only (as Marguerite had at first proposed), but was intended for young people and others whose work left them little time for reading. Clemenceau's style was hardly suitable for such a public, but his name was enough to attract readers, and he was certainly well informed about ancient Greece. (Vladimir d'Ormesson's father, who was ambassador in Greece for eight years, used to say that of all his French guests in that country none had a more exact knowledge of Greek art than was shown by Clemenceau.)

The book was more of a study of Demosthenes's character than an account of his life, and it was notable for its many passages which seemed to recall the Tiger's own experiences. For example, 'He willed, he dared, he saved Athens from the shame of defeatism'; 'Demosthenes answered war with war because submission to brute force could produce only a humiliating peace'; 'If they live too long, men who have known triumphs can see them frittered away, while the vanquished who does not accept defeat can always begin again.' Reviewers were quick to notice the parallels between the author and his subject; so, too, were the publishers, and when a new edition was being prepared in 1928, there was some talk of fabricating a portrait of Demosthenes wearing a skull-cap like Clemenceau's. The Tiger would not allow it. He insisted that he had never intended the book to have any reference to his own life. 'But newspapers make up stories as though they would swallow anything,' he told Marguerite.

The study of Monet, which appeared in 1928 under the title, *Claude*

Monet: Les Nymphéas, was also short. It was not a detailed study of Monet's art, such as their common friend, Gustave Geffroy, had written already; it was rather a memorial to the dead artist, describing his objectives, his style and his reception by critics and public, and dealing at some length with his great series of paintings of *Les Nymphéas,* showing the effects of changing light on the water-lilies in the lake in the artist's garden at Giverny. Thanks to Clemenceau's insistence, Monet had bequeathed to the French nation the second series of these studies, which had been placed on permanent exhibition in the Orangerie at the end of the Tuileries gardens; it was appropriate that he should now publish his affectionate tribute to his dead friend.

The fourth book of Clemenceau's old age was one which he had not meant to write. In 1928 a journalist asked him if he was writing his memoirs, and he answered: 'Write my memoirs? Never! If I wrote what I know about the war, no Frenchman would ever fight for France again!' Yet by the middle of the following year he was hard at work on a book about the war and the peace which was published after his death as *Grandeurs et Misères d'une Victoire.*

It was the death of Foch on 20 March, 1929, which led to the writing of this book. The marshal had never forgiven Clemenceau for failing to secure a Rhine frontier for France in the Treaty of Versailles; in the last years of his life he often discussed the matter with Raymond Recouly, the historian, who published a record of their conversations, entitled *Mémorial de Foch,* after the marshal's death.

Clemenceau had paid due respect to the passing of his old commander-in-chief. Though he had excused himself from attending the funeral ceremonies at Notre Dame and the Invalides he had been to the marshal's home to see him in his coffin and had met Weygand and Madame Foch there. Three weeks later the director of *L'Illustration* sent him an advance proof of an article by Recouly on Foch, which revived the marshal's old complaints about the peace treaty.

Clemenceau at first decided to take no notice of Foch's hackneyed charges. But the article was only a section of Recouly's book, which was published in mid-April. Foch's attacks were here amplified, and Clemenceau was charged with having rashly abandoned France's chief line of resistance and having sacrificed his country's essential interests. He could no longer ignore such a vicious onslaught, even though it came from a dead man. A brief notice appeared in the press: 'Being mentioned in the statements of Marshal Foch, M. Georges Clemenceau announces: "I regret that I am forced into a debate before a coffin; but my silence might seem to be confirmation. I shall reply." '

Recouly's book showed again that Foch had never understood what happened at the peace conference, and never appreciated the intricacies of Clemenceau's hard bargaining with Wilson and Lloyd George. The Tiger, who felt sure the marshal had known that Recouly's book would be published after his death, remarked to Mordacq: 'It's a real Parthian arrow he has let fly at me'; and with the help of Mordacq, Martet and others he plunged into the task of answering the marshal so vigorously that he could report considerable progress by the end of June.

The work was begun in the rue Franklin and continued at Belébat; at the end of July he complained to Martet, 'This book is killing me . . . but not to have written it would have killed me even more.' Early in October he was able to tell Marguerite that he was making the final corrections, though one chapter had still to be written. Probably it was never written, but the book bears no obvious signs of being incomplete.

Grandeurs et Misères d'une Victoire is candidly presented as an answer to Foch's attack on the peace treaty. Clemenceau dismisses Recouly's book as an 'impudent farrago of troopers' tales' and asks regretfully: 'What, my gallant Marshal, are you so insensible to the thrill of the great hours that you took ten years of cool and deliberate meditation to assail me for no other reason than a stale mess of military grousings? . . . Ah, Foch! Foch! my good Foch! Have you then forgotten everything?'

Clemenceau's book rebuts Foch's discredited arguments about the Rhineland and the dismemberment of Germany, and emphasises the impossibility of annexing the Rhineland without destroying the alliance with Britain and America. He goes on to assail Foch for not having called the world's attention to German mutilations of the treaty and not having provided France with adequate frontier defences. He also accused Foch of having lost all interest in France's eastern frontier when once he had failed to detach the Rhineland from Germany.

But the book was not only a refutation of Foch; it was also a warning to France of the resurgence of the German danger. In April he had said to Martet: 'We shall have war before ten years.' He was not so precise in his book, but he put the basic facts clearly before his countrymen:

'*Germany is arming and France disarming*': that is the decisive feature of this moment of history when the two states of mind confront one another in such stark brutality that I defy any sane man to cast doubt on the evidence.

And looking into the future he could say only that 'France will be what the men of France deserve.'

His message came from beyond the grave. The Tiger was dead before the book was published.

THE GOOD EARTH

CLEMENCEAU HAD just passed his eighty-eighth birthday when he began the corrections of *Grandeurs et Misères d'une Victoire*. In the previous year he had told Violet Milner, as they sat among the scabious and sea-holly in the garden of his seaside cottage: 'I am glad to have lived. I do not want to begin again. I should now like to die. Life is a very fine spectacle, only we are badly placed for seeing it, and we do not understand what we see.' And it was beginning to seem as though death were not far away.

Each summer brought a serious bout of illness, Coughs and colds, combined with his diabetes, reduced him to a state of feebleness which brought the anxious Marguerite from the Vosges to Paris in July 1927; yet he made such a good recovery that he was able to attend the wedding of his grandson Georges (son of Michel) at the end of the month. He was seriously ill in July and August 1928, when he was particularly irritated to suffer from lapses of memory, and for a time was quite incapable of either reading or writing; but though the newspapers were getting ready to publish his obituary he again survived. At Belébat in July 1929 he began to complain of feeling tired, and of having 'bad ankles and worse feet'; yet even then he paid many visits to the home of his old cook Clotilde, who was dying, and he attended her funeral.

This was his last summer in the Vendée. He had left Paris on 7 July (the day when Georges Leroy and the four girls from the Conservatoire came to see him off with their flowers and 'crazy letter'), and he returned on 1 October. Piétri and his wife, Madame Monet, Lady Milner and Marguerite were among the guests who stayed at Belébat that summer; some of his other visitors were a general whom he had not seen since 1918, a professor of Greek from the Catholic university of Lille, Douglas and his son, Colonel Alerme (who had been on his military staff at the rue Saint-Dominique), Baschet (of *L'Illustration*), Wormser and Martet, who spent some weeks at the neighbouring seaside resort of La Tranche and came over frequently to help with *Grandeurs et Misères*.

It was a summer in which he was depressed about the weakness of French politicians. 'I shall die unhappy,' he wrote to Marguerite on 19 September, 'on leaving France in the hands of the Briands, the Poincarés, the Tardieus'. And yet, as always, he could spare time to help friends who were in trouble or difficulty.

Two friends who needed his sympathy in August were Madame Sorlin, daughter of his former mistress, Rose Caron, and her husband, who wrote to tell him that their daughter was very ill after an operation for acute appendicitis, and later to say that she had died. Clemenceau sent telegrams of sympathy both to the Sorlins and to Madame Caron, and when the distressed parents went to stay at Madame Caron's house at Monnerville, in the department of Seine-et-Oise, he impulsively decided to call on them on his way back to Paris. Madame Caron was amazed to see him again, and was quite overcome when he said that she was one of his happiest memories; he was pleased to find that she was taking the loss of her granddaughter bravely, but the parents were in despair, and Madame Sorlin burst into tears when they called at the rue Franklin soon after Clemenceau's return to Paris.

For a few weeks he was still able to work on the revision of *Grandeurs et Misères*; but one evening at the end of October the rumour spread round Paris that he was dying. For some hours he seemed on the brink of death; on the next day he was up as usual at five o'clock and resumed his work. 'I am so happy to find you in good health,' a friend said to him two days later. 'You don't look ill at all.' 'I am not ill,' the Tiger answered, 'I am a dying man who is finishing his task.'

The end was near. In the early morning of 24 November, 1929, after two days of great suffering, Clemenceau died at his home in the rue Franklin. No one except the devoted Sister Théoneste, Piétri, Wormser and Martet was allowed at his bedside; even his daughters had to wait in the next room until he had entered his final coma. He had given strict orders that no clergyman should be sent for, but in his last moments Sister Théoneste knelt and prayed for him.

It was over. In his eighty-ninth year death had come at last for the man who had devoted most of a long political and journalistic life to the establishment and preservation of the French Republic, and from 1917 to 1919 had fittingly represented the energy, tenacity and heroism of France. Now the Tiger would roar no more.

At his own request there was no national funeral, and he was buried at his father's side at Colombier, near Mouchamps, in the heart of the Vendean *bocage*. There was no ceremony, no funeral procession, but he had asked that three things should be placed in his coffin—the walking-stick he had had since he was a young man, a casket containing a book which had been his mother's, and the long since withered bunch of flowers which a soldier had given him at the front. Though there was no tombstone over the grave, the site was marked by the erection of a stele, carved by the sculptor Sicard, from a block of stone which the Tiger had brought back from Egypt. It shows a helmeted Pallas Athene, lost in meditation as she leans on her lance.

Clemenceau died, as he had lived, without belief in a life after death. More than thirty years earlier, when the young Violet Maxse was grieving over the death of her old friend, Sir Edward Burne-Jones, Clemenceau wrote to her:

> As for the belief in another life, that can only console those who dare not look at things as they are and who want to anchor their weakness to the primitive images that their imagination creates. . . . No. Let us return with serenity to the good restful earth from whence we come. Content to have emerged from the ocean of things, to see, to know, to love, to suffer, which is the brief record of life.

And it was to the good restful earth of the Vendée that Georges Clemenceau's body returned.

BIBLIOGRAPHY

Manuscript Sources

THE ROYAL ARCHIVES

PEDRONCINI, GUY: *Le Haut Commandement: La Conduite de la Guerre, Mai 1917 à Novembre 1918* (Sorbonne thesis, 1971)

SCHEURER-KESTNER, AUGUSTE: *Journal* (Bibliothèque Nationale, nouvelles acquisitions françaises)

Clemenceau's works
(in order of publication)

De la génération des éléments anatomiques (1865)
La Mêlée Sociale (1895)
Le Grand Pan (1896)
Les Plus Forts (1898)
Au Pied de Sinai (1898)
L'Iniquité (1899)
Vers la Réparation (1899)
Au Fil des Jours (1900)
Contre la Justice (1900)
Le Voile de Bonheur (1901)
Des Juges (1901)
Justice Militaire (1901)
Injustice Militaire (1902)
La Honte (1903)
Figures de Vendée (1903)
Aux Embuscades de la Vie (1903)
L'Eglise, la République et la Liberté (1903)
Notes de Voyage dans l'Amérique du Sud (1911)
Dans les Champs du Pouvoir (1913)
La France devant l'Allemagne (1916)
Demosthène (1926)
Au Soir de la Pensée (1927); English translation, *In the Evening of my Thought* (1929)
Claude Monet: Les Nymphéas (1928)

Grandeurs et Misères d'une Victoire (1930); English translation, *Grandeur and Misery of Victory* (1930)

American Reconstruction (1928): Clemenceau's letters to *Le Temps*, 1865–69, edited by F. Baldensperger
Neuf Conférences par Clemenceau sur la Démocratie (1930); South American lectures reported by Maurice Ségard
Discours de Guerre (1934, revised edition, 1968)
Discours de Paix (1938)
Lettres à une Amie (1970): Clemenceau's letters to Marguerite Baldensperger, 1924–29

Books about Clemenceau

ABENSOUR, LEON: *Clemenceau Intime* (1928)
ADAM, GEORGE: *The Tiger: Georges Clemenceau, 1841–1929* (1930)
AJALBERT, JEAN: *Clemenceau* (1931)
BASTOUL, B.: *Clemenceau vu par un passant inconnu* (1938)
BENJAMIN, RENÉ: *Clemenceau dans la Retraite* (1930)
BRUUN, GEOFFREY: *Clemenceau* (1943)
CHASTENET, JACQUES (and others): *Clemenceau* (1974)
DAUDET, LÉON: *Clemenceau qui sauva la Patrie* (1930)
DAUDET, LÉON: *La Vie Orageuse de Clemenceau* (1938)
DOMINIQUE, PIERRE: *Clemenceau* (1963)
ERLANGER, PHILIPPE: *Clemenceau* (1968)
GEFFROY, GUSTAVE: *Georges Clemenceau, sa Vie, son Oeuvre* (1930)
HALÉVY, DANIEL: *Clemenceau* (1930)
HYNDMAN, H. M.: *Clemenceau: the Man and his Time* (1919)
JACKSON, J. HAMPDEN: *Clemenceau and the Third Republic* (1946)
JUDET, ERNEST: *Le Véritable Clemenceau* (1920)
JULLIARD, JACQUES: *Clemenceau, Briseur de Grèves* (1965)
LECOMTE, GEORGES: *Clemenceau* (1918)
MARTET, JEAN: *Clemenceau* (1930): English version of the two following books
MARTET, JEAN: *Clemenceau peint par lui-même* (1929)
MARTET, JEAN: *Le Silence de M. Clemenceau* (1929)
MARTET, JEAN: *Le Tigre* (1930)
MICHON, GEORGES: *Clemenceau* (1931)
MONNERVILLE, GASTON: *Clemenceau* (1968)
MORDACQ, GENERAL H.: *Clemenceau* (1939)

MORDACQ, GENERAL H.: *Clemenceau au Soir de la Vie.* 2 vols. (1933)
MORDACQ, GENERAL H.: *Le Ministère Clemenceau: Journal d'un Témoin.* 4 vols. (1930–31)
NEURAY, FERNAND: *Entretiens avec Clemenceau* (1930)
ORMESSON, VLADIMIR D'; *Qu'est-ce qu'un Français?* (Clemenceau, Poincaré, Briand) (1934)
PELLETAN, CAMILLE: *Georges Clemenceau* (1883)
RATINAUD, JEAN: *Clemenceau* (1958)
SUAREZ, GEORGES: *Clemenceau.* 2 vols. (1933)
SZEPS, BERTA (Frau Szeps-Zuckerkandl): *Clemenceau tel que je l'ai connu* (1944)
TREICH, LÉON: *Vie et Mort de Clemenceau* (1929)
WATSON, D. R.: *Clemenceau: a political biography* (1974)
WILLIAMS, WYTHE: *The Tiger of France* (1949)
WORMSER, GEORGES: *La République de Clemenceau* (1961)
ZÉVAÈS, ALEXANDRE: *Clemenceau* (1949)

Memoirs and Letters

ASTRUC, GABRIEL: *Le Pavillon des Fantômes* (1929)
BARRÈS, MAURICE: *Mes Cahiers.* 14 vols. (1931–57)
BARRÈS, MAURICE: *Scènes et Doctrines de Nationalisme.* 2 vols. (1925)
BENOIST, CHARLES: *Souvenirs, Vol. III* (1934)
BERTIE OF THAME, LORD: *Diary, 1914–1918.* 2 vols. (1924)
BLAKE, ROBERT (ed.): *The Private Papers of Douglas Haig,* 1914–19 (1952)
BONSAL, STEPHEN: *Heyday in a Vanished World* (1938)
BONSAL, STEPHEN: *Unfinished Business* (1944)
BRANDES, GEORG: *Correspondance.* 4 vols. (1952–66)
BÜLOW, PRINCE VON: *Memoirs, 1849–1897* (1932)
CAILLAUX, JOSEPH: *Mes Mémoires.* 3 vols. (1942–47)
CAMBON, PAUL: *Correspondance.* 3 vols. (1940–49)
CHAMBERLAIN, JOSEPH: *A Political Memoir, 1880–1892* (1953)
CHARLES-ROUX, F.: *Souvenirs Diplomatiques: Rome—Quirinal, 1916–1919* (1953)
CHICHET, ÉTIENNE: *Feuilles Volantes* (1935)
CHURCHILL, WINSTON S.: *Thoughts and Adventures* (1932)
CLEMENCEAU-JACQUEMAIRE, MADELEINE: *Le Pot de Basilic* (1928)
COMBES, ÉMILE: *Mon Ministère: Memoires, 1902–1905* (1956)
DAUDET, LÉON: *Député de Paris, 1919–1924* (1933)
DAUDET, LÉON: *Le Poignard dans le Dos* (1918)
DREYFUS, ALFRED and PIERRE: *The Dreyfus Case* (1937)

FERRY, ABEL: *Les Carnets Secrets, 1914–1918* (1957)

FREYCINET, CHARLES DE: *Souvenirs,* 1877–1893 (1913)

GATINEAU-CLEMENCEAU, GEORGES: *Des Pattes du Tigre aux Griffes du Destin* (1961)

GHEUSI, P.-B.: *Cinquante Ans de Paris.* 2 vols. (1939–40)

GONCOURT, EDMOND and JULES DE: *Journal.* 4 vols. (1956)

GUITRY, SACHA: *If I Remember Right* (1935)

HANKEY, LORD: *The Supreme Command, 1914–1918.* 2 vols. (1961)

HANKEY, LORD: *The Supreme Control at the Paris Peace Conference, 1919* (1963)

HARDINGE OF PENSHURST, LORD: *Old Diplomacy* (1947)

HOUSE, COLONEL E. M.: *Intimate Papers.* 4 vols. (1926–28)

LÉAUTAUD, PAUL: *Journal Littéraire.* 19 vols. (1954–66)

LÉPINE, LOUIS: *Mes Souvenirs* (1929)

LLOYD GEORGE, DAVID: *The Truth about the Peace Treaties.* 2 vols. (1938)

LLOYD GEORGE, DAVID: *War Memoirs.* 6 vols. (1933–36)

LLOYD GEORGE, FRANCES: *The Years that are Past* (1967)

LOUCHEUR, LOUIS: *Carnets Secrets, 1908–1932* (1962)

LOUIS, GEORGES: *Carnets.* 2 vols. (1926)

MARCELLIN, L.: *Politique et Politiciens pendant la Guerre.* 2 vols. (1922)

MILNER, VISCOUNTESS: *My Picture Gallery* (1951)

PALÉOLOGUE, MAURICE: *Journal, 1913–1914* (1947)

PALÉOLOGUE, MAURICE: *My Secret Diary of the Dreyfus Case* (1957)

POINCARÉ, RAYMOND: *Au Service de la France.* 10 vols. (1926–33)

RADZIWILL, PRINCESS CATHERINE: *France from behind the Veil* (1914)

REPINGTON, LIEUT.-COL. C. à C.: *After the War* (1922)

REPINGTON, LIEUT.-COL. C. à C.: *The First World War.* 2 vols. (1920)

RANC, ARTHUR: *Souvenirs, Correspondance, 1831–1908* (1913)

RIBOT, ALEXANDRE: *Journal et Correspondance* (1936)

RIVIÈRE, JACQUES and ALAIN-FOURNIER: *Correspondance, 1905–14,* *Vol. II* (1926)

ROCHEFORT, H. DE: *Les Avertures de ma Vie.* 5 vols. (1896–7)

ROSNY *aîné,* J. H.: *Torches et Lumignons* (1921)

STEED, HENRY WICKHAM: *Through Thirty Years.* 2 vols. (1924)

SZEPS, BERTA (Frau Szeps-Zuckerkandl): *My Life and History* (1938)

STOCK, P.-V.: *Memorandum d'un Éditeur.* 3 vols. (1935–38)

VANSITTART, LORD: *The Mist Procession* (1958)

Biography

ALTIERI, LOUIS: *Nicolas Piétri: l'Ami de Clemenceau* (1965)

ANDREW, CHRISTOPHER: *Théophile Delcassé and the making of the Entente Cordiale* (1968)

BERNANOS, GEORGES: *La Grande Peur des Bien-Pensants: Edouard Drumont* (1931)

BOISDEFFRE, PIERRE DE: *Barrès parmi Nous* (1969)

BURY, J. P. T.: *Gambetta and the making of the Third Republic* (1973)

CALLWELL, MAJOR-GENERAL SIR C. E.: *Field-Marshal Sir Henry Wilson*. 2 vols. (1927)

CHARTERIS, BRIGADIER-GENERAL JOHN: *Field-Marshal Earl Haig* (1929)

CHASTENET, JACQUES: *Gambetta* (1968)

CHASTENET, JACQUES: *Raymond Poincaré* (1948)

CHURCHILL, WINSTON S.: *Great Contemporaries* (1937)

CLADEL, JUDITH: *Rodin* (1936)

COBLENZ, PAUL: *Georges Mandel* (1946)

CURTIS, MICHAEL: *Three against the Third Republic* (Sorel, Maurras, Barrès) (1959)

FLOTO, INGA: *Colonel House in Paris* (1973)

GARVIN, J. L.: *The Life of Joseph Chamberlain, Vol. II* (1933)

GOLLIN, A. M.: *Proconsul in politics: a study of Lord Milner* (1964)

GWYNN, STEPHEN: *Claude Monet and his Garden* (1934)

HALPERIN, V.: *Lord Milner and the Empire* (1952)

HART, B. H. LIDDELL: *Foch: the Man of Orleans* (1931)

LANOUX, ARMAND: *Bonjour Monsieur Zola* (1962)

MAGNUS, PHILIP: *King Edward VII* (1964)

MARSHALL-CORNWALL, GENERAL SIR JAMES: *Foch as Military Commander* (1972)

McCORMICK, DONALD: *Pedlar of Death: the Life of Sir Basil Zaharoff* (1965)

MIQUEL, PIERRE: *Poincaré* (1961)

MORGAN, JOHN H.: *Viscount Morley* (1924)

NEUMANN, ROBERT: *Zaharoff the Armaments King* (1938)

RABAUT, JEAN: *Jaurès* (1971)

RECOULY, RAYMOND: *Le Mémorial de Foch* (1929)

ROSKILL, STEPHEN: *Hankey, Man of Secrets*. 2 vols. (1970-2)

SEAGER, FREDERICK H.: *The Boulanger Affair* (1969)

SHERWOOD, JOHN M.: *Georges Mandel and the Third Republic* (1970)

SORLIN, PIERRE: *Waldeck-Rousseau* (1966)

SUAREZ, GEORGES: *Briand*. 6 vols. (1938-52)

TABARANT, A.: *Manet et ses Oeuvres* (4th edition, 1947)

THARAUD, JEROME and JEAN: *La Vie et Mort de Déroulède* (1925)

THOMAS, ÉDITH: *Louise Michel, ou la Velléda de l'Anarchie* (1971)

VARENNE, F.: *Mon Patron Georges Mandel* (1947)
WORMSER, GEORGES: *Georges Mandel, L'Homme Politique* (1967)
WRENCH, SIR EVELYN: *Alfred, Lord Milner* (1958)

History

ADAM, GEORGE: *Treason and Tragedy: an Account of French War Trials* (1929)
BAINVILLE, JACQUES: *La Troisième République, 1870–1935* (1935)
BALDWIN, HANSON: *World War I* (1962)
BANKWITZ, P. C. F.: *Maxime Weygand and Civil-Military Relations in Modern France* (1967)
BAUMONT, MAURICE: *Gloires et Tragedies de la IIIe République* (1956)
BEAU DE LOMÉNIE, E.: *Les Responsabilités des Dynasties Bourgeoises.* 3 vols. (1943–54)
BERGER, MARCEL and PAUL ALLARD: *Les Secrets de la Censure pendant la Guerre* (1932)
BLET, HENRI: *France d'Outre-Mer* (1950)
BODLEY, J. E. C.: *France* (revised edition, 1899)
BONNEFOUS, GEORGES: *Histoire Politique de la Troisième République, Vols. I–II* (1956–57)
BOUSSEL, PATRICE: *L'Affaire Dreyfus et la Presse* (1960)
BOUVIER, JEAN: *Les Deux Scandales de Panama* (1964)
BROGAN, SIR DENIS: *French Personalities and Problems* (1946)
BROGAN, SIR DENIS: *The Development of Modern France, 1870–1939* (1940)
BROGAN, SIR DENIS: *The French Nation: From Napoleon to Pétain* (1946)
BRYCE, VISCOUNT: *Modern Democracies*, Vol. I (1921)
BURY, J. P. T.: *France, 1814–1940* (4th edition, 1969)
BYRNES, ROBERT F.: *Antisemitism in Modern France* (1950)
CARPENTIER, PAUL and PAUL RUDET: *La Conférence de Doullens* (1933)
CARROLL, E. MALCOLM: *French Public Opinion and Foreign Affairs, 1870–1914* (1931)
CHAPMAN, GUY: *The Dreyfus Case* (1955)
CHAPMAN, GUY: *The Dreyfus Trials* (1972)
CHAPMAN, GUY: *The Third Republic of France: the First Phase, 1871–1914* (1962)
CHASTENET, JACQUES: *Histoire de la Troisième République, Vols. I–V* (1952–60)
CHASTENET, JACQUES: *La France de M. Fallières* (1949)
COOKE, JAMES J.: *New French Imperialism, 1880–1910* (1973)
CORNILLEAU, ROBERT: *De Waldeck-Rousseau à Poincaré* (1926)

DANSETTE, ADRIEN: *Histoire Religieuse de la France Contemporaine,* *Vol. II* (1951)

DANSETTE, ADRIEN: *L'Affaire Wilson et la Chute du Président Grevy* (1936)

DANSETTE, ADRIEN: *Le Boulangisme, 1886–1890* (1938)

DANSETTE, ADRIEN: *Les Affaires de Panama* (1934)

DANSETTE, ADRIEN: *Les Origines de la Commune de 1871* (1944)

DARDENNE, HENRIETTE: *Lumières sur l'Affaire Dreyfus* (1964)

DEFRASNE, JEAN: *La Gauche en France de 1789 à nos Jours* (1972)

EDWARDS, STEWART: *The Paris Commune 1871* (1971)

GAILLARD, JEANNE: *Communes de province, Commune de Paris, 1870–1871* (1971)

GARÇON, MAURICE: *Histoire de la Justice sous la Troisième République.* 3 vols. (1957)

GÉRARD, ALICE: *La Révolution Française, Mythes et Interprétations* (1970)

GIRARDET, RAOUL: *L'Idée Coloniale en France de 1871 à 1962* (1972)

GOGUEL, FRANÇOIS: *La Politique des Partis sous la Troisième République* (1946)

GUILLEMIN, HENRI: *L'Avènement de M. Thiers* (1971)

GUINN, PAUL: *British Strategy and Politics 1914 to 1918* (1965)

HALÉVY, DANIEL: *La République des Ducs* (1937)

HANOTAUX, GABRIEL: *Histoire de la France Contemporaine.* 4 vols. (1903–08)

HART, B. H. LIDDELL: *A History of the Great War, 1914–1918* (1934)

HOUSE, COLONEL E. M. and CHARLES SEYMOUR (ed.): *What really happened at Paris* (1921)

JELLINEK, FRANK: *The Paris Commune of 1871* (new edition, 1971)

JOHNSON, DOUGLAS: *France and the Dreyfus Affair* (1966)

KAYSER, JACQUES: *Les Grandes Batailles du Radicalisme* (1962)

KING, JERE CLEMENS: *Foch versus Clemenceau* (1960)

KING, JERE CLEMENS: *Generals and Politicians* (1951)

LANSING, ROBERT: *The Big Four* (1922)

LARKIN, MAURICE: *Church and State after the Dreyfus Affair* (1974)

LARKIN, MAURICE: *Gathering Pace: Continental Europe, 1870–1945* (1969)

LEFRANC, GEORGES: *Le Mouvement Syndical sous la Troisième République* (1967)

MANÉVY, RAYMOND: *La Presse de la Troisième République* (1955)

MANTEYER, G. DE (ed.): *Austria's Peace Offer, 1916–1917* (1921)

MANTOUX, PAUL: *Les Délibérations des Quatre.* 2 vols. (1955)

MAYER, ARNO J.: *Politics and Diplomacy of Peacemaking* (1968)

McMANNERS, JOHN: *Church and State in France, 1870–1914* (1972)

MELLOR, ALEC: *Histoire de l'anticlericalisme française* (1966)

MICHON, GEORGES: *The Franco-Russian Alliance* (1927)

MIQUEL, PIERRE: *La Paix de Versailles et l'Opinion Publique Française* (1972)

MORDACQ, GENERAL H.: *La Vérité sur le Commandement Unique* (1934)

NEVAKIKI, JUKKA: *Britain, France and the Arab Middle East, 1914–1929* (1969)

NICOLSON, HAROLD: *Peacemaking 1919* (new edition, 1945)

NOWAK, KARL: *Versailles* (1928)

OUSTON, PHILIP: *France in the Twentieth Century* (1972)

PEDRONCINI, GUY: *Les Mutineries de 1917* (1967)

PEDRONCINI, GUY: *Les Négotiations Secretes pendant la Grande Guerre* (1969)

PEDRONCINI, GUY: *Pétain, Général-en-Chef, 1917–1918* (1974)

PICKLES, DOROTHY M.: *The French Political Scene* (1938)

RENOUVIN, PIERRE: *L'Armistice de Réthondes* (1968)

RENOUVIN, PIERRE: *Le Traité de Versailles* (1969)

RENOUVIN, PIERRE: *Les formes du Government de Guerre* (1926)

ROBERTS, J. M.: *Europe, 1880–1945* (1967)

ROLO, P. J. V.: *Entente Cordiale* (1969)

SEIGNOBOS, C. H.: *L'Evolution de la Troisième République (Histoire de la France Contemporaine, Vol. VIII)* (1921)

SHORTER, EDWARD and CHARLES TILLY: *Strikes in France, 1830–1968* (1974)

SOLTAU, ROGER: *French Parties and Politics, 1871–1921* (1930)

SOLTAU, ROGER: *French Political Thought in the Nineteenth Century* (1931)

TANNENBAUM, EDWARD R.: *L'Action Française* (1962)

TARDIEU, ANDRE: *The Truth about the Peace Treaties* (1921)

TAYLOR, A. J. P.: *The Struggle for Mastery in Europe, 1848–1914* (1954)

TERRAIL, G. (under pseud. 'Mermeix'): *Le Combat des Trois* (1922)

THOMPSON, J. M.: *The French Revolution* (1962)

THOMSON, DAVID: *Democracy in France since 1870* (4th edition, 1964)

THOMSON, DAVID: *Europe since Napoleon* (1957)

TINT, HERBERT: *The Decline of French Patriotism* (1964)

WAITES, NEVILLE (ed.): *Troubled Neighbours: Franco-British Relations in the Twentieth Century* (1971)

WATT, RICHARD M.: *Dare Call it Treason* (1964)

WILLIAMS, ROGER L.: *The French Revolution of 1870–1871* (1969)

WRIGHT, GORDON: *France in Modern Times* (1962)

ZELDIN, THEODORE: *France, Vol. I* (1973)

ZÉVAÈS, ALEXANDRE: *Histoire de la Troisième République* (1938)

ZÉVAÈS, ALEXANDRE: *L'Affaire Dreyfus* (1931)
ZÉVAÈS, ALEXANDRE: *Le Scandale de Panama* (1931)

Miscellaneous

BARRÈS, MAURICE: *L'Appel au Soldat* (1900)
BARRÈS, MAURICE: *Les Déracinés* (1897)
BARRÈS, MAURICE: *Leurs Figures* (1902)
BOIS, PAUL: *Paysans de l'Ouest* (1971)
DELL, ROBERT: *My Second Country* (1920)
DRUMONT, EDOUARD: *La Fin d'un Monde* (1899)
FEYDEAU, GEORGES: *Théâtre Complet, Vol. VIII* (1955)
KEYNES, J. M.: *The Economic Consequences of the Peace* (1919)
   L'Intermédiaire des Chercheurs et des Curieu (1921, 1930)
MANTOUX, ÉTIENNE: *The Carthaginian Peace, or the Economic Consequences of Mr. Keynes* (1946)
PÉGUY, CHARLES: *Oeuvres Choisies* (1911)
ROUILLÉ, JOSEPH: *Panache de la Vendée* (1972)
SCOTT, JOHN A.: *Republican Ideas and the Liberal Tradition in France* (1951)
SKINNER, CORNELIA OTIS: *Elegant Wits and Grand Horizontals* (1963)
TOURNÈS, GENERAL R.: *Foch et la Victoire des Alliés* (1936)

Review articles

BALDENSPERGER, FERDINAND: L'Initiation Américaine de Georges Clemenceau (*Revue de Littérature Comparée*, 1928)
BLISS, GENERAL TASKER H.: The Evolution of the Unified Command (*Foreign Affairs*, 1922)
'*CALCHAS*': France as the Keystone of Europe (*Fortnightly Review*, 1908)
CAMBON, JULES: Georges Clemenceau (*Revue des Deux Mondes*, 1929)
GOSSE, SIR EDMUND: The Writings of M. Clemenceau (*Edinburgh Review*, 1919)
JONES, R. B.: Anglo-French Negotiations, 1907: a Memorandum by Sir Alfred Milner (*Bulletin of the Institute of Historical Research*, 1958)
KREBS, ALBERT: Le Mariage de Clemenceau (*Mercure de France*, 1955)
KREBS, ALBERT: Le Secret de Clemenceau (*Miroir de l'Histoire*, 1958)
LÉMERY, HENRY: Clemenceau comme je l'ai vu (*Histoire de Notre Temps*, 1968)
LÉVY, CLAUDE: Un Journal de Clemenceau: *Le Bloc* (*Revue d'Histoire Moderne et Contemporaine*, 1963)

MALARTIC, YVES: Comment Clemenceau fut battu aux élections legislatives à Draguignan en 1893 (*Provence Historique*, 1962)

MARTEL, CHARLES: Souvenirs de *La Justice* (*Grande Revue*, 1909)

MARTET, JEAN: Qui était Georges Clemenceau? (*Revue des Deux Mondes*, 1929)

MILNER, VISCOUNTESS: Clemenceau Intime (*Revue des Deux Mondes*, 1953)

MURARD, PROFESSOR JEAN: Le docteur Clemenceau (*Histoire de la Médecine*, 1972)

PAZ, MAURICE: Clemenceau, Blanqui's Heir (*Historical Journal*, 1973)

PONTY, JANINE: La presse quotidienne et l'Affaire Dreyfus (*Revue d'Histoire Moderne et Contemporaine*, 1974)

RENOUVIN, PIERRE: Le gouvernement français et les tentatives de Paix en 1917 (*Revue des Deux Mondes*, 1964)

RENOUVIN, PIERRE: Les buts de guerre du gouvernement français, 1914–1918 (*Revue Historique*, 1966)

ROBERTS, JOHN: Clemenceau the Politician (*History Today*, 1956)

VALLAT, XAVIER: Pourquoi le 'Tigre' ne logea pas a l'Elysée (*Ecrits de Paris*, 1970)

VARENNE, F.: La Défaite de G. Clemenceau à Draguignan en 1893 (*Revue Politique et Parlementaire*, 1955)

VARENNE, F.: Une célèbre collaboration: Georges Clemenceau, Georges Mandel (*Miroir d'Histoire*, 1958)

WATSON, D. R.: A Note on Clemenceau, Comte and Positivism (*Historical Journal*, 1971)

WATSON, D. R.: The French and Indo-China (*History Today*, 1970)

WATSON, D. R.: The making of French foreign policy during the first Clemenceau ministry (*English Historical Review*, 1971)

Newspapers

La Justice, L'Aurore, La Dépêche de Toulouse, Le Bloc, L'Homme Libre, L'Homme Enchaîné: Le Figaro, Le Monde, Le Temps; New York Times, New York World; The Times.

NOTES

Titles without attribution of author are of Clemenceau's own works. Some of these, and titles of books by authors who have more than one work in the bibliography, are abbreviated if referred to on several cocasions.

CHAPTER 1   THE YOUNG REPUBLICAN

3–4 *Praise of the Vendée*: Cornilleau, 160–9; Rouillé, 106–8
   4 *L'Aubraie: Les Plus Forts*, 5; Martet, *Clemenceau peint par lui-même*, 127–8
   5 *Dr. Clemenceau's influence*: Geffroy, 7; Martet, *op. cit.*, 181
   6 *Dr. Clemenceau's arrest in 1858*: Suarez, *Clemenceau*, I, 29–33; Martet, *op. cit.*, 183
   7 *Parisian students in 1860s*: Sorlin, 83
     Clemenceau's popularity in Latin Quarter: Martet, *op. cit.*, 205, 208; Wormser, *La République de Clemenceau*, 475–6
7–8 *Zola's contribution to* Le Travail: Lanoux, 84–5; Treich, 48
   8 *'Martyrs of history' article*: Zévaès, *Clemenceau*, 16
8–9 *Clemenceau's imprisonment*: Martet, *op. cit.*, 96–7; Suarez, *op. cit.*, I, 60.
   9 *Blanqui's beliefs*: R. L. Williams, 134; Wormser, *op. cit.*, 24–5
  10 *Gustave Jourdan*: Wormser, *op. cit.*, 23–4; Martet, *op. cit.*, 206–9
10–11 *Love for Hortense Kestner*: Scheurer-Kestner, *Journal*, I; Krebs, *Miroir de l'Histoire*, 1958
  11 *Comte and positivism*: Wright, 298–300; MacManners, 16; Watson, *Historical Journal*, 1971
11–12 *Clemenceau's thesis*: *De la Génération des Eléments Anatomiques*, *passim*; Zévaès, *op. cit.*, 20; Martet, *op. cit.*, 199–204
  12 *Letter before leaving France*: Scheurer-Kestner, I

CHAPTER 2   AMERICAN INTERLUDE

  13 *Reading* Robinson Crusoe *in English*: *New York World*, 14 March, 1892
  13 *'Positivist study' of America*: Watson, *loc. cit.*; Martet, *op. cit.*, 231
  14 *Early days in New York*: Baldensperger, *Revue de Littérature Comparée*, 1928; *New York World*, *loc. sit.*, *Declaration of atheism*: Monnerville, 33; Watson, *Clemenceau*, 31
14–15 *Letters to* Le Temps: Baldensperger, *loc. cit.*; *American Reconstruction*, *passim*
  15 *Anti-royalist letter*: Treich, 63
  16 *Miss Aiken's academy*: Krebs, *Mercure de France*, 1955; Martet, *op. cit.*, 192; New York World, *loc. cit.*

16–17 *Clemenceau as teacher*: Wormser, *op. cit.*, 99–100; **Krebs,** *loc. sit.*
17–18 *Courtship and marriage*: Krebs, *loc cit.*; Scheurer-Kestner, I; Martet, *op. cit.*, 192n.
19 *'Belleville manifesto'*: Kayser, 38
   Clemenceau's earnings as doctor: Martet, *op. cit.*, 95–6n.
   Mixed feelings at outbreak of war: Hyndman, 33

CHAPTER 3 MAYOR OF MONTMARTRE

21 *Experiences on 4 September, 1870*: Monnerville, 72
   Appointment as mayor: Martet, *op. cit.*, 159–64
22 *Proclamation*: Mordacq, *Clemenceau*, 2
   National Guard: Edwards, 46–7
22–3 *Circular to schools*: Zévaès, *op. cit.*, 28
23 *Louise Michel in Montmartre*: Thomas, 70–71
   Paris besieged: Brogan, *Development of Modern France*, 50–51
   Balloon letters to Mary: Monnerville, 77
24 *'Cruelly abandoned'*: Chastenet, *Histoire de la Troisième République*, I, 46
   Composition of National Assembly: Beau de Loménie, I, 206–14
24–5 *Opposition to Treaty of Frankfort*: Guillemin, 107; Kayser, 50–51; Treich, 75–6; Carroll, 41–2n
25 *Corsican motion*: Zévaès, *op. cit.*, 312–13; Drumont, *Fin d'un Monde*, 272n.; Caillaux, I, 283; Watson, *Historical Journal*, 1971
   Choice of Versailles for National Assembly: Zévaès, *IIIe République*, 33
26 *National Guard central committee*: R. L. Williams, 86–7; Gaillard, 49
27–30 *Events on 18 March*: Edwards, 124–49; Gaillard, 50–53; Jellinek, 121; Chastenet, *op. cit.*, I, 72–6; Caillaux, I, 280–82; Guillemin, 153–65; (Clemenceau's own account) Martet, *Le Silence de M. Clemenceau*, 259–300
30 *Calm after 18 March*: Guillemin, 163; Edwards, 155 *Deputation to central committee*: Dansette, *Origines de la Commune*, 143–4; Edwards, 165; Hanotaux, I, 176–8
30–31 *Mayors at Versailles*: R. L. Williams, 129
31 *Municipal elections*: Chapman, *Third Republic*, 12–13; Guillemin, 212
   Louise Michel in National Guard: Thomas, 93
   Goncourt's comment on Clemenceau: Goncourt, II, 786
32 *'One of the maddest madnesses'*: Martet, *Clemenceau peint*, 47

CHAPTER 4 DOCTOR AND DEPUTY

33 *Duel after court-martial*: Zévaès, Clemenceau, 34–5
34 *Clemenceau's work as councillor*: Bruun, 28; Hyndman, 55; Michon, *Clemenceau*, 11
   Scheurer-Kestner's parties: Bury, *Gambetta*, 184
   Doctors as deputies: Zeldin, 23, 577
34–5 *Surgery incident*: Le Grand Pan, 230–31
35 *Apartment in rue de Miromesnil*: Clemenceau-Jacquemaire, 77
   Madeleine and Hortense Floquet: Clemenceau-Jacquemaire, 83–5
   1876 election address: Kayser, 93
36 *New Chamber of Deputies*: Bury, *France*, 149
37 *Clemenceau appointed Chamber secretary*: Geffroy, 50
   Correspondence with Louise Michel: Thomas, 168

37–8 *Amnesty speech*: Bury, Gambetta, 297–302; Monnerville, 95–7

38 *Opportunism*: Bury, *op. cit.*, 299; Szeps, *Clemenceau*, 37; Bodley, 599

38–9 *The 'seize Mai'*: Beau de Loménie, I, 300–17; Bodley, 229–30; Kayser, 100n

39 *'Re-plastering'*: Zévaès, IIIe *Republique*, 118

39–40 *Speech at Cirque Fernando*: Kayser, 108–9

40 *Letter from Blanqui*: Paz, *Historical Journal*, 1973 Wormser, *op. cit.*, 137–8; Zévaès, *Clemenceau*, 46–7

41 *'A very old journalist'*: Guitry, 242–3

42 *Staff of* La Justice: Martel, *Grande Revue*, 1909; Rosny *aîné*, 233–4
   Its financial difficulties: Watson, *Clemenceau*, 68; Astruc, 99–100; Goncourt, III, 770

43 *Clemenceau as newspaper director*: Martel, *loc. cit.*; Daudet, *Vie Orageuse*, 40–41; Goncourt, III, 146; Rosny *aîné*, 235

43 *Madeleine's visit*: Martel, *loc. cit.*

CHAPTER 5 MINISTRY-BREAKER

44 *Name retained in medical directory*: Erlanger, 87
   Friendship with Fillis: Astruc, 114
   Foyer de danse: Bodley, 521

44–5 *Apartment in avenue Montaigne*: Cambon, I, 272

45 *Mary Clemenceau in Paris*: Tabarant, 395–7; *New York World*, *loc. cit.*
   Letter consigning children to Herz's care: Martet, *Silence*, 212–13
   No materials for 'vie amoureuse': Ajalbert, 44
   Léonide Leblanc: Ajalbert, 75–6; Drumont, 267; Skinner, 90–91
   Rose Caron: Gheusi, II, 136

46 *Comtesse d'Aunay*: Daudet, *op. cit.*, 75; Radziwill, 310–11; Gatineau-Clemenceau, 65
   Basic political division: Goguel, 17; Roberts, 146
   'Always the same ministry': Ajalbert, 21

47 *Marseilles programme*: Carroll, 80; Beau de Loménie, II, 48–9; Zévaès, *Clemenceau*, 94–6; Seignobos, 78
   Louise Michel's return: Thomas, 182–6

48 *Pelletan on voting systems*: Seager, 17–18

48–9 *Ferry and colonial empire*: Blet, 12–14; Zeldin, 630–31; Mordacq, *Clemenceau*, 229

49 *Clemenceau's anti-colonialism*: Blet, 15–16; Watson, *op. cit.*, 90–91
   Lord Lyons on Bismarck's trap: Adam, *The Tiger*, 83

49–50 *Clemenceau on Tunisian occupation*: Blet, 77–8; Chastenet, *Troisième République*, II, 88; Goguel, 54

50 *Criticised by* Le Siècle: Carroll, 90

50–51 *Speech on Egypt*: Seignobos, 95; Zévaès, *op. cit.*, 59–60; Freycinet, 238

51 *Opponents of Egyptian withdrawal*: Andrew, 21–2

52 *Friendship with Admiral Maxse*: Milner,
   Revue des Deux Mondes: 1953

52–3 *London visit*: Royal Archives; *The Times*, February, 1884
   Senator Waddington on governing France: Soltau, *French Parties*, 22 and n

54 *Commission's report*: Watson, *op. cit.*, 88–9
   Ligue républicaine: Kayser, 126–7; Wormser, *op. cit.*, 157–9

55 *Expansion in Indo-China*: Blet, 204–5; Bainville, 112–13; Brogan, *Development*, 232–5
56 *Clemenceau's attack on Ferry*: Chastenet, *op. cit.*, II, 146; Zévaès, *Clemenceau*, 65; Zévaès, *IIIe République*, 147
  Grévy on Clemenceau: Dansette, *Affaire Wilson*, 46
57 *'Essential text' for colonial controversy*: Girardet, 46–60
  French colonies in First World War: Blet, 250; Mordacq, *op. cit.*, 230

CHAPTER 6 BOULANGER

59–60 *Friendship and share dealings with Herz*: Martet, *Silence*, 212–13, 218–19; Zévaès, *Panama*, 131–3: Drumont, 276–9; Baumont, 234
60 *Comment on 'new men'*: Goncourt, III, 439
61 *Causes of ministerial instability*: Beau de Loménie, II, 112; Bainville, 158–9; Zeldin, 588–9
  Socialist rejection of Radical alliance: Chapman, *op. cit.*, 340; Carroll, 106
62 *Decision to sit for Var*: Monnerville, 155
  Jaurès on 'capital error': Zévaès, *Clemenceau*, 67
63 *Clemenceau's share in Boulanger's appointment*: Zévaès, *op. cit.*, 70; Carroll, 114; Seager, 26; Freycinet, 329–30
  Déroulède's Ligue des Patriotes: Tharaud, 28–34; Byrnes, 36; Carroll, 110–11
64 *Clemenceau 'royally deceived'*: Szeps, *op. cit.*, 101
  Visits to war ministry: Daudet, *op. cit.*, 75
  Boulanger's reforms: Zévaès, *IIIe République*, 169; Brogan, *op. cit.*, 185
  Bismarck's speech: Freycinet, 370–71
64–5 *Schnaebele incident*: Freycinet, 370–71; Taylor, 315 and n.; Brogan, *op. cit.*, 187
65 *'War too serious'*: Saurex, *op. cit.*, I, 181
66 *Clemenceau on gare de Lyon scenes*: Dansette, *Boulangisme*, 95; Seager, 68–9
  Daniel Wilson at Elysée: Dansette, *Affaire Wilson*, 66–9; Chapman, *op. cit.*, 275
66–7 *Attacks on Grévy and Wilson*: Dansette, *op. cit.*, 120–21
67 *'Where is the flag?'* Dansette, *op. cit.*, 125–7
68 *'Les nuits historiques'*: Barnès, *Appel au Soldat*, 103–5; Dansette, *op. cit.*, 187–99; Watson, *op. cit.*, 107–8
68–9 *Sadi Carnot's election*: Barrès, *op. cit.*, 108; Zévaès, *IIIe Republique*, 174; Rochefort, V, 108; Dansette, *op. cit.*, 230–33
69 *Wilson acquitted*: Dansette, *op. cit.*, 261–2
70–71 *Société des Droits de l'Homme*: Ranc, 394; Seager, 159–62; Curtis, 32
71 *Anatole France's comment*: *L'Aurore*, 31 October, 1906
  Floquet's duel: Zévaès, *IIIe République*, 179–80; Rosny aîné, 283; Barrès, *op. cit.*, 168–9; Bonsal, *Heyday in a Vanished World*, 117–20
72 *'Boulangism going down'*: Dansette, *Boulangisme*, 250
  Electoral changes: Zévaès, *op. cit.*, 186–7; Seager, 227
  'Like a second lieutènant': Monnerville, 173

CHAPTER 7 THE PANAMA YEARS

73 *First meetings with Berta Szeps*: Szeps, *op. cit.*, 23
73–4 *First meetings with Violet Maxse*: Milner, *My Picture Gallery*, 22–3, 62–4

74 *Drumont's writings*: Byrnes, 137–42
His abuse of Clemenceau: Drumont, 265–71
75 *The greedy deputy*: Gatineau-Clemenceau, 127; Rosny aîné, 236; Szeps. *op. cit.*, 69; Péguy, 21
Clemenceau and presidency of Chamber: Barrès, *op. cit.*, 105–6
76 *Baron Jacques de Reinach*: Zévaès, *Panama*, 72–3; Chapman, *op. cit.*, 322
Panama canal difficulties: Garçon, II, 52; Zévaès, *op. cit.*, 24–5
77 *Clemenceau sees Fréycinet*: Dansette, *Panama*, 88; Zévaès, *op. cit.*, 87–8
78 *Sardou's 'Thermidor'*: Garçon, II, 279–80; Daudet, *Vie Orageuse*, 98–100;
Zévaès, *Clemenceau*, 85–9; Szeps, *op. cit.*, 67
78–9 *'Bloc' theory of French Revolution*: Zévaès, *op. cit.*, 85–9; Wright, 53;
Gérard, 128–31; *L'Iniquité*, 235–6
79–80 *Speech on Fourmies strike*: Zévaès, IIIe République, 201–3
80 *'Ralliement'*: Soltau, *French Political Thought*, 328–33; Wright, 317; Mellor,
325n; Michon, *Clemenceau*, 19–20; Zévaès, *Clemenceau*, 89–90
81 *Meeting with Crown Prince Rudolf*: Szeps, *op. cit.*, 36–9
'Cossack or Republican?': Carroll, 156
81–2 *Meeting with Chamberlain*: Chamberlain, 295–7; Garvin, II, 457–62;
Taylor, 332–3
83 *Mary Clemenceau divorced*: Goncourt, IV, 528–9; Gatineau-Clemenceau,
27–8; Judet, 176
Her return to America: New York World, 14 March, 1892; Krebs, *Mercure de France*, 1955
83–4 *Destruction of bust*: Szeps, *op. cit.*, 46–7
84 *La Libre Parole*: Byrnes, 327–8; Chastenet, *Troisième République*, II, 307;
Brogan, *French Nation*, 187
85 *Reinach's death*: Dansette, *Panama*, 110–13, 143
85–6 *Déroulède's attack*: Dansette, *op. cit.*, 175–7; Zévaès, *Panama*, 135–44
86–7 *Duel with Déroulède*: Goncourt, IV, 324 and n; Zévaès, *op. cit.*, 146–7;
Ratinaud, 103
87 *Results of Panama scandal*: Chastenet, *op. cit.*, 320–3; Bainville, 172–4
87–8 *Norton forgeries*: Byrnes, 245; Carroll, 162; Zévaès, *op. cit.*, 273–6;
L'Iniquité, 121
88 *Radical Socialist manifesto*: Kayser, 338–40
88–9 *Violet Maxse in Paris*: Milner, 38–9
89–90 *Draguignan campaign*: Daudet, *Vie Orageuse*, 101–7; Brynes, 244–5;
Judet, 223–5; Malartic, *Provence Historique*, 1962; Varenne, *Revue Politique et Parlementaire*, 1955
90 *Speech at Salernes*: Monnerville, 195–201
90–91 *Result of poll*: Malartic, *loc. cit.*; Varenne, *loc. cit.*; Zévaès, *Clemenceau*,
151–2
91 *Pelletan's 'Hamlet' remark*: Szeps, *op. cit.*, 108
Clemenceau's mastery of Chamber: Bodley, 616

CHAPTER 8 THE WRITER'S CRAFT

95 *Journalistic output*: Geffroy, 189; Wormser, *op. cit.*, 512–18
95–6 *Stylistic difficulties*: Ajalbert, 95–7
96 *Sale of paintings*: Geffroy, 73, 78
Collection of Japanese netsuke: Szeps, *My Life*, 67
96–7 *Selma Everdon*: Daudet, *op. cit.*, 143–57; W. Williams, 88–90

97 'Reservoir of Republican strength': Kayser, 209
98 Gosse's criticism: Edinburgh Review, 1919
   Description of execution: La Mêlée Sociale, 409–15
   Pan as activity symbol: Le Grand Pan, lxxxi
99 Comments on strip-tease show: Le Grand Pan, 355–9
   'Literary self-education': Bruun, 210
   Comte d'Aunay's dismissal: Suarez, Clemenceau, II, 19–20
99–100 Comments on Russia: Michon, Franco-Russian Alliance, 85, 95
100 Hopes of writing novel and play: Goncourt, IV, 657
   'The richest are the strongest': Les Plus Forts, 112–13
   'Bourgeois dynasties': Les Plus Forts, 254
101 Wish to write another novel: Szeps, My Life, 162
102 Geffroy on 'Le Voile de Bonheur': Geffroy, 82

CHAPTER 9 DREYFUS

103 German espionage in France: Boussel, 14–15; Bainville, 205
103–4 Clemenceau's first article on Dreyfus: L'Iniquité, 1–3
104 'No case': Johnson, 210
   Reception of Lazare's pamphlet: Chapman, Dreyfus Trials, 86; Boussel, 105; Johnson, 215
105 'Boring me with their Jew': Lanoux, 458
   Clemenceau-Ranc meeting: L'Iniquité, iv–v
   Scheurer-Kestner's views: Boussel, 120
   Mathieu Dreyfus's influence: Wormser, op. cit., 185
106 'Clemenceau's chef d'oeuvre': Geffroy, 92; Halévy, 17
   House in the rue Franklin: Stock, II, 36
107 Zola's reputation: Chapman, op. cit., 125
108–10 Zola's trial: Lanoux, 484–515; Garçon, II, 27–9
109 'Chose jugée': L'Iniquité, 209
110–11 Duel with Drumont: Bernanos, 335–7; Zévaès, Clemenceau, 164–6
112 'The Affair at its height': Barrès, Scènes et Doctrines, I, 48–9; Zévaès, Dreyfus, 116–19; Brogan, Development, 341; Zeldin, 681
   President Faure's death: Paléologue, My Secret Diary, 152–4
   Clemenceau's reception of news: Martel, Grande Revue, 1909; Contre la Justice, 287–8
113 'Nos snobinettes': Barrès, op. cit., I, 211
   Rennes verdict: L'Injustice Militaire, 222–33
113–14 Disappointment with Dreyfus's attitude: Lanoux, 564; Chapman, op. cit., 247; Martet, Clemenceau peint, 178; Miquel, Dreyfus, 108–9
114 Dreyfus's pardon: Chapman, op. cit., 244–5; Miquel, op. cit., 114–15: Dreyfus, 178
115 'Three great defenders': Miguel, op. cit., 81
   Newspapers and 'the affair': Ponty, Revue d'Histoire Moderne et Contemporaine, 1974
   'Weapon for party warfare': Cornilleau, 49

CHAPTER 10 APPROACH TO POWER

116 Letter to Lady E. Cecil: Milner, 156
   'Apart from Waldeck, no one': Sorlin, 456

Déroulède's attempted coup: Barrès, *op. cit.*, I, 242–62; Tharaud, 116–19; *Contre La Justice*, 314–19
'*Civil war*' *warning: Justice Militaire*, 92

116–17 *Rumours of coup d'état: Justice Militaire*, 379; Soltau, *French Political Thought*, 352; Bryce, I, 243: Miquel, *Dreyfus*, 99–100

117 *Barrès's nationalism*: Curtis, 254; Boisdeffre, 110
Clemenceau leaves L'Aurore: Michon, *Clemenceau*, 88–9; Monnerville, 254–5

118 '*Influenza crisis*': Brandes, I, 299–300
Hopes for new paper: Brandes, I, 301; Geffroy, 94–5
Comment on Carlsbad: Au fil des Jours, 243

118–19 *Illness and convalescence*: Rosny aîné, 239–40; Brandes, I, 303

119 *Mary Clemenceau's return to France*: Gatineau-Clemenceau, 28

119–20 *Le Bloc*: Geffroy, 95–6; Lévy, *Revue d'Histoire Moderne et Contemporaine*, 1963

120 *Democratic Republican Alliance*: Soltau, *French Parties*, 45 '*Poincarism*' *article*: Miquel, *Poincaré*, 178–80

121 *Var deputation*: Stock, II, 40–43
Return to L'Aurore: Suarez, *Clemenceau*, II, 56; Wormser, *op. cit.*, 196; Monnerville, 256

122 *Mandel joins staff*: Wormser, *Mandel*, 20–21; Sherwood, 7; Manévy, 138

123 '*Dernier coup de feu*': Brandes, I, 304
1902 general election: Beau de Loménie, II, 336–9; Bainville, 241

123–4 *Clemenceau's opposition to party system*: Kayser, 304–5

124 *Loubet's remark*: Bainville, 245
Combes's fanaticism: Brogan, *Development*, 363

124–5 *Clemenceau on State omnipotence*: Péguy, 22; Dansette, *Histoire Réligieuse*, II, 312; Watson, *Clemenceau*, 158–60

125 *Clemenceau and Combes*: Combes, 95, 203–4
General André and files scandal: Goguel, 118–23; Brogan, *French Nation*, 207–8
'*Board of directors*': Zévaès, *Clemenceau*, 71

125–6 *Anglo-French entente*: Andrew, 213; Blet, 98; Zévaès, *IIIe République*, 270–280

126 *Delcassé and Russian massacre*: Michon, *Franco-Russian Alliance*, 138
France and Morocco: Blet, 88–99; Andrew, 266–72
'*Game of China dogs*': Carroll, 209

126–7 *Coup de Tanger; Delcassé's fall*: Chastenet, *op. cit.*, III, 280–88; Andrew, 273–98

127 *Clemenceau's comments*: Chastenet, *op. cit.*, III, 288

127–8 '*Road to Canossa*': MacManners, 149

128 *Passing of Separation Law*: Mellor, 399; Bury, *France*, 204; Dell, 131–2
Inventory riots: Larkin, *Church and State after Dreyfus*, 193–4; Wright, 231; MacManners, 152; Tannenbaum, 123

CHAPTER 11 MINISTER OF THE INTERIOR

130 '*Sphinx with calf's head*': Chastenet, *Poincaré*, 77
Sarrion's cabinet-making: Suarez, *Clemenceau*, II, 73; Zévaès, *Clemenceau*, 184n.; Bonnefous, 1, 9; Chastenet, *op. cit.*, 78n
Mandel at ministry: Varenne, *Mandel*, 34–6; Sherwood, 8–11

131 *Clemenceau and the bureaucrats*: Treich, 105; Szeps, *Clemenceau*, 153

131–2 *Attitude towards prefects*: Léautaud, II, 125; Daudet, *Vie Crageuse*, 179
132 '*A man of government*': Lépine, 253
    '*Counting candlesticks*': Bonnefous, I, 18; Chastenet, *France de M. Fallières*, 58; MacManners, 156
133 *Article suggesting that ministers should visit scenes of strikes* :*La Mêlée Sociale*, 318–22
    Trade unions' programme: Lefranc, 98
    Remark to Emile Buré: Treich, 111
133–4 *Miners' strike*: Lefranc, 131–4; Shorter and Tilly, 119; Zeldin, 705; Suarez, *op. cit.*, II, 73–85
134 *Parisians' fears*: Lefranc, 134–7; Shorter and Tilly, 122
135 '*In front of the barricade*': Erlanger, 357; Watson, *op. cit.*, 173–5
    '*Ministers are agreed*': Barrès, *Cahiers*, V, 12
136 '*Duel*' *with Jaurès*: Rabaut, 388–94; Bonnefous, I, 23–4; Monnerville, 297–301; Rivière, II, 152
137 *Visit to Vendée*: Cormilleau, 166–9; Mordacq, *Clemenceau*, 194
    Draguignan speech: Bonnefous, I, 34; Watson, *op. cit.*, 182

CHAPTER 12 PRIME MINISTER

138 *Clemenceau in 1906*: Chastenet, *France de M. Fallières*, 41
    His early rising: Louis, I, 43
139 *Picquart as war minister*: Barrès, *Scènes et Doctrines*. I, 199–200; Benoist, III, 129–30
    Ministry of Labour: Lefranc, 145–6, 186
140 *Ministers' nicknames*: Suarez, *op. cit.*, II, 94
    Deputies' salaries: Goguel, 134
140–41 *Acquisition of Western railway*: Bonnefous, I, 161–4
141 '*Full incoherence*': Cornilleau, 171–2; Monnerville, 326–9; Brandes, I, 244
    '*Premier flic de France*': Miquel, *Poincaré*, 214
    Electricity strike: Chastenet, *Troisième République*, IV, 34
141–2 *Civil servants' claim to form unions*: Garçon, I, 217; Lefranc, 158–60; Chastenet, *op. cit.*, IV, 34–5
142 '*Mutes of the harem*': Bonnefous, I, 66–7
142–3 *Wine-growers' protest*: Bonnefous, I, 68–75; Beau de Loménie, II, 379–80; Zeldin, 706–7; Caillaux, I, 243; Rabaut, 405
143 *Clemenceau's ignorance of economics*: Dell, 17
144 *The Villeneuve 'massacre'*: Julliard, 99–100; Beau de Loménie, II, 388–9; Rabaut, 432–3; Lefranc, 161
144–5 *Agents provocateurs*: Dell 87–8
145 *The Métivier affair*: Julliard, 145–50; Rabaut, 432–3; Lefranc, 159n
    Postal workers' strike: Lépine, 254; Brogan, *Development*, 425
    Numbers of strikes: Sherwood, 16–17
146 *Clemenceau's intentions as prime minister*: Watson, *op. cit.*, 210–11
    His patronage of the arts: Lanoux, 585, 606; Chastenet, *France de M. Fallières*, 297n
146–7 *Meeting with Campbell-Bannerman*: Jones, *Bulletin of Institute of Historical Research*, 1958; Hardinge, 140
147 *Talk with Sir Edward Grey*: Hyndman, 219
147–8 *First meetings with Edward VII*: Martet, *Clemenceau peint*, 254; Gatineau-Clemenceau, 186; Magnus, 395; Chastenet, *Troisième République*, IV, 42

148 *Madeleine's illness*: Brandes, I, 272
    War 'inevitable': Louis, I, 21
    1908 meeting with Edward VII: Steed, *The Times*, 24 December, 1920
149 *Compulsory military service reduced*: Bonnefous, I, 77–8
    Relations with Zæharoff: Bruun, 113–14
    Foch's appointment: Treich, 144–5; Marshall-Cornwall, 28–9
149–50 *Casablanca incident*: Chastenet, *op. cit.*, IV, 55–6; Blet, 103
150–51 *Franco-German agreement, 1909*: Watson, *English Historical Review*, 1971;
    Caillaux, I, 277; Brogan, *Development*, 435
151 *British praise of Clemenceau*: *Fortnightly Review*, December, 1908
    Princess Matternich's comment: Barrès, *Cahiers*, V, 283
    Clemenceau's lost support: Soltau, *French Parties*, 48–9; Beau de Loménie, II,
    393–4
152–3 *His fall from power*: Bonnefous, I, 131–8; Benoist, III, 155; Chastenet,
    op. cit., IV, 66; Barrès, *op. cit.*, VII, 247
154 *Madame Arman de Caillavet's comments*: Brandes, I, 255
    End of bloc des Gauches: Bury, *France*, 212

CHAPTER 13 BEFORE THE WAR

155 *Dinner-table quip*: Astruc, 193–4
    Praise for Poiret: Szeps, Clemenceau, 181–2
156 *Last meeting with Edward VII*: Szeps, *op. cit.*, 183–7
    The house at Bernouville: Geffroy, 108
    Quarrel with Rodin: Cladel, 271; Szeps, *op. cit.*, 197–200
    Journal du Var: Varenne, *Mandel*, 38–43
157 *Origin of South American tour*: Astruc, 191
    Details of tour: Notes du Voyage, *passim*
158–9 *Lectures in South America*: Ségard, *passim*; Monnerville, 347–56; Wormser,
    op. cit., 73–81; Thomson, *Democracy in France*, 131
160 *Agadir incident*: Blet, 105–7; Beau de Loménie, II, 421–3
160–61 *Caillaux overthrown*: Poincaré, I, 6–9; Caillaux, II, 179–207; Chastenet,
    Poincaré, 100–6
    Clemenceau left out of Poincaré's ministry: Poincaré, I, 16
161 *Speech on German menace*: Bonnefous, I, 281–2; Erlanger, 413–14
    Clemenceau's operation: Suarez, *op. cit.*, II, 146–7; Barrès, *Cahiers*, IX, 295
    'Things one can do without': Barrès, op. cit., XII, 7
    Clemenceau and Poincaré: Chastenet, *Poincaré*, 80–81; Ormesson, 1–58, 143–6
162–3 *Poincaré's election*: Bonnefous, I, 316–21; Seignobos, 283; Miquel,
    Poincaré, 289–303
163 *Clemenceau's reactions to election*: Bonnefous, I, 321n; Benoist, III, 185
    End of Journal du Var: Sherwood, 13
    Launching of L'Homme Libre: Geffroy, 139–41; Varenne, *Mandel*, 106;
    Daudet, *Vie Orageuse*, 186; Monnerville, 355–6
164 *Briand defeated*: Beau de Loménie, II, 442; Zévaès, *Clemenceau*, 220–23
164 *Clemenceau urges extra year's service*: Champs de Pouvoir, 7–12, 13–18, 40–47, etc.
    'Vouloir ou mourir': Champs du Pouvoir, 115–22
165 *Three years service bill passed*: Miquel, *Poincare*, 324; Carroll, 288
    'Prepare, prepare, prepare!': Hyndman, 243
    'Guilty Austria': Szeps, *op. cit.*, 206, 208
    'Neither defended nor governed': France devant l'Allemagne, 76–9

166 *Madame Caillaux's trial*: Chastenet, *Troisième République*, IV, 174; Marcellin, I, 13
   Two comments on Jaurès's death: France devant l'Allemagne, 85–6; Benjamin, 139

CHAPTER 14   LEADER IN WAITING

169–70 *Malvy and Carnet B*: Daudet, *Le Poignard dans le Dos*, 1–172; Watt, 42–6; Adam, *Treason and Tragedy*, 83–8; Renouvin, *Formes de Gouvernement*, 14–30
   Almereyda: Watt, 44–5; Adam, *op. cit.*, 86–7
170 *Letter to Violet*: *Discours de Guerre*, 43
1707–1 *Clemenceau and the cabinet*: Bertie, I, 23; Chastenet, *op. cit.*, IV, 211; Marcellin, I, 22–3
171 *Poincaré on Clemenceau*: Poincaré, V, 191
171–2 L'Homme Libre *and medical scandals*: Daudet, *Vie Orageuse*, 193; Berger and Allard, 69–70: Adam, *Tiger*, 186
172 L'Homme Libre *becomes* L'Homme Enchaine: Berger and Allard, 70–71; Monnerville, 394–5
   Joffre's GHQ as seat of government: Zévaès, *IIIe Republique*, 295; King, *Generals and Politicians*, 243
   Tributes to poilus: Mordacq, *Clemenceau*, 96
   Onset of diabetes: Murard, *Histoire de Médecine*, 1972; Martet, *Tigre*, 205n.
173 *Unfairness to Poincaré*: Chastenet, *Poincaré*, 171
   Campaign against embusqués: Berger and Allard, 75; Marcellin, I, 69
   'Not a walker-on': Chastenet, *op. cit.*, 175
173–4 *Clemenceau's critics*: Zévaès, *Clemenceau*, 229; Beau de Loménie, III, 59–60; Caillaux, III, 185
174 *'Jusqu'au bout!'*: Chastenet, *Troisième République*, IV, 247–8
   Secret sessions: Bonnefous, II, 126–30; Chastenet, *op. cit.*, IV, 357
174–5 *Parliamentary commissioners*: King, *op. cit.*, 192; Watt, 99–100
175 *Army commission*: Marcellin, I, 277; Monnveville, 404–10
175–6 *Meeting with Sir Henry Wilson*: Callwell, I, 267
176 *Sarrail and Salonika*: Blake, 52 and n; Marcellin, I, 256; Guinn, 132
176–7 *First meeting with Haig*: Blake, 141–2
177 *Breakfast with Wilson*: Callwell, I, 280–81
177–8 *Clemenceau and Foch*: Callwell, I, 285; *Grandeurs et Misères d'une Victoire*, 19; King, *op. cit.*, 205; Hart, *Foch*, 233–4
178 *Poincaré's diary note*: Poincaré, IX, 3
   Censors' leniency towards Clemenceau: Berger and Allard, 233–4
178–9 *Clemenaeau and Russian Revolution*: Michon, *Franco-Russian Alliance*, 315–7; Bernanos, 411
179 *'Wait for the Americans'*: Callwell, II, 364
179–80 *French army mutinies*: Pedroncini, *Mutineries*, 234–42, and *passim*; Chastenet, *op. cit.*, IV, 288; Tint, 157
180–81 *Malvy denounced in Senate*: *Discours de Guerre*, 65–129
181 *Malvy's character*: Lémery, *Histoire de Notre Temps*, 1968
182 *Stockholm conference*: Renouvin, *Revue des Deux Mondes*, 1964; Watt, 209–13
182–3 *Prince Sixtus affair*: Pedroncini, *Negotiations Secrètes*, 50–67; Renouvin, *loc. cit.*; Charles-Roux, 212; Taylor, 552, 560n.
183 *Briand-Lancken peace move*: Renouvin, *loc. cit.*; Chastenet, *op. cit.*, IV, 289 Pedroncini, *op. cit.*, 72; Tardieu, 46n. *Armand-Revertera talks*: Charles Roux, 261–3

184 *Clemenceau and Mordacq*: Mordacq, *Ministère Clemenceau*, I, 1–6
    Poincaré's decision: Poincaré, IX, 321
    Pichon at Elysee: Marcellin, II, 236
185 *'Valet de chambre'*: Marcellin, II, 253
    Piétri takes over L'Homme Libre: Altieri, 39

CHAPTER 15 MAN OF WAR

187 *'Geese who saved the Capitol'*: Suarez, *op. cit.*, II, 207
    Ignace's duties: Mordacq, *Ministère*, I, 48–9
    Mandel as chef de cabinet: *Mordacq, op. cit.*, I, 55; Varenne, *op. cit.*, 127;
    Wormser, *Mandel*, 74–6; Berger and Allard, 275
188 *Clemenceau's day*: Mordacq, *op. cit.*, 27–31
    Poincaré's complaints: Poincaré, X, 10, 28, 41, etc.
    Troops' reactions to Clemenceau's appointment: Pedroncini, *Haut Commandement*, 743
    Confidence on home front: Barrès, *Cahiers*, XII, 159
189 *Attitude of press*: Beau de Loménie, III, 125
    Hankey's note: Roskill, I, 467
190 *Policy speech in Chamber*: Discours de Guerre, 130–49; Churchill, *Great Contemporaries*, 311
191 *Caillaux in war-time*: Caillaux, III, 185–6; Charles-Roux, 150–66; Watt, 122–7
191 *Caillaux loses parliamentary immunity*: Garçon, II, 199–200; Bonnefous, II, 356–7; Marcellin, II, 266
192 *His trial*: Garçon, II, 210–11; Charles-Roux, 144–5
    Comments by Clemenceau and Ybarnégaray: Charles-Roux, 166; Watt, 125
192–3 *'Reign of terror'*: Roskill, I, 535; Sherwood, 22–3; Ferry, 225
193 *Not a dictatorship*: Renouvin, *Formes de gouvernement*, 146–7
    Clemenceau and censorship: Berger and Allard, 236–7, 245
194 *The Fourteen Points*: Berger and Allard, 269–72; Chastenet, *op. cit.*, V, 12; Mordacq, *op. cit.*, I, 123–4
    Matin interview: Berger and Allard, 275n
195 *Meetings with Pershing and House*: Mordacq, *op. cit.*, I, 90, 93
    Sarrail's dismissal: Brogan, *Development*, 505
196 *Clemenceau in the trenches*: Mordacq, *Clemenceau*, 126–8
    Interference with Pétain: Pedroncini, *Haut Commandement*, 421–3, 832–4; Tournès, 56
197 *Haig's high opinion of Clemenceau*: Blake, 289–90
    Haig on unified command: Grandeurs et Misères, 34
    Clemenceau and Lloyd George: Mordacq, *Ministère*, I, 155; Guinn, 288; Blake, 281
197–8 *Proposal for general reserve*: Guinn, 287, 298–300
198 *Clemenceau's contacts with Repington*: Grandeurs et Misères, 91; Guinn, 285–93
198–9 *Changed view of Salonika*: Berger and Allard, 345; Mordacq, *op. cit.*, 187–90
199–200 *Complaint about parliament*: Mordacq, *op. cit.*, I, 197
200 *'Je fais la guerre'*: Discours de Guerre, 163–77

CHAPTER 16 FATHER OF VICTORY

202 *German offensives, 1918*: Baldwin, 144
203 *Haig's telegram to London*: Hart, *Foch*, 270
    Big Bertha: Berger and Allard, 299–301

204 *Lloyd George's claim*: Lloyd George, *War Memoirs*, V, 2892
    Plan to make Clemenceau commander-in-chief: Carpentier, 48–9; Martet, *Clemenceau peint*, 17n
204–5 *Doullens conference*: Carpentier, *passim*; Callwell, II, 77–8; Hart, *World War*, 275; Loucheur, 51–60; Wrench, 342
205 *Foch's retort*: Recouly, 20–21
    Pétain's reaction: Ribot, 256–7; Suarez, *op. cit.*, II, 136
206 *Government removal discussed*: Mordacq, *Ministère*, I, 233; Suarez, *op. cit.*, II, 54; Poincaré, X, 81
206–7 *Clemenceau and Churchill at front*: Churchill, *Thoughts and Adventures*, 165–78
207 *Foch becomes generalissimo*: Hart, *Foch*, 284; Mordacq, *Clemenceau*, 137; Guinn, 302
207–8 *Czernin incident*: Berger and Allard, 306–7; Mordacq, *Ministère*, I, 274–6; Charles-Roux, 297–8; Chastenet, *Troisième République*, IV, 217; Ferry, 228–31; (*Cambon's comment*) Repington, *World War*, II, 281
209 *Staff officer on safety of Chemin des Dames*: *Grandeurs*, 157n
    Battle of Chemin des Dames: Hart, *World War*, 521–9; Baldwin, 143–4
    'We shall fight on the Loire': Mordacq, *op. cit.*, II, 54
    Intrigues in the Chamber: Marcellin, II, 341; Mordacq, *op. cit.*, II, 51
210 *Clemenceau's speech on 4 June*: *Discours de Guerre*, 187–203; *Grandeurs*, 39–42
    Older generals removed: *Grandeurs*, 44–5
211 *The poilus' bouquet*: Mordacq, *Clemenceau*, 143
    Allied successes: Hart, *op. cit.*, 478–80; Baldwin, 148
    Michel Clemenceau at Saint-Mihiel: Mordacq, *Ministère*, 220n
211–12 *'British politicians are fools'*: Callwell, II, 117
212 *Foch at Mass*: Recouly, 318–19
    Clemenceau's exasperation with Chamber: Mordacq, *op. cit.*, II, 159
212–13 *His outbursts at cabinet meetings*: Poincaré, X, 297, 306, 327
213 *Retort to Diaz*: Charles-Roux, 320
213–14 *Quarrels with Lloyd George*: Watson, 367; Nevakiki, 69–70
214 *Foch and the Americans*: Hart, *Foch*, 378–81; Hart, *World War*, 577–85; King, *Generals and Politicians*, 236–7; Marshall-Cornwall, 243
    German request for armistice: Renouvin, *Armistice*, 68; Chastenet, *op. cit.*, IV, 329: Poincaré, X, 365
215 *'Hamstringing troops' letter*: Poincaré, X, 379; Chastenet, *op. cit.*, IV, 329–30; Renouvin, *op. cit.*, 126
    'Building up files for history': Lémery, *Historie de Notre Temps*, 1968
215–16 *Barrére's view of armistice*: Pedroncini, *Negotiations Secrètes*, 133
216 *Foch's comment*: Poincaré, X, 402
    Foch's request for information: Mordacq, *op. cit.*, II, 284; King, *op. cit.*, 239–240
216–17 *Clemenceau's view of armistice*: Renouvin, *op. cit.*, 275
217 *'Task accomplished'*: Mordacq, *op. cit.*, II, 349
    Letter to Colonel House: House, IV, 198
218 *Poincaré's rueful comments*: Poincaré, X, 406
    Clemenceau's ill-health: Mordacq, *Clemenceau*, 176n.; Poincaré, X, 419
    'Kissed by girls': Poincaré, X, 413
218–19 *'Soldier of the ideal'*: *Discours de Guerre*, 227–8
219 *'Winning the peace'*: Mordacq, *Ministère*, III, 6
    Ludendorff on Clemenceau: Mordacq, *op. cit.*, II, 367n

CHAPTER 17 MAKING THE PEACE

221 *Government and Te Deum*: Chastenet, *op. cit.*, V, 14
    Academie de Medecine quip: Mordacq, *op. cit.*, III, 17n
    President Wilson and venue for peace conference: Mayer, 347–53
222 *Clemenceau's reception in London*: Repington, *op. cit.*, II, 486
    Mesopotamia and Syria: Floto, 76–81; Roskill, II, 28–9
    Clemenceau on President Wilson: Mordacq, *op. cit.*, III, 61; *Grandeurs*
222–3 *Clemenceau and Wilson contrasted*: Chastenet, *op. cit.*, V, 14
223 'Between Jesus Christ and Napoleon': Hardinge, 242
223–4 'Noble candour' *speech*: Bonnefous, II, 442; Miquel, *Paix et l'Opinion
    Publique*, 60–61; Floto, 87
224 *Hankey's tribute*; Hankey, *Supreme Control*, 32
    Peace conference organisation: Tardieu, 97; Mayer, 363–4
225 *Wilson's lost power*: Larkin, *Gathering Pace*, 249–50
    Contrast with Congress of Vienna: Thomson, *Europe*, 583
    Differing peace aims: Brogan, *French Nation*, 247
225–6 *Russians and peace conference*: Hankey, *op. cit.*, 51–4; Renouvin, *Traité de
    Versailles*, 112
226 *Kaiser's trial*: Renouvin, *op. cit.*, 99
    Council of Ten: House and Seymour, 93; Tardieu, 100
    Clemenceau's interview with Associated Press: Mayer, 647; Miquel, *op. cit.*, 195n
227 *Balfour at peace conference*: Frances Lloyd George, 94–5
    Attempt on Clemenceau's life: Bonsal, *Unfinished Business*, 65; Mordacq, *op. cit.*,
    III, 133
227–8 *Convalescence and recovery*: Bonsal, *op. cit.*, 66–9; Mordacq, *op. cit.*, II, 134–156
228–9 *Rhineland problem*: King, *Foch v. Clemenceau*, 3–5, 17–18; Recouly, 180
229 *Clemenceau-Tardieu memorandum*: Renouvin, *op. cit.*, 68
229–30 *Anglo-American guarantee*: Renouvin, *op. cit.*, 69–71; Loucheur, 71–3;
    Floto, 131
231 *Clemenceau in Council of Four*: Lansing, 27
231–2 *Rhineland frontier proposals*: King, *op. cit.*, 47–9; Larkin, *op. cit.*, 252;
    Martet, *Silence*, 245–6; Tardieu, 203; Renouvin, *op. cit.*, 71
232 'Leaving politics for ever': Tardieu, 263
    Germans' idea of justice: Mantoux, *Délibérations des Quatre*, I, 70
    Wilson 'a pro-German': House and Seymour, 464
    Saar settlement: Waites, 80
232–3 *Clemenceau and Foch*: Miquel, *op. cit.*, 352; Callwell, II, 183–7; Recouly,
    188–9
233 *Plenary session of 6 May*: Miquel, *op. cit.*, 401–2
    Senators' manifesto: Mayer, 630–32
233–4 *Reparations difficulties*: House and Seymour, 259–90: Keynes, *passim*
234 'War guilt clause': Keynes, 139–40
    End of reparations: Thomson, *op. cit.*, 569
    Clemenceau's comment on Klotz: Vansittart, 223
    'Langues de chat': Frances Lloyd George, 155
235 'A kind of Lloyd George': Ratinaud, 237
    Trianon Palace meeting: Mayer, 767; Monnerville, 658–9
235–6 *Clemenceau and Rhineland separatism*: King, *op. cit.*, 82–106
236 'Deuxième flic de France': Sherwood, 31
    Proposed march to Berlin: Hart, *Foch*, 427

236–7 *Signing of peace treaty*: Monnerville, 660–61; Mordacq, *op. cit.*, III, 304; Callwell, II, 201
237 *Treaty presented to Chamber*: Monnerville, 662–3
237–8 *'Keynote' of treaty*: Grandeurs
238 *Clemenceau keeps war ministry*: Mordacq, *op. cit.*, III, 319
238–9 *Verdicts on treaty*: Renouvin, *op. cit.*, 115–17; Chastenet, *op. cit.*, V, 63–4; Martet, *Silence*, 304–5; Watson, 362–5

CHAPTER 18 DEFEAT

240 *Mandel's handling of strikes*: Sherwood, 31–3
  Clemenceau's fatigue: Mordacq, *op. cit.*, IV, 111
241 *His medicines*: Barrès, Cahiers, XII, 186–7
  Ratification debates: *Discours de Paix*, 165–222, 233–81; Miquel, *op. cit.*, 561–5
242 *Election programme*: Sherwood, 42–3; Soltau, *French Parties*, 55
241–2 *'No miracle of the peace'*: Miquel, *op. cit.*, 548
242–3 *'Horizon blue Chamber'*: Chastenet, *op. cit.*, V, 59–64; Soltau, *op. cit.*, 62–3; Bryce, I, 323
243 *Mandel's speech*: Sherwood, 45
  Joking with Benoist: Benoist, III, 379
  And with Lloyd George: Roskill, II, 137
  Belébat: Mordacq, *op. cit.*, IV, 186; *Lettres à une Amie*, 81n
244 *Initial refusal to stand for presidency*: Wormser, *République de Clemenceau*, 394
  Tardieu's insistence: Wormser, *Mandel*, 89n
  Deschanel as candidate: Zévaès, *Clemenceau*, 279–80
244–5 *Briand's anit-Clemenceau campaign*: Chastenet, *op. cit.*, V, 62; Suarez, *Briand*, V, 66
245 *Clemenceau and the Catholics*: Mordacq, *op. cit.*, 279–82: Beau de Loménie, III, 256
  Maurras's prestige: Vallat, *Ecrits de Paris*, 1970
246 *Clemenceau's letter of withdrawal*: Barrès, *Cahiers*, XII, 246–7
  Deschanel's call at war ministry: Suarez, *Clemenceau*, II, 301
  Comments by Poincaré and Mandel: Poincaré, X, 425, 430
246–7 *How Clemenceau would have acted as president*: Mordacq, *op. cit.*, 278; Martet, *Clemenceau peint*, 214
247 *Why he was defeated*: Barrès, *op. cit.*, XII, 249; Ormesson, 186
  Lloyd George's remark: Mordacq, *op. cit.*, 293n.
  Last speeches to Supreme Council and to his staff: Mordacq, *op. cit.*, IV, 295, 297
  Transfer of power to Millerand: Martet, *op. cit.*, 218

CHAPTER 19 PRIVATE CITIZEN

249 *'Sphinx hunt'*: Wormser, *République de Clemenceau*, 438
  Comment on pyramids: Mordacq, *Clemenceau au Soir de la Vie*, I, 17
  Capus's tribute: Wormser, *op. cit.*, 438–9
249–50 *Visit to India*: Mordacq, *op. cit.*, I, 17–145
250 *Tiger-shooting*: Altieri, 69–70; (*'the one with the gun'*) Hardinge, 255
  Temple of thousand Buddhas: Wormser, *op. cit.*, 440n
251 *Repington's visit*: Repington, *After the War*, 186–7
  Oxford degree: Wormser, *op. cit.*, 441n
  Visit to Corsica: Monnerville, 688–90

252 *L'Echo National*: Wormser, *op. cit.*, 442–7; Mordacq, *op. cit.*, II, 13–14; Sherwood, 71; (*Sir Basil Zaharoff rumour*) McCormick, 226

252–3 *Visit to America*: New York Times, 12 November, 1922; King, *Foch v. Clemenceau*, 120–21; Monnerville, 690–700;

254 *Last meeting with Woodrow Wilson*: Bonsal, *Unfinished Business*, 256

255 *Refusal to stand for Senate*: Suarez, *op. cit.*, II, 315
'*Poverty and loneliness*': Suarez, *op. cit.*, II, 325; Brogan, *French Nation*, 250; ('*too many visitors*') Lettres à une Amie, 203

256 *House in rue Franklin bought by American admirer*: Lettres, 271–5; (*and re-painted*) Martet, *Silence*, 34

256–7 *Meeting with Marguerite Baldensperger*: Lettres, iii–xvi

257 *Madame de Gennes*: Lettres, 540

258 *Sister Théoneste's call*: Lettres, 576
Madame Rostand's poem: Lettres, 574; Martet, *Tigre*, 21
Madame Callot's visit: Lettres, 453–60

259 *Comment on Madeleine*: Lettres, 217
Censoring 'Le Pot de Basilic': Lettres, 282
Casual visitors at Belébat: Lettres, 60, 106, 321, etc.
'*The most bitter years*': Wormser, *op. cit.*, 465

260 *Letter to President Coolidge*: Grandeurs, 369–72
On short skirts: Martet, *Tigre*, 97
'*Toute petite gymnastique*': Lettres, 598

261 *Object of 'Au Soir de la Pensée'*: In the Evening of my Thought (English translation), I, 11
Daudet's opinion of the book: Daudet, *Vie Orageuse*, 277
Justifying atheism: In the Evening, I, 263, II, 328, etc.

261–2 *Singing mice*: In the Evening, II, 318n

262 '*Demosthène:*' Lettres, viii, xiii, 49, 117, 119, 124, 125, 495
Knowledge of ancient Greece: Ormesson, 28

263 '*Write memoirs? Never!*': Léautaud, VI, 287
Seeing Foch in his coffin: Martet, *op. cit.*, 87; Lettres, 381
Decision to answer Recouly's book on Foch: Martet, *op. cit.*, 99–106

264 '*Parthian arrow*': Mordacq, *op. cit.*, II, 228
'*This book is killing me*': Martet, *op. cit.*, 299
One chapter still needed: Lettres, 649
Foch rebutted: Grandeurs, ii–iv and *passim*
Risk of another war: Grandeurs, 336–7; Martet, *op. cit.*, 118
'*France will be . . .*': Grandeurs, 348

CHAPTER 20   THE GOOD EARTH

265 *Reflection on life*: Milner, 70
Illness in 1928: Lettres, 543
At Clotilde's funeral: Lettres, 631

265–6 '*I shall die unhappy*': Lettres, 640

266 *Last meeting with Rose Caron*: Lettres, 630–32, 646–7; Gheusi, I, 76–7
'*A dying man*': Treich, 251–2
Clemenceau's death: Monnerville, 744–5

267 *No belief in life after death*: Milner, 70

INDEX